PSALMS

Also by James Montgomery Boice

Witness and Revelation in the Gospel of John

Philippians: An Expositional Commentary

The Sermon on the Mount

How to Live the Christian Life (originally, *How to Live It Up*)

Ordinary Men Called by God (originally, *How God Can Use Nobodies*)

The Last and Future World

The Gospel of John: An Expositional Commentary (5 volumes in one)

"Galatians" in the *Expositor's Bible Commentary*

Can You Run Away from God?

Does Inerrancy Matter?

The Foundation of Biblical Authority, editor

The Epistles of John

Genesis: An Expositional Commentary (3 volumes)

The Parables of Jesus

The Christ of Christmas

The Minor Prophets: An Expositional Commentary (2 volumes)

Standing on the Rock: Biblical Authority in a Secular Age

The Christ of the Open Tomb

Foundations of the Christian Faith (4 volumes in one)

Christ's Call to Discipleship

Transforming Our World: A Call to Action, editor

Ephesians: An Expositional Commentary

Daniel: An Expositional Commentary

Joshua: We Will Serve the Lord

Nehemiah: Learning to Lead

Romans (4 volumes)

Amazing Grace

Mind Renewal in a Mindless Age

PSALMS

Volume 1
Psalms 1–41

JAMES MONTGOMERY BOICE

BakerBooks

A Division of Baker Book House Co
Grand Rapids, Michigan 49516

Published by Baker Books
a division of Baker Book House Company
P.O. Box 6287, Grand Rapids, MI 49516-6287

Fourth printing, November 2000

Printed in the United States of America

Library of Congress Cataloging-in-Publication Data

Boice, James Montgomery, 1938–
    Psalms: an expositional commentary / James Montgomery Boice.
      p. cm.
    Includes bibliographical references and indexes.
    Contents: v. 1. Psalms 1–41.
    ISBN 0-8010-1077-2 (v. 1)
    1. Bible. O.T. Psalms—Commentaries. 2. Bible. O.T.
Psalms—Homiletical use. I. Title.
BS1430.3.B64 1994
223'.2077—dc20   93-36246

For information about academic books, resources for Christian leaders, and
all new releases available from Baker Book House, visit our web site:
http://www.bakerbooks.com/

To
Jesus Christ,
God's King
in Zion

Contents

Preface

There is no more wonderful portion of Scripture than the psalms. They have been a blessing to God's people through many generations, first in the Old Testament period when they were sung by the people of Israel in their worship at the temple in Jerusalem and now in the New Testament period when they are recited, sung, memorized, and cherished by Christians (as well as Jews) literally around the world. Ever since the days when they were first written, beginning in the age of the early monarchy under King David, they have been used in the worship of God more consistently and more frequently than any other portion of the Bible.

Some of the best known parts of the Bible are psalms or parts of psalms. We think at once of Psalm 1, Psalm 23, Psalm 46, Psalm 90, Psalm 100, and the longest Bible chapter of all, Psalm 119. The psalms are frequently memorized. Psalms 1, 23, and 100 are chief examples. They have contributed noteworthy ideas and poetic phrases to much of the world's literature. Hundreds of books have received their titles from some well-tuned phrase in this great collection of ancient Hebrew verse.

For years I have wanted to preach through the psalms—studying them carefully, applying them to contemporary problems, and eventually publishing them for the benefit of today's church. But I hesitated for a long time because I knew how profound and deeply spiritual the psalms are, and I was fully aware, as so many before me have also been aware, that I was in no way wise enough or spiritual enough to do them justice. In the end I decided to proceed because it occurred to me that I was getting older—I do not have an unlimited number of years to do Bible exposition—and there are many, many psalms.

And there is also this factor: At the same time I have been working on the psalms I have also been preaching through the Book of Romans, and I remember that these were the two books Martin Luther was chiefly studying and teaching in the years leading up to his posting of the Ninety-five Theses on the door of the castle church at Wittenberg. This means that they were the scriptural foundation for the teachings that produced the Reformation. I do not suppose that my own studies will be blessed in like manner, but I anticipate significant blessing in many lives as these two sets of books are released over the years by Baker Book House, which has been most helpful in publishing them.

My studies of the psalms will appear in three volumes. It is difficult to know where to make a division since the psalms have been grouped in the Bible into five books, and these vary substantially in length. Charles Haddon Spurgeon's great work on the psalms, *The Treasury of David,* is in three volumes today, but originally it was in seven volumes. Several contemporary works on the psalms are in one or two volumes. The plan I am following is this. The first of my volumes contains the first of the Psalter's five books, that is, Psalms 1–41. The second volume will contain books 2, 3, and 4—Psalms 42–106. The third volume will contain studies of the Psalter's fifth book, namely, Psalms 107–150. This means that my volumes will be of somewhat unequal length, but they will have the advantage of following the Psalter's own divisions.

When I was preaching on the minor prophets some years ago, I found that the material was so profound and demanded such practical response from those who studied them that I could not simply rush through the books in one preaching series. I had to spread the exposition over several years. Exactly the same thing has been my experience preaching through the psalms. The sermons appearing in this volume were preached in relatively short segments between the winter of 1989 and the fall of 1991 and were aired on the Bible Study Hour in special winter and summer series in 1992–93.

As in all my books, I want to thank the Session and congregation of Tenth Presbyterian Church for allowing me to spend so much of my time in Bible study and the writing of sermonic material. I also want to thank the staff, particularly the ministerial staff, who ably attend to many of the demands of a thriving church that I do not have time for personally. I owe special thanks to Miss Joan Borgard, my executive assistant, who handles my schedule and carries forward much of my work.

It is my prayer that these studies may be a source of rich spiritual nurture, grace, instruction, and comfort to you as you read them. And may he who gave them to us for exactly those ends bless you as by your study you increasingly learn to love and better serve him.

"Praise be to the LORD, the God of Israel, from everlasting to everlasting. Amen and Amen" (Ps. 41:13).

Book One of the Psalter

Psalm 1

The Fast Lane or the Right Path

Blessed is the man
    who does not walk in the counsel of the wicked
or stand in the way of sinners
    or sit in the seat of mockers.
But his delight is in the law of the LORD,
    and on his law he meditates day and night.
He is like a tree planted by streams of water,
    which yields its fruit in season
and whose leaf does not wither.
    Whatever he does prospers.

Not so the wicked!
    They are like chaff
    that the wind blows away.
Therefore the wicked will not stand in the judgment,
    nor sinners in the assembly of the righteous.

For the LORD watches over the way of the righteous,
    but the way of the wicked will perish.
                                        verses 1–6

The first psalm is among the best known, if not the best known, psalm in the entire Psalter, and rightly so, for it stands as a magnificent gateway to this extraordinary ancient collection of

Hebrew religious verse. To use another image, it is a text of which the remaining psalms are essentially exposition. Psalm 1 is a practical psalm. Since it leads the collection, we are taught at once that study of the Psalter must have practical effects if the psalms are to achieve the purpose for which God gave them to us. Psalm 1 introduces us to the way in which we may find happiness and fulfillment in life. It is by meditation on and delight in the law of God. The psalm also warns us of sure, eventual, and eternal ruin if we do not.

Divergent Ways

Psalm 1 introduces us to the doctrine of the two ways, which is a very common concept. Most Americans are acquainted with Robert Frost's use of the idea in the poem "The Road Not Taken."

> Two roads diverged in a wood, and I—
> I took the one less traveled by,
> And that has made all the difference.[1]

Those who know literature a bit more thoroughly are aware that the idea of paths diverging in a wood is also found in Dante Alighieri, the Florentine poet of the Middle Ages, whose *Divine Comedy* begins,

> Midway this way of life we're bound upon,
> I woke to find myself in a dark wood,
> Where the right road was wholly lost and gone.[2]

But there are biblical examples too. The most important is the use of the idea by Jesus toward the end of the Sermon on the Mount as recorded by Matthew. The last section of the sermon lists a series of contrasts, between which choices must be made: two gates and two roads, two trees and their two types of fruit, two houses and two foundations. The part regarding the two ways says, "Enter through the narrow gate. For wide is the gate and broad is the road that leads to destruction, and many enter through it. But small is the gate and narrow the road that leads to life, and only a few find it" (Matt. 7:13–14). Psalm 1 is the clearest, most carefully developed, and first full expression of this idea in the Bible.

But let me back up slightly.

The psalms have been classified in a variety of types or genres, about seven of them,[3] and one of them is "wisdom psalm," which is what this is. It portrays the way the wise man chooses. But Psalm 1 is more than this. It is the father of all the wisdom psalms. Saint Jerome, the translator of the Latin Vulgate, calls Psalm 1 "the preface of the Holy Spirit" to the Psalter. The great Baptist preacher Charles Haddon Spurgeon, who also calls Psalm 1 a "Preface Psalm," adds, "It is the psalmist's desire to teach us the way to blessedness, and to warn us of the sure destruction of sinners. This then, is the matter of the first psalm, which may be looked upon in some respects, as the text upon which the whole of the psalms make up a divine sermon."[4]

In his helpful introduction to the psalms Tremper Longman III, an associate professor of Old Testament at Westminster Theological Seminary, writes, "Psalm 1 deliberately [draws] two portraits in our minds: the portrait of the wicked man and the portrait of the wise man. The question then is posed: Which are we? As we enter the sanctuary of the psalms to worship and petition the Lord, whose side are we on?"[5]

The Two Ways Described

The first verse of Psalm 1, and therefore also the first verse of the Psalter, begins with the word *blessed*. This is important certainly, for it is a way of saying that the psalms (as well as all Scripture) have been given to us by God to do us good. *Blessed* means supremely happy or fulfilled. In fact, in Hebrew the word is actually a plural, which denotes either a multiplicity of blessings or an intensification of them. The verse might correctly be translated, "O the blessednesses of the man who does not walk in the counsel of the wicked."

At first glance it might seem surprising that the idea of the blessed or the happy man is followed immediately by a description of the wicked man, particularly since a description of the way of the wicked also appears later in verses 4 and 5. But it is actually an excellent device. By starting in this way the poet achieves three important things.

First, he begins where we are. None of us automatically starts out being righteous. We start out being sinners, and if we do eventually enter by the straight gate upon the narrow road that leads to life, it is by God's grace. No one, either in the Old Testament or in the New Testament period, was saved in any other way. Second, the poet is able to introduce the doctrine of the two ways from the start. We do not have to wait until verse 4 to read that there is a way other than the way of the godly. Third and finally, the author says something important about godliness. He is going to present godliness positively as the way of the one who delights in the law of the Lord. But any positive affirmation, to have meaning, must have a negative to go with it. Thus, in order to say what the way of the godly man is, we must also be able to say what it is not, and that is what the first verse of the first psalm accomplishes.

How beautifully it does it! The most striking feature of Hebrew poetry is what is known as parallelism, that is, saying the same thing or a variety of the same thing, in two linked lines. That is what we have here, only in this verse there are three linked lines and there are three parallel terms in each line: set 1, "walk, stand, sit"; set 2, "counsel, way, seat"; and set 3, "wicked, sinners, mockers."

Because of this common feature of Hebrew poetry, a number of writers are reluctant to see any special progression in these terms.[6] But it is hard to believe that the phrases are not saying that the way of the wicked is downhill and that sinners always go from bad to worse. Certainly Spurgeon thought so. He said, "When men are living in sin they go from bad to worse. At first they merely *walk* in the counsel of the careless and *ungodly,* who forget God—the evil is rather practical than habitual—but after that, they become habituated to evil, and they *stand* in the way of open *sinners* who willfully violate God's commandments; and if let alone, they go one step further, and become themselves pestilent teachers and tempters of others, and thus they *sit in the seat of the scornful.* They have taken their degree in vice, and as true Doctors of Damnation they are installed."[7]

This interpretation is built into the psalm. The psalm does not merely describe the lifestyle of the wicked; it shows the fruit of that way of life and its end. To the unsaved, "the way of sinners" may seem wonderful and exciting. It is the track they want to be on. But the psalmist warns that it is actually a fast track to emptiness and frustration here as well as judgment in the life to come.

What about the other way, the way of the righteous? We might expect, since the wicked man has been described in terms of his associations, that the godly man will now be described in terms of his associations too, that is, as a person who associates with the godly. But that is not the case. Instead, he is described as one whose "delight is in the law of the LORD" on which "he meditates day and night" (v. 2).

That is a powerful expression: to "delight" in the law of the Lord. But it is also somewhat puzzling, at least at first glance. The British scholar and Christian apologist C. S. Lewis found it to be so. In *Reflections on the Psalms* he describes how at first he found the psalmist's delight in God's law "utterly bewildering" and "mysterious." Lewis said he could understand how one could delight in God's mercies, visitations, and attributes, but not how one could delight in God's law. You do not delight in law, not really. Rather law is something you respect and (one hopes) obey.

I would argue that it *is* possible to delight in a good law, one that is both well written and effective in promoting righteousness. But I think Lewis is also right when he suggests that more than this is involved. He finds the clue to the psalmist's meaning in the idea of meditation on God's law. This makes the law a subject of the righteous man's study. So, for the ancient Jew, saying that he delights in the law is much like what we might mean if we said that we love history or physics or archaeology. But, of course, it is even more than that. For when we study the Bible—the word *law* is used to refer to the whole of God's inscripturated revelation—we are really learning, not about human beings or nature primarily (which is what the other disciplines teach us), but about God. And, as Lewis says, "The Order of the Divine mind, embodied in the Divine Law, is beautiful." The language of the poet is "not priggery nor even scrupulosity; it is the language of a man ravished by a moral beauty."[8]

John R. W. Stott adds wisely that this delight "is an indication of the new birth, for '. . . the sinful mind is hostile to God. It does not submit to God's law, nor can it do so' (Rom. 8:7). As a result of the inward, regenerating work of the Holy Spirit, however, the godly find that they love the law of God simply because it conveys to them the will of their God. They do not rebel against its exacting demands; their whole being approves and endorses it. . . . Delighting in it, the godly will *meditate* in it, or pore over it, constantly, day and night."[9]

The contrast between the two ways may be put like this. It is the difference between those who are in love with sin and those who love God. The first class love sin's ways and follow it. The second love God and seek him in Scripture, where he may be found.

Flourishing or Fruitless

When most people think of the results of upright or godly living they think of rewards. That is, they think that if they do what God tells them to do, he will reward them, but that if they do not, they will be punished. There is an element of truth in this; it is what is involved in the doctrine of the final judgment. But what the psalmist actually says here is quite different. He is talking about "blessedness," the blessedness of the man "who does not stand in the way of sinners" but whose "delight is in the law of the LORD." His point is that this is not a reward but rather "the result of a particular type of life."[10]

The poet uses two images to show the result of these two ways. The first is a fruitful tree. It describes the man who delights in the law of God and draws his spiritual nourishment from it as a tree that draws its nourishment from an abundantly flowing stream. The land about might be quite dry and barren. The winds might be hot. But if the tree is planted by the stream, so that it can sink its roots down and draw nourishment, it will prosper and yield fruit. This is the godly man.

> He is like a tree planted by streams of water,
>   which yields its fruit in season
> and whose leaf does not wither.
>   Whatever he does prospers.

Years ago a couple who had gone to China as missionaries used this image to describe their life there after the communists had taken over China at the end of the Second World War. Their name was Matthews, and they were the last missionaries of the China Inland Mission to escape from that country. They were under communism for two years, during which time they lived with their young daughter Lilah in a small room. Their only furniture was a stool. They could not contact their Christian friends for fear of getting them into trouble. Except for the smallest trickle, their funds were cut off by the government. Heat came from a small stove which they lit once a day to boil rice for dinner. The only fuel they had was dried animal refuse that Art Matthews collected from the streets. These were indeed dry times. But afterward, when they wrote their testimony to God's grace in the midst of such privations, they called their book *Green Leaf in Drought Time,* because they found that those who delight in the Word of God do not wither but instead produce the Holy Spirit's fruit.

The second illustration the psalmist uses is chaff, to which he compares the wicked. The picture here is of a threshing floor at the time of the grain harvest. The threshing floors of Palestine are on hills that catch the best breezes. Grain is brought to them, is crushed by animals or by threshing instruments that are drawn over it, then is pitched high into the air where the wind blows the chaff away. The heavier grain falls back to the threshing floor and is collected. The chaff is scattered or burned, and it is what the psalmist says those who live wickedly are like.

The wicked are like chaff in two senses. Chaff is worthless, and chaff is burned. This pictures the futile, empty, worthless life of the godless, as well as their inevitable judgment.

If only those who are running away from God could see this! But they cannot, because they will not listen to God and the world is shouting the exact opposite of the Bible's teaching. The world says that to be religious is foolishness. Religious people never have any fun or accomplish anything, the wicked say. If you want to amount to something and enjoy yourself doing it, get on the fast track of sin, reach out for whatever you want, and take it. Be happy. That is what the world teaches. But it is all a lie, which is exactly what Paul calls it in Romans 1 where he analyzes this fast downward spiral (v. 25).

In Eden, the devil told Eve that if she disobeyed God by eating of the forbidden tree, her eyes would be "opened" and she would be "like God, knowing good and evil" (Gen. 3:5). But she did not become like God; she became like Satan. And her eyes were not opened; they had been open. Now she (and her husband) became blind to spiritual realities.

Do not believe the devil's lie. Do not follow the world when it tries to draw you from righteous living by beguiling falsehoods.

Two Final Ends

Verse 6 is a fitting end to the psalm and a proper thematic statement from which to proceed on into the Psalter. It distinguishes between the final end of the righteous and the final end of the wicked, saying,

> For the LORD watches over the way of the righteous,
>   but the way of the wicked will perish.

The verse describes the destiny of these two groups of people. Wise King Solomon wrote,

> There is a way that seems right to a man,
> but in the end it leads to death (Prov. 14:12).

That is the way of the wicked. The way of the righteous is the way of the Lord Jesus Christ, who described himself as "the way and the truth and the life" (John 14:6) and promised to keep those who follow him (Matt. 28:20).

I do not want to read too much prophecy into the psalms, though there is some, and I do not want to suggest that the author of this psalm, whoever he may have been, was looking forward to the coming of the Lord Jesus Christ when he wrote it. I do not believe he was. Nevertheless, it is hard not to notice, as Arno C. Gaebelein, an excellent devotional writer on the psalms, has said, that "the perfect man portrayed in the opening verses . . . is . . . the Lord Jesus."[11] He is the only one who was really like this.

Let me close with this story. Harry Ironside, the Bible teacher, told of a visit to Palestine years ago by a man named Joseph Flacks. He had an opportunity to address a gathering of Jews and Arabs and took for the subject of his address the first psalm. He read it and then asked the question: "Who is this blessed man of whom the psalmist speaks? This man never walked in the counsel of the wicked or stood in the way of sinners or sat in the seat of mockers. He was an absolutely sinless man."

Nobody spoke. So Flacks said: "Was he our great father Abraham?"

One old man said, "No, it cannot be Abraham. He denied his wife and told a lie about her."

"Well, how about the lawgiver Moses?"

"No," someone said. "It cannot be Moses. He killed a man, and he lost his temper by the waters of Meribah."

Flacks suggested David. It was not David.

There was silence for a long while. Then an elderly Jew arose and said, "My brothers, I have a little book here; it is called the New Testament. I have been reading it; and if I could believe this book, if I could be sure that it is true, I would say that the man of the first Psalm was Jesus of Nazareth."[12]

Jesus is that man, of course. He is the only perfect man who ever lived, and he is the sinner's Savior. It is he who stands at the portal of this book to show us the way to live and help us do it.

Psalm 2

The Wrong Path and Its Consequences

Why do the nations rage
    and the peoples plot in vain?
The kings of the earth take their stand
    and the rulers gather together
against the LORD
    and against his Anointed One.
"Let us break their chains," they say,
    "and throw off their fetters."

The One enthroned in heaven laughs;
    the Lord scoffs at them.
Then he rebukes them in his anger
    and terrifies them in his wrath, saying,
"I have installed my King
    on Zion, my holy hill."

I will proclaim the decree of the LORD:

He said to me, "You are my Son;
    today I have become your Father.
Ask of me,
    and I will make the nations your inheritance,
    the ends of the earth your possession.
You will rule them with an iron scepter;
    you will dash them to pieces like pottery."

> *Therefore, you kings, be wise;*
> *be warned, you rulers of the earth.*
> *Serve the LORD with fear*
> *and rejoice with trembling.*
> *Kiss the Son, lest he be angry*
> *and you be destroyed in your way,*
> *for his wrath can flare up in a moment.*
> *Blessed are all who take refuge in him.*
>
> *verses 1–12*

There is a debate among Old Testament scholars as to whether Psalm 2 can be considered messianic. That is, does it speak specifically of Jesus Christ? This is a complicated question with which we will deal again in the expositions of other psalms. But I say at the outset that if any psalm can rightly be regarded as messianic, it is this one. Psalm 2 speaks of the rebellion of the world's rulers against God's Anointed—the actual word is *Messiah*[1]—and of the Father's decree to give him dominion over them. This determination, plus the psalm's ready and obvious application to the hostile circumstances of their day, made Psalm 2 one of the psalms most quoted by the writers of the New Testament.

In the most extensive New Testament reference, the first two verses were cited by the earliest Christians in a thanksgiving prayer following the release of Peter and John by the Sanhedrin: "Sovereign Lord, . . . You spoke by the Holy Spirit through the mouth of your servant, our father David:

> 'Why do the nations rage
> and the peoples plot in vain?
> The kings of the earth take their stand
> and the rulers gather together
> against the Lord
> and against his Anointed One.'"

In the next verse they identified this rebellion with the conspiracy of "Herod and Pontius Pilate . . . with the Gentiles and the people of Israel . . . against . . . Jesus" (Acts 4:24–27).

The author of Hebrews applied verse 7 to Jesus twice, saying, "For to which of the angels did God ever say,

> 'You are my Son;
> today I have become your Father'?" (Heb. 1:5).

And again, "So Christ also did not take upon himself the glory of becoming a high priest. But God said to him,

> 'You are my Son;
>> today I have become your Father.'" (Heb. 5:5).

Psalm 2 is referred to frequently in Revelation. Examples: "Jesus Christ . . . the ruler of the kings of the earth" (Rev. 1:5); "He will rule them with an iron scepter; he will dash them to pieces like pottery" (Rev. 2:27); "She gave birth to a son, a male child, who will rule all the nations with an iron scepter" (Rev. 12:5); and other less specific references.

Augustine called Jesus *iste cantator psalmorum* (himself, the singer of the psalms). That is explicitly true of Psalm 2, since this psalm is not only *about* Jesus, but he himself speaks in it.

A Second Introductory Psalm

The specifically messianic psalms are not numerous. They include Psalms 22, 45, 72, 110, and some others. But among even this relatively small number Psalm 2 stands out dramatically. That is probably why it has been placed where it is, as the second introductory psalm to the Psalter.

There is some evidence in both Jewish and Christian traditions that Psalm 2 was at one time joined to Psalm 1, both psalms together being considered the first psalm. In the Jewish tradition Rabbi Johanan is quoted in the Talmud as having said: "Every chapter that was particularly dear to David he commenced with 'Happy' and terminated with 'Happy.' He began with 'Happy,' as it is written, 'Happy is the man,' and he terminated with 'Happy,' as it is written, 'Happy are all they that take refuge in him'" (*Ber.* 9b). These references are to Psalm 1:1 and Psalm 2:12, which indicates that the two psalms were at that time considered a single literary unit.

Similarly, in the oldest Greek texts of Acts 13:33, Psalm 2:7 is referred to as being from Psalm 1. Modern versions change the reference to Psalm 2, which is appropriate in view of the psalms' present numbering. But the fact that the oldest texts called Psalm 2, Psalm 1 indicates that at one time the two were together.[2]

This throws light on how Psalm 2 should be taken. For if the psalm is messianic, and if it was originally linked with Psalm 1, then the doctrine of the two ways introduced in Psalm 1 is here carried forward but at a higher pitch. On the one hand, the way of sinners in Psalm 1 now becomes a cosmic revolt of the nations against God and his Anointed. It becomes an unfolding of the wrong path and its consequences. On the other hand, the righteous man of the opening psalm is now explicitly seen to be God's Son, the Lord Jesus Christ, which I suggested at the close of the previous chapter. It is by taking refuge in Jesus that the judgment awaiting the wicked can be avoided by them.

Part One: The Narrator Speaks

The outline of Psalm 2 is straightforward. It divides into four nearly equal parts, each uttered by a different speaker or speakers. In the first section, verses 1–3, the speakers are the rebellious rulers of this earth, introduced by the narrator. He asks why they engage in anything as useless as trying to throw off the rule of God's Anointed.

Since the earlier years of this century, when European scholars such as Hermann Gunkel, Sigmund Mowinckel, and Artur Weiser published their influential studies on the psalms, it has been customary to look at Psalm 2 as a "royal" or a "coronation psalm" of Israel. This means that scholars consider the psalm to have been written on the occasion of the ascension of a Jewish king, either David or one of his successors, to the throne. Accordingly, it is only in a remote or a secondary sense that the psalm can be thought of as messianic.

But is this so? Is the one against whom the nations, people, and kings of the earth rage so furiously really David?

The chief arguments for this scholarly view are of two kinds. First, there have been studies of the coronation literature of other ancient peoples, and it has been argued that Psalm 2 matches this other material and must therefore be written of an earthly king, as the other poems have been. But that does not follow. The form of a psalm does not predetermine its meaning. In fact, nothing would be more natural than that the form of a hymn written to praise an earthly monarch should be taken over to praise one who is the King of Kings. What verse form could be more appropriate?

The second type of argument is based on the supposed similarity between Psalm 2 and the promises given to David through Nathan's oracle recorded in 2 Samuel 7:5–16. But the parallels are not great. And what is of maximum significance is that the oracle itself makes a distinction between the promises made to David, which are what might be expected of a merely human monarch (vv. 5–11a), and the promises that concern David's great future descendant whose kingdom will be established forever (vv. 11b–16). Indeed, all the real parallels to Psalm 2 occur in this second section, which itself proves that the psalm is not written of David or his merely human descendants but of the future divine Messiah. Promises of an eternal reign are false if they concern human beings only, as David himself recognized (cf. v. 19).

This means that we cannot understand this psalm until we realize that it is an expression of the rebellion of the human heart against God and not a limited revolt of some merely human Near Eastern king or kings against David or his successors. There is danger in reading too many Christian allusions into strictly Jewish psalms. They are not all about Jesus. Nevertheless, in this case, we are right in saying that the righteous one of Psalm 1, who is the Lord Jesus Christ, is not wanted by these rulers. And since Jesus is God's Son, their rebellion against him is actually a rebellion against God the Father.[3]

Charles Haddon Spurgeon was right when he said, "We have, in these first three verses, a description of the hatred of human nature against the Christ of God."[4]

Part Two: God the Father Speaks

In the second section of the psalm, verses 4–6, the speaker is God the Father, though the narrator sets up his words, just as in the opening section he set up the arrogant words of the rebelling monarchs.

What is God's reaction to the haughty words of these pygmy human rulers? God does not tremble. He does not hide behind a vast celestial rampart, counting the enemy and calculating whether or not he has sufficient force to counter this new challenge to his kingdom. He does not even rise from where he is sitting. He simply "laughs" at these great imbeciles.

This is the only place in the Bible where God is said to laugh, and it is not a pleasant laugh. It is a laugh of derision, as the next verb shows: "the Lord scoffs at them" (v. 4). This is what human attempts to throw off the rule of the sovereign God deserve. It is understandable that sinners should want to reject God's rule. That is what sin is: a repudiation of God's rule in favor of one's own will. But although it is understandable, the folly of this attempt surpasses belief. How can mere human beings expect to get rid of God?

After laughing at such foolishness, God speaks to rebuke and to terrify these rulers. He tells of the appointment of his Son to be King in Zion and foretells his triumph.

Spurgeon pointed out that in the late third and early first centuries the emperor Diocletian (A.D. 245–313), a great foe of Christianity, struck a medal which bore the inscription: "The name of Christianity being extinguished." Diocletian extended the frontier of the empire westward into Spain, where he erected two monuments proclaiming:

> Diocletian Jovian Maximian Herculeus Caesares Augusti
> for having extended the Roman Empire in the east and the west
> and for having extinguished the name of Christians
> who brought the Republic to ruin

and

> Diocletian Jovian Maximian Herculeus Caesares Augusti
> for having everywhere abolished the superstition of Christ
> for having extended the worship of the gods.

But Diocletian had not abolished Christianity. On the contrary, at the time Christianity was growing stronger than ever, and eventually it triumphed over Caesar's throne.

Spurgeon quotes an earlier preacher, William S. Plumer:

Of thirty Roman emperors, governors of provinces and others in high office, who distinguished themselves by their zeal and bitterness in persecuting the early Christians, one became speedily deranged after some atrocious cruelty, one was slain by his own son, one became blind, the eyes of one started out of his head, one was drowned, one was strangled, one died in a miserable captivity, one fell dead in a manner that will not bear recital, one died of so loathsome a disease that several of his physicians were put to death because they could not abide the stench that filled his room, two committed suicide, a third attempted it but had to call for help to finish the work, five were assassinated by their own people or servants, five others died the most miserable and excruciating deaths, several of them having an untold complication of diseases, and eight were killed in battle, or after being taken prisoners.

Among these was Julian the Apostate. In the days of his prosperity he is said to have pointed his dagger to heaven, defying the Son of God whom he commonly called the Galilean. But when he was wounded in battle, he saw that all was over with him, and he gathered up his clotted blood and threw it into the air, exclaiming, "Thou has conquered, O thou Galilean."[5]

So has it been throughout history. So will it be to the end.

Part Three: The Son Speaks

The third section of the psalm, verses 7–9, contains the words of God's Anointed, the Lord Jesus Christ.

Scholars who see Psalm 2 chiefly as a psalm of coronation for a Davidic king take the words "You are my Son; today I have become your Father" (v. 7) as a formula for the symbolic adoption of the Jewish king by God at the time of his inauguration. But aside from the fact that nothing like this is ever said or suggested in the Old Testament, the Bible's own handling of the words is always in regard to Jesus. The words "You are my Son" or "This is my beloved Son" were spoken of Jesus by the Father twice during his earthly ministry: once at his baptism and once at the transfiguration. At the baptism a voice from heaven said, "This is my Son, whom I love; with him I am well pleased" (Matt. 3:17; cf. Mark 1:11; Luke 3:22). At the transfiguration God said, "This is my Son, whom I love; with him I am well pleased. Listen to him!" (Matt. 17:5; cf. Mark 9:7; Luke 9:35).

The other part of the verse in Psalm 2—"today I have become your Father"—is used by Paul in a way consistent with the Gospels' use of the first part. In the first of his sermons recorded in Acts, he refers it to Jesus' resurrection (Acts 13:33). That is, he refers "today" not to Jesus' eternal begetting by the Father, which is wrapped up with the doctrine of the Trinity, but with God's raising him from the dead by which he became what is else-where called "the firstborn from among the dead" (Col. 1:18).

Verses 8 and 9 have special bearing upon our obligation to tell others about Jesus Christ today. This is because, although verse 6 speaks of God *having* established his King on Zion (past tense), verses 8 and 9 speak in a future sense, saying,

> Ask of me,
>> and I *will* make the nations your inheritance,
>> the ends of the earth your possession.
> You *will* rule them with an iron scepter;
>> you *will* dash them to pieces like pottery (italics added).

This is an acknowledgment of what the author of Hebrews says in apply-ing another psalm to Jesus. In chapter 2, he quotes Psalm 8:4–6, noting that the Father has placed everything under Jesus' feet. But he says, "At present we do not see everything subject to him" (Heb. 2:8). Jesus is Lord. But there are still many, like the rulers of the psalm's opening lines, who resist him.

Here is the great missionary challenge of the church. It is for us, the grateful subjects of Jesus' divine kingdom, to make his name known among the nations, until every ear shall hear and every knee shall bow. Harry Ironside wrote, "I never come to a missionary meeting but I feel as though there ought to be written right across the entire platform, 'Ask of me, and I shall give thee the heathen for thine inheritance, and the uttermost parts of the earth for thy possession.'" He continued, "It is the will of God that his Son should have a great heritage out of the heathen world, the godless Gentiles."[6] Our assignment is to carry the message of God's decree and Christ's rule to them. It is to proclaim the rule of King Jesus.

Part Four: The Narrator Speaks Again

In the final section of this psalm, verses 10–12, the narrator speaks again, uttering words of warning and entreaty to those who have not yet bowed before God's Son. Since the author of the psalm is not specifically identi-fied, it is perhaps not overly whimsical to follow Ironside at this point too, since he speaks of "four voices" in the psalm: those of the world, God the Father, God the Son, and God the Holy Spirit. It is the role of the Holy Spirit to draw us to Jesus, which is what the individual I have called the nar-rator is doing here. Ironside calls his "a very gentle, a very loving, a very ten-der voice."[7]

What does this gentle, loving, and tender voice call on these rebellious human beings to do? A number of things: to "be wise," to "be warned," to "serve the LORD with fear," to "rejoice with trembling" (vv. 10–11). But chiefly they are to "kiss the Son" in grateful, loving submission.[8]

That is what these rulers will not do, of course. It is why they are in danger of a final, fierce destruction. Make sure you are not among them. The rulers of the world rage against Christ. But why should you? The hands he holds forth for you to kiss are hands that were pierced by nails when he was crucified in your place. One day he is coming as the great judge of all. On that day the wicked will be punished, but today is the day of his grace. He invites you to come to him. The final verse says, "Blessed are all who take refuge in him." It is a reminder that the only refuge from the wrath of God is God's mercy unfolded at the cross of Jesus Christ.

Psalm 3

New Day Dawning: A Morning Psalm

O LORD, how many are my foes!
  How many rise up against me!
Many are saying of me,
  "God will not deliver him."   Selah

But you are a shield around me, O LORD,
  you bestow glory on me and lift up my head.
To the LORD I cry aloud,
  and he answers me from his holy hill. Selah

I lie down and sleep;
  I wake again, because the LORD sustains me.
I will not fear the tens of thousands
  drawn up against me on every side.

Arise, O LORD!
  Deliver me, O my God!
Strike all my enemies on the jaw;
  break the teeth of the wicked.

From the LORD comes deliverance.
  May your blessing be on your people.   Selah
                                    verses 1–8

After Psalms 1 and 2, which are foundational psalms—the first stressing the importance of the law of God in one's life, the second stressing the ultimate triumph of the Messiah—a number of psalms deal with various circumstances that come into the godly man's life in which he must trust God. Psalm 3, which heads the list, describes a person who is in great physical danger as a new day dawns.

It has been called a morning psalm because of verse 5: "I lie down and sleep; I wake again, because the LORD sustains me." At first glance this does not seem sufficient reason to call Psalm 3 a morning psalm, as most commentators both past and present do. But I am convinced that, if the introductory title is taken seriously, as I want to show it should be, the psalm does describe a specific dangerous morning in the life of King David and is a testimony to how he gained confidence and courage at that time and in those dangerous circumstances by his faith in God. Because of that setting, the psalm seems to have become thought of, in time, as a general morning prayer and therefore was placed appropriately at this early position in the Psalter.

It is followed in a balanced fashion by an evening psalm, Psalm 4, which ends, "I will lie down and sleep in peace, for you alone, O LORD, make me dwell in safety" (v. 8).

What a Morning!

Psalm 3 begins with an introductory title: "A psalm of David. When he fled from his son Absalom." It is the first title to a psalm in the Psalter, and it contains a number of other important firsts too. (1) This is the first time the word *psalm* has occurred. The Hebrew word is *mizmor,* meaning a poem to be sung to musical accompaniment. (2) This is the first poem of which "David" is said to be the author. (Generally, the psalms ascribed to David occur in the first two books of the Psalter, Psalms 1–72, but some also occur later.[1]) (3) This is the first psalm which is given a historical setting, namely, "When he [David] fled from his son Absalom."

Is this historical setting to be taken seriously? Since the titles of the psalms are in the canonical text of the Hebrew Bible (though, strangely enough, they are omitted in many English translations), the position I hold is that they are to be taken with absolute seriousness throughout. But even apart from this dogmatic consideration, there are ample reasons for viewing Psalm 3 as arising out of the situation in David's life to which the title alludes.[2]

The chief reason is the appropriateness of the psalm to that setting. The story of David's flight is told in 2 Samuel 15 and 16. While David had been occupied with the affairs of government, his son Absalom stole the hearts of the people and raised a rebellion in the nearby town of Hebron. The revolt was so sudden and unexpected that David had no recourse but to flee Jerusalem with whatever leaders remained faithful to him. He retreated down the steep descent from the capital, crossed the Kidron Valley, and made his way up over the Mount of Olives to the temporary safety of the desert. The narrative says that he went weeping and barefoot, his head covered in sorrow. Along the way David was loudly and openly cursed by Shimei, a Benjamite who had remained loyal to the house of David's predecessor Saul. Shimei cried, "Get out, get out, you man of blood, you scoundrel! The LORD has repaid you for all the blood you shed in the household of Saul, in whose place you have reigned. The LORD has handed the kingdom over to your son Absalom. You have come to ruin because you are a man of blood!" (2 Sam. 16:7–8).

This is the situation Psalm 3 describes. It is true that there are no references to the specific details of David's grim retreat from Jerusalem. Very few of the psalms are specific in this way, obviously so that they might be used by people in similar though not identical situations. Still, what is said in Psalm 3 fits 2 Samuel 15 and 16.

The late Lutheran commentator H. C. Leupold refers to the parallels:

> Note that the opponents of the author are numerous (vv. 1, 2, 6); note the same situation in 2 Samuel 15:13. Again, the attitude of some of David's opponents was that he had forfeited all right to hope for divine aid; cf. 2 Samuel 16:8. Verse 2 of our psalm says the same thing. That David directs his prayer to the holy hill (v. 4) agrees well with the situation as outlined in 2 Samuel 15:25, where David has taken steps to have the ark, which marked the presence of God on the holy hill, returned to Jerusalem rather than have it taken along with him on his flight. Lastly, the thought that the issues of this whole experience rested with God (cf. v. 9 [v. 8 in our numbering]) is the very thought expressed in 2 Samuel 15:25. Besides, the author is a man of some eminence. Nothing of moment can be adduced to remove any of these points of correspondence between the history of David and the contents of the psalm.[3]

A second reason for taking the title of the psalm literally is that the images of the psalm are military, which fits the situation in 2 Samuel well. P. C. Craigie is not inclined to take words that identify a psalm as David's at face value, but in this case he does. He writes, "the military language is entirely in harmony with the superscription linking the psalm with David's flight from Jerusalem."[4] Examples are:

1. The reference to "foes" (v. 1) and "enemies" (v. 7).
2. The references to victory (vv. 3, 8).
3. God is described as a "shield" (v. 3).

4. "People" (v. 8) may be employed with the nuance "army" and probably should be in this context.
5. People are deployed (v. 6) against the psalmist.
6. The expression "Arise, O LORD" (v. 7) is parallel to the words spoken on the departure of the Ark of the Covenant for war (cf. Num. 10:35).
7. "From the LORD comes deliverance" (v. 8) sounds like a battle cry.

These examples of military language as well as general correspondence between the psalm and the condition of David described in 2 Samuel 15 and 16 suggest strongly that the title "when he fled from his son Absalom" should be taken literally. In fact, it might be possible to be even more specific. Leupold suggests that the psalm was composed the second day after the rebellion was staged or, if written afterward, was at least meant as a reflection of David's thoughts at that time.[5]

So the psalm is not speaking of a vague problem or disappointment but rather of a specific danger David faced that specific far-off morning.

A World of Foes

I am sure that many people can identify with that. Perhaps you are one. You may not be facing an imminent military battle when you wake up most mornings, but you are facing a battle. The climate in the department of the company for which you work may be one of open warfare: Everyone is trying to defeat everyone else. The conditions are cutthroat. The weapons are rumors, lying, gossip, misrepresentation, even violence, bribes, or stealing. A friend told me how he had gone on a vacation, leaving his business in the hands of his partner. When he came back after only two weeks the partner had managed to steal it away, leaving him with significant debts. How can any honest person survive in such a jungle?

Again, you may not be facing thousands of enemies, as David was. But how many enemies does it take to make life miserable and possibly lead even to the loss of your job? One will do, if he or she is determined enough. And you probably have more than that! In fact, the more prominent you are, the more enemies you will have and the more vulnerable you will be to them.

Or what about bureaucracy? Bureaucracy is a formidable enough enemy for anyone, particularly if you work in a state or government agency.

Or again, you may not be attacked by soldiers commanded by your son, as David was attacked by Absalom. But your children may hate you or may have betrayed what you stand for. For that matter, your husband may have done it, or your wife. You thought your spouse was an ally, but he or she has become part of that frightening force arrayed against you. It may even be that some of your foes are saying, as they said of David, "God will not deliver him" (v. 2). Charles Haddon Spurgeon wrote, "It is the most bitter of all afflictions to be led to fear that there is no help for us in God."[6]

I want you to think about whatever distress you may be having or whatever danger you may be in before going on with your study of this psalm,
because it is in the midst of precisely that danger that God will appear to
you and deliver you. The text urges us to do this when it interrupts the
poem at this point by the word *selah*.[7]

The Psalmist's Confidence in God

Much happens in this psalm in the space between the first two stanzas,
marked out by *selah*. The first stanza is an expression of the crisis that has
come into the psalmist's life because of the enemies who have risen up
against him. The second stanza is a quiet expression of his confidence in
God. What has produced this abrupt but obvious change? The answer is
that he has turned his attention from his enemies to God.

When a believer gazes too long at his enemies, the force arrayed against
him seems to grow in size until it appears to be overwhelming. But when he
turns his thoughts to God, God is seen in his true, great stature, and the
enemies shrink to manageable proportions.

This principle was illustrated by the difference between the ten and
the two spies when they were first sent into Canaan at the time of the
Jewish conquest. Ten of the spies were overwhelmed with the strength
and stature of the Canaanites, especially the descendants of Anak, who
were giants. They said, "We can't attack those people; they are stronger
than we are. . . . All the people we saw there are of great size. We saw the
Nephilim there (the descendants of Anak come from the Nephilim). We
seemed like grasshoppers in our own eyes, and we looked the same to
them" (Num. 13:31–33). The other two spies, Caleb and Joshua, said,
"We should go up and take possession of the land, for we can certainly
do it" (v. 30).

What was the difference? Had they seen different things? No. The land
was the same. Both groups had seen the giants. But the ten looked only at
the giants and forgot about God, with the result that they seemed in their
own eyes to shrink to the size of grasshoppers. The two kept their eyes on
God, and for them it was the giants who appeared small.

So also with David. As soon as David turned his thoughts to God he was
reminded of how strong God is, and his foes, even the formidable armies
then flocking to the side of his rebellious son, seemed manageable. He
tells us three things about God. First, God was a "shield" around him. God
had been a shield for him on earlier occasions; he would prove himself to
be so again. Second, God would "lift up" his head, even when he was
severely cast down. Sin beats us down; God always lifts us up. We can
expect God to do that for us, even if we do not see him doing it right now.
Third, God "answers" the psalmist when he cries aloud to him. God always

answers, though not always at once and not always as we wish. Spurgeon wrote, "We need not fear a frowning world while we rejoice in a prayer-hearing God."[8]

If you are not fully aware of what you have in God—a shield against foes, a lifter-up of your drooping head, a responder to prayer—this is a good time to think about it. Note the second *selah!*

"Though This World with Devils Filled"

To many people the most appealing part of this psalm is the third stanza, the part in which David tells how he was able to lie down and sleep even in the midst of the sudden great danger occasioned by Absalom's rebellion. It is a beautiful picture of one so trusting of God that he is able to sleep soundly even while the treacherous seek his life. Leupold calls it "the high point of faith reached by the psalm."[9]

> I lie down and sleep;
>> I wake again, because the LORD sustains me.
> I will not fear the tens of thousands
>> drawn up against me on every side (vv. 5–6).

Actually, the confidence expressed in these verses is the confidence of the next morning. The psalmist went to sleep trusting God. Now he has awakened with the events of the day (as was the case with the events of the previous night) firmly in God's hands. He is saying, "I had a good night's rest, and now I am not afraid to face the terrors of this new day. I will not fear the thousands drawn up against me."

It reminds one of Martin Luther on his way to Worms. Luther had been called to Worms by the emperor and the papal legate to answer for his "heretical" teachings. He had been promised a safe-conduct. But his friends had heard the Reformer's enemies say that the safe-conduct of a heretic ought not to be honored, and they feared for his life. After all, John Huss had been given a safe-conduct not long before, and he had been burned at the stake. As Luther approached the city, a messenger arrived with a warning from his friend Georg Spalatin: "Do not enter Worms!" Luther told the messenger, "Tell your master that even if there should be as many devils in Worms as tiles upon the housetops, still I would enter it."

Years later, a few days before his death, Luther said of that moment, "I was then undaunted. I feared nothing."

It must have been true, too, because it was in Worms that Luther gave his classic reply to the Diet: "Unless I be persuaded by the words of Scripture and sound reasoning I cannot and will not recant. Here I stand. I can do no other. God help me. Amen." Where had Luther found such courage? He had found it where David had found it, in God.

A Confident Cry for Deliverance

The last section of the psalm is a confident cry for God's deliverance—confident because the psalmist knows that God has heard him and that he will provide the needed deliverance.

David's words are actually a war cry, as I suggested earlier. In Numbers 10:33–36 we are told that when the hosts of Israel broke camp, they did so because the cloud of the Lord, which normally rested over the Ark of the Covenant in the midst of the camp, had risen up and gone before them. Then Moses would cry,

> Rise up, O LORD!
> May your enemies be scattered;
> may your foes flee before you.

Whenever the cloud came to rest, Moses would say, "Return, O LORD, to the countless thousands of Israel."

Regardless of the speaker, the words "Rise up, O LORD" always carried this connotation. So when David said them he was making a victorious call to battle, knowing that the Lord was going before him and would give him the victory.

And God did! God caused Absalom to listen to bad advice and thus fail to pursue and defeat his father when he was most vulnerable. Then, when the battle was finally engaged, after David had been able to gather strength and prepare for it, David's troops achieved a great victory. It took place in the forest of Ephraim, where twenty thousand men were killed, including Absalom.

The final verse of Psalm 3 contains a testimonial—"From the LORD comes deliverance"—followed by a blessing. The testimonial reminds us of Jonah 2:9, which reads, "Salvation comes from the LORD." It is what Spurgeon called, "the sum and substance of [true or] Calvinistic doctrine." Spurgeon said,

> Search the Scripture through, and you must, if you read it with a candid mind, be persuaded that the doctrine of salvation by grace alone is the great doctrine of the word of God. . . . This is the great point concerning which we are daily fighting. Our opponents say, "Salvation belongeth to the free will of man; if not to man's merit, yet at least to man's will." But we hold and teach that salvation from first to last, in every iota of it, belongs to the Most High God. It is God that chooses his people. *He* calls them by his grace; *he* quickens them by his Spirit, and keeps them by his power. It is not of man, neither by man: "not of him that willeth, nor of him that runneth, but of God that showeth mercy."[10]

That is all quite true. God is indeed the author of salvation from beginning to end. If he were not, no one would be saved. Neither you nor I. Salvation *is* of the Lord. But if that is true—if God has saved you in this great matter of salvation—why should you tremble before the lesser, physical dangers of this life, however imposing and frightful they may seem? You should triumph by faith in God, as David did.

Psalm 4

An Evening Psalm

Answer me when I call to you,
  O my righteous God.
Give me relief from my distress;
  be merciful to me and hear my prayer.

How long, O men, will you turn my glory into shame?
  How long will you love delusions and seek false gods? Selah
Know that the LORD has set apart the godly for himself;
  the LORD will hear when I call to him.

In your anger do not sin;
  when you are on your beds,
  search your hearts and be silent.   Selah
Offer right sacrifices
  and trust in the LORD.

Many are asking, "Who can show us any good?"
  Let the light of your face shine upon us, O LORD.
You have filled my heart with greater joy
  than when their grain and new wine abound.
I will lie down and sleep in peace,
  for you alone, O LORD,
  make me dwell in safety.

verses 1–8

It is tempting to seek a historical setting for Psalm 4, just as for Psalm 3, but there is little justification for it. The setting for Psalm 3 is indicated by the title: "A psalm of David. When he fled from his son Absalom." When we studied that psalm, I argued that the setting indicated by the title should be taken literally if for no other reason than that the title is part of the canonical Hebrew text. We do not have the same situation in Psalm 4. The title says merely: "For the director of music. With stringed instruments. A psalm of David."

In spite of this, a number of commentators link the psalm with the one preceding and therefore carry the setting of Psalm 3 over to Psalm 4. Charles Haddon Spurgeon and Franz Delitzsch assume the connection.[1] H. C. Leupold argues it as follows: "To refer the psalm to the days when David fled before Absalom certainly fits the words of the psalm in a number of striking ways: the author is obviously in distress; his honor is assailed; he seeks to set his erring son and those that err with him aright; a paternal type of admonition is used such as David might well have used over against the rebel son; and lastly, the author manifests a courageous faith such as is often noted in the life of David."[2]

Those connections between the psalm and David's flight from Jerusalem are tenuous, however, and in some cases they are even questionable. But the chief reason for doubting that Psalm 4 has to do with David's flight is that the problems in the two are quite different. The problem at the time of David's flight from Absalom, reflected in Psalm 3, was one of physical danger. Thousands of troops had aligned themselves against David. He needed God to be his "shield" against these armed enemies.

This is not the problem in Psalm 4. In this psalm the problem is one of malicious slander and lies. It is the psalmist's reputation rather than his person that is being attacked, and what he needs is a sense of the presence and approval of God rather than physical deliverance.

The Agony and the Ecstasy

Earlier, in our study of Psalm 1, I mentioned that scholars speak of various types or genres of psalms, pointing out that there are perhaps seven types in all. The seven genres are usually referred to as hymns, laments, psalms of thanksgiving, psalms of confidence, psalms of remembrance, wisdom psalms, and kingship (possibly messianic) psalms.[3] Psalm 4 could be classified in two ways and is perhaps best seen as a combination of two genres. It is a psalm of individual lament, but it is also a psalm of confidence. In fact, it moves from one to the other, from distress to quiet confidence in God.

P. C. Craigie says, "It is not a psalm of penitence, arising out of the recognition of sins committed; there are other psalms for that purpose. It is rather a psalm which reflects the anguish of the innocent and oppressed, or of the righteous sufferer. And thus it is a particularly important kind of psalm, for it addresses a fundamental human experience, the experience of injustice, suffering and oppression."[4]

Is there such a thing as a totally righteous sufferer? Is anyone ever really innocent? The answer is: of course not, unless we are thinking of the Lord Jesus Christ, which is the way some scholars have interpreted Psalm 4. But that is not the point here. None of us is ever utterly innocent, but there are nevertheless times of relative innocence in which evil people really do heap injustices on us. There are times when we are falsely accused. At other times we are slandered. Someone may want to advance himself by getting us out of the way. Or an attack may be occasioned by pure envy.

When a citizen of Athens was asked why he had voted for the condemnation of Aristides, called "the Just" (c. 530–468 b.c.)—he was one of the most outstanding statesmen that nation had produced—the citizen replied, "I voted against him simply because I was tired of hearing him called 'the Just.'"

Perhaps you have experienced something like that. In fact, I would be surprised if in this sinful world you had not. All are slandered at one time or another. All have their reputations attacked. Although the attacks on you probably have not been accompanied by actual physical danger, they have nevertheless probably hurt you a lot. When we were children and our friends and playmates said nasty things about us, we were taught to say,

> Sticks and stones can break my bones,
> But names will never hurt me.

But it was not true, as we probably found out. Names do hurt. To be falsely accused is agony, and we have to rise above it.

But how? How do we rise above it? In this psalm, David, the target of many false accusations, shows how.

The psalm falls into three parts. First, there is an urgent plea to God for help in distress (v. 1). This is a real distress, requiring genuine relief. David needs an answer from God, which is why he is praying. Second, there is a moving remonstrance addressed to the psalmist's enemies (vv. 2–5). In these verses David shows a surprisingly kind attitude to his enemies and gives advice that not only would solve his difficulty but also would help them. His enemies would become different people if they would do what he advises. Third, there is a final expression of the psalmist's security in God (vv. 6–8). This enables him to say, as he closes,

> I will lie down and sleep in peace,
>   for you alone, O Lord,
>   make me dwell in safety.

It is because of these words that Psalm 4 has been called an evening psalm.

We are going to study this psalm according to this obvious three-part outline. But I need to say at the outset that what is important about the psalm is not the outline but rather what happens to the psalmist as he prays. What happens is that he changes. He moves from anxiety because of his accusers to quiet trust in God, which is to say in modern jargon that prayer is his therapy. It does him good.

Since all of us have had the psalmist's experience at some time or another, perhaps regularly, Craigie is certainly right when he says, "There are days in the lives of all human beings which require a psalm like this at their end."[5]

An Appeal to God

Whom do you turn to when you hear of an unjust accusation that someone has been making against you? You are at work, and the secretary down the hall stops by your desk and says, "Do you know what so-and-so said about you yesterday?" Then she pours out the story, perhaps even embellishing it a little. Or a business associate circulates a memo in which you are pictured in an unjust light. What do you do? Whom do you tell? Most of us would go to our friends and complain, looking for sympathy. We might even start a slander campaign of our own. It might go: "Well, the only reason she said that is because she. . . ."

This is not what David did. Instead of turning to friends for sympathy or even attacking his enemies, David turned to God.

> Answer me when I call to you,
>   O my righteous God.
> Give me relief from my distress;
>   be merciful to me and hear my prayer.

David knew that his only help was in God, which strikingly is where the psalm also ends. The last words of the psalm say: "You *alone*, O LORD, make me dwell in safety" (v. 8, italics added).

Notice two important things about this appeal.

David's appeal is honest. If David were presenting his case before some other person, he might have pretended something other than what he really felt—or at least, that is what we probably would do. We would pretend that we were less affected by the attack than we were. We would try to keep up appearances. However, David is coming to God, who knows the situation perfectly anyway, and thus he does not need to keep up appearances. He can tell it as it is. He indicates that his enemies are significant men, not people who can safely be ignored. This is implied by the Hebrew words *beni ish,* rather than the more common *beni adam.*[6] Again, he is deeply distressed by their actions. The next verse describes what is happening. His enemies are dishonoring him by ruining his reputation (turning his "glory into shame"). Why are they doing this? It is because they love lies ("delusions") and are opposed to his religious convictions (they "seek false gods").

Do you know the advantage of coming to God with your troubles? It is an important one. To come to God means that you do not need to pretend. You can tell him exactly where you hurt and how you feel.

David's appeal is balanced. I mean by this that although he is conscious of the injustice of his enemies' accusations and is appealing to God for relief on the basis of God's righteousness ("O my righteous God"), the psalmist is nevertheless also aware of his own sin in relation to God. This is why he speaks of mercy, saying "be merciful to me and hear my prayer." Isn't that an interesting combination of ideas? Before other men and in comparison with his enemies he is righteous. He can properly appeal to God for relief. But in relationship to God he is a sinner like everyone else and can only ask God to intervene mercifully.

We will have to remember this when we begin our study of the difficult imprecatory psalms.

An Appeal to His Enemies

The most interesting part of this psalm is the second section (vv. 2–5), in which David relates to those who are harming him. They are wrong. He is right. He is asking God to help him. Nevertheless, although slandered and injured by them, David speaks of his enemies kindly and tries to win them from their errors. And there is this: in trying to help them, he unintentionally but inevitably helps himself.

We see how this works in verse 3. In this verse David reminds his enemies of a truth that is very important, namely, that "the LORD has set apart the godly for himself." This is something the enemies of the righteous do not want to hear. It refers to election, which they hate. In David's case, the statement was a reminder that he had become king by the sovereign choice of God, not by man's authority. Therefore, he could not be attacked with impunity. His enemies would have resented that a great deal. In our case, the statement is a reminder that we have been brought into the company of God's people by God's choice and actions, not our own. That too is a doctrine widely hated. *But it is nevertheless true.* And it follows from the truth of election that, if God "has set apart the godly for himself," he will obviously not abandon them. He will stick by them, for "he who began a good work in you will carry it on to completion until the day of Christ Jesus" (Phil. 1:6). The ungodly need to be reminded of this, because it means that their attacks upon God's people will not ultimately be successful.

How does that help David? In this way. As soon as he reminded his enemies that the Lord protects his people, David must have realized afresh that what he was telling his enemies applied to him. He was one of God's people. God had set him apart and would not abandon him. Therefore, as he says in the second half of the very same verse, "the LORD will hear when I call to him."

Do you see how it is working? David began with a cry of real anguish:

> Answer me when I call to you,
>   O my righteous God.
> Give me relief from my distress;
>   be merciful to me and hear my prayer.

Now, having reminded his enemies that God cares for his own, David turned what began as a prayer into a statement of confidence: "the LORD *will* hear when I call to him" (italics added).

Are you confused by attacks upon you? Go through David's procedure. In your thoughts remind your enemies that God will take care of you, and you will find that the very act of reminding them will strengthen your own confidence. You will quiet your distress by this exercise.

This same thing—David himself benefiting by the way he expresses concern for his enemies—occurs again in the psalm's second half. It grows out of David's advice to them in verses 4 and 5.

Verse 4 is a bit of a problem, however. There are two ways the words "in your anger do not sin" can be interpreted. The first is the meaning given to the words in the Septuagint (the Greek translation of the Old Testament) and then apparently picked up by the apostle Paul and quoted in Ephesians 4:26. It is, in effect: "Be angry, but do not let your anger carry over into sinful acts." Paul seems to mean this, because his next words in Ephesians are, "Do not let the sun go down while you are still angry"—that is, deal with your problem in the anger stage.

However, the verb *be angry* can also mean "tremble," which is the way H. C. Leupold takes it. Tremble in what way? Well, it could mean tremble in anger, which is why most versions use the word *anger* to translate it. But it could also mean tremble before God, which is what Leupold thinks it means. That is, "Stand in awe of God, and because you are in awe of him cease sinning as you have been doing." This makes good sense in the psalm, for the thought would then be: "The evil you are planning should be abandoned, because God is against you in it. You should be able to see this when you are upon your beds searching your hearts silently."[7]

I do not know which is the right answer, but I incline to the second view because of what comes next. Verse 5 says,

> Offer right sacrifices
> and trust in the LORD.

These sacrifices must be sacrifices for sin. So verse 4 probably does not mean, "deal with your anger and do not sin," but rather, "tremble before

God and cease from the sin you are committing." It would follow from the latter that, having recognized the sin as sin, the enemies of the psalmist would then offer the proper sacrifices of atonement for it.

The final step would be for them then to live as those who "trust in the LORD" rather than in their own devices (v. 5).

The Psalmist's Trust in God

Were David's enemies likely to follow his advice, tremble before God, offer sacrifices for their sin, and begin to trust the Almighty? It was not very likely! It is not even likely that David spoke these words to them. They are part of the psalm, words that David spoke to God and would have liked to have spoken to his enemies but probably did not have the chance to utter. But here is the important thing: although his enemies did not come to trust God, David did. He had trusted God in the past. He had laid before him his grief over the false accusations of his enemies. Now God provided the peace he was seeking by doing three things.

God assured him of his favor (v. 6). In their distress the people around David were asking, "Who can show us any good?" In their opinion, there was nothing good about their circumstances at all. But God brought to David's mind the well-known Aaronic blessing of Numbers 6:24–26.

> The LORD bless you
>   and keep you;
> the LORD make his face shine upon you
>   and be gracious to you;
> the LORD turn his face toward you
>   and give you peace.

He remembers it in an abbreviated form in verse 6. Thus, he was reminded that the one who had shown him good in the past can be counted on to show him good again, even God himself.

God filled him with joy, greater than the joy of those reaping an abundant harvest (v. 7). Joy floods our hearts when we are conscious of the Lord's favor.

God gave him peace even in the turmoil (v. 8). This is the final blessing that came to David as he tried to help those who were his enemies. As Craigie says, "At the end, the psalmist has seen that he is better off than his adversaries. He has advised them to lie still on their beds, in an attempt to curtail their evil (v. 5 [v. 4, our numbering]), but he could lie on his bed and sleep the sleep of peace which came from God."[8] It is always that way. If we leave our problems with God, he will shoulder them. And he will enable us to sleep in peace.

Psalm 5

A Prayer for Coming to God's House

Give ear to my words, O LORD,
   consider my sighing.
Listen to my cry for help,
   my King and my God,
   for to you I pray.
In the morning, O LORD, you hear my voice;
   in the morning I lay my requests before you
   and wait in expectation.

You are not a God who takes pleasure in evil;
   with you the wicked cannot dwell.
The arrogant cannot stand in your presence;
   you hate all who do wrong.
You destroy those who tell lies;
   bloodthirsty and deceitful men
   the LORD abhors.

But I, by your great mercy,
   will come into your house;
in reverence will I bow down
   toward your holy temple.

Lead me, O LORD, in your righteousness
  because of my enemies—
  make straight your way before me.

verses 1–8

Banish them for their many sins,
  for they have rebelled against you.

But let all who take refuge in you be glad;
  let them ever sing for joy.
Spread your protection over them,
  that those who love your name may rejoice in you.
For surely, O LORD, you bless the righteous;
  you surround them with your favor as with a shield.

verses 10–12

I have called this psalm "a prayer for coming to God's house" because of verse 7: "But I, by your great mercy will come into your house; in reverence will I bow down toward your holy temple." However, we must not think of it as restricted to a formal worship setting. This is actually a generic prayer showing how we must approach God, if we would be heard by him, and what we can expect of him when we do.

An outline is helpful for understanding the text. Psalm 5 consists of five strophes or stanzas. In three of these (the first, third, and fifth) the psalmist is standing face-to-face before God with only God in view. In the two alternating stanzas (the second and fourth) he glances sideways at the wicked, as it were, and develops contrasts between God and the wicked (in stanza two) and the righteous and the wicked (in stanza four). These interlocking contrasts give movement and power to the psalm. Here is how P. C. Craigie describes it: "Psalm 5 illustrates with clarity the polarity and tension which characterize certain dimensions of the life of prayer. On the one side, there is God: on the other, evil human beings. And the thought of the psalmist alternates between these two poles. He begins by asking God to hear him, but recalls that evil persons have no place in God's presence. He turns back to God again, expressing his desire to worship and his need of guidance, but then is reminded of the human evils of the tongue. Eventually, he concludes in confidence, praying for protection and blessing."

Craigie adds that "the prayer is not only for protection *from* wicked persons, but also a prayer for protection from becoming *like them.*"[1]

Psalm 5 is another morning psalm (v. 3), like Psalm 3. Since the following psalm is another evening psalm ("all night long I flood my bed with weeping," Ps. 6:6), we therefore have prayers for morning and evening, morning and evening in Psalms 3–6. It is a way of saying that our entire day, from the rising to the setting of the sun, should be prayerful.

Charles Haddon Spurgeon said, "Prayer should be the key of the day and the lock of the night. Devotion should be both the morning . . . and the evening star."[2]

An Appeal for God to Listen

The first three verses are an appeal for God to listen to the psalmist's prayer. Many psalms begin in this way. Psalm 4 is one. It begins, "Answer me when I call to you, O my righteous God" (v. 1). Psalm 5 begins,

> Give ear to my words, O LORD,
>   consider my sighing.
> Listen to my cry for help,
>   my King and my God,
>   for to you I pray.
> In the morning, O LORD, you hear my voice;
>   in the morning I lay my requests before you
>   and wait in expectation.

Have you ever been stopped in your prayers by doubts about whether you are approaching God rightly? Almost everyone has had doubts like this. If you have, notice what these verses teach us. They teach three things.

The Spirit in Which We Should Pray

One characteristic of this prayer is its *urgency* expressed in the imperatives: "give ear," "consider," and "listen." They mean that David was not merely going through a prayer routine. He was intensely serious, and all prayer should be serious. In the New Testament James refers to the case of Elijah who, he says, was "a man just like us." But "he prayed earnestly that it would not rain, and it did not rain on the land for three and a half years. Again he prayed, and the heavens gave rain, and the earth produced its crops" (James 5:17–18). James says rightly, thinking of Elijah, "The prayer of a righteous man is powerful and effective" (v. 16).

A second characteristic of prayer is *persistence*, seen in the repeated phrase "in the morning" (v. 3). It carries the ideas of "as soon as it is morning" and "every morning." It reminds us of the Lord's teaching about the unjust judge who did not want to help a poor widow but who eventually gave her justice just to escape her constant petitions. Jesus concluded, "And will not God bring about justice for his chosen ones, who cry out to him day and night? Will he keep putting them off?" (Luke 18:7). His point was that we are to persist in prayer even if, for reasons unknown to us, the answer of God is delayed. God will not refuse to act forever.

George Mueller, the founder of the great faith orphanages in England in the nineteenth century, saw great answers to prayer even though some of the answers were delayed. When he was quite young he began to pray for two of his friends. He prayed for them every day for more than sixty years. One was converted just before Mueller's death at what was probably the last preaching service Mueller held. The other was converted within a year of Mueller's passing. Clearly we ought always to "pray and not give up" (Luke 18:1).

A third characteristic of this prayer is *an expectant spirit,* which is how verse 3 ends: "I . . . wait in expectation." This means that the psalmist was praying in faith, for, having laid his requests before God, he expected God to answer. It is as James says, "If any of you lacks wisdom, he should ask God, who gives generously to all without finding fault, and it will be given to him. But when he asks, he must believe and not doubt" (James 1:5–6).

The Types of Prayers That Can Be Uttered

Most commentators call attention to three types of prayers in these verses: prayer by "words," inarticulated prayers or "sighing," and prayer which is a "cry." Most often we pray by words. That is, we express ourselves in proper, well-reasoned terminology. Sometimes we are in such distress that our prayers are only desperate cries for God to help us. At still other times we cannot find words adequate to express our feelings or voice what we need, though we are nevertheless still praying. But here is the encouraging thing: God hears all kinds of prayers. The Psalter itself contains various types of prayer. Besides, we have the New Testament teaching that, although we often "do not know what we ought to pray, . . . the Spirit himself intercedes for us with groans that words cannot express" (Rom. 8:26).

The Relationship That We Must Have with God

In these three opening verses David calls God his "LORD" twice (vv. 1, 3) and "my King and my God" once (v. 2). The latter phrase reminds us of the way Thomas greeted Jesus when he saw him after the resurrection. Before this Thomas had been told about the resurrection but had refused to believe it. He had demanded physical evidence: "Unless I see the nail marks in his hands and put my finger where the nails were, and put my hand into his side, I will not believe it" (John 20:25). But after Jesus had appeared to him and had invited him to make the test he had demanded, Thomas fell at his feet exclaiming, "My Lord and my God!" (v. 28). That is the faith the psalmist shows in these verses.

Notice the pronouns: "*my* King and *my* God." They show that the faith of the psalmist was genuine faith and not mere superstition. Spurgeon calls these pronouns "the pith and marrow of the plea."[3] Derek Kidner says, "The covenant relationship expressed by the repeated 'my' . . . gives the prayer a firm footing."[4]

God Does Not Listen to the Wicked

The second stanza (vv. 4–6) is a reflection on the wicked, growing out of the psalmist's approach to God in verses 1–3. Each of the preceding psalms has spoken of the wicked, though differently in each psalm. Psalm 1 considers "the way of the wicked" as opposed to "the way of the righteous" (v. 6). Psalm 2 traces the rebellion of the wicked against God, particularly that of the kings and rulers of the earth (v. 2). In Psalm 3 the psalmist has been attacked by wicked persons and asks God for protection from them (v. 7). In Psalm 4 the wicked have slandered the psalmist, and he is asking God for vindication. In the psalm we are studying now, David refers to wicked people as those whose prayers the Lord will not hear and in whom he has no pleasure.

David is distinguishing himself from evil persons, reminding himself that he must be different if he would be heard by God. Another psalmist will say, "If I had cherished sin in my heart, the Lord would not have listened." But since he has not done this the later psalmist adds, "God has surely listened and heard my voice in prayer" (Ps. 66:18–19).

We take sin too lightly. If we did not, we would not sin as grievously or as frequently as we do. Someone told me recently of a lapel button that reads: "How much sin can you get away with and still go to heaven?" Imagine a thought like that! The answer to the question is that you cannot get away with any sin. You must be holy, and the secret to being holy is to see sin as God himself sees it and to draw close to him.

This is what David himself does as he prays this second stanza. He does it in two ways. First, he reviews the types of evildoers, moving from terms that are general to those that are stronger and more descriptive: "the wicked" (v. 4), "the arrogant" (v. 5), "all who do wrong" (v. 5), "those who tell lies" (v. 6), "bloodthirsty and deceitful men" (v. 6). We sense that he is growing in his awareness of how sinful sin is in these verses. Second, he reminds himself of how God views sin, and again the words grow in intensity. The first expression is a negative, pointing out that "God [does not take] pleasure in evil" (v. 4). But this moves to the stronger expression "you *hate* all who do wrong" (v. 5) and to the even stronger words: "You *destroy* those who tell lies; bloodthirsty and deceitful men the LORD abhors" (v. 6, italics added).

This is a good way to measure how well you are praying and whether, as you pray, you are drawing close to God or are merely mouthing words. If you are drawing close to God, you will become increasingly sensitive to sin, which is inevitable since the God you are approaching is a holy God.

We need this sensitivity. H. C. Leupold was thinking along these lines when he wrote, "Prayers of this kind may have more value than our age is inclined to admit." He explains, "they are surely born out of a deep sense of the sinfulness of sin and out of the conviction that the only one who can stem the tide of sin is the Almighty."[5]

"'Tis Mercy All"

One of the complaints unbelievers make against Christians is that their understanding of sin causes them to think of themselves as better than other people. But that is not actually the case. In fact it is the opposite. The next stanza of Psalm 5 shows what really happens (vv. 7–8).

Remember that David has approached God properly and has been led by that to reflect on the sinfulness of sin and on the fact that God will not hear the ungodly. In these verses he turns back to God again. If the objection of unbelievers were true, we would expect David to be saying: "But I am different from the evildoers I have mentioned. I am a good man, and it is because I have tried to live a good life that I ask you to hear me." Actually, he does nothing of the sort. Instead of pleading his own righteousness as grounds for coming to God, he pleads God's mercy.

> But I, by your great mercy,
>   will come into your house;
> in reverence will I bow down
>   toward your holy temple.[6]

I cannot emphasize too much how important this is, since it is by the mercy of God alone that any human being may approach him. We must not forget Jesus' parable of the Pharisee and the tax collector. The Pharisee was an ostensibly righteous man. He prayed—and we have no reason to disbelieve him—"God, I thank you that I am not like other men—robbers, evildoers, adulterers—or even like this tax collector. I fast twice a week and give a tenth of all I get" (Luke 18:11–12). The tax collector, who was standing at a distance, did not consider himself worthy even to look up to heaven but only prayed, "God, have mercy on me, a sinner" (v. 13). In a situation like this the world will always side with the visibly righteous man. But Jesus said, "I tell you that this man [the tax collector], rather than the other [the Pharisee], went home justified before God. For everyone who exalts himself will be humbled, and he who humbles himself will be exalted" (v. 14).

Of the psalm, Craigie says, "Though evil persons are excluded from God's presence because of their sin, it does not follow that the psalmist is admitted by virtue of his own goodness. The psalmist's entrance into God's house would be based only upon 'the abundance of your loving kindness' (v. 8; [v. 7, our numbering]); that is to say, it was only God's grace and covenant love *(hesed)* toward his people which made entrance into his presence possible."[7]

Verse 8 contains the first actual petition in the psalm, which means that over half has been spent on preparation. And now that the request occurs it is simply for guidance—that God would "lead" the psalmist in righteousness and make his way "straight" before him.

God's Rejection of the Wicked

At this point David turns to the wicked again. Earlier he had spoken of them as "those who tell lies," but this was only one descriptive phrase among many. In these verses (vv. 9–10) he describes them in terms of their wicked speech or words, probably because he had just prayed for guidance (v. 8) and was thinking of how the words of the wicked cannot be trusted.

Ah, but it is even worse than that. Their words are destructive, and those who follow them will perish. Perhaps this is why the apostle Paul quoted part of verse 9 in his great summary of the sin of the race in Romans 3:10–18. In that summary he quotes four psalm passages in succession (Ps. 14:1–3 [par. 53:1–3]; 5:9; 140:3; 10:7). Then, after adding a text from Isaiah (Isa. 59:7–8), he ends with another psalm quotation: "There is no fear of God before their eyes" (Ps. 36:1). His point is that the human race is utterly and incurably wicked: "there is no one who does good, not even one" (Rom. 3:12).

Verse 10 contains the second petition of the psalm (after v. 8) and is the Psalter's first imprecatory prayer. That is, it is a prayer asking for judgment on the wicked. Prayers like this present a difficulty for many people, and for that reason we will consider them in detail later where more extensive examples occur. In this case, it is necessary to note only that David's vexation with the wicked is not personal. (Few people in the Bible were more forgiving in response to personal attacks than he.) Rather, his concern is that they have rebelled against God (cf. Ps. 2), and his request is for God's condemnation of their sin. David asks God to condemn sin rather than justifying sinful behavior and to see to it that the stratagems of the wicked fail and that they are banished while they are in such a state of rebellion. It is exactly the kind of prayer we should be able to pray when we see the effects of evil in our fallen world.

The Joy and Blessings of the Righteous

The final stanza is a happy one in which the concerns of the psalmist broaden to include all the righteous. He encourages them to "take refuge" in God and "be glad," to "sing for joy." He also asks God to "spread [his] protection over them"—which he is certain God will do.

The last words say,

> For surely, O LORD, you bless the righteous;
>   you surround them with your favor as with a shield.

When Martin Luther was making his way to Augsburg to appear before Cardinal Cajetan, who had summoned him to answer for his heretical opinions, one of the Cardinal's servants taunted him, asking, "Where will you find shelter if your patron, the Elector of Saxony, should desert you?"

"Under the shelter of heaven," Luther answered.

That was the psalmist's shelter. It should be yours also.

Psalm 6

A Psalm of Repentance

O Lord, do not rebuke me in your anger
  or discipline me in your wrath.
Be merciful to me, Lord, for I am faint;
  O Lord, heal me, for my bones are in agony.
My soul is in anguish.
  How long, O Lord, how long?

Turn, O Lord, and deliver me;
  save me because of your unfailing love.
No one remembers you when he is dead.
  Who praises you from the grave?

I am worn out from groaning;
  all night long I flood my bed with weeping
  and drench my couch with tears.
My eyes grow weak with sorrow;
  they fail because of all my foes.

Away from me, all you who do evil,
  for the Lord has heard my weeping.
The Lord has heard my cry for mercy;
  the Lord accepts my prayer.
All my enemies will be ashamed and dismayed;
  they will turn back in sudden disgrace.

verses 1–10

P salm 6 is the first of the penitential psalms, that is, psalms in which the author confesses his sin and asks God for his mercy and forgiveness. The other penitential psalms are Psalms 32, 38, 51, 102, 130, and 143, the best known being Psalm 51, titled "A psalm of David. When the prophet Nathan came to him after David had committed adultery with Bathsheba." It was the custom in the early church to sing these psalms on Ash Wednesday.

But there is a question about how to classify this psalm accurately. I have called it "a psalm of repentance," following the tradition of the early church and what I suppose to be the majority of the commentators. But others— P. C. Craigie is one—see it as "a prayer in sickness." In defense of this alternate view, it is worth noting that the psalm contains no explicit confession of sin and no explicit repentance. In this respect it is very different from Psalm 51, which is quite explicit in acknowledging the author's "sins," "iniquity," and "transgressions" and in asking for cleansing from sin and for spiritual renewal. On the other hand, Psalm 6 does not sound like it is dealing with sickness so much as with grief over wrong done. We can understand the psalmist's physical problems as the outworking of his spiritual grief, but it is hard to understand the petition "do not rebuke me in your anger or discipline me in your wrath" if sickness was his only problem.

Probably a sense of sin, though unspecified, is basic, and the physical afflictions flowed from it, the result being what the old writers called "the dark night of the soul."

If you have been through such a dark night, you will know exactly what that phrase means and will readily identify with David as he gives expression to his feelings. In my counseling I have come across people who have been troubled by similar depressions and who could have said, as David does,

> I am worn out from groaning;
> all night long I flood my bed with weeping
> and drench my couch with tears (v. 6).

The great English preacher D. Martyn Lloyd-Jones was so aware of this problem among the people of his congregation after World War II that he preached a series of sermons on it. They are printed in *Spiritual Depression: Its Causes and Cure*.[1] More recently, Multnomah Press published "A Critical Concern Book" in which a Baptist minister tells of his own severe depression, his hospitalization, and his recovery. It is called *Depression: Finding Hope and Meaning in Life's Darkest Shadow*.[2]

I do not suggest by linking these books with this "psalm of repentance" that depression is always caused by sin. Depression has many causes. But since we are all sinners, depression is seldom utterly divorced from sin. In any case, a sense of sin often leads to a feeling of having been abandoned by God or of being chastised by him, which results in depression. This seems to have been true of David at the time of the writing of Psalm 6.

The Psalmist's Distress

In the New International Version the psalm is divided into four stanzas, which is right. But in terms of its content the psalm is best considered in two parts. In the first (vv. 1–7) David is in great distress. His whole person—body, soul, and spirit—is in anguish. He senses the anger of God upon him for sin. He cannot sleep. In the second section (vv. 8–10) he suddenly becomes aware of God's presence once again and moves out of his deep depression into new faith and bold conduct.

The best way to handle the first section is to go through it with care, noting its chief features and asking what points of our own experience, past or present, match his.

A Sense of God's Disapproval or Wrath

The starting point is the psalmist's sense of God's disapproval or wrath, for he asks God not to "rebuke" him in "anger" or "discipline" him in "wrath" (v. 1). From the point of view of what he is feeling, it matters little whether he has sinned in some striking way and so senses God's judgment on him for this sin or whether he is simply depressed by circumstances and merely feels that God is disciplining him in general. The sense of anguish is the same. The point is that he feels overwhelmed by what is happening.

Have you ever felt like that? Do you feel like that now? Maybe you have done something wrong and know it. You know God is disrupting your life because of your sin. On the other hand, you may be overwhelmed by what is going on around you or is happening to you. Let me suggest some possible situations. You may be young, and your parents are getting a divorce. That is traumatic. Everything you used to consider stable is falling apart, and you think that somehow it is all your fault. "What have I done to cause this?" you are asking. "What can I do to make things right again?" In your case, you are not to blame at all, but that does not keep you from feeling that you are to blame. You want to say, "O Lord, do not rebuke me in your anger or discipline me in your wrath."

Maybe you have suffered reversals at work. Perhaps you have even lost your job, and you may be at an age when finding another one will be difficult. God seems to be punishing you. But for what? You find yourself thinking, "Maybe I got out of God's will somehow. Maybe I wasn't reading my Bible enough. Maybe I didn't give my job high enough priority." There are dozens of maybes in a situation like that, and there are no easy responses to any of them. Quite possibly what happened is not due to failures in you at all. At any rate, I do not know the answers any more than you do. But you are still praying, "O Lord, do not rebuke me in your anger or discipline me in your wrath."

Maybe your husband has left you. Or maybe your wife. "God, what are you doing to me?" you are asking. "What have I done?"

Maybe you have gotten very sick, and for this reason your circumstances particularly parallel those of the psalmist. You do not know whether God is punishing you for some sin or trying to develop character in you by the things you are suffering. Paul wrote, "we know that suffering produces perseverance; perseverance, character; and character, hope" (Rom. 5:3–4). That may be it. But how do you know? And what does it matter as long as you are feeling as downcast as you are? All you want is that God should hear you and relieve your distress, if that is possible. "O Lord, do not rebuke me in your anger or discipline me in your wrath," you pray.

A Loss of a Sense of God's Presence

A sense of being disproved of by an angry God is bad enough, but sometimes in our depression things seem even worse than this. What if God should not even be present? Suppose he has turned away from us or withdrawn himself? This is what David was feeling, which he indicates by the word *return* in verse 4. The New International Version says *turn*, but this weakens the statement. What David actually prays is that God will turn back to him, since he senses that God's presence has been withdrawn. Haven't you felt like that? Recently I talked with a woman who was suffering severe depression. She felt that God had abandoned her, and her complaint was: "God is not answering my prayers."

Loss of Sleep

After speaking of such things as being abandoned by God or being disciplined by him, it may seem trivial to speak of sleep. But it is not at all trivial to those who are unable to sleep due to the kind of distress I am describing. P. C. Craigie wrote, "For most sufferers, it [is] in the long watches of the night, when silence and loneliness increase and the warmth of human companionship is absent, that . . . pain and grief [reach] their darkest point."[3] One man who went through a particularly black period described himself as dragging through his day's work, hardly able to function, and then getting into bed at night and lying awake through the long, dark hours until the dawn came and it was time to begin the whole desperate process all over again. Nights like this are often filled with deep soul groanings and tears.

Listen to David:

> I am worn out from groaning;
>> all night long I flood my bed with weeping
>> and drench my couch with tears.
> My eyes grow weak with sorrow;
>> they fail because of all my foes.

If you are experiencing something like this, the last thing you want is an easy dismissal of your problem. But it may help to remember that these words were written, not by some unsuccessful or weak person naturally inclined to depression, but by King David. If anyone was ever strong or successful, it was he. Yet sometimes, it would seem, the strong in particular have this problem. Martin Luther was inclined to depression, at times even doubting his salvation or the rightness or value of the Reformation. Charles Haddon Spurgeon was likewise affected. It is good to know that one is not alone in having such afflictions.

A Sense of Spiritual and Bodily Fatigue

If you have been long in such a condition, you will know the feeling of utter weariness and fatigue that David describes. He speaks about it in verse 2 when he says, "Be merciful to me, LORD, for I am *faint*" and in verse 6, "I am *worn out* from groaning" (italics added). In times like these we feel that we are too tired to do those many countless things that urgently need to be done. We are

- too tired to get out of bed and get dressed
- too worn out to get into the car and go to work
- too exhausted to get the kids off to school
- too weary to clean the house
- too depressed to go to church
- too burdened to read the Bible
- too sluggish even to pray

Perhaps the only thing you can pray is the prayer David utters in verse 3: "How long, O LORD, how long?" Spurgeon, in his great *Treasury of David*, tells us that this was a favorite prayer of John Calvin's: *"Domine, usque quo"* (O Lord, how long?). It was wrung from him again and again by the countless burdens and responsibilities he bore, the physical ailments he suffered, the dangers he faced, and the misunderstandings he endured.[4]

The Psalmist's Hope

Yet, in spite of the extremely black picture I am painting, the situation was not quite as hopeless as even the psalmist thought. Nor is it as hopeless as you might think. It may be that David felt under God's fierce disapproval and wrath. I am sure he did. I am sure that he felt that God had hidden his face and was nowhere to be seen or found. But God was still there, and he was David's God in spite of everything.

Have you noticed how often in this psalm, even in the midst of his great anguish, David calls upon God? Five times in the first four verses. That is, once or more than once in each verse! And the name he uses for God is *Jehovah,* which characterizes God particularly as our Redeemer or Deliverer.

> O LORD, do not rebuke me in your anger
>   or discipline me in your wrath.
> Be merciful to me, LORD, for I am faint;
>   O LORD, heal me, for my bones are in agony.
> My soul is in anguish.
>   How long, O LORD, how long?
>
> Turn, O LORD, and deliver me;
>   save me because of your unfailing love (italics added).

If there is a turning point in this psalm, this is certainly it. It is when David, whether by training, habit, or sheer discipline, called upon the name of the Lord. Learn from David at this point. In times of victory, call upon God. Praise him. In times of defeat, call upon God. Ask for help. In times of temptation, call upon God. Seek deliverance. In the dark night of the soul, call upon God. Request light. God is our pathway through the darkness. He is our one sure hope in life and in death. He is our hope even when we are unaware of his presence.

The Psalmist's Prayer

When we were studying the preceding psalm I noted that, even when David is conscious of being set apart from evildoers, he appeals to God not on the basis of his righteousness but on the basis of God's mercy. It is the same here. David's plea, uttered in the midst of his anguish, has nothing to do with merit.

What he asks for is mercy: "Be merciful to me, LORD." And the basis of his plea, if it can be called a basis, is his need. He expresses it in three parallel statements: "I am faint [weak]"; "My bones are in agony"; and "My soul is in anguish." It is never wrong to ask for mercy on the basis of our weakness. We are told in Scripture, "He knows how we are formed, he remembers that we are dust" (Ps. 103:14). In verse 4 the plea to God to "deliver me" and "save me" is on the same basis. It is "because of your unfailing love." The reference to "the grave" or Sheol in verse 5 parallels and reinforces the references to the psalmist's weakness in verses 2 and 3. So throughout the psalm, it is because he is such a poor, perishing creature that David asks God to be merciful.[5]

God's Answer to the Psalmist

The second half of the psalm, which begins with verse 8, contains such a radical change of mood that many commentators seem to be without any adequate explanation. They have supposed that something, perhaps an oracle given to the psalmist by one of the priests, intervenes.[6] This is an unnecessary and mechanical explanation. What happened, quite simply, is that God answered David's prayer.

> . . . the LORD has heard my weeping.
> The LORD has heard my cry for mercy;
> the LORD accepts my prayer.

God made himself known to David once again and restored his confidence. And this had immediate results. In verse 4 he had asked the Lord to "turn back" to him. Now, using the same verb, he tells his enemies to "turn back," that is, to leave him. He is on the right track already.

Surely Derek Kidner is correct when he says, "This sudden access of confidence, found in almost every suppliant psalm, is most telling evidence of an answering touch from God."[7]

Do you remember the Baptist pastor I referred to earlier, the one who experienced such severe depression, was delivered, and later wrote about it in order to help others? His name is Don Baker. After months of therapy and soul-searching, he was by himself near a lake, where his family had a cottage. He had been praying for a long time and with many tears, and here is what happened.

I continued to kneel by that couch long after the tears had dried and the prayer was finished.

I noticed as I remained there that things felt different. Nothing ecstatic or noisy. Nothing high-powered or sensational. I just felt different.

As I examined that feeling, I became aware of strength in my limbs, of objects before my eyes. I saw, I felt, I heard. Was it possible? Was the cloud finally gone? Had my world come alive again?

I stood and moved carefully at first. The feeling, the sensations, the awareness, the strength—was it real? Was it back to stay? I began thanking and praising God, singing and laughing.

I put on my shoes and ran down the hillside—more falling than running from Arnie's cabin to where carpenters were building a new dining hall. One of my deacons was there. I shouted to him, "Jerry, I'm all right! Thank you for praying." He looked bewildered and unbelieving. He needed time; but eventually he, too, would rejoice at the reality of what had finally come full circle.

I continued to walk with vigor for the full three miles around the lake. I sang. I cried. I laughed. I prayed. I quoted Scripture. I talked to the birds. I talked to the trees.

To this day I'm grateful no one saw me. I would have been shipped back to Ward 7E for sure.[8]

Exceptional? Perhaps, but nevertheless real. It is what happens for those who turn back to God. Because he is still there! He is always there—even though, for a time, we may not be aware of it.

Psalm 7

Cry Justice!

O LORD my God, I take refuge in you;
*   save and deliver me from all who pursue me,*
or they will tear me like a lion
*   and rip me to pieces with no one to rescue me.*

O LORD my God, if I have done this
*   and there is guilt on my hands—*
if I have done evil to him who is at peace with me
*   or without cause have robbed my foe—*
then let my enemy pursue and overtake me;
*   let him trample my life to the ground*
*   and make me sleep in the dust.*   Selah

Arise, O LORD, in your anger;
*   rise up against the rage of my enemies.*
*   Awake, my God; decree justice.*
Let the assembled peoples gather around you.
*   Rule over them from on high;*
let the LORD judge the peoples.
Judge me, O LORD, according to my righteousness,
*   according to my integrity, O Most High.*

O righteous God,
  who searches minds and hearts,
bring to an end the violence of the wicked
  and make the righteous secure.

verses 1–9

He who is pregnant with evil
  and conceives trouble gives birth to disillusionment.
He who digs a hole and scoops it out
  falls into the pit he has made.
The trouble he causes recoils on himself;
  his violence comes down on his own head.

I will give thanks to the LORD because of his righteousness
  and will sing praise to the name of the LORD Most High.

verses 1–17

I f you have been paying close attention to the psalms preceding Psalm 7 and have been comparing them, you may have noticed a growth in the intensity of feeling on David's part. The first two psalms are introductory and are not written by David, so far as we know. But the next ones, indeed, almost all the psalms in the Psalter's first division (Pss. 1–41), are written by David, and it is the earliest of these that show the growth I am talking about.

Psalm 3 is a prayer for deliverance, apparently from physical or military danger. This was a serious danger, but the psalmist is not in any great distress about it. Instead he shows quiet confidence in God. Psalm 3 is called a morning psalm, because David says, "I lie down and sleep; I wake again, because the LORD sustains me" (v. 5). Psalm 4 is an evening psalm. In this psalm David *is* distressed. It is true that he comes to a condition of trust and peace, but this is only after a struggle, and at the psalm's end. Psalm 5 is filled with expressions of intense sighing and cries for God's help (v. 1), and David's enemies are described, not merely as political foes, but also as those who "do wrong" and "tell lies." They are "bloodthirsty and deceitful men" (vv. 5–6). By Psalm 6 the psalmist is in deep personal anguish (vv. 2–3). He says that he is worn out from his groaning and weeping that last throughout the night (vv. 6–7).

Psalm 7 is the longest psalm thus far. In it David is so overcome with his enemies' harsh injustice to him that he cries out for divine vindication. "Awake, my God; decree justice" is his cry (v. 6).

False Accusations

The specific details of David's problem are alluded to in the psalm's title, which describes it as a lament sung "to the LORD concerning Cush, a Benjamite." We have no other information about Cush, but the fact that he was from the tribe of Benjamin fits well with what we know of the opposition David faced from this tribe. David's predecessor, King Saul, was a Benjamite. So when Saul was killed by the Philistines and David became king of Israel, a process that spanned nearly eight years, it was natural that the new king's chief source of opposition was Saul's tribe.

It seems to have lasted for a long time too. For when David was forced to flee Jerusalem years later on the occasion of his son Absalom's rebellion, a man named Shimei of Benjamin cursed him as he left the city. He accused David of being a "man of blood" and a "scoundrel." He cried out, "The LORD has repaid you for all the blood you shed in the household of Saul, in whose place you have reigned" (2 Sam. 16:7–8). Still later, when David had returned to Jerusalem after Absalom's death and the defeat of his armies, another Benjamite named Sheba led a revolt against him (2 Sam. 20:1–2). Neither of these men can be identified with the Cush of Psalm 7, but it is easy to understand how the slander described in the psalm could have emerged from the smoldering hostility of this tribe.

David does not report the accusation in detail. But it seems, from verses 3 and 4, that he had been accused of doing evil to one whom he had no cause to regard as an enemy and of robbing one whom, though he was an enemy, he had no cause to abuse.

There are two things we need to note about this specifically. First, a slander like this was a serious matter for one in David's position. It was not trivial. We tend to regard most verbal accusations as unimportant, at least when they are directed at someone else. "Sticks and stones can break my bones, but names will never hurt me," we say. But lies are not always inconsequential, even for us, and they were certainly not a matter of unimportance for King David. The king was the chief administrative and legislative officer for Israel. He was responsible for seeing that right was upheld and that justice was dispensed. An accusation that attacked his integrity undermined the moral basis of the kingdom. It was a first step to moral anarchy and, possibly, armed rebellion.

The second thing we need to note is the difficulty of dealing with false accusations. It is here that the problem touches us closely. Most of us are not in so influential a position that something big will go to ruin if a false charge against us is allowed to run on unchecked—though it may hurt our families or damage our standing in the workplace. But we all, nevertheless, know the problem of overcoming slander. What do we do when we are attacked falsely?

Should we respond in kind? We can't do that, because that brings us down to our accuser's level.

Do we protest openly and widely? That tends only to fan the flame. Moreover, people suspect wrongdoing when commotion occurs. "Where there's smoke, there's fire," we say. Or sometimes we quote William Shakespeare: "Methinks he doth protest too much."

How do you vindicate yourself or get out from under such false and unjust accusations? If you are innocent of the fault, you cannot even repent of it and make restoration.

What can you do?

There is only one thing to do, and that is to take your problem to God, as David does. We can appeal to God for justice. The one good thing about a false accusation, as P. C. Craigie says, is that "whereas [a false accusation] may deceive and convince our fellow human beings, it cannot deceive God."[1]

Is Anyone Ever Innocent?

When we turn to Psalm 7 to see how David dealt with the problem of false accusations, we discover two surprising features, which for us are problems in themselves. The first is David's protestation of innocence. We find this in verses 3–5 and 8. It is extreme. David tells God,

> . . . if I have done this
>   and there is guilt on my hands—
> if I have done evil to him who is at peace with me
>   or without cause have robbed my foe—
> then let my enemy pursue and overtake me;
>   let him trample my life to the ground
>   and make me sleep in the dust.   *Selah*

> Judge me, O LORD, according to my righteousness,
>   according to my integrity, O Most High.

"Innocent?" we object. "Who is ever innocent?" We have been taught, "There is no one righteous, not even one" (Rom. 3:10). We have been taught that, even when we have done our best, "We are [at best] unworthy servants" (Luke 17:10). (We will encounter this troubling theme again and again as we go forward in our studies of the psalms, but this is the first time it has occurred explicitly.)

There are three things to keep in mind as we think about this problem. First, although David is expressing himself as perhaps we would not, his words do not mean that he is perfect, only that he is innocent of the crime of which he was charged. This is a very important distinction, the kind that is made every day in courts of law. Indeed, it is the kind of distinction David would himself have been called upon to make regularly as head of the nation. The question is not whether David was morally perfect but whether he was innocent of this particular slander. And he was! David was known for his integrity and for his generous conduct toward enemies. H. C. Leupold says, "Only the man who is sure of his innocence in the sight of God would venture to call for such a doom upon himself in case he had been guilty of the thing wherewith he is charged. David, therefore, represents the cause of the righteous who are unjustly persecuted, as the church always is."[2]

The second thing to keep in mind is that David does not take vengeance into his own hands, which he might well have been able to do, being king. Instead he submits his case to God, who alone has the ultimate right to judge and who alone can judge perfectly.

This is an important example for us. In his exposition of the psalm, Arno C. Gaebelein observes, "The godly in time of trouble always flee to him who gives shelter and has the power to deliver."[3] But do we? Or do we take matters into our own hands and retaliate, perhaps doing even more damage to our enemy than he or she did to us?

The third thing to notice is that, although David is pleading for justice in his own case, he does not separate his prayer from the concern that God will also exercise judgment over the peoples of the earth. In fact, the cry "let the LORD judge the peoples" and the appeal "Judge me, O LORD" are placed side by side in verse 8. This is not a selfish concern on David's part. It is the personal side of a broader and perfectly proper concern.

Justice or Mercy?

The second surprising feature of Psalm 7, which is also a problem for us, is David's appeal to God for justice in verses 6–9. Gaebelein suggests that over this psalm should be written the sentence: "Shall not the Judge of all the earth do right?" referring to Abraham's prayer in the face of God's threatened destruction of Sodom and Gomorrah.[4] But David is not pleading for Sodom or Gomorrah or any other third party. He is pleading for himself. "Judge me, O LORD, according to *my* righteousness, according to *my* integrity" is his sharp cry (v. 8, italics added).

And his cry is urgent. Look at the imperatives: "arise," "rise up," "awake," "decree" (v. 6), "rule" (v. 7), "judge" (v. 8), and, eventually, "bring to an end" and "make secure" (v. 9). We have been taught to believe that only fools ask for justice from God and that what we need from God is not justice but mercy.

In my opinion, this is a point at which C. S. Lewis makes an important contribution. In his *Reflections on the Psalms,* Lewis begins by distinguishing between two kinds of justice: ultimate or heavenly justice, which is most commonly in the Christian's mind when he considers justice; and limited or earthly justice, which was the primary preoccupation of the Jew. These two understandings produce two different attitudes toward judgment. On the one hand, the Christian trembles at the thought of God's judgment, because he thinks of himself as the defendant and knows that he is not innocent. Apart from the substitutionary atonement of Christ, he knows that he stands to be condemned. The Jew, thinking of earthly justice, does not tremble at judgment but seeks or desires it. What is more, he does not think of himself as the defendant. He is the plaintiff. The Christian hopes for acquittal or a pardon. The Jew hopes for a resounding triumph with heavy damages.

When justice is distinguished in this way, Christians naturally embrace the more recent and (perhaps) higher conception. But Lewis rightly asks us to yearn for earthly justice also, and work for it.

For one thing, to do this puts us on the side of those who traditionally have had difficulty obtaining justice. The Oxford (and later Cambridge) don rightly reminds us of the Lord's parable in which the poor widow cries for justice from a judge who is unwilling to hear her. This is because she has nothing to bribe him with. According to the parable, the judge finally does hear her but only because of her persistence or importunity (Luke 18:1–8). Lewis reminds us that in most countries of the world this is a very real problem. The poor are abused because they cannot bribe those who are able to see that their cases are heard or those who actually give judgment. And it is not only in other countries that this problem exists. Injustice resulting from a person's poverty is far more common in the West, even under our "enlightened" judicial systems, than we may care to admit.

But there is another issue, and this is earthly justice itself and our responsibilities as Christians to be concerned for it. Is it not true that preoccupation with a final, heavenly judgment, at which we hope to be acquitted through the work of Christ, has often made us indifferent to the need for justice now? I think it has. Even more, we have sometimes focused on the importance of a forgiving attitude in this life to the detriment of actually working for justice.

Lewis gives an illustration. He imagines two boys fighting over a pencil.

> The question whether the disputed pencil belongs to Tommy or Charles is quite distinct from the question which is the nicer little boy, and the parents who allowed the one to influence their decision about the other would be very unfair. (It would be still worse if they said Tommy ought to let Charles have the pencil whether it belonged to him or not, because this would show that he had a nice disposition. That may be true, but it is an untimely truth. An exhortation to charity should not come as a rider to a refusal of justice. It is likely to give Tommy a lifelong conviction that charity is a sanctimonious dodge for condoning theft and whitewashing favoritism.)[5]

If these distinctions are valid, as I believe they are, they speak to us of three great needs today:

Champions for the poor or disadvantaged. Who will help them? They are
unable to help themselves.

Upright conduct. We cannot honestly pursue justice for others if we do not
practice it ourselves.

Vindication of the righteous. We must see that those who do good are
acknowledged to be good and that the wicked are identified as such.

Who can dispute any of these needs? Or the responsibility to work at
them? To ignore these needs is to abandon the poor, disgrace our calling,
and encourage wickedness.

In your personal religious experience you may not be at this point yet.
You may still be struggling with the matter of eternal or heavenly justice.
And if that is the case, I counsel you to disregard what I am saying for now
and stick with the simple gospel. Do not veer from that track until you know
that your sin has been atoned for by the blood of Jesus Christ and that you
stand before God in his righteousness. On the other hand, if you know that
you have been saved by Christ and are mature in faith, having gotten
beyond mere justification, let me insist that a passionate concern for earthly
justice on your part is essential. It is part of what it means to be a Christian.

And do not be deterred by the cheap shots of those who want to turn
your concerns aside and make you ineffective: "You just think you're better
than everyone else," or "Why don't you show a little more of the forgiving
spirit of Jesus?" The first is untrue, or should be. The second is beside the
point. Justice is important all by itself, particularly so when it involves
another person.

Confidence in God

The second half of Psalm 7 (vv. 10–17) is an expression of David's deep
confidence in God. It expresses thoughts not much different from what he
has said in several preceding psalms and will say many more times in those
that follow.

David says that God will protect him, being his shield against foes; God is
righteous, expressing his wrath against evil every day; God will judge his
accusers if they do not repent; and God has arranged things so that evil
eventually brings judgment on itself. For this latter assertion, he employs a
bold image later used by the apostle James, saying that the wicked conceive
trouble, become pregnant with evil, and eventually give birth to disillusionment (v. 14; cf. James 1:15). He adds that the wicked dig a hole to trap others but eventually fall into it themselves.

The psalm's last words say, "I will give thanks to the LORD because of his
[that is, God's, not David's] righteousness and will sing praise to the name
of the LORD Most High" (v. 17).

The seventh psalm is a great testimony. Yet here is the striking thing. It is uttered at a time when, so far as we know, David had not yet obtained the earthly justice from God that he was seeking. He had come to God with his problem, which was the right and wise thing to do. In doing so, he has provided us with an example of what we can do in similar circumstances. Yet in spite of these many right attitudes and actions we do not know if David was actually vindicated in this life. Craigie says, "We do not know from the psalm whether the falsely accused was finally vindicated or his name was cleared; we know only that he came into such a knowledge of God that he could accept his lot. . . ." Yet, since he did accept it, we learn from this that "it is better to maintain integrity and continue to suffer injustice, than to sell out to evil and form ranks with the unrighteous."[6]

Cry justice? Yes, we must do that, and work for it. But above all, we must continue to live righteously, because it is right to do so and because goodness and integrity are their own rewards.

Psalm 8

Our God, Our Glory

O LORD, our Lord,
how majestic is your name in all the earth!

You have set your glory
above the heavens.
From the lips of children and infants
you have ordained praise
because of your enemies,
to silence the foe and the avenger.

When I consider your heavens,
the work of your fingers,
the moon and the stars,
which you have set in place,
what is man that you are mindful of him,
the son of man that you care for him?
You made him a little lower than the heavenly beings
and crowned him with glory and honor.

You made him ruler over the works of your hands;
you put everything under his feet:
all flocks and herds,
and the beasts of the field,

> *the birds of the air,*
> *and the fish of the sea,*
> *all that swim the paths of the seas.*
>
> *O Lord, our Lord,*
> *how majestic is your name in all the earth!*
> *verses 1–9*

I t would be difficult to say anything negative about any one of the psalms, since each is a part of sacred Scripture and is given to us by God for our benefit. Every psalm in the Psalter has undoubtedly been of great spiritual benefit to many millions of persons. Yet we cannot escape feeling that some of them stand out. This is true of Psalm 23, probably the most beloved psalm in the Psalter. It is true of the first psalm, which we have already studied, Psalm 19, Psalm 51, Psalm 100, and more. It is true of Psalm 8, to which we come now.

C. S. Lewis called Psalm 8 a "short, exquisite lyric."[1] Derek Kidner, in his excellent two-volume study of the psalms, says, "This psalm is an unsurpassed example of what a hymn should be, celebrating as it does the glory and grace of God, rehearsing who he is and what he has done, and relating us and our world to him, all with a masterly economy of words, and in a spirit of mingled joy and awe." He adds rightly, "The range of thought takes us not only 'above the heavens' (1) and back to the beginning (3, 6–8) but, as the New Testament points out, on to the very end."[2] The psalm's theme is the greatness of God and the place of man within God's universe.

I call it "our God, our glory."

The hymn has four obvious parts: celebration of the surpassing majesty of God (vv. 1–2); confession of the insignificance of man (vv. 3–4); astonishment at the significance of man (vv. 5–8); and a concluding refrain that repeats the psalm's first lines (v. 9).

"Jehovah, Our Adonai"

The most striking feature of Psalm 8—and its dominant theme, if we count verses—is its description of man and his place in the created order. But the psalm does not begin by talking about man. It begins with a celebration of the surpassing majesty of God, and this places men and women within a cosmic framework. It is a way of saying from the outset that we will never understand human beings unless we see them as God's creatures and recognize that they have special responsibilities to their Creator.

One responsibility is to praise God, of course, which is what David does. Indeed, he does it grandly, beginning the psalm with two great names for God: Jehovah *(Yahweh)* and *Adonai* (Lord), literally "O Jehovah, our *Adonai.*"

In later ages of Israel's history, the Jewish people considered the name Jehovah to be so sacred that they would not pronounce it. So when they came to it in their reading of the Old Testament, as here, for example, they would say *Adonai* instead. In fact, when the Masoretes came in time to provide the vowel pointing for the consonantal Hebrew text, they wrote the vowels for *Adonai* whenever the name Jehovah occurred, as a reminder of what should be said. So when he read this verse, the pious Jew would say, "O *Adonai,* our *Adonai,*" meaning "Lord, Lord."

There is none of this belabored piety with David. Jehovah is his God. So he begins with that name, maintaining that Jehovah is so majestic and his glory so great that the latter is "above the heavens." This means, as David's son Solomon would say later in his great prayer at the dedication of the temple: "The heavens, even the highest heaven, cannot contain you. How much less this temple I have built!" (1 Kings 8:27). The reason the creation, wonderful as it is, cannot exhaust the glory of God is that God is its maker. So although creation expresses his glory, revealing his existence, wisdom, and great power, as well as other attributes, it is only a partial revelation of the surpassingly greater God who stands behind it. If God has set his glory above the heavens, it is certain that nothing under the heavens can praise him adequately.

Yet this is what men and women have the privilege of doing. In fact, even infants and children can praise God, and do, according to verse 2.

Psalm 8 is quoted a number of times in the New Testament, on one occasion by Jesus. He had entered Jerusalem in triumph on what we call Palm Sunday. While he was in the temple area, healing the blind and lame who came to him, the children who had observed the triumphal entry continued to praise him, crying, "Hosanna to the Son of David." This made the chief priests and teachers of the law indignant. But Jesus replied, referring to Psalm 8, "Have you never read, 'From the lips of children and infants you have ordained praise'?" (Matt. 21:16). If these leaders of the people had been indignant before, they must have become nearly catatonic now. For by identifying the praise of the children of Jerusalem with Psalm 8, Jesus not only validated their words, showing them to be proper. (He was, indeed, the "son of David," the Messiah.) He also interpreted their praise as praise not of a mere man, which a mere "son of David" would be, but of God, since the psalm says that God has ordained praise for himself from children's lips.

Jesus also placed the scribes and teachers, who resisted his claims to be the unique Son of God, in the category of "the foe and the avenger," thereby identifying them as God's enemies.

What Is Man?

The bulk of the psalm is about man, however. And the first thing that is asserted about man is his insignificance in the vast framework of creation. This grows out of the opening verses. For when the psalmist thinks of the glory of God exceeding the greatness of creation and thus thinks of creation, he is struck with how small man is by comparison.

I suppose this beautiful section of the psalm grew out of David's memory of lying in the fields at night staring at the stars, in the days when he cared for his family's sheep. Not many of us have this experience today. Most of us live where light from a city blocks out most of the stars' light. But if you live in the country, you know how majestic the heavens really are. This was especially true for David. In the east the air is very clear, and, for those who look up at them, the stars seem to be almost overwhelming in number and to hang nearly within reach of the outstretched arm of the observer. "What is man that you are mindful of him?" asked David when he recalled the stars' vast array.

Sometimes we experience this emotion too. True, we do not often have David's opportunities to lie back and wonder at the heaven's greatness. But we have our scientific knowledge and know, at least mathematically, much more than he. We know that the earth, which is vast enough, is only a small planet in a relatively small solar system toward the outer edge of one of the billions of solar systems in the universe. And we know something of the distances. We know that light coming to us from the most distant parts of the universe takes billions of years to get here. In fact, even within our solar system the distances are great. Recently our Voyager II spacecraft reached Neptune, the last of four planets it passed and photographed on its astonishing voyage to outer space. Neptune is not even the outermost of the planets. Pluto is beyond it. But the radio waves sent back to earth from Neptune at the speed of light (186,000 miles per second) took four hours to get here. So a single set of communications from earth to the spacecraft and back to us took one third of a day.

How small we are in this vast cosmic setting! How astonishing that the God of this vast universe, the God who made it and orders it, should think of us and care for us!

Looking Up or Looking Down

Yet that is what God does. And not only that. Not only does God think of us and care for us, which is what verse 4 asserts, he has also crowned us with "glory and honor" (v. 5). This means that he has given human beings, mere specks in this vast universe, a significance and honor above everything else he has created.

David makes this point in two striking ways. First, he uses the word *glory,* which he first used of God, of mere man. Verse 1 says, "You have set *your*

glory above the heavens" (italics added). This is a glory that surpasses even
the great and overwhelming glory of the heavens. But then in verse 5 he
says, speaking of men and women, "You . . . crowned *him* with glory and
honor" (italics added). This is an effective way of identifying man with God
and of saying that he has been made in God's image, reflecting God's glory
in a way other parts of the creation do not.

The second way David emphasizes man's special significance is by speaking of his role as "ruler" over the world and its creatures. Rule is something
normally ascribed to God. He is the "blessed and only Ruler, the King of
kings and Lord of lords," according to the apostle Paul (1 Tim. 6:15). Psalm
8 says that God shared this rule with man, making him ruler over creation,
particularly in respect to intelligent life on earth.

In my opinion, the most interesting aspect of Psalm 8 is the way in which
it places man in what has been called "a mediating position" in the universe. Thomas Aquinas, the great Roman Catholic theologian, was one of
the first to stress this, saying that Psalm 8 places man midway between the
angels, which are above him, and the beasts, which are below. Man is a
spirit/body being, according to Aquinas. Angels have spirits but no bodies.
Animals have bodies but no spirits. Man, however, has both a spirit and a
body and so comes between. He is midway on the scale of intelligent creation. This is exactly what Psalm 8 describes. It begins and ends with God
("How majestic is your name in all the earth!"). It speaks of the heavens.
Then it says, speaking of man,

> You made him a little lower than the heavenly beings
>   and crowned him with glory and honor.
>
> You made him ruler over the works of your hands;
>   you put everything under his feet:
> all flocks and herds,
>   and the beasts of the field,
> the birds of the air,
>   and the fish of the sea,
>   all that swim the paths of the seas (vv. 5–8).

In this section of the psalm the allusions to the first chapter of Genesis are
inescapable, which shows that David was thoroughly acquainted with this
book.

But here is the interesting thing. When the psalm gets around to describing man specifically, it describes him as being "a little lower than the heavenly beings" rather than "a little higher than the beasts." It could have been
written the other way around. If man really is a mediating being, as the
psalm maintains, it would have been equally accurate to have described him
as slightly higher than the beasts rather than as slightly lower than the

angels. But it does not, and the reason it does not is that, although men and women have been given a position midway between the angels and the beasts, it is nevertheless humanity's special privilege and duty to look upward to the angels (and beyond the angels to God, in whose image women and men have been made), rather than downward to the beasts. The result is that they become increasingly like God rather than increasingly beast-like in their behavior.

The fact that human beings have been made in God's image and are to become increasingly like God is even clearer in Hebrew than in our English versions. For in the Hebrew text the word in verse 5 translated "heavenly beings" is actually *Elohim,* the plural word for God.

This is an interesting fact. In some places *elohim* obviously does mean "spirit beings," as in 1 Samuel 28:13, where the witch of Endor says that she sees "spirits" *(elohim)* emerging from the ground. Psalm 82 also uses the word in this way (cf. vv. 1, 6). For this reason, and perhaps also for the sake of modesty, not wanting to say that men and women are only "a little lower than God," the Septuagint translators of the Old Testament used the Greek word for "angels" in Psalm 8. It was this translation that the author of Hebrews picked up when he referred the text to Jesus, saying that in the incarnation God made him a little lower than the angels for the purpose of achieving our salvation. This translation probably also influenced the New International Version in its similar rendering of Psalm 8:5.[3]

"Nevertheless, the translation *God* is almost certainly correct," as Craigie and other commentators maintain.[4] This is because the allusions of verses 5–8 are drawn from Genesis 1. Not only is *Elohim* the word exclusively used for God there, the emphasis of the chapter (so far as man is concerned) is on his being made in God's image. "Then God *(Elohim)* said, 'Let us make man in our image, in our likeness, and let them rule over the fish of the sea and the birds of the air'" (Gen. 1:26). In light of that chapter there can be little doubt that David is linking men and women to God, being slightly less than him in whose image they are made.

But here is the sad thing. Although made in God's image and ordained to become increasingly like the God to whom they look, men and women have turned their backs on God. And since they will not look upward to God, which is their privilege and duty, they actually look downward to the beasts and so become increasingly like them.

The great example here is King Nebuchadnezzar of Babylon, whose story is told in Daniel. Nebuchadnezzar turned his back on God, saying as he looked out over the great capital of his empire, "Is not this the great Babylon I have built as the royal residence, by my mighty power and for the glory of my majesty?" (Dan. 4:30). It was a classic statement of what we today call secular humanism, describing creation as *of* man, *by* man, and *for* man's glory. The words were still on his lips when a voice came from heaven saying, "This is what is decreed for you, King Nebuchadnezzar: Your royal authority has been taken from you. You will be driven away from people and will live with the wild animals; you will eat grass like cattle. Seven times will pass by for you until you acknowledge that the Most High is sovereign over the kingdoms of men and gives them to anyone he wishes" (vv. 31–32).

And so it was. Nebuchadnezzar became insane—it is insanity to take the glory of God for oneself, putting oneself in the place of God—and then was driven out to live with and behave like the wild animals.

I have noticed that this is the way our society increasingly regards itself. Western society has lost sight of God. It no longer sees man as a creature made in God's image, whose chief end is "to glorify God and enjoy him forever." It has eliminated God from its collective conscience. But then, because it no longer looks to God to derive its sense of identity and worth from him, it looks in the only other direction it can look. It looks downward to the beasts and derives its identity from the animal kingdom.

This is what evolution is all about. Eliminate God, and evolution is the only theory left. We are only slightly advanced beasts, according to this theory. Besides, since we see ourselves as beasts, we begin to behave like beasts. Indeed, we behave worse than beasts, for we end up doing things the animals would not even dream of doing.

"But We See Jesus"

So what does God do? We know what he does, because he has done it. God sends his own Son, the Lord Jesus Christ, to save us from our willful ignorance and rebellion, and to fulfill Psalm 8 as we have not. That is why the author of Hebrews uses the psalm as he does in chapter 2. He applies it to Jesus, saying that he was made a little lower than the angels (in order to die for us) and that, as a result, the Father has "crowned him with glory and honor and put everything under his feet," adding, "In putting everything under him, God left nothing that is not subject to him" (Heb. 2:7–8). It is a parallel statement to that great hymn of the church recorded for us by Paul in Philippians 2:

> And being found in appearance as a man,
>   he humbled himself
>   and became obedient to death—
>   even death on a cross!
> Therefore God exalted him to the highest place
>   and gave him the name that is above every name,
> that at the name of Jesus every knee should bow,
>   in heaven and on earth and under the earth,
> and every tongue confess that Jesus Christ is Lord,
>   to the glory of God the Father (vv. 8–11).

The fullness of that great destiny is still future, as Hebrews notes: "At present we do not see everything subject to him" (2:8). But although we do not see everything subject to Jesus yet, there is one thing we do see. "We see Jesus . . . now crowned with glory and honor because he suffered death, so that by the grace of God he might taste death for everyone. . . . Therefore, holy brothers, who share in the heavenly calling, fix your thoughts on Jesus" (Heb. 2:9; 3:1).

What happens when we do? The answer is obvious. At this point we are looking up again—by the grace of God—and the grace of God, which has saved us and redirected our affections, now begins the work of once again conforming us to his likeness. We end Psalm 8 where David himself ended it, crying, "O LORD, our Lord, how majestic is your name in all the earth!"

Psalm 9

Praise the Lord!

I will praise you, O Lord, with all my heart;
    I will tell of all your wonders.
I will be glad and rejoice in you;
    I will sing praise to your name, O Most High.

My enemies turn back;
    they stumble and perish before you.
For you have upheld my right and my cause;
    you have sat on your throne, judging righteously.
You have rebuked the nations and destroyed the wicked;
    you have blotted out their name for ever and ever.
Endless ruin has overtaken the enemy,
    you have uprooted their cities;
        even the memory of them has perished.

The Lord reigns forever;
    he has established his throne for judgment.
He will judge the world in righteousness;
    he will govern the peoples with justice.
The Lord is a refuge for the oppressed,
    a stronghold in times of trouble.

Those who know your name will trust in you,
for you, LORD, have never forsaken those who seek you.

Sing praises to the LORD, enthroned in Zion;
proclaim among the nations what he has done.
For he who avenges blood remembers;
he does not ignore the cry of the afflicted.

verses 1–12

The wicked return to the grave,
all the nations that forget God.
But the needy will not always be forgotten,
nor the hope of the afflicted ever perish.

Arise, O LORD, let not man triumph;
let the nations be judged in your presence.
Strike them with terror, O LORD;
let the nations know they are but men.   Selah
verses 17–20

I f you were to ask any normal church-going person to define a psalm, I suppose that he or she would most naturally compare it to a hymn. A prayer, perhaps, but chiefly a hymn in which David or one of the other authors of the psalms praises God. And the person would be right! For, more than anything else, the psalms in our Bibles are hymns of praise.

But have you noticed that there have not been any purely praise psalms until now? At the end of the Psalter the psalms are nearly all praise psalms. The last five each begin and end with the words "Praise the LORD," for instance. Here at the beginning it has been different. The first psalm celebrates the doctrine of the two ways—the way of the righteous and the way of the wicked. The second is a messianic psalm, anticipating the victorious rule of God's coming king. These first two psalms are introductory. The next psalms ask for help or deliverance or justice, all in varying ways. The psalm closest to being a praise psalm thus far is Psalm 8, which begins and ends, "O LORD, our Lord, how majestic is your name in all the earth!" But even that psalm was chiefly a celebration of man's place in the created universe, as we saw when we studied it. Psalm 9 is the first psalm that is chiefly a song of pure praise.

Yet I say *chiefly*, because the psalm has two main parts and only the first is exclusively devoted to praise. The first part (vv. 1–12) contains praise for past deliverance. The second (vv. 13–20), which grows out of it, is prayer for future deliverance. Yet so confident is this second part that it seems largely to be praise also.

A Technical Problem

Before we begin a careful study of this first praise hymn, there is a technical problem that we need to look at, involving this psalm and Psalm 10. It arises from the fact that in some versions of the Bible Psalm 9 and Psalm 10 are printed together as one psalm. Is that right? Does Psalm 9 belong with Psalm 10? Were they originally one? Should they be put back together as one? Or should they be kept separate?

Here are the arguments in favor of their being one composition:

1. As I have just mentioned, some versions of the Old Testament treat them as one. The Greek translation of the Old Testament, the version known as the Septuagint, does this, and so does the Latin Vulgate, the translation made by Saint Jerome, which was for years the chief version of the Roman Catholic Church. As a result, the numbering of the psalms differs between some Roman Catholic Bibles and virtually all Protestant ones. In versions stemming from the Septuagint, the numbering is the same up to Psalm 8. But here the numbers begin to vary, and they do not get back together again until Psalm 148.[1] Clearly some ancient scholars considered Psalms 9 and 10 to be one unit.

2. Psalm 10 lacks an introductory title, which is unusual for the first book of the Psalter (Pss. 1–41). With the exception of Psalms 1, 2, 10, and 33, all the other psalms in Book 1 have titles. This suggests that Psalms 9 and 10 might originally have been together.

3. The strongest argument for joining the two psalms is the existence of an acrostic pattern that begins in the first psalm and continues in the second. An acrostic psalm is one in which lines or stanzas of the psalm begin with consecutive letters of the Hebrew alphabet. The best known of these is Psalm 119, which contains twenty-two units of eight verses each, each beginning with the proper sequential letter of the alphabet. In the New International Version the Hebrew letters are used as headings for each section. But there are also other acrostic psalms, some utilizing the entire alphabet, others doing so incompletely. Psalms 37, 111, 112, and 119 are complete. Psalms 9–10, 25, 34, and 145 have partial alphabets.

In Psalms 9 and 10 the situation is this. Psalm 9 contains verses beginning with the alphabet's first eleven letters (that is, half of them), but omitting *daleth* (D). Psalm 10 uses the second half of the alphabet, beginning with *lamedh* (L), but three letters are missing and two are reversed.[2]

What are the arguments in favor of Psalms 9 and 10 originally being separate? There are two:

1. They are separate in the Hebrew text. This is an important point since, whatever the versions may or may not have done, the Hebrew is clearly the original text. The acrostic pattern may be explained by supposing that at

one time there was an original, longer poem containing all or even most of what we have in Psalms 9 and 10, but that at some point it was divided and perhaps altered. Even if that was the case, it was done before our present Hebrew text was solidified, which means that the original "canonical" version had two psalms.

2. The most important argument is that the themes of the two psalms are strikingly different. Psalm 9 is a praise hymn, as I have indicated. Psalm 10 is what is usually called a lament. In it the psalmist grieves over the success and prosperity of the wicked and calls on God to arise and rebuke them and deliver the righteous. I am treating Psalms 9 and 10 separately chiefly because of these two distinct emphases.

Praise for Past Deliverance

The tone of Psalm 9 is set by the first two verses, which declare David's intention of praising God verbally, with words and in song, and with his whole heart. This exuberant note of praise begins and ends the psalm's first section (vv. 1–2).

Here we need to stop and apply David's example to ourselves, for it is often the case that we do neither of these things. We do not praise God with our lips very much, if at all. And when we do, if we do, we praise him half-heartedly. Tenth Presbyterian Church, which I serve as a senior pastor, is an exception to this—for which I am very thankful. Our church knows how to sing God's praises, and our members do speak of God and his blessings often. But in many churches the hymns are rather mumbled than sung, and no one under any circumstances actually praises God in words. It is more often true that Christians complain of how God has been treating them, carry on excessively about their personal needs or desires, or gossip. This should not be. Christian worship should be more like the exuberant worship of ancient Israel than it is.

Let me tell you about one thing I have started to do as a result of my study of the psalms. Recognizing that they are open in their praise of God (as well as emotive in their articulation of pain or grief), I decided to make a point every day of acknowledging God's goodness in some area to some person. That does not seem like much. But when I began to think along these lines I realized how much time frequently went by without my having praised God for anything. And I discovered something else. Once I had begun to make a point of acknowledging God's goodness, I began to think of his goodness more often, and I actually developed a more positive and spiritual frame of mind. This is not mere psychological conditioning, though it works that way perhaps. It is actually a recognition (not always easy to achieve) that God is constantly active in our lives and that, as the apostle Paul put it, "in all things God works for the good of those who love him" (Rom. 8:28).

David knew this. Therefore, although he expressed dismay when the events of his life seemed to run contrary to his being the object of God's goodness, the characteristic themes of his psalms are nevertheless true praise.

> I will praise you, O LORD, with all my heart;
>   I will tell of all your wonders.
> I will be glad and rejoice in you;
>   I will sing praise to your name, O Most High (vv. 1–2).

What is it that David praises God for in this psalm? There are three things, each of which we should properly expect from a man God had made king over Israel.

Victory over Enemies (vv. 3–6)

Enemy nations had marched against Israel, but God had turned them back, causing them to stumble and eventually perish in their headlong retreat. David sees this as God upholding his cause and judging righteously. He rejoices that even the very name of his enemies has been forever blotted out. God has brought them to ruin.

We need to say here that we cannot imagine an identical situation involving ourselves. We are not kings or queens. Most of us have not been charged with defending our land from foreign enemies, though this might apply to military commanders in times of war. Moreover, even though we might have real enemies in some area of our lives or employment, we would not want God utterly to destroy them, blotting out their name from the earth, as David says God did here. We are instructed rather to pray for our enemies and to do good to those who use us wrongly (Matt. 5:44; Luke 6:27–36).

There is one area in which we can echo David's words wholeheartedly, however, and that is in the Lord Jesus Christ's victory over Satan. Satan is our great spiritual enemy, a ruthless enemy. But Jesus has defeated him. Satan is active, yet he is a defeated foe; we can praise God for that.

The Working Out of Justice and Right Judgment on Earth (vv. 7–8)

As the chief executive officer and judge of Israel, David was responsible for seeing that justice was done in civil matters. Therefore, it is appropriate that he should praise God for having established the divine throne for judgment and for ruling justly.[3]

This is something Christians in our day should be increasingly concerned about. Do you remember Micah 6:8? It says, "What does the LORD require of you? To act justly and to love mercy and to walk humbly with your God." I am impressed with each of those requirements, but particularly the first, which requires us to act justly and to be concerned with justice elsewhere. Above all, it means to be concerned with justice for other persons. All too often Christians, particularly evangelical Christians, seem to be concerned with justice only for themselves or their pet causes. And the world fears that if evangelicals should gain political power, here or elsewhere, the rest of the population would suffer at the Christians' hands. I fear it too. I think that in many cases the concern of the world at this point is fully justified.

We need to be on guard against that possibility and praise God as much as David did for wherever and by whomever justice is done.[4]

Refuge from the Wicked (vv. 9–10)

The third thing for which David praises God is his having been a refuge for the oppressed in times of trouble. David had known much trouble during the years he had been forced to hide from King Saul, but God had been a refuge for him. Consequently, this is a dominant theme in the psalms: Psalms 11, 16, 18, 40, and 46, for example. David is not without personal experience to back up his words when he says, "You, LORD, have never forsaken those who seek you" (v. 10).

Any Christian who cannot echo those words should be ashamed. Has God not said, "Never will I leave you; never will I forsake you" (Heb. 13:5; cf. Deut. 31:6)? Did Jesus not say, "Surely I am with you always, to the very end of the age" (Matt. 28:20)?

At the end of this first section David praises the Lord again, echoing the verses with which the psalm began. It is striking that in each part the psalmist combines singing with preaching. And it is interesting to remember that great periods of church history have always been marked by both. At the time of the Protestant Reformation, Martin Luther's hymns were on the lips of the German people as much as his words were in their hearts. At the time of the Wesleyan Revival in Great Britain, the recovery of the gospel was accompanied by an equally stirring recovery of gospel singing, as the hymns of John and Charles Wesley, Augustus Toplady, William Cowper, John Newton, and others show.

Charles Haddon Spurgeon notes this connection in his study of Psalm 9 and concludes, "[So] sing on brethren, and preach on, and these shall both be a token that the Lord still dwelleth in Zion."[5]

Prayer for Future Deliverance

The second part of Psalm 9 (vv. 13–20) is a prayer for future deliverance based on the praise of God for past deliverance recounted in part one. This section begins and ends with prayer, just as the first part began and ended with praise. There are two petitions.

A Prayer for Mercy (v. 13)

This is a foundational petition, showing that David never approached God on the basis of any supposed goodness in himself or any achievement for which he believed he should be rewarded. He came always as a sinner seeking mercy.

A Prayer for God to Arise in Judgment on the Nations (vv. 19–20)

The ground for assurance in this petition is that this is what God has done so admirably in the past, as the first part of the psalm has been saying. It is because of past deliverance that David expects present and future deliverance from God.

In a number of places Psalm 9 seems to refer to Psalm 7, and one of them is in this section. In verse 15 David speaks of the nations having "fallen into the pit they have dug" and of their feet being "caught in the net they have hidden." Similarly, in Psalm 7 he said, "He who is pregnant with evil . . . digs a hole and scoops it out [and] falls into the pit he has made" (vv. 14–15). I do not know if David had any particular examples in mind as he wrote, but it is hard to read what he says without thinking of some ourselves. In fact, we can think of one example, perhaps the clearest and most powerful in the entire Bible, that was not even known to David.

Years after David's reign, when the Jews had been carried off to Babylon by Nebuchadnezzar, there was a time when an enemy of the people named Haman concocted a plot against them. He tricked the king, whose name was Xerxes, into signing a law according to which, on a certain day, all the Jews in the kingdom were to be killed and their goods confiscated. What Haman did not know was that Esther, who had become Xerxes' queen, was a Jewess. She was the adopted daughter of a man named Mordecai. When Mordecai learned that Haman had plotted to have his people killed, he persuaded Esther to intercede for them with Xerxes. Haman, the villain, had built a gallows on which he planned to hang Mordecai, his enemy. But when the plot was uncovered and Xerxes had intervened to spare the Jews' lives, Haman was hanged on the very gallows he had himself constructed. Thus, as Psalm 9 suggests, Haman fell into the pit he had dug and was caught in the net he had hidden.

Man's Chief End

Another point in this last section is worth drawing attention to in closing. It is the reason David gives for praying for mercy in verse 13, his first petition. What is that reason? That he might escape hell? That he might have a comfortable life here and now? That he might prosper above others? No. David prays for mercy specifically so that

> . . . I may declare your praises
> in the gates of the Daughter of Zion
> and there rejoice in your salvation (v. 14).

It is a way of saying that man's chief end is not to enjoy this life or even to escape the punishment due us for our many sins, but to praise God.

"What is the chief end of man?"

You know the answer: "Man's chief end is to glorify God and to enjoy him forever" (*Westminster Shorter Catechism,* question and answer 1). And those are not separate things. To glorify God is to enjoy him, and the enjoyment of God always results in the praise of his people. We never come closer to our true and ultimate destiny as redeemed persons than when we do that, just as David has done so beautifully in this psalm. So praise the Lord! Praise the Lord always and with your whole heart!

Psalm 10

Practical Atheism

Why, O LORD, do you stand far off?
Why do you hide yourself in times of trouble?

In his arrogance the wicked man hunts down the weak,
who are caught in the schemes he devises.
He boasts of the cravings of his heart;
he blesses the greedy and reviles the LORD.
In his pride the wicked does not seek him;
in all his thoughts there is no room for God.
His ways are always prosperous;
he is haughty and your laws are far from him;
he sneers at all his enemies.
He says to himself, "Nothing will shake me;
I'll always be happy and never have trouble."
His mouth is full of curses and lies and threats;
trouble and evil are under his tongue.
He lies in wait near the villages;
from ambush he murders the innocent,
watching in secret for his victims.
He lies in wait like a lion in cover;
he lies in wait to catch the helpless;
he catches the helpless and drags them off in his net.

His victims are crushed, they collapse;
they fall under his strength.
He says to himself, "God has forgotten;
he covers his face and never sees."

Arise, LORD! Lift up your hand, O God.
Do not forget the helpless.
Why does the wicked man revile God?
Why does he say to himself,
"He won't call me to account"?
But you, O God, do see trouble and grief;
you consider it to take it in hand.
The victim commits himself to you;
you are the helper of the fatherless.
Break the arm of the wicked and evil man;
call him to account for his wickedness
that would not be found out.

The LORD is King for ever and ever;
the nations will perish from his land.
                                        verses 1–16

A number of years ago George Gallup, president of the American Institute of Public Opinion, wrote a report of his research into the religious beliefs of Americans entitled "Is America's Faith for Real?" He was struck by a strange anomaly. On the one hand, the answers to his questions indicated that America is unusually religious. But on the other hand, the same research showed that America's religious beliefs make little difference in how people actually live and act.

Here is the positive side:

Eighty-one percent of Americans claim to be religious, which places them second only to Italians, whose rating is eighty-three percent.

Seventy-one percent believe in life after death.

Eighty-four percent believe in heaven.

Sixty-seven percent believe in hell.

A large majority says it believes in the Ten Commandments.

Nearly every home has at least one Bible.

Half of all Americans can be found in church on an average Sunday morning.

Only eight percent say they have no religious affiliation.

Most say that religion plays an important role in their lives. One-fourth
   claim to lead a "very Christian life."
Ninety-five percent believe in God.

But listen to these percentages:
Although 95 percent believe in God and four out of five say they are
religious, only one in five says that religion is the most influential factor in
his or her life. Most want some kind of religious instruction for their children, but religious faith ranks far below many other traits parents would
like to see developed in their sons and daughters. Only one in eight says
he or she would consider sacrificing everything for religious beliefs or God.
Gallup records "a glaring lack of knowledge of the Ten Commandments,"
even by those who say they believe in them. He observes "a high level of
credulity, . . . a lack of spiritual discipline," and a strong "anti-intellectual
strain" in the religious life of most Americans. Only one in eight
Americans says that religion makes a significant difference in his or her
life.[1]
This is practical atheism, and it is extremely widespread. In fact, according to Gallup and his statistics, it is the religion of most of today's
Americans. It is the philosophy of the wicked who are described by David in
Psalm 10.

Two Kinds Of Atheism

There are two kinds of atheism in the psalms. One is a theoretical atheism, the kind we normally think of when we use the words *atheist* or *atheism.*
It is described in Psalms 14 and 53, for instance. These psalms are almost
identical. They begin with the well-known words, "The fool says in his heart,
'There is no God.'" This person really believes that God does not exist,
though the psalmist says he is a fool to think so.
The other kind of atheism is a functional or practical atheism. The
practical atheist might acknowledge that there is a God. "Of course there
is a God," he might say. "Only a fool would deny it." A person like this
might go to church and even take an active role in church affairs. But
so far as his or her life is concerned, God might as well be non-existent.
P. C. Craigie says rightly, "The functional atheist is not concerned so
much with the theoretical question as to the existence of God; rather, he
lives and behaves *as if* God did not exist."[2] It is this person that Psalm 10
describes. According to David, "In all his thoughts there is no room for
God" (v. 4).
What a description this is! Martin Luther was correct when he said,
"There is not, in my judgment, a psalm which describes the mind, the man-
ners, the works, the words, the feelings and the fate of the ungodly with so
much propriety, fullness and light, as this psalm."[3]

The Practice of Atheism

What are the chief characteristics of those who practice atheism? There are five of them, according to David.

Arrogance (vv. 2–4)

The characteristics of the practical atheist overlap in David's description, but if we take them in the order they appear, the first notable mark is arrogance. David uses the word itself in verse 2: "In his arrogance the wicked man hunts down the weak, who are caught in the schemes he devises." Then he fleshes out his description with the words *boasting* ("He boasts of the cravings of his heart") and *pride* ("In his pride the wicked does not seek him," that is, God) in verses 3 and 4. This haughty, boasting, vain, arrogant person shows contempt for both God and man, and does it by both actions and words. He exploits the weak and crushes them. As for his words,

> He says to himself, "Nothing will shake me;
>   I'll always be happy and never have trouble.
>
> He says to himself, "God has forgotten;
>   he covers his face and never sees" (vv. 6, 11).

Prosperity (v. 5)

The godly person might expect the practical atheist to be struck down by a resentful and avenging deity, but for a time at least the opposite seems to be the case. Instead of experiencing God's judgment, the atheist prospers. In fact, his prosperity makes his arrogance both possible and offensive. "His ways are always prosperous," says David. "He is haughty and your laws are far from him; he sneers at all his enemies."

If an unsuccessful person throws his weight around, everyone laughs at him. But when this arrogant person drives a Maserati, wears designer suits, and flys off for vacations to all the hot spots of the jet-set world, it is different, particularly when he laughs at us for our old-fashioned morality. "Forget all that," he says. "There may be a God; but if there is, he doesn't have anything to do with practical life. If you're going to get ahead, you're going to have to do it yourself. God won't help you. And in this world only the strong succeed. If you're not successful, it's your own fault. The poor are poor because they want to be."

Haven't you heard that? Of course you have. It is a well-articulated philosophy in today's culture.

Security (v. 6)

The third characteristic of the practical atheist is his apparent security, which his prosperity seems to guarantee. David quotes him as saying, "Nothing will shake me; I'll always be happy and never have trouble."

During the Second World War the fascist premier and dictator Benito Mussolini was shot at and nearly killed on one occasion. But he laughed it off, saying, "The bullet has never been made that can kill me." That is the attitude of the "secure" atheist. No one can touch him. And as far as any divine retribution is concerned, well, if God has even seen what he has done, he has forgotten. God doesn't interfere.

Vile speech (v. 7)

The fourth characteristic of the practical atheist is a surprising element for most of us, but it is nevertheless in many of the psalms: vile or destructive speech. In words later quoted by the apostle Paul (in Rom. 3:14) as uniquely descriptive of the ungodly, David says,

> His mouth is full of curses and lies and threats;
>   trouble and evil are under his tongue.

I call this surprising, because most of us think of truly bad *acts* as wicked and of *words* as harmless and unimportant. C. S. Lewis says that at first he found it surprising too. "I had half expected that in a simpler and more violent age when more evil was done with the knife, the big stick, and the firebrand, less would be done by talk. But in reality the psalmists mention hardly any kind of evil more often than this one, which the most civilized societies share. . . . It is all over the Psalter. One almost hears the incessant whispering, tattling, lying, scolding, flattery and circulation of rumors. No historical readjustments are here required, we are in the world we know."[4]

And if we think about it, the psalmist clearly is right and we are wrong. Cursing, lying, threatening, and troubling and evil speech are all destructive. They flow from one who does not believe that God will hold him or her accountable.

Violence (vv. 8–11)

The last characteristic of the practical atheist is violence, which has been mentioned in one form or another all along but is developed explicitly in verses 8–11. Verses 8 and 9 portray the violent person by three images. He is an assassin or murderer (v. 8), a lion (v. 9), and a hunter (v. 9). The characteristic that holds these three images together is that each involves the perpetrator lying in wait or hiding to seize his unsuspecting prey. Verse 10 describes the result of this undeserved and sudden violence. It is successful! The arrogant man is able to crush his victims, who "fall under his strength."

Verse 11 describes the conclusion the godless man draws. He reasons that God either does not see him or else quickly forgets his evil actions.

A Problem for the Righteous

The problems the wicked create for their victims are obvious. Because they are weak, the victims of these people are "caught in the schemes" they devise and are "crushed." But David was not one of these weak persons. He was a strong military commander and later king of Israel. Nevertheless, the success of these practical atheists created a problem for David also. What is it? It is God's apparent toleration of the wicked, and the suspicion that their boasts about God's not seeing or not caring might be true.

Haven't you ever thought that way, perhaps when you have looked about at the practical atheism of our age? When you have been down about what seems to be a great injustice done either to you or to someone close to you, haven't you sometimes doubted whether God actually does see and care, as you have been taught to believe? Haven't you thought that God does seem to be unresponsive and even unfair? Or at least that it looks that way?

Here is how Craigie puts it.

It is easy to say that God exists, to affirm that morality matters, to believe in divine and human justice, but the words carry a hollow echo when the empirical reality of human living indicates precisely the opposite. The reality appears to be that the atheists have the upper hand, that reality really does not matter and that justice is dormant. At the moment that this reality is perceived, in all its starkness, the temptation is at its strongest to jettison faith, morality and belief in justice. What good is a belief and a moral life which appear to be so out of place in the harsh realities of an evil world? Indeed, would there not be a certain wisdom in the oppressed joining ranks with the oppressors?[5]

The Response of Godly People

That may be worldly wisdom, of course, and many have bought into it. But it is not the response of those who know God, as David did. In this psalm David's response to those who show their contempt of God by taking advantage of the poor is threefold. We find it in the psalm's second half (vv. 12–18).

First, David asks God to act: "Arise, LORD! Lift up your hand, O God. Do not forget the helpless" (v. 12). Many times God does not act or does not seem to act. We look on and cannot understand his silence or inactivity. We are puzzled, distraught. In such times it is never wrong to ask God to intervene. He may not do it when we ask him to, but it is still right to ask. We can pray for ourselves in such circumstances, asking for God's intervention and deliverance, and we can certainly intercede for others. This seems to be the heart of David's concern. He saw injustice being done and prayed for God's intervening help for the victims.

Second, David reminds himself that, although God does not seem to see what is happening—the wicked say that "God . . . covers his face and never sees"—God nevertheless does see, is concerned, and eventually does intervene. God's retributive actions are often delayed. That is why David intercedes for the suffering. But when he does intercede, he does so confidently because of his knowledge of what God is like and how he operates.

> But you, O God, do see trouble and grief;
>   you consider it to take it in hand.
> The victim commits himself to you;
>   you are the helper of the fatherless (v. 14).

Finally, David thinks of an eventual judgment of the wicked. "The LORD is King for ever and ever; the nations will perish from his land" (v. 16).

In David's mind this was probably an earthly judgment. We have already seen how judgment in this life, rather than judgment in the life to come, is the major concern of the psalmists. There are grounds for this confidence. Arrogance against God and man frequently oversteps itself. The mighty are often caught in their own devices and brought down. The words "How the mighty are fallen!" have been uttered more than once in human history (see David's moving lament for Saul and Jonathan, 2 Sam. 1:19–27). Nevertheless, for a final balancing of accounts we must await the final judgment.

Never mind that the wicked scoff at it.

The apostle Peter spoke of people who would be like this. They too would be practical atheists. He wrote,

> You must understand that in the last days scoffers will come, scoffing and following their own evil desires. They will say, "Where is this 'coming' he promised? Ever since our fathers died, everything goes on as it has since the beginning of creation." But they deliberately forget that long ago by God's word the heavens existed and the earth was formed out of water and by water. By these waters also the world of that time was deluged and destroyed. By the same word the present heavens and earth are reserved for fire, being kept for the day of judgment and destruction of ungodly men. . . . But the day of the Lord will come like a thief. The heavens will disappear with a roar; the elements will be destroyed by fire, and the earth and everything in it will be laid bare (2 Peter 3:3–7, 10).

In other words, the proof of the final judgment is the fact that God has already judged the world once in the great flood of Noah's day. God's wrath may be delayed, but it is not canceled. The final judgment is no less certain than the former one.

In the meantime, what shall the righteous do? Habakkuk had the answer. God told him of extremely bad times that were coming. The Babylonians were going to overrun his country and carry the people into slavery. But, said God, in such times, "The righteous will live by his faith" (Hab. 2:4).

This is not always easy to do, but it is what Habakkuk did and what David did too. In this psalm is as in many of these psalms, we do not see the answer the psalmist was expecting. David asked God to "break the arm" (that is, the power) of the wicked. But we do not know that David lived to see it in the cases he was troubled about. Or even if he did, we know that there would soon have been other practical atheists to take the places of those who had fallen. Still David trusted God. He lived by faith and was therefore confident of the ultimate ends of the righteous and the wicked.

> Though the fig tree does not bud
>> and there are no grapes on the vines,
> though the olive crop fails
>> and the fields produce no food,
> though there are no sheep in the pen
>> and no cattle in the stalls,
> yet I will rejoice in the LORD,
>> I will be joyful in God my Savior (Hab. 3:17–18).

That was Habakkuk's testimony, and it is David's, too. God's timing is not our timing. But we will be able to live joyfully even in times of trouble, if we carry our troubles to the King of Kings.

Psalm 11

What Can the Righteous Do?

In the LORD I take refuge.
How then can you say to me:
"Flee like a bird to your mountain.
For look, the wicked bend their bows;
they set their arrows against the strings
to shoot from the shadows
at the upright in heart.
When the foundations are being destroyed,
what can the righteous do?"

The LORD is in his holy temple;
the LORD is on his heavenly throne.
He observes the sons of men;
his eyes examine them.
The LORD examines the righteous,
but the wicked and those who love violence
his soul hates.
On the wicked he will rain
fiery coals and burning sulfur;
a scorching wind will be their lot.

For the LORD is righteous,
he loves justice;
upright men will see his face.

verses 1–7

Psalm 11 contains faith's response to fear's counsel. The psalmist is in danger from the wicked, who are bending their bows and shooting at him, and either his friends or his enemies are advising him to take flight. "Flee to the mountains," they say. But he refutes their advice, asserting that his true refuge is in God.

In the midst of this psalm, probably as a despairing question asked by David's fearful but well-meaning friends, we have a classic question. You have probably heard it many times. "When the foundations are being destroyed, what can the righteous do?" (v. 3). More than fifty years ago the great Bible teacher Arno C. Gaebelein called this "the burning question of our day."[1] But if that was so in 1939, when his study was copyrighted, it is a thousand times more true today. What shall we do when the laws are not upheld, when morality is undermined and evil sweeps on unchecked? What shall we do when the Bible is undermined and its teachings disregarded—when even churchmen seem to support the rising tide of secularism? What shall we do when family values are crumbling and the tide of frequent divorce sweeps forward with increasing damage to children, parents, and society alike? What can we do when everything around us seems to be giving way? Some counsel hiding, that is, running away from what is happening. David's response was to take refuge in the Lord. It is this—what it means and how it is done—that we must consider in this study.

Was there a situation in David's life that fits this psalm? Two possibilities are often presented by commentators: first, the years in which David was opposed by King Saul, and second, the period in which he was fleeing from Absalom. Charles Simeon and Charles Haddon Spurgeon suggest the first possibility. Franz Delitzsch prefers the second. Neither of these fit the psalm very well, however, because in both cases David actually fled to the mountains rather than resisted the advice of his friends to do so. Probably we cannot fix upon a single appropriate setting in David's life. Yet this is not bad, because it opens the possibility of interpreting the psalm more broadly.

There are three parts to Psalm 11. Verses 1–3 describe the temptation David faced. Verses 4–6 describe his reaction to it. Verse 7, the last verse, describes the result.

What Shall We Do?

As I say, we do not know what this particular crisis in David's life was, but the nature of the crisis is made clear enough by the image of hidden enemies and the advice of his friends to flee to the mountain strongholds. We would say, "Your enemies are lying in wait for you. You won't even see the blow coming. The best thing you can do is get out of their reach for the time being."

The most intriguing part of the opening stanza (vv. 1–3) is the classic question of verse 3:

> When the foundations are being destroyed,
>   what can the righteous do?

It is intriguing, first, because it is a question the righteous have asked again and again in bad times and, second, because a good answer to it is hard to find. In times of stable government or strong faith, the righteous appeal to the country's law or to established standards of faith or morality. But in bad times these do not exist. "What shall I do?" becomes a pressing and overwhelmingly important question. Let me give some illustrations.

First, an illustration from David's time. In 1 Samuel 22 we are told of a particularly vile atrocity by King Saul. David had been warned by his friend Jonathan of Saul's determination to kill him, and David had fled from Jerusalem without time to prepare for the journey. His flight brought him to the city of Nob, where he presented himself to Ahimelech, the city's priest. Ahimelech, assuming that David was still in Saul's service, was surprised that he had arrived without his division of the army. But David replied that he was on urgent royal business and asked for the priest's help. Ahimelech gave him consecrated bread to eat and Goliath's sword, which had been in the priest's custody.

A short time later Saul was told that Ahimelech had assisted David, even inquiring of the Lord for him. Saul called Ahimelech to Gibeah, where he was holding court, and accused him of treason. Ahimelech denied that he was guilty of any such thing. He said that he had honored David's requests as he always had, believing him to be Saul's servant. Saul would not believe him. "You will surely die, Ahimelech, you and your father's whole family," he said abruptly.

Saul ordered his guards to kill Ahimelech and the other priests of Nob who had accompanied him, but they would not. They were afraid to lift their hands against the Lord's anointed. Saul turned to one of his servants named Doeg, who then killed eighty-five of the priests, after which he also turned on the town of Nob and had all its men, women, children, infants, and animals exterminated. It was one of the darkest moments of that grim period of history. The king, who was responsible for maintaining and enforcing law and order, was himself destroying it.[2]

Those who lived in that time might well have asked,

> When the foundations are being destroyed,
>   what can the righteous do?

Here is another example, closer to us because it is from our own time. In Columbia, South America, the government of President Vigilio Vargas was under attack by the country's notorious drug cartel. The government had been trying to enforce the country's laws by stopping the drug traffic, and the cocaine barons fought back by a long series of terrorist explosions at banks, businesses, and newspapers and by assassinations of important persons. Among those brutally assassinated were a Medellin police chief, several judges, and Columbian presidential candidate Luis Carlos Galan. When the government began to extradite leaders of the cartel to the United States to stand trial on various drug charges, the cartel threatened to kill ten Columbian judges for every accused drug trafficker extradited.

Justice Minister Monica de Greiff came to Washington for help, denying rumors that she would soon resign because of threats against her and her family. "The law is under siege in Columbia," she said. "We must protect it in every way we can."[3] But two weeks later she did resign due to the mounting dangers. Columbia was in near anarchy.

The righteous might well say,

> When the foundations are being destroyed,
> what can the righteous do?

Nor is it entirely different in the United States. The drugs prepared in Columbia and other South and Central American countries are for the American market, and few communities are unaffected by it. In major cities drugs are sold openly on street corners, and violence follows in the wake as dealers fight with each other for control of their drug turf. Frequently, innocent people are killed. In Philadelphia, six-year-old Ralph Brooks was paralyzed by a stray bullet fired in a feud between two drug dealers in the area of Twentieth and Tasker Streets. In New York City Maria Hernandez, a thirty-four-year-old mother of three who had been resisting the intrusion of drug dealers into her Brooklyn neighborhood, was shot to death through the window of her home, presumably by order of the drug dealers. Ten days earlier her husband had been stabbed in a confrontation with a dealer on the street.

And crime? Much of it is caused by those seeking objects to sell to buy drugs. In Philadelphia cars are regularly broken into and their radios or other salable objects stolen. It is not uncommon for cars regularly parked on the streets to bear handwritten signs, saying: "No $$. No radio. No valuables. No nothing." And if a car is broken into (or stolen), the police do not even want to come to investigate, so hopeless is the chance of arresting anyone.

> When the foundations are being destroyed,
> what can the righteous do?

What *can* the righteous do? They can go on being righteous. And they can stand against the evil of their society, as many in the situations I have described are attempting to do.

The one thing they must not do is "flee to the mountains."

Where Should We Look?

I want to answer the question of verse 3 ("What can the righteous do?") with another question. That question is: To whom shall the righteous look? The answer is: To the Lord. He is the only one to whom we can look when the foundations are shaken, and he is the one to whom we must look if we are to stand firm in unsettling times.

Charles Wesley knew it. He wrote of such times:

> Other refuge have I none,
> Hangs my helpless soul on thee;
> Leave, ah! leave me not alone,
> Still support and comfort me.
> All my trust on thee is stayed,
> All my help from thee I bring;
> Cover my defenseless head
> With the shadow of thy wing.

This is what David does, of course. It is what the second part of the psalm, the part that contains the answer, is about.

Do you remember Psalm 8 and the description it contains of man and his place in the created universe? Men and women are in a mediating position. They are midway between the angelic beings, who are above them, and the beasts, who are below. Yet they are described as being "a little lower than the heavenly beings" (v. 5) rather than "a little higher than the beasts." When we were studying that psalm, I pointed out how significant this description is. Being made in God's image, it is humanity's privilege and responsibility to look upward to the heavenly beings and beyond them to God, and so become increasingly like God, rather than downward to the beasts with the result that the one looking down becomes like them. I showed how our society is becoming increasingly beast-like, since it will not acknowledge, look to, or worship God.

But the righteous do look to God. That is, they look upward. Where is he that they might look to him? The answer is: "in his holy temple" and "on his heavenly throne" (v. 4).

Whenever we see the word *temple* in the Old Testament, we tend to think of Solomon's great gilded temple or the temple of Herod that was in Jerusalem in the time of Jesus Christ. But that is not what David is thinking of here. For one thing, the temple had not been built in David's time. And although it is true that the word *temple* is sometimes used of the wilderness tabernacle, usually in retrospect by those who witnessed the later temples and saw the tabernacle as their forerunner, the context of Psalm 11 makes clear that David is thinking of the temple of God in heaven from which the Almighty looks down upon "the sons of men" to "examine them."

The temple was associated with the holiness of God; the earthly temple (tabernacle) contained the Holy Place and the Most Holy Place. So when David looks to the Lord, who is "in his holy temple," he is looking to the Lord as the moral standard by which the thoughts and intents, words and actions of all men and women will be judged.

This leads to the second directional statement: "the LORD is on his heavenly throne." The throne is the place from which God, the judge of the earth, renders judgment. When David looks to the Lord on his throne, he is looking to him to render just judgment, much as he has done in other psalms we have studied. This important upward look convinces David of three things, all having to do with God.

God *observes* all that people do. "He observes the sons of men; his eyes examine them," says David. The words remind us of the well-known Anglican collect that speaks of him "before whom all hearts are open, all desires known." Or of Proverbs 15:3, which says, "The eyes of the LORD are everywhere, keeping watch on the wicked and the good." When David speaks of God observing people, he is reminding himself of God's omniscience. This is particularly apt in a psalm that began with a warning against those who "shoot from the shadows at the upright in heart" (v. 2). They hide so they might not be seen or known. But although the righteous may not see them, the all-seeing God sees them. Their deeds are as apparent to him as if they were performed in bright daylight.

God *examines* the upright. The word *examine (bahan)* in verse 5 is the same word as in the preceding verse ("his eyes examine them"). Some versions translate it differently in verse 4 from verse 5 because the word can have two meanings. It can mean "try" or "test." If "test" is the meaning, it would involve God's testing of the righteous by the difficult times the first verses of the psalm describe. Craigie thinks along these lines when he says, "The testing of the righteous (v. 5a), though it might involve great hardship, would culminate in purity and the removal of dross."[4] Spurgeon thinks the same, when he writes that God "refines [the righteous] with afflictions."[5] On the other hand, the word can mean "try" in the sense of inspecting and approving. Leupold holds to this view when he writes, "The Lord . . . finds them to be what they claim and aim to be. . . . His divine approval rests upon them."[6]

The two ideas may be related, of course. But little in the psalm suggests that David views the temptations of the righteous as a trial by which they are perfected. Rather the context is one of judgment, and the contrast with the wicked (in the second half of verse 5) suggests a trial in which the righteous are approved and the wicked condemned. The verse teaches that God not only sees people's deeds, which is what verse 4 affirms, but that he also pronounces a verdict on them.

God *prepares his judgments* for the wicked. They may be preparing to shoot at the righteous from the shadows. But the Lord will protect the righteous, and in the end the wicked will themselves be shot at and destroyed.

None of this is fantasizing or mere wishful thinking on David's part. For when he refers to God raining down "fiery coals and burning sulfur" on the wicked, he is thinking of God's destruction of Sodom and Gomorrah by that means. He thus reminds himself that God's judgments do come, though they may often be delayed. Sodom is a great biblical example of judgment. David may even be reminding us that God sometimes spares the wicked for the sake of the righteous, as he promised to do in the case of Sodom if only ten righteous persons could have been found there (see Gen. 18:32).

Where Will We Be?

What can the righteous do? There is one more thing. David had looked around at the wicked. He had looked up to God. Now he looks ahead, to the future, concerned at this point not with the destiny of his enemies but with his own destiny and that of all who trust God. The last verse means: *because* "the LORD is righteous [and] loves justice, upright men will see his face" (v. 7).

This last phrase is an anticipation of nothing less than the beatific vision, the ultimate aspiration of the Old Testament saints: to see God face to face. Strangely, many commentators seem reluctant to admit this, pleading the incomplete and uncertain view of the afterlife Old Testament believers are supposed to have had. But although Old Testament understandings are obviously less developed than those of the New Testament, based as the latter are upon the resurrection and explicit teaching of Jesus, and although the idea of seeing God's face could mean only that the light of his favor will shine upon the upright, it is nevertheless hard to suppose that David is not thinking here of the believer's ultimate reward and bliss.[7] Why? He has just spoken of a future judgment on the wicked: "On the wicked he will rain fiery coals and burning sulfur" (v. 6). What is called for now is a parallel statement of what the same all-seeing and just God will do for those who are righteous.

They will see God! How glorious!

Remember how Moses asked that favor of God and was told he could not see him? God said, "I will put you in a cleft in the rock and cover you with my hand until I have passed by. Then I will remove my hand and you will see my back; but my face must not be seen" (Exod. 33:22–23). "You cannot see my face, for no one may see me and live" (v. 20).

Yet this is what the Old Testament believers continued to seek. They pray for it many times in the Old Testament. Wishful thinking? Something nice, but actually impossible? Not at all. Because, when we come to the end of the New Testament, to the letters of the apostle John, who gazed often on the face of the earthly Jesus, we find him promising, "When he [that is, the heavenly, glorified Jesus] appears, we shall be like him, for *we shall see him as he is*" (1 John 3:2, italics added). The upright really will see God's face.

Psalm 12

False Words or Faithful Words

Help, LORD, for the godly are no more;
the faithful have vanished from among men.
Everyone lies to his neighbor;
their flattering lips speak with deception.

May the LORD cut off all flattering lips
and every boastful tongue
that says, "We will triumph with our tongues;
we own our lips—who is our master?"

"Because of the oppression of the weak
and the groaning of the needy,
I will now arise," says the LORD.
"I will protect them from those who malign them."
And the words of the LORD are flawless,
like silver refined in a furnace of clay,
purified seven times.

O LORD, you will keep us safe
and protect us from such people forever.
The wicked freely strut about
when what is vile is honored among men.

verses 1–8

P salm 12 is about human speech, as used by lying men and as employed by God in biblical revelation. It is about the use and the abuse of words. The principle involved is that the higher or finer a thing is, the more vulnerable it is to perversion. Love is the greatest quality in life. Yet love can be terribly abused. So also with words. On the lips of an Abraham Lincoln or a Winston Churchill words can inspire and challenge. They can lift people to times of extraordinary greatness. But in the mouth of an Adolf Hitler they can sweep the world into a destructive war.

Words are both our glory and our shame.

The psalm begins by describing the use of words by wicked persons in order to deceive and to oppress others, and in this respect it is a commentary on a theme introduced in the two preceding psalms. In Psalm 10 the writer is describing the wicked, one prominent feature of such persons being how they use words. They boast (v. 3) and sneer (v. 5). They say, "Nothing will shake me; I'll always be happy and never have trouble" (v. 6). The psalmist concludes his description with words later alluded to by the apostle Paul in Romans, saying, "His mouth is full of curses and lies and threats; trouble and evil are under his tongue" (v. 7; cf. Rom. 3:14).

In a similar way, Psalm 11 speaks about the destruction of society's foundations by wicked people (v. 3), and we know that one of the ways they do this is with their tongues. "When the foundations are being destroyed, what can the righteous do?" asks David. When we were studying that question, I said that the righteous turn to the Lord in such times. David did this in Psalm 11. He also does it in Psalm 12. In fact, it is the way the psalm begins.

> Help, LORD, for the godly are no more;
> the faithful have vanished from among men (v. 1).

Like many psalms, this one is divided into two main parts, followed by a concluding response on the writer's part. In my judgment, the response is of special importance. It is the application of the "sermon." So I consider the psalm in three sections here: the words of the wicked (vv. 1–4); the words of the Lord (vv. 5–6); and the response of the psalmist to God's words, which show the way to live a faithful and prosperous life in bad times (vv. 7–8).

The Words of the Wicked

As we begin this psalm, we find that the psalmist feels isolated, like Elijah in the desert, where he fled after his great victory on Mount Carmel. "The Israelites have rejected your covenant, broken down your altars, and put your prophets to death with the sword. I am the only one left, and now they are trying to kill me too" (1 Kings 19:10). Elijah was mistaken, of course, and David probably was too. God told Elijah that there were yet seven thousand who had not bowed down to Baal. Still, that was only a small remnant, and there are times when those who love God and want to be faithful to him really do feel alone.

Haven't you felt that way at times? Perhaps you were trying to do the right thing at work, and everyone ignored you because they did not want to be judged by your standards. You may have felt isolated at home or at school. People in government say they often feel that "the godly are no more" and that "the faithful have vanished from among men."

Psalm 12 is said to have been written by David, and there were surely many times in his life when David felt like this. But it is striking that the psalm contains nothing of a strictly personal note. There is no first person language, no *I, me,* or *my.* H. C. Leupold says, "This is one of the many instances when the psalms rise above the purely personal and local and look to the later needs of the church of God."[1] In other words, we can identify easily with what Psalm 12 describes.

What is the situation? The writer is surrounded, not by upright and trustworthy people, but by "people of the lie." He is surrounded by people who use words not to advance truth but to advance their own evil ends. They do four things.

They Lie

This is the most embracing expression for the misuse of words in these verses, but it does not mean exactly what the word *lie* means to us in English. To us a lie means falsehood, a distortion of truth. The Hebrew word, while it includes this idea, actually means "emptiness," thus including also the additional ideas of insincerity and irresponsibility.[2] Our best expressions for this are "empty (or vain) talk" and "vanity." This is the essence of most cocktail-party conversations.

They Flatter

Flattery goes a step beyond mere emptiness, because it contains the additional element of a corrupt or an evil motive. People flatter others for bad purposes—to get something out of them, deceive them, or cheat them. There have been periods of history when flattering speech has been developed to a high degree, as in diplomatic or courtly language. King Solomon must have endured a great deal of it at his court, because the Book of Proverbs, which he wrote, warns often against flattery (e.g., Prov. 26:28; 28:23; 29:5). Daniel says that flattery will be a tool of that wicked world ruler who will arise at the last day (Dan. 11:32). Jude links flattery to the ways of the ungodly who will be condemned in the final judgment (v. 16).

We have plenty of this today. The Hebrew word actually means "smooth," and there is much smooth talk about us. Smooth talk is glib, facile, false, pleasing, and deadly.

They Deceive

The Hebrew text is idiomatic at this point, for it says literally, "They speak with a heart and a heart" (v. 2). It is the Hebrew way of describing double-talk or, as we would say, "talking out of both sides of our mouths." It is using a word that means one thing to advance something that is its exact opposite.

In no area of modern life is this more obvious than in the misuse of language to legitimize abortion. Abortion is killing a baby while it is still in the womb. In past generations there were some who would do this, as today, but they were not deceived in what they were doing. They knew they were killing the child. Today we have abortions on a large scale. But because murder, even of the frailest members of the human race, is still unacceptable to most people, there has been a concerted attempt to rename what is done. First, the baby became a fetus, then only tissue. No one can get disturbed about aborting tissue; that is like removing a mole. Then even the word *abortion* was changed. People do not talk so much about abortions now. Rather, it is a "surgical procedure" or, even worse, a heroic exercise of the right of free choice by the mother.

I saw a new debasement of language in this area not long ago. A pro-abortion group was holding a rally against Pennsylvania Governor Robert Casey, a Democrat who opposes abortion. Casey was soon to sign a Pennsylvania law that would restrict abortions after twenty-four weeks into a pregnancy, except to save the life of the mother, would ban abortions for sex selection, would establish a twenty-four-hour waiting period to deter precipitous action, and would do a few other wise things. The signs for the rally read:

> The Reproductive Rights Robber
> is coming to town.
> Protest anti-choice Governor Casey.

I do not mind the protest itself. This is a free country in which the right of free speech is properly protected. I do not even mind a specific protest against Casey by those who oppose his position. But I do mind the language. "Reproductive Rights Robber"? Whatever were they thinking of? Abortion may be many things, but one thing it is not is the protection of reproductive rights. People have the right to reproduce. They have it whether they are married or unmarried, young or old. The issue in abortion is whether they also have the right to kill the ones thus reproduced.

Say, "It is more important to protect the freedom or convenience of a female adult than the life of a baby," if you will. That is wrong, but it is at least an honest description of what is happening. But do not say, "We want our *reproductive* rights," when what is actually being called for is the right to kill babies.

And what of the word *robber?* That was deceptive also. The governor was accused of theft, when actually his concern was for the saving of life—and by legal means. It is the abortionists who are robbers, for they are robbing the lives of children yet unborn.

They Boast

The third bad use of language described in Psalm 12 is boasting, an outward expression of the deadly sin of pride. David reports the boasts of those surrounding him by listing their three claims: "We will triumph with our tongues"; "We own our lips"; and "Who is our master?" The first claim justifies the means by the end: winning justifies deceit. The second claims autonomy: "We have the right to say anything we please." The last boast means, "And if we lie when we speak, who is there who can call us to account?" It is a denial of any higher standard or accountability.

The French atheist Voltaire made these claims openly. He once said, "In twenty years Christianity will be no more. My single hand shall destroy the edifice it took twelve apostles to rear." He wrote that in fifty years no one would remember Christianity. But the year he wrote that, the British Museum paid the Russian government five hundred thousand dollars for a Bible manuscript while one of Voltaire's books was selling in the London book stalls for just eight cents. Fifty years after his boast, the house in which Voltaire wrote his atheistic literature was the headquarters of the Geneva Bible Society and was therefore being used to disseminate the Christian Scriptures.

The nurse who attended Voltaire in his last illness said, "For all the wealth in Europe I would not see another infidel die."

His physician's name was Trochim. He was with the great Voltaire when he died and reported that his last words were: "I am abandoned by God and man! I will give you half of what I am worth if you will give me six months' life. Then I shall go to hell; and you will go with me. O Christ! O Jesus Christ!"[3]

How misleading human words can be! The most famous words of communism are the opening of Karl Marx's *Communist Manifesto:* "Workers of the world, unite." But in demonstrations in Moscow on the occasion of the seventy-second anniversary of communism in Russia, people carried signs that read, "Workers of the world, we're sorry" and "72 years leading nowhere."

The Words of the Lord

This brings us to the second half of Psalm 12. After reviewing the destructive words of wicked persons, the psalmist turns to the words of God and acknowledges that they are quite different. In verse 5 he quotes God directly: "Because of the oppression of the weak . . . I will now arise." It is the first oracle in the psalms. Then he says that the words of God are "flawless, like silver refined in a furnace of clay, purified seven times" (v. 6). Silver refined seven times would be completely pure.

This speaks to the struggle over the authority of the Bible in our day. There are three basic views.

The first view is that the Bible is the Word of God, which it claims to be, and that, because it is the Word of God, it is without flaw in whatever it teaches. This is the classic, evangelical view that has prevailed throughout church history. There have been many debates about doctrine in church history, even about such items as the deity of Jesus Christ, the nature of the Trinity, and the way of salvation. But whenever such debates erupted it was always the Bible to which the disputing parties turned. Even heretics viewed the Bible as the Word of God. They erred in their interpretation of it and had to be corrected as the church studied the issue, allowing the Holy Spirit to speak to them through the Word. But all acknowledged that the Bible is God's Word and that it is therefore inerrant.

The second view is that the Bible is the words of mere men. This is the outlook of liberalism and neo-orthodoxy, even though many neo-orthodox theologians have given serious attention to the Bible and have been willing to be guided by it. Liberalism says that the Bible is man's word only—helpful perhaps, but by no means utterly authoritative or inerrant. Neo-orthodoxy says that God is so transcendent that he cannot speak to us in human words but rather reveals himself nonverbally. The Bible is a book in which men testify in their own words to what they believe God has revealed in this fashion.

The third position is the one we are especially wrestling with today, that the Bible is the Word of God and the word of man combined. These are combined, not in the sense that the Bible is the Word of God in words of men especially chosen and inspired to be such channels, which is accurate, but in the sense that, when we read the Bible, we find things that have come to us from God and are therefore truthful. But there are also (so the argument goes) things that are not truthful, things which we know to be in error; because we know that God cannot speak lies, the only possible conclusion is that these are not from God but are from men only. The Bible is thus a combination of divine and merely human words. It is the task of scholarship to sort them out for us.

But what happens in this framework is that the scholar himself becomes God. That is, he becomes the authority who tells us what is true and what is not true, what is of God and what is not of God. And because the sinful heart of man, even that of scholars, prefers its own misunderstandings to God's truth, there is always a tendency to reject what we most need to hear, calling it mere human teaching or error. Thus the reforming Word of God is dismissed, we continue in our sins, and the vitality of the church suffers.[4]

The Bible has been "tried and found flawless." It has been tested by unbelievers and believers alike, and it has always survived unscathed. *Time* acknowledged this some years ago in a cover story:

> The breadth, sophistication and diversity of all this biblical investigation are impressive, but it begs a question: Has it made the Bible more credible or less? Literalists who feel the ground move when a verse is challenged would have to say that credibility has suffered. Doubt has been sown, faith is in jeopardy. But believers who expect something else from the Bible may well conclude that its credibility has been enhanced. After more than two centuries of facing the heaviest guns that could be brought to bear, the Bible has survived—and is perhaps the better for the siege. Even on the critics' own terms—historical fact—the Scriptures seem more acceptable now than when the rationalists began the attack.[5]

Charles Haddon Spurgeon said the same thing more than a century earlier. In his comments on Psalm 12:6, Spurgeon wrote, "The Bible has passed through the furnace of persecution, literary criticism, philosophic doubt, and scientific discovery, and has lost nothing but those human interpretations which clung to it as alloy to precious ore. The experience of the saints has tried it in every conceivable manner, but not a single doctrine or promise has been consumed in the most excessive heat."[6]

That is absolutely true. The infidels of the ages have beat upon this rock. But the Word of God stands firm, and in the end, like Voltaire, unbelievers are broken by the rock rather than breaking it.

Standing on the Rock

At the end of Psalm 12, we find something characteristic of many psalms. We find that there is no change in the circumstances. The wicked are still "freely strut[ting] about" (v. 8).[7] There is as much lying, flattering, deceiving, and boasting as there ever was. But the psalmist has changed. He began with a despairing cry for God's help: "Help, LORD, for the godly are no more; the faithful have vanished from among men." God answered, and the psalmist now realizes that, regardless of what others do, he has the word of the reliable God as his rock and is able to stand on this firm foundation.

> O LORD, you will keep us safe
> and protect us from such people forever (v. 7).

I think here of J. C. Ryle, that great nineteenth-century bishop of the Church of England who did so much for evangelical Christianity in his day.

He lived in a time when rationalistic theories were bursting on the church like a flood and many were being swept away. The attacks were outdistancing the answers. Believing scholars were hard pressed to keep up. But Ryle was unshaken by the attacks. He declared, like David, "Give me the plenary, verbal theory of biblical inspiration with all its difficulties, rather than the doubt. I accept the difficulties and humbly wait for their solution. But while I wait, I am standing on the rock."[8]

Psalm 13

How Long?
How Long?

How long, O LORD? Will you forget me forever?
How long will you hide your face from me?
How long must I wrestle with my thoughts
and every day have sorrow in my heart?
How long will my enemy triumph over me?

Look on me and answer, O LORD my God.
Give light to my eyes, or I will sleep in death;
my enemy will say, "I have overcome him,"
and my foes will rejoice when I fall.

But I trust in your unfailing love;
my heart rejoices in your salvation.
I will sing to the LORD,
for he has been good to me.

verses 1–6

You may have noticed in your study of the psalms that certain places in the Psalter reveal increasing intensity and even apparent desperation. We find this movement as we pass from Psalm 12 to Psalm 13.

In Psalm 12 David feels himself to be alone, in the sense that godly or faithful persons seem to have disappeared. Instead of upright persons, he is surrounded by "people of the lie." This is bad enough, of course. If we feel alone in any trying situation, we feel desperate. But when we read Psalm 13, we find that David feels abandoned now not only by godly or faithful men, but even by God himself! Can anything be worse than that? It is hard to think so. When Jonah was trying to get away from God, he thought that being abandoned by God would be desirable. But when he was thrown into the sea, was swallowed by the great fish, and finally did sense himself to be abandoned by God, he found that he did not like the feeling at all. He compared his state of abandonment to Sheol or hell and cried out in distress, asking God to save him (cf. Jonah 2).

Before beginning to explore Psalm 13 in detail, I have two observations to make about feeling abandoned by God.

The first is this. As a result of counseling people over more than two decades of my ministry, I am convinced that a feeling of abandonment is far more common than it appears to be. Many people feel abandoned—by others, first, but ultimately also by God, which makes this a spiritual problem and not only a psychological one. Moreover, I find that counselors confirm this. A psychiatrist friend says that she deals with it frequently in her practice, particularly when someone feels depressed. She says, "The amount of despair and false guilt result in a feeling of a deep chasm between the person and God." The person feels that no one cares about him or her, and since no person cares, God must not care either. God seems to have left such persons to themselves.

Here is the second observation. Although this is a common problem, I have not been able to find much helpful literature about it, particularly by Christians. Even D. Martyn Lloyd-Jones in *Spiritual Depression: Its Causes and Cure* does not specifically deal with feelings of abandonment.[1]

Why do you suppose this is? I think it is because we have been taught that Christians are not to experience such things, that we are only to have "life more abundantly" or to "live victoriously." In the last chapter I quoted the dying French atheist Voltaire, who said, "I am abandoned by God and man." We are not surprised to hear an unbeliever say that. But if any of us should admit to such feelings, many of our friends would look askance at us, shake their heads, and wonder whether we are Christians. Isn't that true? Isn't that the chief reason why you do not talk to other Christians about this or about many other problems?

How good then to find that David does talk about it! David is a giant in Scripture, a person "after [God's] own heart" (1 Sam. 13:14). Yet described here is a time when David felt that God had left him entirely. And he doesn't cover up his feelings. To use Howard Cosell's famous phrase, David "tells it like it is." He feels abandoned by God and says so. Well, if he says so, we can say so too. Even more importantly, we can learn from him and can experience the same good movement from despair to settled trust in God that this psalm shows.

Three-Part Outline

Psalm 13 has a simple but important outline, which we need to keep in mind. There are three parts, each consisting of two verses. Verses 1 and 2 express David's feeling of abandonment. Verses 3 and 4 are a prayer in which he asks God to turn his face toward him and to answer his questions. Verses 5 and 6 express David's recovered trust in God and have a tone of rejoicing. In these verses David recalls that God has been good to him in the past and says that he is sure God will be good to him again.

We need to note the place of prayer in this psalm. It occurs in the middle and is the turning point. That is an important thing to know.

And there is also a minor, technical point to consider: the number of lines per stanza. The first stanza of the psalm has five lines. The second stanza has four lines. The third stanza has three lines in reality, although in the New International Version the last line has been broken into two parts to make a four-line stanza. This means that the form of the poem, as well as the subject matter, moves from the tumultuous and emotional beginning (expressed in five lines), through an increasingly calm prayer (expressed in four lines), to a final expression of trust in God and harmony (expressed in three lines). Franz Delitzsch, one of the great nineteenth-century commentators on the psalms, wrote, "This song, as it were, casts up constantly lessening waves, until it becomes still as the sea when smooth as a mirror, and the only motion discernible at last is that of the joyous ripple of calm repose."[2]

Abandonment and Dejection

We turn to the psalm itself then, and the first thing we find is the poet's expression of his intense feeling of abandonment.

> How long, O LORD? Will you forget me forever?
>   How long will you hide your face from me?
> How long must I wrestle with my thoughts
>   and every day have sorrow in my heart?
> How long will my enemy triumph over me?

It reveals a number of reasons for his feelings.

A Prolonged Struggle

The first thing to note about this stanza is the obvious one. The most important words "How long?" are repeated four times: "How long, O LORD . . . will you forget me . . . ?" "How long will you hide your face from me?" "How long must I wrestle with my thoughts and every day have sorrow in my heart?" and "How long will my enemy triumph over me?" It is an effective way of saying that the struggle being described has continued for a long time.

I do not hesitate to say that this is an important cause, perhaps even the most frequent cause of a feeling of abandonment. In the short term we do not think this way. We may be unaware of God's presence or be puzzled about his apparent silence where a particular prayer of ours is concerned. But we trust that God has reasons for being silent, and we try to be patient. We still believe God is there. It is different when the short-term experience becomes a long-term pattern, and we begin to wonder whether God's silence may endure "forever." For that is the term David uses: "Will you forget me *forever?*" (italics added). We begin to imagine that the end of this period of distressing and painful abandonment will never come.

One commentator writes, "Well must David have understood what this was, when, hunted by Saul, he knew not where to betake himself, at one time seeking refuge among the Moabites, at another in the wilderness of Ziph; now an outlaw hiding himself in the cave of Adullam, and anon a captain in the service of the King of the Philistines; and amid all his projects, haunted by the mournful conviction, 'I shall now one day perish by the hand of Saul.'"[3]

Andrew Fuller, another of the earlier commentators, said, "It is not under the sharpest, but the longest trials, that we are most in danger of fainting. . . . When Job was accosted with evil tidings, in quick succession, he bore it with becoming fortitude; but when he could see no end to his troubles, he sunk under them."[4]

Lack of Apparent Blessing

A second cause of depression, leading to feelings of abandonment, is an extension of the first: a prolonged period in which the blessings of God given in an earlier time seem to have been removed. I think this is what David is talking about in the second line when he asks, "How long will you hide your face from me?" This means more than merely being forgotten by God, which is what the first question addresses. To say that the face of God is shining upon us is a way of saying that God is being favorable to us or blessing us. So, if God is hiding his face, what this must mean is that the times of blessing or favor seem to have ceased.

Let me suggest a few areas of our lives in which this happens.

It happens in family relationships. It may be that the happiness of the early days of a marriage has been replaced by the stress of trying to work out personality conflicts or other difficulties. You may be wondering if God has ceased to bless your marriage. Again, your problems may involve children. You remember the early days when it was comparatively easy to rear them. Your family had many good times together. But now one or more of your children is antagonistic and rebellious, and everyone else in the family suffers under the inevitable strain. Nobody has fun anymore. Has God forgotten? Have the blessings of God been taken away forever?

It happens in our work. Perhaps in the early days of your business you seemed to make rapid progress and succeeded at almost everything you touched. But you have entered a middle period of your career in which your early successes have leveled off and your business is stagnant.

It can happen in church work, too. Growth levels off. Times of harvest give way to times of reorientation or testing, to seasons of hard plowing and sowing. Where are God's blessings?

It can happen in our spiritual lives. There may have been years when you saw many spiritual victories and could chart rapid spiritual progress. But for many months now you have been in a deepening slump. You know that God deals with us by grace. But the lack of blessing has continued for so long that you have become morbidly introspective. You have been dredging up past sins and have been wondering, "Is God punishing me for what I did then? I confessed the sin and believed he forgave me. But maybe he is bringing it up again and putting me on hold because of it." In extreme situations you may even think, "God has abandoned me forever."

Dark Thoughts and Uncontrollable Emotions

The third time David asks, "How long?" he refers to a combination of what we would call dark thoughts and uncontrollable emotions. When we no longer sense that God is blessing us, we tend to ruminate on our failures and get into an emotional funk. And when our emotions take over it is always hard to get back onto a level course. This is because the best means of doing this—calm reflection and a review of past blessings—are being swept away. We discover that we cannot settle ourselves long enough to complete the exercise.

Let me make two more points here.

First, some people are more prone to morbidity than others, and it is helpful to know this, especially if you are among them. Martyn Lloyd-Jones begins his book on depression by saying that "foremost" among all causes of spiritual depression is "temperament."[5] Knowing that you are temperamentally inclined to depression may not cure the depression, but it is an important factor to weigh when evaluating your condition.

Second, a plunge into disquieting thoughts and emotions can be caused by physical factors—illness, for example. Charles Haddon Spurgeon was one of the greatest evangelical leaders of the last century, but he suffered from severe bouts of depression. Why? The main reason is that he suffered from gout, marked by painful inflammation of the joints and an excess of uric acid in the blood. It was common in the last century, and it drained Spurgeon's energies.

Into this same category can be placed all forms of physical tiredness, mental fatigue, and strain. A woman who is up half the night with a colicky baby and is exhausted by it should not be blamed if she feels abandoned. It is hard to be attuned to God when you are wrung-out physically.

Another physical factor is the let-down following some effort. A good example is the depression experienced by Elijah after he had accomplished the great victory on Mount Carmel. While the battle was on he stood tall. But after it was over he sank to such a low state that he supposed he was the only faithful person left in Israel. What Elijah needed was rest and nourishment, which was exactly what God provided for him (1 Kings 19).

Enemies

When Elijah told God that it would be better for him to die than to live, it was not only the acute emotional let-down following his victory that had affected him. There was also the presence of his enemies, Ahab and Jezebel. This is why he said, "I am the only one left, and now they are trying to kill me too" (1 Kings 19:10). In the same way, David knew what it was to be pursued by his relentless enemy King Saul and perhaps by others too. It is why he says, "How long will my enemy triumph over me?"

Most of us probably do not have literal human enemies, at least not serious enemies. But if you are a Christian, you do have one great spiritual enemy who is worse than any human enemy imaginable. This is the devil, whom the apostle Peter compared to "a roaring lion looking for someone to devour" (1 Peter 5:8). Lloyd-Jones says of this foe, "The devil [is] the adversary of our souls. He can use our temperaments and our physical condition. He so deals with us that we allow our temperament to control and govern us, instead of keeping temperament where it should be kept. There is no end to the ways the devil produces spiritual depression. We must always bear him in mind."[6]

Turning the Corner

Reviewing this long list of causes of feeling abandoned by God is helpful, because it shows us that these feelings are not unique to us. David had them, and so have countless others throughout the long ages of the church. But this is not all we need, of course—to know that others have also felt abandoned. We also need to get out of our depression and recover a sense of God's presence.

At the end of Psalm 13, David has obviously gotten to this point. He says that he is trusting in the Lord's unfailing love, rejoicing in the Lord's salvation, and looking forward to the day when he will again sing to the Lord of his goodness.

How did David get to this position? The turning point was prayer.

> When all things seem against us,
>   To drive us to despair,
> We know one gate is open
>   One ear will hear our prayer.

For the true child of God there is always some awareness of this truth, regardless of how deep his or her depression may be. We may be depressed even to the point of feeling utterly abandoned. But the fact that we feel abandoned itself means that we really know God is there. To be abandoned you need somebody to be abandoned by. Because we are Christians and have been taught by God in Scripture, we know that God still loves us and will be faithful to us, regardless of our feelings.

So what do we do? We pray, as David does. This does not exclude seeking help professionally if our depression is severe. We often need help in order to hang on and begin to work through our dark feelings. But above all, we need to pray. We need to pray consistently and urgently, especially about our feelings of abandonment.

David's prayer has three requests: "Look on me"; "Answer"; and "Give light to my eyes." His feelings tell him that God has turned away from him, hiding his face. So the first thing he asks God to do is turn around and look in his direction once again. His feelings tell him that God is no longer speaking to him and will never speak again. So the second thing he asks God to do is answer his questions. His feelings have told him that all is lost and that his enemy will triumph, no doubt meaning that his enemy will eventually succeed in killing him. So he asks God to give light to his eyes, that is, to preserve him and to restore him to full physical and mental health.

And God does, at least to this extent. David recovers his trust in God and looks forward to the day when he will be able fully to praise him for his goodness. H. C. Leupold says at this point, "Faith has climbed out of the lowest depths of despair where it had well-nigh perished into the full sunlight of godly hope." Now "it can wait for the help to come, for it is sure that it will not fail him."[7]

Come, Lord Jesus

I close with two scenes from the Book of Revelation. In chapter 6 the souls of those who were martyred for their testimony and are now with God in heaven cry out, "How long, Sovereign Lord, holy and true, until you judge the inhabitants of the earth and avenge our blood?" (Rev. 6:10). These saints are distressed at God's seeming reluctance to act. Yet although these are the souls of martyrs, they are told to be patient, to wait "a little longer." If they can be asked to be patient, we who know so much less obviously can be asked to be patient too.

The second scene comes at the end of the book. Here we are not told what the saints are saying explicitly, but they must be longing for the end, yearning for the return of Christ, who seems to be far from them, because Jesus speaks several times to reassure them that the end will be not long delayed. His words are: "Behold, I am coming soon!" (Rev. 22:7), "Behold, I am coming soon!" (v. 12), and "Yes, I am coming soon" (v. 20), to which they reply, "Amen. Come, Lord Jesus" (v. 20).

If you are suffering from a sense of feeling abandoned by God, which is what this psalm is about, I cannot tell you when the emotional oppression will lift. But it will lift. The curtain of your despair will rise, and behind the veil you will see the blessed Lord Jesus Christ, who has been with you and has loved you all the time.

Psalm 14

Ship of Fools

The fool says in his heart,
"There is no God."
They are corrupt, their deeds are vile;
there is no one who does good.

The LORD looks down from heaven
on the sons of men
to see if there are any who understand,
any who seek God.
All have turned aside,
they have together become corrupt;
there is no one who does good,
not even one.

Will evildoers never learn—
those who devour my people as men eat bread
and who do not call on the Lord?
There they are, overwhelmed with dread,
for God is present in the company of the righteous.
You evildoers frustrate the plans of the poor,
but the LORD is their refuge.

Oh, that salvation for Israel would come out of Zion!
When the LORD restores the fortunes of his people,
let Jacob rejoice and Israel be glad!

verses 1–7

The Bible is a big book, but not many things in the Bible are said, word for word, more than once. If the words are repeated, it is for emphasis. They are important. How then if they are repeated more than once? What if they are found three times? This is the case with Psalm 14. Psalm 14 is repeated almost entirely in the Book of Psalms itself. Psalm 53 is a nearly exact duplication; only verses 5 and 6 are changed. Then the most important part of Psalm 14 is repeated in Romans 3:10–12. In fact, the great first chapter of Romans is actually an explanation of these words.

Anything God says once demands attention.

Anything he says twice demands our most intent attention.

How then if he says something three times, as he does in this case? This demands our keenest concentration, contemplation, assimilation, and even memorization. These are words which, to use the often-quoted phrase of the collect from the Book of Common Prayer, we are to "read, mark, learn and inwardly digest."

The Fool Speaks about God

This psalm is about atheism, of both a theoretical and a practical kind. In the first verse are the fool's words about God. As far as he is concerned, God does not exist. Our text quotes him as saying, "There is no God," but we should note that in the Hebrew text the words *there is* are not present. They have been added to the English to make the psalm read smoothly. The fool actually says, "No God!" That is, "No God for me." So his is a practical as well as a theoretical atheism. Not only does he not believe in God, he also acts on his conviction.

This is a position of extreme folly, of course. That is why the psalm begins, "The fool. . . ." But it is worth asking why a person who denies the existence of God is called a fool in Scripture, rather than being regarded as a mistaken person who does not know any better. Why is one who denies the existence of God a fool?

The answer lies in Paul's magnificent exposition of this world's atheism in Romans 1, which, as I said, is actually a commentary on Psalm 14. He is a fool because he knows there is a God and yet chooses to deny it. If a person knew there were no God and said so, he would be wise and perhaps even courageous for standing against the nearly universal but mistaken opinions of the human race. If he did not know whether there were a God and said so, he would at least be an honest skeptic or agnostic. If a person is convinced there is no God when actually there is one, he is merely mistaken. But none of these is the case, according to Paul's careful exposition. The reason the person is a fool and not merely mistaken is that he knows there is a God and yet chooses to believe and act as if there is none.

Here are two important questions.

First, how does the person actually know there is a God? The answer Paul gives is: because of God's revelation of himself in nature. It is not an extensive revelation. In fact, as Paul states, it consists of two things only: God's "eternal power and divine nature," what we would call his power and mere existence (Rom. 1:20). Nothing in nature reveals God's saving qualities: his love, mercy, and compassion. But what is revealed—these two important elements—is sufficient to prove to any honest man or woman that God truly does exist and to lead that person to conclude that every member of the human race owes this God praise and thanksgiving. To refuse to acknowledge him is not only wrong; it is the height of folly.

But perhaps the evidence for God is not clear, one might object. Or perhaps the human being just does not have the capacity for perceiving or understanding the revelation. That will not do, says Paul, for God has made the revelation of himself so clear that it has been clearly seen and understood by all. They are without excuse for failing to seek God out and then praise and thank him. His words are: "What may be known about God [that is, from nature] is plain to them, because God has made it plain to them. For since the creation of the world God's invisible qualities—his eternal power and divine nature—have been clearly seen, being understood from what has been made, so that men are without excuse" (vv. 19–20).

According to these verses, the revelation of God in nature is not hidden so that only a highly skilled scientist may find it. It is open and manifest to everyone. A child can see it. There is enough evidence of God in a snowflake, a fingerprint, a flower, a drop of water to lead any honest member of the human race to believe in God and worship him. Every single object in the world shouts "God" to humanity.

Here is the second question. If that is so, if the revelation of God in nature is as clear as Paul declares it to be, why would any sane person reject it? Why would anyone be so foolish as to say, "There is no God"?

Romans answers this question too. In verse 18 Paul argues that people "suppress the truth" about God by or because of their "godlessness and wickedness." This means that they try to live without God because they do not like him. Everything about him is an offense to them. He is sovereign; they are not, though they wish they could be. He is holy; they are not. His holiness is a condemnation of their sin. He is omniscient; they are not. They find his knowledge of them to be unsettling. He is love; they are filled with hatred. He is gracious; they are ungracious. He is wise; they are foolish.

They are so foolish that they suppress what they really do know about him and cry, often with great heat and sometimes even with great sophistication, "There is no God."

The result, as both the apostle and the psalmist declare, is corruption. Paul unfolds it at length in Romans 1, showing three sharp downward steps in the progressive degeneration of the race. David says the same thing, though more succinctly:

> They are corrupt, their deeds are vile;
> there is no one who does good (Ps. 14:1).

Hebrew, like English, has quite a few words for describing those who are unwise. They correspond to words like simple, silly, simpleton, fool, and madman.[1] The word used in this verse is *nabel,* which embraces the idea of a foolish but also an aggressively perverse personality. Folly expresses itself in evil acts. There is a man in the Bible who was called Nabal. He was the husband of Abigail, who later became the wife of King David. Nabal was churlish and perverse, so much so that he almost got himself killed by David, though he was saved by his wife's intercession on his behalf. Abigail herself said of him, "He is just like his name—his name is Fool, and folly goes with him" (1 Sam. 25:25). Nabal perished suddenly and miserably.

It is always this way. H. C. Leupold rightly says, "Atheism bears its proper fruit in rotten conduct."[2]

God Speaks about the Fool

Having allowed us to listen in as the fool speaks about God, David now permits us to listen as God speaks about the fool. This true and discerning judgment is expressed in the next two verses, where David describes the Almighty literally "bending over to look down [from heaven] upon" such folly (vv. 2–3, author's translation). The words remind us of God descending from heaven to observe the folly of those building the tower of Babel (Gen. 11:5) or looking down upon the wickedness of the race prior to his judgment by the flood (Gen. 6:5).

There are two important things to notice about this judgment. Both concern the scope of the corruption.

First, the folly of the opening verse of the psalm, which we might have imagined to be restricted to a single class of people (fools), is now viewed as characteristic of all people in their natural or unrepentant state. This is unmistakable. It is seen in the description of God looking down on "the sons of men," that is, on all persons and not merely on those we might choose to term *atheists* or *fools.* It is also seen in the tumbling cascade of inclusive terms in these verses: "any," "any," "all," "[all] together," "no one," and "not even one." Up to this point we might have excused ourselves from the judgments of verse 1. "After all, we are not atheists!" we might say. But now, as we are let in on God's perspective, we see that we too are included. In other words, the outspoken atheist of verse 1 is only one example of mankind in general. As P. C. Craigie notes, "The fool is not a rare sub-species within the human race; all human beings are fools apart from the wisdom of God."[3]

This is what Paul says in Romans, too, though he does it differently. For the issue in Romans is not whether or not people say they believe in God or whether they actually worship some god in some way. The issue is their actual relationship to the true and only God, and in this respect they have all gone astray and are corrupt, according to Paul's teaching. They are all true atheists, even when, as is sometimes the case, they are excessively religious.

The second thing to notice about the inclusive nature of God's assessment of humanity in these verses is that it concerns not merely a single part of people's makeup but rather everything about them. It involves their spiritual understanding, their seeking after (actually their failure to seek after) God, and their morality, the same items Paul mentions in his great summary of the race's corruption in Romans 3.

> The LORD looks down from heaven
> > on the sons of men
> to see if there are any who understand,
> > any who seek God.
> All have turned aside,
> > they have together become corrupt;
> there is no one who does good,
> > not even one (Ps. 14:2–3; cf. Rom. 3:10–12).

Apart from God's special illuminating work in the human heart by means of the Holy Spirit, there is no one who understands spiritual things (1 Cor. 2:14). We do not even understand ourselves. We think we are seeking God when we are running away from him. We think we are righteous when we are most corrupt. Rightly considered, said Charles Haddon Spurgeon, "Humanity, fallen and debased, is a desert without an oasis, a night without a star, a dunghill without a jewel, a hell without a bottom."[4]

Obviously, if there is going to be any hope or salvation for people such as ourselves, it is going to have to come from God himself, which is where the psalm ends.

The Way of the Fool

The third stanza of Psalm 14 describes the way of the fool, which we have now seen to be the way of the entire human race apart from God's special, saving intervention. There are two things said about us.

First, we never seem to learn. We are practical materialists; that is, we are relentless in our efforts to use others for our advantage, profiting from them. We will not learn that "man does not live on bread alone but on every word that comes from the mouth of the LORD" (Deut. 8:3; cf. Matt. 4:4; Luke 4:4). And we are prayerless. We "do not call on the LORD," because we believe that we can manage very well without him.

Here are two illustrations of this truth. I once heard Dr. Joel Nederhood, a radio preacher of the Christian Reformed Church, tell of being in Moscow and attending a booksellers' convention. The fascinating thing about this convention was that, in the age of *glasnost* (the openness in the last days of the Soviet Union), the American Bible Society was present and was giving away Bibles. A long line of people patiently waited to receive these Bibles and, as Nederhood told it, the line stretched several hundred feet out into the display area, where it passed in front of a neglected booth manned by seventy-year-old Madalyn Murray O'Hair, the most famous of American atheists, who sat there glowering.

She must have been thinking, "What fools these Russians are to stand in line for Bibles. They should be buying books about atheism from me." But it was she, not they, who was the fool. For they had tried atheism and had found it wanting. She had lived about as long as communists had ruled Russia, but she had learned nothing.

I found another illustration of our inability to learn in these areas in an essay by Joseph Addison, the eighteenth-century prose writer, who is quoted by Spurgeon in his *Treasury of David*. Addison had been on shipboard with a particularly vile person when the ship was overtaken by a gale. The passenger was the only one severely frightened. But he was so frightened that he went to the chaplain, fell on his knees, and confessed that he had been a denier of God and an atheist ever since he had come of age. It soon got around the ship that there was an atheist on the upper deck, and the common sailors who, said Addison, had never heard the word *atheist* before, at first supposed that it was a rare kind of fish. But when they learned that it is a man who denies God they were frightened themselves and suggested, not quietly, that "it would be a good deed to heave him overboard." However, the ship soon came near land. When the penitent man saw that they were not going to perish after all, he repudiated his conversion, begging the passengers not to say a word of what had happened to anyone, and went back to his openly wicked ways.

That part of the story alone would make my point, but there is more. After two days on shore this man ran into one of the other passengers again, and the passenger reminded him of his new-found piety. The atheist denied it, and the argument got so fierce that it ended in a duel in which the atheist was run through with his opponent's sword. Addison said that at this point he "became as good a Christian as he was at sea—till he found that his wound was not mortal," at which point he relapsed again. The last Addison heard of him he had become what in those days was called "a free thinker" and was writing foolish books about religion.[5]

This amusing story also illustrates the second thing that is said about us in this stanza, namely, that we are occasionally also "overwhelmed with dread" (v. 5).

The psalmist expresses this in a strange way, saying literally, as the New International Version indicates: "*There they are,* overwhelmed with dread" (italics added). This has led some writers to wonder what specific "there" he is referring to. Where does this take place? When is the moment at which those who deny God are so moved? Some have suggested that this is fear which will emerge only at the final judgment. It is what Jesus seemed to speak of when he described the ungodly crying out for the mountains and hills to fall upon them and cover them in that day (Luke 23:30). Others have suggested that it is fear evoked by some calamity, as in Addison's story about the panicked passenger.

I think it is none of these but is rather what we would call an inner psychological dread. In proof, I cite Psalm 53:5. Psalm 53 is the psalm that is an almost exact repetition of Psalm 14, as I said earlier. But at this verse there is an important variation, an addition. After the words "There they were, overwhelmed with dread," Psalm 53 inserts "where there was nothing to dread." In other words, the fear described is an inner fear, occasioned by no visible cause.

To put it another way, no one is threatening these unbelieving persons. They seem secure, as the wicked often do. But in their quiet moments, deep in their hearts, they sense that if this is a moral universe, as they suspect it must be, then they are guilty of many sins and will undoubtedly suffer for them. They are unnerved by this and shudder violently.

Calm Hope of Deliverance

The psalmist is not shuddering, however. And the reason is that he has learned what unbelievers have not learned, namely, that "God is present in the company of the righteous" and that "the LORD is their refuge" (vv. 5–6). He concludes with a prayer so tranquil that it is almost a sigh. It is a prayer for deliverance.

> Oh, that salvation for Israel would come out of Zion!
> When the LORD restores the fortunes of his people,
> let Jacob rejoice and Israel be glad! (v. 7).

It is not possible for us to get to that quiet position of trust and confidence by ourselves. If we have understood this psalm rightly, we know that we are in the exact position of those who cry out, "There is no God," unless God himself makes his person and ways known to us.

How does he do it? He does it in Jesus Christ. In the first chapter of 1 Corinthians the apostle Paul is talking about wisdom. He is contrasting the true wisdom of the gospel with the apparent wisdom of the wise, who regard the gospel as foolishness. God has destroyed this human wisdom, he says. And he has given us Jesus, "who has become for us wisdom from God—that is, our righteousness, holiness and redemption" (1 Cor. 1:30). That is it exactly! Left to ourselves, our minds run to utter foolishness, and we act the fool too. But in Christ we find a wisdom from God which is able to save us and lead us in the way of righteousness.

Psalm 15

A Man after God's Own Heart

LORD, *who may dwell in your sanctuary?*
Who may live on your holy hill?

He whose walk is blameless
  and who does what is righteous,
who speaks the truth from his heart
  and has no slander on his tongue,
who does his neighbor no wrong
  and casts no slur on his fellowman,
who despises a vile man
  but honors those who fear the LORD,
who keeps his oath
  even when it hurts,
who lends his money without usury
  and does not accept a bribe against the innocent.

He who does these things
  will never be shaken.

verses 1–5

About the time I was preparing a study of this psalm I also preached on Romans 8:4, pointing out that the end for which God saves us is not merely that we might escape from hell

121

but that we might live righteous lives. The words of the text say that God condemned sin in Christ "in order that the righteous requirements of the law might be fully met in us, who do not live according to the sinful nature but according to the Spirit."

Shortly after preaching that sermon I received a note from someone, asking, "What is this righteous requirement of the law we are to meet? What exactly is required of us?"

It was a good question, and I answered it as you might expect. The law is the law given to us in the Old Testament, and the righteous requirements of the law are what we normally call the moral law. The moral law is summarized in the Ten Commandments, interpreted by the rest of the Bible. The best explanation of the moral law is given by Jesus, who spoke of it in terms of the first and second great commandments. The first: "Love the Lord your God with all your heart and with all your soul and with all your mind." The second: "Love your neighbor as yourself" (Matt. 22:37, 39; the commands are from Deut. 6:5 and Lev. 19:18). This is the standard to which God is leading his people. What God wants for us is that we might be like Jesus Christ.

The Question of the Psalm

Apparently, this is the question David was also asking when he composed the fifteenth psalm, inquiring, "LORD, who may dwell in your sanctuary? Who may live on your holy hill?" (v. 1). That is, what is the character of the person God approves? Or we could also say, How must we live to enjoy the fullness of fellowship with God? This is a direct, simple question, and because it is the outline of the psalm, the psalm is also quite simple. First, David asks the question. Then, he provides a series of representative answers.[1]

However, we have to understand a few things before we begin.

First, this is a question about godly living and not a question about justification. The two are related, of course, but they are not the same. If we ask, "How can a man or woman become right with God?" there is only one answer: It is by faith in Jesus Christ as one's own personal Lord and Savior. The Old Testament saints looked forward to his coming; we look back. But if we ask, "What is the character of the woman or man God approves?" the answer clearly involves the moral law. The justified person is not made right with God by keeping the moral law. Justification is by the work of Christ. But if a person has really been justified, he or she will necessarily begin to keep it, moving increasingly in this direction. This is because no one is ever justified apart from regeneration, and regeneration means that the Spirit of God is at work in us to bring us into increasing conformity to the character of Christ.

The second thing we need to understand is what I hinted at earlier when I said that David responds to the question of verse 1 with *representative* answers. This means that the items listed in verses 2–5 are not all-inclusive.

One way we know this is to compare this list with the lists provided to almost identical questions in Psalm 24:3–4 and Isaiah 33:14–17. Psalm 24 asks, "Who may ascend the hill of the LORD? Who may stand in his holy place?" It answers, "He who has clean hands and a pure heart" and does not serve idols. There is some overlap here with Psalm 15, but the points are not identical. In a similar way, Isaiah 33 asks, "Who of us can dwell with the consuming fire? Who of us can dwell with everlasting burning?" He replies:

> He who walks righteously
>   and speaks what is right,
> who rejects gain from extortion
>   and keeps his hand from accepting bribes,
> who stops his ears against plots of murder
>   and shuts his eyes against contemplating evil (v. 15).

Again, the parallels are close, but the details vary. Each passage supplies a representative list of character traits to work on.

Hebrew Parallelism

There is one more introductory item, and it has to do with the way the answers provided in Psalm 15 are to be handled. How many are there, for instance? Some commentators find ten items and seem attracted to this number, probably because it suggests the Ten Commandments.[2] Stewart Perowne counts eleven particulars.[3] In my opinion the best way to approach the answers is by giving attention to the Hebrew parallelism.

English poetry is most often marked by rhyme and meter, but neither of these is in Hebrew. There is a certain kind of emphasis in the lines, which corresponds to our meter, but there is no rhyme at all. The chief characteristic of Hebrew verse is its parallel lines. Usually the idea of the first line is repeated in the second with slight variations, but it is not always that simple. Sometimes the lines involve mere repetition, as in the first part of verse 2.

> He whose walk is blameless
>   and who does what is righteous . . .

Sometimes they express a contrast, as in the couplet that ends verse 2 and begins verse 3.

> who speaks the truth from his heart
>   and has no slander on his tongue . . .

Sometimes they have the form: Not only this, but also that. The second half of verse 4 is an example of this construction.

> who keeps his oath
>   even when it hurts . . .[4]

I deal with parallelism here for two reasons. First, although there have been many examples in the psalms thus far, this is the first psalm in which this feature has been so prominent and in which, therefore, it is easy to see some of the important variations. Second, and more important, to recognize the parallelism gives us a proper way to handle the material in the psalm. When we recognize that the verses have this paired construction, we see at once that there are six couplets and that each contains an independent idea. In other words, each couplet introduces a separate characteristic of the person who is approved by God. The couplets are the psalm's outline.

The Person God Approves

What do these six couplets cover? They cover the approved man's character, speech, conduct, values, integrity, and use of money. A person who has these representative characteristics is one who is after God's heart.

His Character

The first couplet containing an answer to David's question seems at first glance to be a contrasting parallel. The first line is expressed negatively: "He whose walk is blameless," that is, "without blame." The second line is expressed positively: he "does what is righteous." But in fact, the two halves are about as close as they can get, since the word translated "blameless" in our text is the Hebrew word *tamim,* which is not negative at all but means rather that which is "whole" or "sound." It refers to a person whose character, as we might say, is morally well-rounded and grounded. This person is not just strong in one area and weak in others. He strives to keep all the commandments. What is more, he does not vacillate in his commitment to them. He is the same Monday through Saturday as on Sunday morning.

When I say that the two halves of the couplet are as close as they can get, I do not mean that the second half is nothing but repetition. The second part of a parallel almost always adds something to the original thought, and in this case the new element is the verb *does.* The upright person not only has a passively upright character, as it were. He or she is also actively engaged in doing righteousness. To use a New Testament expression of the idea, the person is one who feeds the hungry, gives drink to the thirsty, welcomes the stranger, clothes the naked, cares for the sick, and visits the prisoner (Matt. 25:34–39).

James, the Lord's brother, was talking about the same thing in that well-known discussion of the relation of faith to works, which says: "What good is it, my brothers, if a man claims to have faith but has no deeds? Can such faith save him? Suppose a brother or sister is without clothes and daily food. If one of you says to him, 'Go, I wish you well; keep warm and well fed,' but does nothing about his physical needs, what good is it? In the same way, faith by itself, if it is not accompanied by action, is dead" (James 2:14–17).

It is the point I made earlier. Justification can never be separated from regeneration, and regeneration that produces genuine faith always also expresses itself in right action.

His Speech

The second couplet deals with the approved person's speech and *is* a contrast. The first line tells what he does, the second line what he does not. What he does is "speak the truth." Whenever you talk with such a person, you know that he or she is "telling it like it is." He is not just saying what you want to hear. She is not using speech to flatter you in order to get something out of you. We remember that complaints about these wrong uses of speech have already been found in Psalms 10 and 12.

There are also a few other things here. First, although in Hebrew the word *truth* includes the idea of what is correct or accurate as opposed to what is false, the essential idea is bigger than that, coming closest to what we might call "being trustworthy." Truth is something you can count on. Therefore, the one who speaks truth is a trustworthy person. That is why God the Father is described as the "true God" (John 17:3), Jesus termed himself "the way and the truth and the life" (John 14:6), the Holy Spirit is named "the Spirit of truth" (John 14:17), and the Word of God is called "truth" (John 17:17). Because of this, a person can rely on God the Father, God the Son, God the Holy Spirit, and God's Word. Obviously, God's people are to be like him in this important characteristic.

Second, a person who is like this does not slander others. He does not gossip. Isn't this a chief sin in the church of Jesus Christ today? Aren't many bold in gossiping about and harming others with their tongues? I am not speaking here about the unsaved, though they certainly gossip too, but about Christians. I think more damage has been done to the church and its work gossip, criticism, and slander than by any other single sin. So I say, don't do it. Bite your tongue before you criticize another Christian. The great seventeenth-century commentator Matthew Poole wrote, "Pity your brethren; let it suffice that godly ministers and Christians are loaded with reproaches by wicked men—there is no need that you should combine with them in this diabolical work."[5]

His Conduct

The third couplet is also almost a parallel to the second, for there is much in common between speaking the truth and not slandering another (in couplet two) and doing a neighbor no wrong and casting no slur on him (in couplet three). But there is a difference too, and the difference seems to be that in this parallelism the idea moves beyond mere words to actions. This is clear in the first half: "who does his neighbor no wrong." It is probably also what is meant in part two, for although casting a slur usually suggests verbal abuse to us, a slur can also be cast—perhaps more often is cast—by how we actually treat another person.

The question is: Do you treat other people with respect, especially those who have a less important position in life than you do? Or do you snub them? Do you talk down to them? Are you mean? These verses tell us that these things displease God and are a barrier to fellowship with him.

His Values

The fourth couplet, like the third, also deals with our responses to other people. But here the idea is not so much how we treat them but how we regard them. It has to do with values. I would express it by asking: Who are your models? Who do you look up to? Whose actions and character do you find offensive?

This is one of the saddest things about today's younger generation. A few years ago a government commission in Canada studied the characteristics of today's young people, and one of the things they discovered is that the youth of today have no heroes. This is hard for most older people to appreciate, for we did and do have heroes. There are people we have looked up to and have tried to be like. But the youth of today generally have no heroes, no models. Without heroes they tend to drift along.

But there is one thing worse than having no models, and that is having the wrong ones. And I suspect that, in spite of the Canadian study, many young people are actually drifting in this direction now. They admire the rock singer who has an abominable lifestyle but is nevertheless rich and famous. They admire the crack dealer who prances around in fancy clothes and sports gold jewelry. And the upright people? People who work hard for a living? Fathers who provide for their families? Mothers who are faithful in caring for and rearing their children? People who sacrifice for others? The young couldn't care less about such people.

In fact, many older people don't think much of such people either. One social critic says, "We have reached a point in our day where people would rather be envied than admired." Not so the righteous! We are told in the psalm that he who God approves "despises a vile man but honors those who fear the Lord."

His Integrity

The fifth couplet contains an incomplete parallelism in which two additional parts need to be supplied mentally. As it stands, the couplet is the simple phrase "who keeps his oath even when it hurts." If it were given a fuller form, it would read something like this:

> who keeps his oath [at all times],
>   [and is faithful] even when it hurts . . .

The effect of the omissions is to shorten the phrase and highlight part of it, in this case the words "even when it hurts." That is the important thing. No one has much trouble keeping his or her word when to do so is to the person's own advantage. You would have to be unbalanced not to. But how about when the conditions have changed and the promise, agreement, or contract is no longer to your advantage? Do you honor your promise then? Do you fulfill the contract? Or do you try to find some way to get out of what you had committed yourself to? The psalmist says that God approves people who keep their oaths even when it hurts them to do so.

His Use of Money

The final characteristic of the person who is after God's heart is that he or she has a right approach to money. I put it this way, because I am convinced that the concern of this verse is not with receiving interest for money loaned, though it seems to say that, but rather with whom the interest is taken from. In other words, the verse concerns greed eclipsing justice.

The reason the first half of verse 5 is not a simple denunciation of lending money for interest is that the Old Testament prohibited this only in the case of Jews taking interest from other Jews (Deut. 23:19–20), and this is usually explained as a prohibition against a wealthy person taking advantage of one who is needy (Exod. 22:25; Lev. 25:35–37). Also, the Lord's parables about talents suggest that God did not prohibit borrowing money for legitimate business matters. The best Old Testament illustration of the abuse verse 5 is talking about is in Nehemiah 5, where the wealthy were taking advantage of the poor among the exiles when all should have been helping one another. The poor complained to Nehemiah, "We have had to borrow money to pay the king's tax on our fields and vineyards. Although we are of the same flesh and blood as our countrymen and though our sons are as good as theirs, yet we have to subject our sons and daughters to slavery. . . . We are powerless, because our fields and our vineyards belong to others" (Neh. 5:4–5). The problem was that those who had money were putting their personal gain before the well-being of their neighbors. They were putting money before people.

The second example in verse 5 is also a case of putting money before people, taking bribes. Here the offense is also against justice, since bribery is a crime and corrupts the criminal and civil courts.[6] Putting these two wrongs together gives us a picture of one who uses money wrongly, and gets money wrongly, too. The upright do not do that.

Here then is the portrait of one who pleases God. It is a picture of the virtues God wants to see in you. Does he see them? Are they developing in you? They must be, if you are his. But notice: If you aspire to this, the psalm ends with an encouraging promise for you. It says, "He who does these things will never be shaken." This means, in response to the opening question, that not only will such a person dwell in God's sanctuary, on his holy hill. In addition, nothing will ever shake him or her out of it. If you are God's, you may be shaken, but you will never be shaken loose.

Psalm 16

A Prophecy of the Resurrection

Keep me safe, O God,
for in you I take refuge.

I said to the LORD, "You are my Lord;
apart from you I have no good thing."
As for the saints who are in the land,
they are the glorious ones in whom is all my delight.
The sorrows of those will increase
who run after other gods.
I will not pour out their libations of blood
or take up their names on my lips.

LORD, you have assigned me my portion and my cup;
you have made my lot secure.
The boundary lines have fallen for me in pleasant places;
surely I have a delightful inheritance.

I will praise the LORD, who counsels me;
even at night my heart instructs me.
I have set the LORD always before me.
Because he is at my right hand,
I will not be shaken.

Therefore my heart is glad and my tongue rejoices;
  my body also will rest secure,
because you will not abandon me to the grave,
  nor will you let your Holy One see decay.
You have made known to me the path of life;
  you will fill me with joy in your presence,
  with eternal pleasures at your right hand.
                                    verses 1–11

On the first Lord's day, following hard upon the resurrection of Jesus Christ, two people were walking to their hometown of Emmaus from Jerusalem. They were disciples of Jesus, and the name of one of them was Cleopas (Luke 24:18). If this Cleopas was the same man as the Clopas of John 19:25 (which seems likely since the names are nearly identical), and if both were disciples of Jesus and were in Jerusalem at this time (which we know to be the case), then the other of these two disciples was probably Mary, Clopas's wife.

Cleopas and Mary were despondent because of the death of their master. They had heard reports of an empty tomb and of angels who had told some of the women that Jesus was "risen, just as he said." Yet they did not doubt that Jesus was really dead and that their dream of a messiah who should reign upon the throne of his father David, the dream that had inspired them for the three long years of Christ's ministry, was over. While they were making their sad way along their homeward path, Jesus appeared to them. They did not recognize him. "What are you discussing together as you walk along?" he asked them kindly.

They replied by an offhand reference to the "things" that had taken place in Jerusalem.

"What things?" Jesus asked.

"About Jesus of Nazareth," they answered. "He was a prophet, powerful in word and deed before God and all the people. The chief priests and our rulers handed him over to be sentenced to death, and they crucified him; but we had hoped that he was the one who was going to redeem Israel."

Jesus chided them for their slowness to believe all that the prophets had spoken. "Did not the Christ have to suffer these things and then enter his glory?" he asked them. Then, "beginning with Moses and all the Prophets, he explained to them what was said in all the Scriptures concerning himself" (see Luke 24:13–27).

That was a sermon I very much wish I could have heard. It was the Lord's own sermon on the resurrection, a sermon in which he expounded the Old Testament texts that had bearing on his prophesied triumph over the grave on Easter morning.

What texts do you suppose Jesus spoke of?

We cannot know the full answer to that question, of course, though we have strong indications of what some of the texts were, due to the way they were later used by the early disciples in their preaching.[1] But one text we can be certain of is Psalm 16:10. This is because Peter used a section of this psalm to preach the resurrection in his great sermon on Pentecost (Acts 2:25–28, citing Ps. 16:8–11) and because Paul likewise used a shorter portion of it in his sermon to the Jews in the synagogue of Antioch early in his ministry (Acts 13:35–37, citing Ps. 16:10). Psalm 16:10 says,

> You will not abandon me to the grave,
>   nor will you let your Holy One see decay.

If ever there was a clear Old Testament prophecy of the resurrection of the Lord Jesus Christ, it is this statement. It makes Psalm 16 the third specifically messianic psalm in the Psalter, after Psalm 2 and (somewhat less directly) Psalm 8.

Jesus' Resurrection

The reason verse 10 is such a clear prophecy of Jesus' resurrection is the startling claim found in its second half. The first part is strong and impressive but not startling. It is a declaration based on faith that God will not abandon the psalmist to the grave. This is a high attainment for faith, of course, but it might have been spoken by any one of the Old Testament saints. It matches Job's declaration:

> I know that my Redeemer lives,
>   and that in the end he will stand upon the earth.
> And after my skin has been destroyed,
>   yet in my flesh I will see God;
> I myself will see him
>   with my own eyes—I, and not another (Job 19:25–27).

Although the first half of verse 10 is strong and impressive, it is not an impossible statement for any one of the Old Testament saints to have uttered. Any one of them could have spoken of God preserving him or her beyond the grave.

But that is not true of the second part of this verse, and it is this that makes it a remarkable prophecy of Jesus' resurrection. That part says: "nor will you let your Holy One see decay." When we die our bodies do decay, even if we are waiting for the resurrection. David's body decayed. But the body of Jesus did not decay. God preserved Christ's body from corruption while it was lying in the tomb and then breathed life back into it on Easter morning. And that is why the verse cannot apply to David or to any other mere human being—even though the rest of the psalm can—and why it is a prophecy of Jesus' resurrection.

When Peter referred to the text he said, "Brothers, I can tell you confidently that the patriarch David died and was buried, and his tomb is here to this day. But he was a prophet and knew that God had promised him on oath that he would place one of his descendants on his throne. Seeing what was ahead, he spoke of the resurrection of the Christ, that he was not abandoned to the grave, nor did his body see decay" (Acts 2:29–31).

Paul's use of the text was even clearer. He said, "For when David had served God's purpose in his own generation, he fell asleep; he was buried with his fathers and his body decayed. But the one whom God raised from the dead did not see decay" (Acts 13:36–37).

Our Portion in Life and Death

This great prophecy grew out of the life and times of King David. I stress this because there have been attempts to see Psalm 16 as a prophecy about Jesus throughout. That is, each verse has been taken as referring to something specific in his life. One commentator has connected each passage to Jesus' thoughts and experiences during the hours he spent praying in Gethsemane.[2] This is farfetched and unnecessary. Since the psalm seems to have been written by David—the heading says so—most of it should be understood as referring to his life rather than to Jesus' life.

H. C. Leupold suggests that the best setting of the psalm is those years in the life of David when he was forced to flee from King Saul. Leupold gives the psalm a title: "Jehovah—the Psalmist's Portion in Life and His Deliverer in Death." It has four primary concerns.

The Psalmist's Relationship to God (vv. 1–2)

The opening verses begin with a statement of the psalmist's relationship to God. The essence of that relationship is in the names for God he uses. The first word is *el,* translated simply "God" in verse 1. *El* is the most common name for God. But the unique quality of this name is that it delineates God as "the Strong (or Mighty) One." It is appropriately chosen in verse 1, for it is in God as the Mighty One that the psalmist takes refuge.

The second name is Jehovah, translated "LORD" in the first part of verse 2. This is the personal name of the great God of Israel. It was revealed to Moses at the burning bush. "Moses said to God, 'Suppose I go to the Israelites and say to them, "The God of your fathers has sent me to you," and they ask me, "What is his name?" Then what shall I tell them?'

"God said to Moses, 'I AM WHO I AM. This is what you are to say to the Israelites: "I AM has sent me to you"'" (Exod. 3:13–14). Since this name is the covenant name for God in relation to his chosen people, it is appropriate that David's confession, "apart from you I have no good thing," is in this verse, where the name is mentioned, rather than in verse 1.

The third name for God is *Adonai,* translated "Lord" in the first part of verse 2. *Adonai* can designate an earthly Lord as well as God. So when the psalmist says, as he does, "I said to the LORD [Jehovah], 'You are my Lord [*Adonai*],'" he is saying that the God of Israel is his master. That is, God is not only the strong, powerful God in whom he can take refuge but also the one who is able to—and does—order his life and direct what he should do. We have an equivalent of this in our common New Testament way of speaking when we say that Jesus is our Lord and Savior. Savior corresponds to *el,* since it is as "the Strong One" that Jesus saves us. Lord is the equivalent of *Adonai.* It means that Jesus is also Master of our lives.

Is Jesus your Lord and Savior, your Master? If he is, you should be able to say, as David does, "apart from you I have no good thing."

This means that God is the source of all good. James says, "Every good and perfect gift is from above, coming down from the Father of the heavenly lights, who does not change like shifting shadows" (James 1:17). It means that if we do not have God himself, even the best things of life will be valueless to us. Jesus said, "What good will it be for a man if he gains the whole world, yet forfeits his soul?" (Matt. 16:26). It means that, having come to know God as our refuge, redeemer, and Lord, nothing hereafter can ever mean as much to us as God does.

The Immediate Result of the Psalmist's Relationship to God (vv. 3–4)

Since God is the one by whom the psalmist measures all else, it follows that the immediate result of his relationship to God is its bearing on his relationships to others. On the one hand, the psalmist is drawn to the righteous, whom he calls "the saints who are in the land." He says, "they are the glorious ones in whom is all my delight." On the other hand, he is turned away from the wicked. He says of them,

> The sorrows of those will increase
> who run after other gods.
> I will not pour out their libations of blood
> or take up their names on my lips.

This is a practical matter, for it is a way by which we can measure our relationship to the Lord. Do you love other Christians? Do you find it good and rewarding to be with them? Do you seek their company? This is a simple test. Those who love the Lord will love the company of those who also love him. Those who find their "good" in God will also find good in those who likewise seek him. Again, do you find it uncomfortable to be with those who sin openly? Are you troubled by their values, shocked by their desires, repulsed by their blasphemies? Or are you at ease among them? If, like

Peter, you have no difficulty warming your hands at the fire of those who are hostile to your Master, it is because you are far from him. You had best get back to him before you deny him, as Peter did.

The Psalmist's Present Blessings (vv. 5–8)

The third part of the psalm describes the psalmist's present blessings. There are four of them.

First, "you have assigned me my portion and my cup." The word *portion* can have two meanings. It can refer to one's portion in the land, that is, one's estate or inheritance. Or it can refer to one's daily portion of food, a ration. Since it is linked to the word *cup* in this verse and since the idea of an inheritance in the land occurs in the next verse, the *portion* in verse 5 is probably the singer's daily ration of food or, by extension, other necessities. It is what we ask for in the Lord's Prayer when we recite, "Give us this day our daily bread." It means that we are looking to God for our provisions.

Second, "you have made my lot secure." A lot can be one's portion in life or one's land. But again, since the idea of a land inheritance occurs in verse 6, this passage in verse 5 probably is speaking about the psalmist's general circumstances. The point is his security in them. With the Lord defending him, he is not going to be uprooted or cast out.

Third, "the boundary lines have fallen for me in pleasant places; surely I have a delightful inheritance." Isn't it interesting that the psalmist is content with what God has meted out to him, especially since so many people are discontent? Discontent is one of the most striking characteristics of our time. It is particularly a mark of the so-called Baby Boomer or Yuppie generation. One child of the fifties wrote, "Baby boomers are not very content. Because our expectations are so much higher than our reality, we tend to be discontent, restless and bored."[3] There is no cure for this except in God.

Fourth, "the Lord . . . counsels me." David needed counsel; his official decisions affected thousands of his subjects. He needed counsel he could trust. So do we! Our decisions may not affect as many people as David's did, but they affect the one person who matters most to us, namely ourselves, and they generally also affect others, sometimes many, who depend on us. God provides such counsel if we will ask him. The Bible says, "If any of you lacks wisdom, he should ask God, who gives generously to all without finding fault, and it will be given to him" (James 1:5).

Having reviewed these blessings, David reaffirms the commitment to God with which he began and upon which his felicity rests.

> I have set the Lord always before me.
> Because he is at my right hand,
> I will not be shaken (v. 8).

The Psalmist's Future Hope (vv. 9–11)

The first part of the psalm has been a strong statement of the psalmist's commitment of his entire life to God and the difference this has made for him. But nothing said thus far is as remarkable as what follows. Having spoken of the present blessings that result from his relationship to God, the writer now turns to the future and expresses his confidence in what God will do for him in death and even beyond death. This is where the verse that prophesies the resurrection of the Lord Jesus Christ comes in.

Did David consciously prophesy the Lord's resurrection? He may have, but it is not necessary to think so. To be sure, Peter termed him a prophet in Acts 2. But later in his first letter, Peter wrote that the prophets "searched intently and with the greatest care, trying to find out the time and circumstances to which the Spirit of Christ in them was pointing when he predicted the sufferings of Christ and the glories that would follow" (1 Peter 1:10–11). This means that David did not necessarily understand that he was writing of Jesus' resurrection when he composed verse 10.

Yet if he was not writing of Christ, the verse is in some ways even more remarkable. In that case, David was writing of his own hope, expecting that God would not abandon him to the grave and would preserve him. He did not have the resurrection of Jesus before him as a sample of what he had in mind or proof of what God can and will do, as we who live on this side of the resurrection do.

How did David get to this point? There is only one answer. It was by the logic of faith. He reasoned that if God had blessed him and kept him in this life, then God, who does not change, would undoubtedly keep him and bless him in the life to come.

One commentator has written, "The boldness of it all almost leaves the reader breathless. How can a man see all men dying and note that all the children of men before him have died without exception and still say: God cannot let that happen to me! It appears like sheer being carried away into rhapsody of bold assertions. But still, in the last analysis, must not faith draw the conclusion that, if you hold to God, God will take care of you perfectly."[4]

Faith Is the Victory

I have said that David achieved this great pinnacle of trusting God in death through the logic of faith. But the victory itself was achieved by Jesus about whom David perhaps only unintentionally prophesied. It was Jesus' victory that won salvation for us all.

Reuben A. Torrey, a Bible teacher of an earlier generation, tells the story of four men who were climbing the most difficult face of the Matterhorn. A guide, a tourist, a second guide, and a second tourist were all roped together. As they went over a particularly difficult place, the second tourist lost his footing and went over the side. The sudden pull of the rope carried the second guide with him, and he carried the other tourist along also. Three men were now dangling over the cliff. But the guide who was in the lead, feeling the first pull upon the rope, drove his ax into the ice, braced himself, and held fast. The first tourist then regained his footing, the guide regained his, and the second tourist followed. They went on in safety.

So it is in this life. As the human race ascended the lofty cliffs of life, the first Adam lost his footing and tumbled headlong over the abyss. He pulled the next man after him, and the next, and the next, until the whole human race hung in deadly peril. But the second Adam, the Lord Jesus Christ, kept his footing. He stood fast. Thus all who are united to him by a living faith are secure and can regain the path.[5]

Psalm 17

The Prayer of a Righteous Man

Hear, O LORD, my righteous plea;
  listen to my cry.
Give ear to my prayer—
  it does not rise from deceitful lips.
May my vindication come from you;
  may your eyes see what is right.

Though you probe my heart and examine me at night,
  though you test me, you will find nothing;
  I have resolved that my mouth will not sin.
As for the deeds of men—
  by the word of your lips
I have kept myself
  from the ways of the violent.
My steps have held to your paths;
  my feet have not slipped.

I call on you, O God, for you will answer me;
  give ear to me and hear my prayer.
Show the wonder of your great love,
  you who save by your right hand
  those who take refuge in you from their foes.

Keep me as the apple of your eye;
  hide me in the shadow of your wings
from the wicked who assail me,
  from my mortal enemies who surround me.

verses 1–9

Rise up, O LORD, confront them, bring them down;
  rescue me from the wicked by your sword.
O LORD, by your hand save me from such men,
  from men of this world whose reward is in this life.

You still the hunger of those you cherish;
  their sons have plenty,
  and they store up wealth for their children.
And I—in righteousness I will see your face;
  when I awake, I will be satisfied with seeing your likeness.

verses 13–15

Commentators on the psalms frequently distinguish between various types of psalms, which they call genres. A typical classification might be hymns, laments, thanksgiving psalms, psalms of remembrance, psalms of confidence, wisdom psalms, and kingship (possibly messianic) psalms.[1]

Hymn psalms usually begin with a call to worship and continue by giving reasons why God should be praised and then by praising him. Laments express the writer's distress at some problem or calamity and ask God to help. Sometimes they also contain a confession of sin. They usually move to expressions of confidence that God has heard the prayer and will answer it. Thanksgiving psalms thank God for some blessing, often his response to a prior complaint. Psalms of remembrance and confidence are just what they sound like. A wisdom psalm usually compares two contrasting ways of life, one to be followed and the other to be shunned. The chief example of this is Psalm 1, which begins:

Blessed is the man
  who does not walk in the counsel of the wicked
or stand in the way of sinners
  or sit in the seat of mockers.
But his delight is in the law of the LORD,
  and on his law he meditates day and night (vv. 1–2).

Kingship psalms focus on the Jewish monarchy, not infrequently looking beyond it to the reign of God's promised Messiah. Psalm 2 is an example.

What kind of a psalm is Psalm 17? Fit into the categories I have listed, it is more of a lament than anything else. The psalmist is in danger and is crying to God for protection and deliverance. But mostly Psalm 17 is a prayer. In fact, it is the first psalm explicitly called "a prayer" in the Psalter ("a prayer of David").

As we begin to study Psalm 17, I want to suggest that it is a model prayer. It is urgent, perceptive, moving. But, most of all, it models prayer by the way the psalmist uses arguments to make his appeal to God. He does not merely ask for what he wants or needs. He argues his case, explaining to God why God should answer. This is something preachers in an earlier day used to urge on members of their congregations. Charles Haddon Spurgeon often did this. They recommended arguments, not because God needs to be persuaded to help his children—he does not—but because arguments force us to carefully think through what we are asking and to sharpen our requests. Spurgeon said of David, "David would not have been a man after God's own heart if he had not been a man of prayer. He was a master in the sacred art of supplication."[2]

The Psalmist's Innocence

Since Psalm 17 is a request for God's protection and deliverance, it contains urgent appeals to God to hear the psalmist's prayer. We find these in verses 1 ("hear," "listen," and "give ear") and 6 ("give ear to me and hear my prayer"). And we could rightly add to this list David's appeals to God to act quickly and decisively: "Show the wonder of your great love" (v. 7); "Keep me as the apple of your eye" (v. 8); "Hide me in the shadow of your wings" (v. 8); and "Rescue me from the wicked by your sword" (v. 13).

But what is most striking about this psalm is that from the first line David protests his innocence, arguing that God should hear his prayer and should answer it because his plea is right and his life is above reproach. This is his first argument, in verses 1–5.

David does not make this argument in timorous language either. In fact, his claims to innocence are so forceful that we, who live in a more introspective and self-conscious age, are easily troubled by them. Consider what he says. In the first line he claims that the plea he is about to make is "righteous." Do we dare to say that when we approach the holy God? In the same verse David argues that his prayer "does not rise from deceitful lips." In the next verse he calls for vindication, because God sees him and therefore sees "what is right."

The second stanza is even more extreme:

> Though you probe my heart and examine me at night,
>   though you test me, you will find nothing;
>   I have resolved that my mouth will not sin.

As for the deeds of men—
  by the word of your lips
I have kept myself
  from the ways of the violent.
My steps have held to your paths;
  my feet have not slipped (vv. 3–5).

This is a claim to innocence both in word and deed, both positively and negatively. Some of these words remind us of the first psalm, which makes us think that David must be claiming that he is the "righteous" man of Psalm 1. He has not walked "in the counsel of the wicked" or stood "in the way of sinners" or seated himself "in the seat of mockers." On the contrary, his delight is in God's law. We say, "How can any mere human being claim such innocence?" We have been taught to pray, "Forgive us our sins" (Luke 11:4) and to say, even in our triumphs, "We are [at best] unworthy servants" (Luke 17:10).

One important answer to our question is to see that David is not claiming a perfect innocence in these lines, only innocence of the wrongs of which he has been charged. He wants "vindication" (v. 2). We discussed this distinction earlier in our study of Psalm 7.

Still, I do not want to dismiss this matter quite that easily. In Psalm 17 we are seeing how David uses arguments in prayer, and one of these arguments, an important argument, is that the life of the praying person is above reproach. In other words, this is the positive side of the warning found in Isaiah 59:1–2. "Surely the arm of the LORD is not too short to save, nor his ear too dull to hear. But your iniquities have separated you from your God; your sins have hidden his face from you, so that he will not hear." Open and unconfessed sin is a great prayer barrier. An upright life is a strong basis for appeals.

Consider God's evaluation of Job. Job was certainly not sinless. But when God called Satan's attention to his servant, his words were, "Have you considered my servant Job? There is no one on earth like him; he is blameless and upright, a man who fears God and shuns evil" (Job 1:8). At the end of the book God says that he will accept Job's prayer, because Job had not spoken folly as his comforters had (Job 42:8).

This is the sense in which David is claiming innocence, and it is what we are also to possess as a foundation for our requests. In fact, one of the most important exercises of prayer is self-examination to determine whether we are approaching God rightly and whether our prayers are righteous prayers or not. It is along these lines that Paul told the Corinthians to "examine" themselves before participating in the Lord's Supper (1 Cor. 11:28).

Here are some areas in which we should conduct self-examination:

Are we being disobedient? This is what Isaiah 59 is talking about when it says that God will not hear us if we cherish sin in our hearts. Are you doing something that you know is wrong? Are you defying God's moral law? Are you neglecting the Lord's day? Have you been stealing? Committing sexual sins? Lying? Coveting something that is not yours? If you have been doing these things (or others that you know are wrong), should you be surprised if your prayers seem powerless and perfunctory? You need to change what you are doing. You need to renounce the sin. Remember how Jesus asked, "Why do you call me, 'Lord, Lord,' and do not do what I say?" (Luke 6:46).

Are we being selfish? It is right to pray for our own needs, of course. David is doing just that in this psalm—praying for God's protection and deliverance. But our prayers for ourselves often go beyond what is fitting and right and become mere selfishness. One correction for this is to pray for others' needs before our own.

Are we neglecting some important duty? Sins of neglect are real sins, just as sins of commission are. Remember the collect for "Morning Prayer" from *The Book of Common Prayer* that says, "We have left undone those things we ought to have done, and we have done those things which we ought not to have done, and there is no health in us." If you are neglecting some duty, make it right. Above all, if there is someone you should be caring for but are not, attend to that responsibility. Paul told Timothy, "If anyone does not provide for his relatives, and especially for his immediate family, he has denied the faith and is worse than an unbeliever" (1 Tim. 5:8). Why should God listen to such a person's prayers?

Is there a wrong we should first make right? Maybe your sin *is* a sin of commission. Jesus had words for this. He said, "If you are offering your gift at the altar and there remember that your brother has something against you, leave your gift there in front of the altar. First go and be reconciled to your brother; then come and offer your gift" (Matt. 5:23–24). You cannot claim that yours is a "righteous plea" if you have wronged another person and have failed to make the wrong right.

Are our priorities in order? David speaks of his priorities in verses 3–5, arguing that he has determined not to sin with words or walk in the ways of violent men, but rather to hold steadfastly to the path God has given him to walk. If we have our priorities in order, these will also be our determinations, and we will be able to claim an upright life as the first reason for God to answer our petition.

The Love of God

The second of David's arguments for why God should hear and answer his prayer is expressed in verses 6–8. It concerns the character of God, in these verses particularly his covenant-keeping love. These verses say:

> I call on you, O God, for you will answer me;
> give ear to me and hear my prayer.

> Show the wonder of your great love,
>> you who save by your right hand
>> those who take refuge in you from their foes.
> Keep me as the apple of your eye;
>> hide me in the shadow of your wings.

Verse 7, which appeals to the covenant-keeping love of God, stands at the center of the psalm and is the heart of David's appeal. It is more powerful in Hebrew than in English, for the word translated "love" is actually *hesed,* which refers to a covenant. It is not just a general benevolence, the kind God shows to the just and the unjust alike. This is the love by which he enters into a favorable relationship with his people, promising to be their God and the God of their children forever. The New International Version translates the word rather weakly as "great love." Other versions translate it "lovingkindness," "steadfast love," or "true love." It is the love by which God entered into a relationship with Abraham and his descendants. It is the covenant-keeping love revealed to Moses, David, and other Old Testament believers.

Although it is not evident at first glance, we need to see that verses 6–9 echo two of the "Songs of Moses" from the Pentateuch. The first is the victory song of Exodus 15. Again, the connection is more evident in Hebrew than in English, but even in English there are obvious parallels. Three terms stand out: "show the wonder" (Ps. 17:7) and "working wonders" (Exod. 15:11); "your great love" (Ps. 17:7) and "your unfailing love" (Exod. 15:13); and "by your right hand" (Ps. 17:7) and "your right hand" (Exod. 15:12). The translations vary somewhat, but in the Hebrew each pair of words is the same. In the same way, there are echoes in Psalm 17 of the "Song of Moses" recorded in Deuteronomy 32. Here is where the phrase "apple of your eye" and the idea of God hiding the psalmist "in the shadow of [his] wings" (Ps. 17:8) come from (cf. Deut. 32:10–11).

Each of these songs celebrates God's faithfulness to his covenant, which he demonstrated by delivering his people from their many enemies. Therefore, when David echoes their language in the psalm, he is appealing to what God has already revealed himself to be like. God has kept his covenant in the past. He is unchanging. Therefore, he can be expected to do the same for David in his parallel and equally dangerous circumstances. It is no accident that this is also the most confident section of the psalm. We find David saying, "I call on you, O God, for *you will answer me*" (v. 6, italics added).

God's covenant-keeping love is a marvelous thing. How marvelous? The great Baptist preacher Spurgeon suggested that it is "marvelous in its antiquity, its distinguishing character, its faithfulness, its immutability, and above all, marvelous in the wonders which it works."[3] It is this same covenant-keeping love that has reached out to us and saved us through the wonder-working death and resurrection of Jesus Christ.

The Danger Involved

The third of David's reasons why God should hear him seems a bit hum-drum compared with the first two, but it was not humdrum to the psalmist. It is the danger in which he found himself. He speaks about it in verses 10–12. This is the first time in the psalm in which David speaks specifically about his problem: he has enemies, and they are threatening him. He says three things about them. First, "they close up their callous hearts" (literally, "they are enclosed in their own fat"). He probably means that they are implacable. They have no mercy. Second, "their mouths speak with arro-gance." David has denounced this type of speech in earlier psalms (Pss. 5:5; 10:2–13; 12:3). Third, "they have tracked me down, they now surround me, with eyes alert, to throw me to the ground." He means that they are intent on his destruction.

This is a sound basis for a prayer appeal, if we know that we really are God's and are serving him. One Bible teacher was in the habit of praying when under attack, "Lord, your property is in danger." We are never on such strong ground as when we can pray that God's property and work are in danger and that we need his deliverance.

A Final Appeal

After making these three urgent arguments for God's intervention in his danger, David ends with a final appeal. It has an interesting form. When we were studying Psalm 15, I included a brief discussion of parallelism as the chief characteristic of Hebrew poetry. I said that there are different kinds of parallelism and gave illustrations. One type which I did not mention is called chiasm, from the Greek letter *chi* which is written like an X. A chias-mic parallel has the form: A, B; B, A. There was an example in Psalm 15:3:

> who does his neighbor no wrong
> and casts no slur on his fellowman . . .

The form is noun (subject), verb; verb, noun (object).

I mention this here because entire compositions have this pattern, as does Psalm 17. In the first part of the psalm David has protested his inno-cence, after which he has described his enemies. As he closes, in verses 13–15, he reverses the order by describing his enemies a second time and then restating his claim of innocence: "And I—in righteousness I will see your face" (v. 15). In this way the psalm ends precisely where it began.

It is a great blessing to be able to pray like this—not to be sinless, of course, but to be so close to the Lord that we can approach him with an upright heart and then, having prayed, can go back to the affairs of this world still knowing that we are right before him.

In Harry Ironside's brief but sometimes helpful study of the early psalms, he says that there are three verses that he likes to link together: Psalm 18:30 ("As for God, his way is perfect"), Psalm 103:15 ("As for man, his days are like grass"), and Psalm 17:15 ("As for me, I will behold thy face in righteousness" [KJV]). The first teaches that no matter what comes into our lives— sickness, financial trouble, family problems—whatever it is, God makes no mistakes. His ways with us are flawless. But man? Well, says David in effect, "'As for man,' I have learned not to expect much from him: 'his days are like grass.'" And therefore, "'As for me,' I will put my hope in God, knowing that 'in righteousness I will see [his] face' and that, when I awake from the sleep of death, 'I will be satisfied with seeing [his] likeness.'"[4]

That is the prayer of a righteous man, and like the righteous themselves it is strong and prevailing. Such prayers always are. This is what James was speaking about when he wrote, "The prayer of a righteous man is powerful and effective" (James 5:16).

Psalm 18

My God Is
My Rock: Part 1

My Fortress

I love you, O LORD, my strength.

The LORD is my rock, my fortress and my deliverer;
my God is my rock, in whom I take refuge.
He is my shield and the horn of my salvation, my stronghold.
I call to the LORD, who is worthy of praise,
and I am saved from my enemies.

The cords of death entangled me;
the torrents of destruction overwhelmed me.
The cords of the grave coiled around me;
the snares of death confronted me.
In my distress I called to the LORD;
I cried to my God for help.
From his temple he heard my voice;
my cry came before him, into his ears.

verses 1–6

144

He reached down from on high and took hold of me;
  he drew me out of deep waters.
He rescued me from my powerful enemy,
  from my foes, who were too strong for me.

verses 16–17

Psalm 18 is the first long psalm in the Psalter. There are others, of course. Psalm 119 is known for being the longest chapter in the Bible. Yet Psalm 18, with fifty verses, is the longest thus far. Before this the longest was Psalm 9, with twenty verses. Because Psalm 18 is exceptionally long, I will discuss it in two parts, a pattern I will follow more than once from this point forward.

Psalm 18 is a thanksgiving song.[1] It follows naturally upon Psalm 17, which is a lament. Thanksgiving psalms seem to follow laments. In his lament David described himself as being surrounded by callous enemies who were intent on his destruction. They were like lions "hungry for prey" (v. 12). He cried out for deliverance, and at the end of the psalm he is found confidently expecting that God will come to his aid. In Psalm 18 we find David looking back over a lifetime of such saving interventions by God and praising him for them.

At the same time, Psalm 18 is also a kingship psalm. It is a rehearsal of God's many blessings on the king and his kingdom. This means that it could have been sung, not only by David, but by anyone who had experienced the blessings of David's rule or the rule of many who later followed him to the throne.

Some of the kingship psalms have elements that look beyond the earthly king to God's promised Messiah. That is the case here. In fact, we have biblical justification for seeing the psalm this way, since in his letter to the Romans the apostle Paul quotes verse 49 as the first of four prophecies to show that Christ came for the Gentiles as well as for the Jews (Rom. 15:9). Derek Kidner summarizes the situation well when he says, "Although every Davidic king might make this psalm his own, it belonged especially to David whose testimony it was, and to Christ who was his 'offspring.'"[2]

The Historical Setting

There is another, interesting feature of Psalm 18 which we see as soon as we turn to it: the title is unusually long. In fact, it is the second longest in the Psalter, exceeded only by the title to Psalm 60. This is not just a quaint observation. It is an important one since it leads us to 2 Samuel, which is the psalm's historical setting. When we go to 2 Samuel, surprisingly, we find that Psalm 18 is duplicated almost exactly in 2 Samuel 22. In fact, even the title is from that chapter (vv. 1–2). No one is sure which of the two came first—whether an original, independent psalm was incorporated into 2 Samuel or whether a psalm originally written for the historical book was later extracted and made a separate composition. But it is certainly significant that in both settings the psalm is identified as a composition of King David, which tends to lend it special authenticity and authority.

What is the setting in 2 Samuel? In that book, the psalm appears almost as David's final words. Hence, it is a summary thanksgiving for God's many deliverances of him through his long life of service. These deliverances fall into three categories.

First, and most dramatic, there were the deliverances of David from King Saul during the long years David had to hide from him in the wilderness. The second half of 1 Samuel tells this story, beginning with Saul's jealousy of David because of the way the people of Israel praised him. While David was still at court Saul tried to kill him on more than one occasion, and when he fled first to the land of the Philistines and later to the cave at Adullam and other wilderness fortresses, Saul pursued him and tried to kill him there. These years contain amazing accounts of how God more than once brought Saul to a place where David could have killed him, and they report that David did not do it. David spared Saul, and God spared David. Thus, at the end of 1 Samuel, Saul dies by his own hand after a disastrous battle with the Philistines, and at the start of 2 Samuel David becomes king, first over the large southern tribe of Judah and then over all Israel.

Second, God delivered David during his years of fighting against Israel's enemies and gave him numerous victories. This was the period in which David established the kingdom. Second Samuel 8 lists David's victories over the Philistines, Moabites, Arameans of Damascus, and Edomites.

Third, God delivered David from the hand of his son Absalom. The young man had plotted to drive his father from Jerusalem and take the kingdom for himself, and he succeeded to the extent that David had to flee his capital and take refuge again in the vast rocky wilderness. A battle followed in which the armies of Absalom were defeated and Absalom was himself killed. David was delivered again, though he said he would that he had been killed rather than his son. Psalm 18 comes in 2 Samuel 22 after this moving recital of the events of David's life and is a fitting expression of thanksgiving to God for his protection and deliverance during many dangerous years.

Section One: Praise to God

Although there are various ways of dividing the material in this psalm, it is clear that the first three verses stand together as an opening section or prelude. In them David professes his love for God, who has shown himself to be his deliverer and to be worthy of his praise. Two kinds of metaphors are used to portray God in these verses. One kind relates to David's military victories, picturing God as his "strength," "shield," and "horn of salvation." The other type relates to the times David was forced to flee from his enemies. These images picture God as David's "rock," "fortress," "deliverer," and "stronghold." There are seven metaphors in all.

The most important of these, the theme of the psalm, is that the Lord was David's "rock." This metaphor occurs twice in verse 2, but it also appears later, in verses 31 and 46. The four form a meaningful sequence.

> The LORD is my rock.
> My God is my rock.
> Who is the Rock except our God?
> Praise be to my Rock!

Obviously, this is the dominant theme of the composition.

More than twenty years ago the great professor of classics at Auckland University, E. M. Blaiklock, wrote a series of articles for *Eternity* entitled "New Light on Bible Imagery." One of the images he wrote about was *rock*. He showed that it has several uses. First, it is an image for protection and shade. In the hot, sandy lands of the Bible the struggle of life against the merciless elements is intense in a way we can hardly appreciate in our more temperate climes. When the spring rains come a light carpet of green, doomed to be scorched by the sun and then covered with sand in just a few short weeks, will emerge on the desert's edge. But set a rock in the sand, and soon a small oasis develops on the boulder's leeward side. The desert's feeble life prospers under the rock's protection. Similarly, a man traveling through the desert during the hottest hours of the day can find shade in the rock's shadow and can survive and continue his journey. These ideas are present in verses like Isaiah 32:2, which describes the king as "the shadow of a great rock in a thirsty land." Protected by a righteous king, many weaker people may prosper. Yet the king is himself sheltered by God, as David confesses in Psalm 18. It is because the Lord was his rock that David thrived.

The second use of this image is to portray God as a refuge for his people. This idea is prominent in Psalm 18, because David is thinking of God's protection during the years he was forced to hide from Saul and later Absalom. David knew every cranny, crack, and secret hiding place in the vast, rocky wilderness. So when he fled to the rocks, he knew that he would be safe in their protection. From the height of some great rock David could look down into the canyon below and watch as his enemies pursued him hopelessly.

The vision of David perched on some high rock suggests the third biblical use of this image: having a sure foundation beneath one's feet. Here a rock is contrasted with mire and sand, as in Psalm 40:2:

> He [the LORD] lifted me out of the slimy pit,
>   out of the mud and mire;
> he set my feet on a rock
>   and gave me a firm place to stand.

Jesus used this image in the closing lines of the Sermon on the Mount, in which he contrasted the person who builds his life on sand with the person who builds on rock. The person who builds on sand suffers the loss of everything when the rains come. His house is swept away. The house that is built on rock stands firm against the rains, flood, wind, and storm "because it had its foundation on the rock" (Matt. 7:25).[3]

Psalm 18 is one long testimony to the faithfulness of God in each of these aspects. He is a shelter, a stronghold, and a firm foundation for all who build on him.

Section Two: The Psalmist's Deliverance

The next section of Psalm 18 is a longer one, encompassing verses 4–19. It is the first of two sections in which David tells what God did for him. The second, which we will examine in the next chapter, embraces verses 30–45.

David begins by recalling his former deadly perils at the hands of his enemies (vv. 4–6), and at once we are reminded of Psalm 17. In the previous psalm David speaks of his enemies tracking him down and surrounding him so he would not be able to escape, intending to overthrow him and devour him like a lion hungry for prey. In this psalm he speaks differently, saying, "The cords of death entangled me; the torrents of destruction overwhelmed me. The cords of the grave coiled around me" (vv. 4–5). But it is the same thing. Moreover, each psalm describes David responding in the same way in his distress. Psalm 18 says, "In my distress I called to the LORD; I cried to my God for help" (v. 6). In Psalm 17 he is actually crying out:

> Hear, O LORD, my righteous plea;
>   listen to my cry.
> Give ear to my prayer (v. 1).

What is most impressive about this section of Psalm 18 is the magnificent way the psalmist describes God rising from his throne in heaven in response to his servant's cry, parting the clouds, and descending to fight the king's battles accompanied by earthquakes, thunder, storms, and lightning. This is poetic writing. (The second long section of the psalm, verses 30–45, describes the same deliverance in more natural terms and from the king's own perspective.) So far as we know, David never experienced a literal display of God's presence in these exalted ways. But this does not mean that David merely made these things up. A careful comparison of Bible passages will show that these terms were all borrowed from the accounts of God's self-manifestation in Egypt, at Sinai, and during the days of Joshua and the judges.

Verses 7–11 use language associated with the descent of God to Mount Sinai to give the law through Moses. This was accompanied by a shaking of the earth, dark clouds, and lightning. The author of Hebrews describes Sinai as "a mountain . . . burning with fire; . . . darkness, gloom and storm," so terrifying that even Moses said, "I am trembling with fear" (Heb. 12:18–21).

Verses 12–14 refer to God's intervention in the battles against the Canaanites at the time of the Jewish conquest, particularly against the southern confederation in the battle described in Joshua 10. That is the occasion on which God sent hailstones against the Jews' enemies.

The exposure of the sea valleys described in verses 14 and 15 undoubtedly refers to the parting of the Red Sea at the time of the exodus from Egypt and the parting of the waters of the Jordan River at the time of the crossing over into Canaan. What is happening in these verses is what Spurgeon describes in a portion of his comments on the psalm: "David has in his mind's eye the glorious manifestations of God in Egypt, at Sinai, and on different occasions to Joshua and the judges; and he considers that his own case exhibits the same glory of power and goodness, and that, therefore, he may accommodate the descriptions of former displays of the divine majesty into his own hymn of praise."[4]

This also means that the God of Moses, Joshua, and the judges is his God too, which is the point we saw in studying Psalm 17, where we treated it in terms of the covenant. There David explicitly alluded to the two "Songs of Moses" in Exodus 15 and Deuteronomy 32. Therefore the God Moses praised is declared to be David's God also. Here David accomplishes the same thing by reference to the special manifestations of God's presence and power in past victories.

And God did deliver him, which is what the next subsection, verses 16–19 describes. It is the specific answer to the cry of Psalm 17.

> He reached down from on high and took hold of me;
>   he drew me out of deep waters.
> He rescued me from my powerful enemy,
>   from my foes, who were too strong for me.
> They confronted me in the day of my disaster,
>   but the LORD was my support.
> He brought me out into a spacious place;
>   he rescued me because he delighted in me.

Section Three: Why God Delivered David

The third of the six major sections has five verses and explains why God delivered David (vv. 20–24). This also takes us back to Psalm 17, for the point is that God delivered David because of the upright manner in which he lived, which is the first basis for his appeal for God's help made earlier. In Psalm 17 David says, "Though you probe my heart and examine me at night, though you test me, you will find nothing; I have resolved that my mouth will not sin" (v. 3). Here he says, "The LORD has dealt with me according to my righteousness; according to the cleanness of my hands he has rewarded me. For I have kept the ways of the LORD; I have not done evil by turning from my God" (vv. 20–21).

Since this psalm is supposed to have been written late in David's life as a summary of God's repeated deliverances of him, these words immediately raise a question of how David could say this in light of his sin with Bathsheba and against her husband Uriah. How could he claim to have been "blameless" and to have "kept [himself] from sin" in view of this sad episode?

It is a good question, but the answer is probably to be seen in the following verses, which we will consider more fully in the next chapter. In those verses David broadens what he says about himself in verses 20–24 to express the principle that God honors righteousness and judges sin even in this life. This is not a promise that the righteous will always prosper. Some suffer the experience of Job. It does not even mean that there is anyone who does right all the time. But as a general principle, when we live for God and try to go in his way, he cares for us and blesses us. When we go our own way, we bring misery and destruction on ourselves. This is all David is saying.

If we were to remind David of his sin with Bathsheba, he would claim it as an illustration and a proof of this principle since he suffered in a variety of ways as a consequence of that great sin. But even though that happened, just as similar transgressions are committed by us all, on the whole he was nevertheless a man after God's own heart and was greatly blessed by God. He tried to serve God, and God was faithful to him throughout his long and prosperous rule over Israel.

Their Rock and Our Rock

There is more to this psalm, as I have been suggesting—an important second half, which we will look at soon. But I want to end this chapter with a different observation.

One of the great sermons of the great American evangelist D. L. Moody was on God being our Rock, though it was not based on Psalm 18 but on Deuteronomy 32:31, which (in the version used by Moody) read, "For their rock is not as our Rock, even our enemies themselves being judges" (KJV). What caught Moody's imagination was the second part of that verse: "even our enemies themselves being judges." For he argued that in times of trouble the objects trusted by unbelievers fail them, and they concede that they do not find the help in their gods that Christians find in ours. Moody pursued this by talking about atheists, pantheists, and infidels, claiming that in the hour of their death they do not turn to their atheism or pantheism but rather, if they turn to anything at all, they ask a minister to pray for them. "I have never heard of an infidel going down to his grave happily," claimed Moody. They have nothing to hang on to. "Their rock is not as our Rock," and they confess it.[5]

How different it is for Christians! We do not live perfect lives, and we stumble many times, sometimes dreadfully. But when we come to the end of life and look back on it, as David has done in this psalm, we confess that whatever our failings may have been, our God has not failed us. We confess as a true saying: "if we are faithless, he will remain faithful, for he cannot disown himself" (2 Tim. 2:13).

There is no rock like our Rock. Praise be to the Rock of our salvation!

Psalm 18

My God Is
My Rock: Part 2

The Rock Cleft for Me

To the faithful you show yourself faithful,
*   to the blameless you show yourself blameless,*
to the pure you show yourself pure,
*   but to the crooked you show yourself shrewd.*
You save the humble
*   but bring low those whose eyes are haughty.*
You, O LORD, keep my lamp burning;
*   my God turns my darkness into light.*
With your help I can advance against a troop;
*   with my God I can scale a wall.*

As for God, his way is perfect;
*   the word of the LORD is flawless.*
He is a shield
*   for all who take refuge in him.*
For who is God besides the LORD?
*   And who is the Rock except our God?*

It is God who arms me with strength
and makes my way perfect.

verses 25–32

The LORD lives! Praise be to my Rock!
Exalted be God my Savior!
He is the God who avenges me,
who subdues nations under me,
who saves me from my enemies.
You exalted me above my foes;
from violent men you rescued me.
Therefore I will praise you among the nations, O LORD;
I will sing praises to your name.
He gives his king great victories;
he shows unfailing kindness to his anointed,
to David and his descendants forever.

verses 46–50

In the preceding chapter, I pointed out a number of interesting things about Psalm 18. For instance, it is the first long psalm in the Psalter, which is why I am studying it in two parts. Again, it is a psalm of thanksgiving which is also a kingship psalm. Third, it has the second longest introductory title, second only to the title of Psalm 60. Fourth, it is found in almost the same form in 2 Samuel 22, which gives it an important historical setting toward the end of David's life. It appears to have been written after David's deliverance from Saul, the kings of the many hostile states that surrounded Israel, and the armies commanded by David's rebellious son Absalom.

Another interesting feature of the psalm is its structure. It has six parts, as I have pointed out: praise to God (vv. 1–3); the psalmist's deliverance (vv. 4–19); the reason God delivered David (vv. 20–24); an important principle (vv. 25–29); the story of David's deliverance told again (vv. 30–45); and praise to David's Rock (vv. 46–50). But what is interesting about this structure is that the second half, parts 4–6, repeats the first half, though in reverse order. Part 4 repeats part 3, broadening or universalizing the principle. Part 5 repeats part 2, this time telling the story of David's deliverance from his rather than God's perspective. Part 6, the last, repeats part 1. So the psalm begins with praise, describes the deliverance for which God is being praised, establishes a principle concerning God's blessing of the righteous, and then moves back through each of these three themes to end, as it began, with praise to God.

The fact that the second half of the psalm repeats the outline of the first half does not mean that the content is mere repetition, however. I have suggested some of the changes in my descriptions of the six sections. And there is another change too, an important one. In the second half of the psalm we begin to pick up messianic overtones until, as we get to the next to last verse (v. 49), we find a statement that is actually quoted by the apostle Paul in Romans as referring to Jesus Christ. It is possible to have missed these allusions before. But when we get to this point and are aware of the text in Romans, we are encouraged to look back over the whole psalm to see the ways it forecasts Jesus' rejection and deliverance.

Some treatments of the psalm, by commentators like H. A. Ironside, Arno C. Gaebelein, and Saint Augustine, focus almost exclusively on these anticipations. Thus, Gaebelein writes,

> We find utterances and experiences here which cannot be matched in David's life. Some of these utterances have been described as "bold poetic figures," but they are more than figures of speech. These utterances and experiences which cannot be applied to David, though faintly foreshadowed in his sufferings and deliverances, are prophetic. The true Anointed One of God, Christ our Savior, in his sufferings, and the deliverances from above, as well as his exaltation and his coming kingdom, constitute the deeper, prophetic meaning of this great, inspired hymn. The eighteenth Psalm is therefore a Messianic Psalm.[1]

The many messianic allusions found in Psalm 18 by these writers are overdone, in my opinion. But there is something to them, as we will find when we come to the concluding section.

Section Four: An Important Principle

In order to understand section four of this psalm (vv. 25–29), we need to back up to section three where David explained the reason for his deliverances by God. He said that the Lord dealt with him and rewarded him "according to [his] righteousness; according to the cleanness of [his] hands" (v. 20). It was because he had "kept the ways of the LORD" and had not "done evil by turning from [his] God" (v. 21).

When we looked at that explanation in the last chapter I asked how David could make those claims, particularly since these words were written toward the end of his life and thus following his great sin with Bathsheba. But I said that what he claims for himself in section three (vv. 20–24) must be understood in conjunction with the general principle now unfolded in section four (vv. 25–29). The principle is that, as Leupold puts it,

God very appropriately deals with every man as that man deals with him. God lets man, as it were, choose the pattern after which he will be dealt with. . . . If a man keeps faith with God, he will find that God "keeps faith" with him (v. 25). If a man's conduct is blameless—and it should be noted that this is a typically biblical mode of speaking also in the New Testament (Luke 1:6)—he will never find a thing that he can blame God for. The same holds true with regard to a "pure" man (v. 26) or, as we might say, a sincere man. God is bound to meet him with an approach that is in turn entirely pure.[2]

The principle applies for the opposite characteristics too.

Translators have had difficulty rendering the second half of verse 26 ("to the crooked you show yourself shrewd"), probably because David himself had difficulty writing it. It is easy enough to say that when a man exhibits a good characteristic toward God, God shows the same good characteristic to him. But if man shows a bad or evil characteristic, can God really show a *bad* characteristic back? Hardly! God cannot do evil. So David expresses the second half of the parallel by a somewhat ambiguous word, the root meaning of which is "twisted." The verse actually says, "To the twisted (or crooked) you will show yourself twisted (or crooked)." But even that doesn't sound quite right, which is why the New International Version translators used the word *shrewd* in place of the second *twisted*. The idea seems to be that if a person "insists in going devious ways in his dealings with God, God outwits him, as that man deserves."[3]

I repeat that this is a *general* principle. It does not cover situations like that of Job, who was a righteous man (Job 1:8; 2:3), or the man born blind of whom Jesus said, "Neither this man nor his parents sinned, but this happened so that the work of God might be displayed in his life" (John 9:3). The principle simply means that unless other, special factors are involved, the righteous person will be blessed and protected by God while the ungodly will be judged.

This does not mean that the ungodly may not prosper for a time either. Often they do. Dictators sometimes rule for decades. Still, justice frequently does come, as it recently has for Panama's Manuel Noriega and Romania's Nicolae Ceausescu. A few years after the end of World War II, the great English historian Herbert Butterfield wrote a book called *Christianity and History,* in which he argued that the fall of Hitler followed this same observable pattern, namely, that the wicked do not prosper forever and that the good are rewarded.[4] This is all David is saying here. It is his own testimony—but a testimony that many should be able to repeat. When we go God's way, God protects and prospers us. We are like the flourishing, productive tree of Psalm 1. The wicked are not like this. They are soon swept away.

Section Five: The Story Retold

The fifth section of Psalm 18 (vv. 30–45) is the most obvious repetition of earlier material, in this case a repetition of verses 4–19. But it is neither a mere repetition nor a vain repetition. Charles Haddon Spurgeon said, "Second thoughts upon God's mercy should be and often are the best."[5]

The first time David told the story of his deliverances by God it was from God's perspective. As we saw when we studied verses 4–19, the language is borrowed from the accounts of God's appearance to Moses on Mount Sinai, his deliverance of the people from their enemies in the battles under Joshua at the time of the conquest, and the exodus from Egypt. The account describes God rising from the throne of his glory in heaven, parting the clouds, and descending to earth, accompanied by thunder, smoke, fire, darkness, and earthquakes. The result was that David was drawn "out of deep waters" and "rescued from" powerful enemies (vv. 16–17).

In the second telling (vv. 30–45) David describes in common terms what this intervention by God meant to him personally. It meant, in short, that God provided for his every need.

The terms are physical. First, his feet: "He makes my feet like the feet of a deer; he enables me to stand on the heights" (v. 33). The words are almost identical to the ending of the book of the minor prophet Habakkuk (Hab. 3:19). Second, his hands: "He trains my hands for battle" (v. 34). Third, his arms: "my arms can bend a bow of bronze" (v. 34). Fourth, his ankles: "You broaden the path beneath me, so that my ankles do not turn" (v. 36). Interspersed with these acknowledgments are verses that say that God armed him with strength (v. 32) and gave him his own shield of victory (v. 35). As a result, David was always able to achieve a full victory over all his enemies.

Verses 37–42 describe the extent of these victories. They were complete and total. Then, lest the reader get the impression that somehow this was David's own achievement, verses 43–45 make clear once again that his victories were due to God's intervention and provision. In other words, these verses link the second telling of David's deliverance to the first.

David was a king and a military commander, so he needed strength for and victory in battle. We do not usually need these things. But the principle holds true for us anyway, since, whatever we need, God, the same God, provides it. Is it wisdom? God is the source of wisdom, and we are told to pray for it. "If any of you lacks wisdom, he should ask God, who gives generously to all without finding fault, and it will be given to him" (James 1:5). Is it peace in the midst of trouble? God is the source of peace. Jesus said, "Peace I leave with you; my peace I give you" (John 14:27). Is it love? Joy? Patience? The Bible says, "the fruit of the Spirit is love, joy, peace, patience, kindness, goodness, faithfulness, gentleness and self-control" (Gal. 5:22–23). Paul wrote, "And my God will meet all your needs according to his glorious riches in Christ Jesus" (Phil. 4:19).

Wise people have found this to be true and have therefore learned to turn to God for their needs, rather than turning to the false promises of the surrounding evil world.

There is another interesting thing about these verses. David begins by saying, quite rightly, "As for God, his way is perfect" (v. 30). But then, just two verses further on, he adds, ". . . and [he] makes my way perfect" (v. 32). So it is! A life well-ordered is a life that follows after and is obedient to the Lord.

Section Six: Praise to My Rock

In the final five verses (vv. 46–50) we come back to the point from which we started out, namely, praise to God. And the theme of God being our rock reappears. Verse 2: "The LORD is my rock" and "my God is my rock." Now, verse 46: "The LORD lives! Praise be to my Rock! Exalted be God my Savior!"

Verse 49 is the verse Paul uses in Romans 15 to show that Jesus brought salvation to the Gentiles as well as to Jews. It is one of four texts, the others being Deuteronomy 32:43, Psalm 117:1, and Isaiah 11:10. Paul writes,

For I tell you that Christ has become a servant of the Jews on behalf of God's truth, to confirm the promises made to the patriarchs so that the Gentiles may glorify God for his mercy, as it is written:

> "Therefore I will praise you among the Gentiles;
>   I will sing hymns to your name."

Again, it says,

> "Rejoice, O Gentiles, with his people."

And again,

> "Praise the Lord, all you Gentiles,
>   and sing praises to him, all you peoples."

And again, Isaiah says,

> "The Root of Jesse will spring up,
>   one who will arise to rule over the nations;
> the Gentiles will hope in him" (Rom. 15:8–12).

At first glance the use of Psalm 18:49 might seem inappropriate, since David seems to be saying that *he* will praise Jehovah to the Gentile nations because of the victories God had given *him*. But it is not inappropriate at all, since verse 50 makes clear that David is also thinking of the victories God will yet give, not only to him, but to "his descendants forever." As Leupold says, "David was given victory to make possible the greater victories of his Greater Son."[6]

This is the point at which we are encouraged to look back over the entire psalm for messianic meanings. The most extensive treatment along these lines is by Arno C. Gaebelein, who sees five areas of prophecy concerning Christ.

His death (vv. 1–6). Gaebelein acknowledges that these words are indeed David's and that they can be ours also. But he feels that they are especially Jesus' words, since, in Gaebelein's judgment, they praise God for delivering him from death ("Sheol," v. 5).

His resurrection (vv. 7–18). Gaebelein sees the description of God's manifestations of himself in verses 7–18 as Jesus' resurrection. But it is a foretaste of an even fuller revelation of Jesus at the final judgment.

His exaltation (vv. 19–27). The verses in which David protests his innocence are applied exclusively to Christ by Gaebelein, since no mere human being is ever entirely righteous. He views the reward of verse 24 as Jesus' exaltation by God the Father, along the lines of Philippians 2:9–11.

His victory (vv. 28–42). This section describes the subjection of Jesus' enemies. Gaebelein recognizes that it is primarily a description of the victories God gave David, but he adds that "in this he is the type of Christ under whose feet all things will be put."

His kingdom (vv. 43–50). The final verses describe Jesus as "the head of nations." Gaebelein refers the phrase "people I did not know" to the Jews, who were "unknown" by him in their unbelief but will be "known" again in their future repentant state (v. 43). "Foreigners" are Gentiles (v. 44). The "violent man" (singular, although NIV has "men") is the Antichrist.[7]

I find that Gaebelein reads too much into the psalm, as I said earlier. But although David did not intend these allusions, the correspondence between his experiences and Christ's are nevertheless suggestive.

And here is one link more, which brings us back to where we started. The dominant theme of Psalm 18 is that God is our Rock! In the previous chapter, I pointed out that this means he is a shelter beside which we can be protected and prosper, a fortress into which we can run and be safe, a firm foundation upon which our shaking feet can stand and upon which we can build. But I remember also the way in which the great eighteenth-century preacher and songwriter Augustus M. Toplady (1740–1778) handled it in what has since become one of the best-known hymns in our language: "Rock of Ages." Toplady was traveling in the country when a storm came upon him and he was forced to take shelter in the cleft of a great rock. While he was waiting for the storm to pass he reflected on the situation spiritually, and the words of a hymn began to form in his mind. Looking down at his feet, he discovered a playing card that someone who had been there earlier had dropped. So he picked it up and used it to record these words. The card is still in existence.

> Rock of Ages, cleft for me,
> Let me hide myself in thee;
> Let the water and the blood,
> From thy riven side which flowed,
> Be of sin the double cure,
> Cleanse me from its guilt and power.
> Rock of Ages, cleft for me,
> Let me hide myself in thee.

We do not know how much of Christ's future work his lesser ancestor, King David, foresaw. But we, who stand on this side of the cross, know what Jesus Christ did. We know that he was smitten for us, crucified, that we might be saved from sin and protected from all harm. Are you "in him"? Are you sheltered in the cleft of that Rock? If you are, you can sing David's song with full reference to the cross and resurrection. You can sing,

> The LORD lives! Praise be to my Rock!
> Exalted be God my Savior! (v. 46).

Psalm 19

The Big Book and the Little Book: Part 1

The Revelation of God in Nature

The heavens declare the glory of God;
*   the skies proclaim the work of his hands.*
Day after day they pour forth speech;
*   night after night they display knowledge.*
There is no speech or language
*   where their voice is not heard.*
Their voice goes out into all the earth,
*   their words to the ends of the world.*

In the heavens he has pitched a tent for the sun,
*   which is like a bridegroom coming forth from his pavilion,*
*   like a champion rejoicing to run his course.*
It rises at one end of the heavens
*   and makes its circuit to the other;*
*   nothing is hidden from its heat.*

verses 1–6

Whaen I first began to preach through
the psalms as part of the Sunday evening services of Tenth Presbyterian
Church, which I have served as pastor since 1968, I decided whenever possible to end the services with a hymn based on the psalm being studied. At
first I did not know whether our hymnal would have many hymns based on
the psalms, but I was surprised to find that it did. The hymnal we used at
that time, Trinity Hymnal, contained 730 hymns in all—not a great number. But I discovered that in one way or another several hundred of these
hymns either paraphrase or are developed from 117 of the 150 psalms.
Most psalms had only one hymn or at best two hymns based on them, of
course. But when I came to Psalm 19, I discovered no fewer than seven
hymns developed from this one passage.

Here is a list (with authors) identified by their first lines:

"The spacious firmament on high" (Joseph Addison)
"The heavens declare thy glory" (Thomas Birks)
"The heavens declare thy glory, Lord" (Isaac Watts)
"Lord, thy Word abideth" (Henry Baker)
"Jehovah's perfect law restores the soul again" (*Psalter*, 1912)
"The law of God is good and wise" (Matthias Loy)
"Most perfect is the law of God" (*Psalter*, 1912)

This tells us a number of things about Psalm 19. For one thing, it is
clearly great poetry, a judgment confirmed by no less a master of literature
than C. S. Lewis, who called it "the greatest poem in the Psalter and one of
the greatest lyrics in the world."[1]

But just because a verse is great poetry does not necessarily mean
that we adapt it to make hymns. It must also contain important theological and spiritual truths, which Psalm 19 does, of course. This is why
it has been formed into the many hymns I mentioned. What it contains is a profound (and moving) statement of the doctrine of divine
revelation. And like the Bible's teaching elsewhere on this subject, it
divides this revelation into two main categories: general revelation,
which refers to the revelation of God in nature, and special revelation,
in this case the revelation of God in Scripture. The first of these is discussed in verses 1–6, the second in verses 7–11. Then there is a concluding section or coda in which the psalmist applies this revelation to
himself (vv. 12–14).

I have called these two parts of God's revelation "The Big Book and the
Little Book," the big book being the universe and the little book the
Bible. I will consider the first of these in this chapter and the second in
the next.

General Revelation

General revelation is the term theologians most often use to refer to the revelation of God in nature, which is where Psalm 19 begins.

> The heavens declare the glory of God;
>   the skies proclaim the work of his hands (v. 1).

Here the psalmist is thinking of the stars, which are visible by night, and the sun, which he will introduce specifically in verses 4b–6. His teaching is that the heavens, which contain these created objects, witness to the existence of their Creator. But more than that, they also witness to his "glory." The stars and the sun are so glorious that the one who made them must be more glorious still.

Clearly, this is a limited revelation. Alexander Maclaren notes this in his commentary, arguing that in this psalm *glory* has no "moral element."[2] That is, it does not testify to God's moral qualities—attributes like justice, mercy, love, wrath, goodness, grace, compassion. But the creation certainly testifies to God's existence and power. Indeed, this is exactly what the apostle Paul writes in Romans 1, in a passage that probably has the nineteenth psalm in mind, even though it is not directly quoted.

In Romans Paul says, "For since the creation of the world God's invisible qualities—his eternal power and divine nature—have been clearly seen, being understood from what has been made, so that men are without excuse" (v. 20). This is the meaning of *glory* in Psalm 19—a revelation of God's existence and power so great that it should lead every human being on the face of the earth to seek God out, to thank him for bringing him or her into existence, and to worship him.

But that is what we do not do. What Paul says in Romans is that, apart from God's special intervention in our lives to save us, all human beings actually suppress the truth of God's general revelation, either denying his existence altogether or else erecting a lesser god, an idol, in the true God's place. As a result of this, the wrath of God has been revealed against us and our truth-suppressing cultures.

The Nature of This Testimony

It is not only the fact of general revelation that we find in Psalm 19. That would be significant enough, coming as it does in this relatively early stage of the biblical revelation. However, in addition to the mere truth of general revelation, we also have some profound statements about its nature and extent. Verses 2 and 3 say three things about it.

General Revelation Is Continuous

The psalmist says of the heavens that "day after day they pour forth speech" and of the skies that "night after night they display knowledge"

(v. 2). In other words, they are not an intermittent revelation, as if God were to send a prophet one year and then let many silent years go by before sending another. The skies reveal the glory of God every single night of the week, every week of the year, year after year, and they have done this since their creation, which scientists tell us was about twenty billion years ago. There has never been a moment in the much shorter history of the human race when the heavens were not testifying to us about God. This is what Joseph Addison captured so brilliantly in the third verse of his hymn based on Psalm 19.

> What though in solemn silence all
> Move round this dark terrestrial ball?
> What though no real voice nor sound
> Amidst their radiant orbs be found?
> In reason's ear they all rejoice,
> And utter forth a glorious voice;
> Forever singing, as they shine,
> "The hand that made us is divine."

General Revelation Is Abundant

In the words of the psalm, it pours forth speech (v. 2). This is stronger in the Hebrew text than it appears to be in English, for the image is literally of a gushing spring that copiously pours forth the sweet, refreshing waters of revelation.

This is true in two ways, though I am not certain in what sense David meant the statement. First, every individual part of nature testifies to its Creator, so that whatever part you happen to be looking at will pour forth knowledge. If you look at the stars, they testify to a God of great power who made them. If you study the human body, you will find that the body testifies to an all-wise Creator. The petals of a flower, a blade of grass, a snowflake, the intricacies of the atom, the nature of light, physical laws like gravitational attraction, the second law of thermodynamics, or relativity—all testify abundantly to a divine mind that lies behind them.

Moreover, this is quite plain. We should almost say self-evident. The witness lies on the surface. It does not require extensive technical investigation to see it. As Paul says in the corresponding passage in Romans 1, "what may be known about God is plain to them, because God has made it plain to them. For since the creation of the world God's invisible qualities—his eternal power and divine nature—have been clearly seen, being understood from what has been made, so that men are without excuse" (vv. 19–20).

However, there is a second way in which the heavens pour forth abundant revelation. Whenever we do investigate them by scientific or other means, we soon find the testimony of nature even stronger than we at first surmised. In other words, the existence of a creator is not a facile but erroneous judgment naively made by the uneducated, a judgment quickly disproved as soon as one looks into the evidence carefully. On the contrary, the more one looks, the more the heavens gush forth knowledge.

This has been true even of the most recent investigations of the heavens by the greatest scientific minds the human race has produced. Until well into this century the prevailing scientific cosmology was what is called the "steady state" theory, which holds that the universe had no beginning and is eternal. The theory satisfied scientists with its corollary that everything has a cause and every cause can be investigated. That view has been entirely overthrown, and the inescapable conviction of today's scientific community is that the universe did indeed have a beginning about twenty billion years ago. The new view thinks of the origin of the universe as a gigantic fireball explosion known popularly as the "big bang."

The story of this Copernican-like scientific revolution in cosmology is interesting. It began in 1913 with astronomer Vesto Melvin Slipher's discovery that about a dozen galaxies relatively close to the earth were moving away from us at high speeds, up to two million miles per hour. During the next decade a younger astronomer named Edwin Hubble carried Slipher's observation further, measuring the velocities of scores of galaxies and formulating the laws for an expanding universe. Hubble discovered that the further away a galaxy is, the faster it is moving. By measuring the speed of these retreating galaxies and plotting them against their distance from us, Hubble was able to pinpoint a moment in the past when all the matter of the universe must have been together, in other words, the moment of creation. It was apparently between fifteen and twenty billion years ago. Finally, in 1965 two scientists from the Bell Telephone Laboratories, Arno Penzias and Robert Wilson, discovered the leftover radiation or echo of that big bang.

Many scientists did not like this discovery because it pointed to God and to a moment of creation beyond which they could not and would never be able to penetrate. Sir Arthur Eddington, a British astronomer, wrote in 1931, "The notion of a beginning is repugnant to me."

The German chemist Walter Nernst said, "To deny the infinite duration of time would be to betray the very foundations of science."

Phillip Morrison of the Massachusetts Institute of Technology remarked of the big bang theory, "I would like to reject it."

Even Albert Einstein, whose theory of relativity itself predicted an expanding universe (though he did not recognize it at the time), said, "The circumstance [of an initial moment of creation] irritates me. To admit such possibilities seems senseless." However, after examining Hubble's work he declared himself convinced.

Robert Jastrow, the founder and director of NASA's Goddard Institute for Space Studies, was amused at these reactions of his fellow scientists and has written a book about it called *God and the Astronomers*. The book concludes wittily, "For the scientist who has lived by his faith in the power of reason, the story ends like a bad dream. He has scaled the mountains of ignorance; he is about to conquer the highest peak; as he pulls himself over the rock, he is greeted by a band of theologians who have been sitting there for centuries."[3]

General Revelation Is Universal

It is known everywhere. Psalm 19 says of the skies and heavens,

> There is no speech or language
> where their voice is not heard.[4]
> Their voice goes out into all the earth,
> their words to the ends of the world (vv. 3–4).

This is the basis for the universal ascription of guilt to humanity by Paul in Romans 1. For although everyone in every land and of every human language has "heard" this general revelation—no one is exempt from it—none have of themselves followed up on it in order to seek the true God out and worship him. Instead they suppress the knowledge of the true God and make idols of a lesser god more to their liking. It is because of this general revelation (and not a special revelation which, of course, numerous peoples and cultures do not have) that God is just in punishing the heathen as well as those who, having the special revelation, also sin against their greater light.

The Glory of the Sun

In his brief comments on this psalm, John R. W. Stott calls the sun "a particular example" of the universal witness to God by the heavens.[5] But, of course, it is more than this. As David describes the sun in verses 4b–6, from his perspective it is "the crowning achievement of God's creation."[6]

A "tent for the sun" is probably to be understood as the darkness into which the sun retreats each night and from which it emerges boldly each new day. David compares the sun to a vigorous young man in two aspects: "like a bridegroom coming forth from his pavilion" and "like a champion rejoicing to run his course." In each case, the image conveys the ideas of youthful strength, energy, and physical joy. Naturally, David did not know all we know about the sun—how it is a ball of gases, chiefly hydrogen, burning itself up in a vast nuclear reaction, yet destined to continue burning for at least six billion years more, how it is so far away from earth that light radiating from its surface takes eight minutes to get here. Yet strangely, though knowing less about the sun than ourselves, David nevertheless praised God more. He knew that the sun is God's handiwork and that it displays his glory.

C. S. Lewis has rightly pointed out that the key line in this description is the last, which says that "nothing is hidden from [the sun's] heat" (v. 6). The line links the witness of the physical creation to the witness of the Word, for the Scriptures are likewise penetrating, warming, and lifegiving, while also searching, testing, and purifying.

The Two Revelations

In the second half of the psalm, David is going to move abruptly to talk about God's revelation of himself in Scripture, thus laying the second half of this great doctrine before us. The two appear together so naturally in this psalm that even in this chapter a few observations are called for.

First, there is no conflict between natural and special revelation, nor can there be. Unbelievers and skeptics often talk this way, suggesting that no scientific mind can honestly accept the Bible's teachings. But many able scientists have embraced both the Bible and science and have argued that scientific study of the cosmos actually points in the same direction as does the Book of Genesis. Years ago, Harry A. Ironside wrote rightly, "There is no conflict whatever between the testimony of nature and the testimony of the Word of God."[7] If we think there is, we are misunderstanding nature, the Bible, or both.

Charles Haddon Spurgeon said, "He is wisest who reads both the world-book and the Word-book as two volumes of the same work, and feels concerning them, 'My Father wrote them both.'"[8]

Second, nature, like Scripture, points to God but is not itself God. Lewis is particularly helpful at this point, arguing that a doctrine of creation such as we find in this psalm, "while it brings God and Nature into relation, also separates them. What makes and what is made must be two, not one. Thus the doctrine of Creation in one sense empties Nature of divinity."[9] Liberal scholars have imagined echoes of pagan hymns of worship of the stars and sun in Psalm 19, but nothing could be farther from the psalm's intent. The psalmist is actually protesting against pagan worship. For the heavens are pointing to God, not themselves, and the sun, while glorious, only fulfills a function and follows a course prescribed for it by its divine maker.

"But in another sense," as Lewis likewise points out, "the same doctrine which empties Nature of her divinity also makes her an index, a symbol, a manifestation of the Divine." Nature is now "the bearer of messages."[10] It is a defect in the modern scientific mind, not an achievement, that it has so much difficulty seeing this.

Third, if we value creation, as many in our day obviously do—witness the environmental lobby groups and others who work to purify and preserve our water, air, and wild lands—we should cherish the written revelation of God in Scripture even more. David did. That is why the psalm will go on to speak of the value and beneficial functions of God's law. David reveled in God's law, just as he obviously did in nature, and we should too. If we value nature, we should value the Bible even more, and equally important, we should make it the object of our most careful, searching, devout, thankful, and obedient meditation every day.

Psalm 19

The Big Book and the Little Book: Part 2

The Revelation of God in Scripture

The law of the LORD is perfect,
    reviving the soul.
The statutes of the LORD are trustworthy,
    making wise the simple.
The precepts of the LORD are right,
    giving joy to the heart.
The commands of the LORD are radiant,
    giving light to the eyes.
The fear of the LORD is pure,
    enduring forever.
The ordinances of the LORD are sure
    and altogether righteous.
They are more precious than gold,
    than much pure gold;
they are sweeter than honey,
    than honey from the comb.
By them is your servant warned;
    in keeping them there is great reward.

Who can discern his errors?
  Forgive my hidden faults.
Keep your servant also from willful sins;
  may they not rule over me.
Then will I be blameless,
  innocent of great transgression.

May the words of my mouth and the meditation of my heart
  be pleasing in your sight,
O LORD, my Rock and my Redeemer.

verses 7–14

In the first chapter of 2 Peter there are verses that have bearing on Psalm 19. Peter is an old man at this point (cf. v. 14), and he has been reflecting on the time he and two other disciples saw the Lord Jesus Christ transfigured before them on the mountain. It was a great experience. "We were eyewitnesses of his majesty," he says. We heard "this voice that came from heaven" (vv. 16, 18). It was an experience comparable to that of Moses meeting with God on Mount Sinai. Nevertheless, in spite of having seen the Lord's glory and having heard the very voice of God from heaven, saying, "This is my Son, whom I love; with him I am well pleased," Peter says that there exists an even greater witness to the truth. "We have the word of the prophets made more certain," is his testimony (vv. 17, 19). The Authorized Version of the Bible calls this witness a "more sure word of prophecy," that is, more sure even than the voice from heaven.

This has bearing on Psalm 19, as I say. For the verses in 2 Peter 1 are a New Testament equivalent of the transition from verses 1–6 in Psalm 19, which talk about the general revelation of God in nature, to verses 7–11, which talk about the special revelation of God in Scripture. The revelation of God in nature is glorious, just as the visible transfiguration of Jesus and the heavenly voice were glorious. But glorious as it is, it cannot compare to the written revelation. It is that "more certain" or "more sure" revelation that concerns David in the second half of this psalm.

One Psalm or Two?

The movement from the first part of this psalm to the second is so abrupt that some scholars have used the differences to argue that Psalm 19 was originally two separate psalms. This is a typical example of the workings of the liberal mind, and the reasons for it are not hard to discover. If the two sections were originally separate, then the first half of the psalm, in which the psalmist writes of nature, can be compared to the many nature hymns of the ancient pagan world: the Babylonian hymns to Shamash,

Egyptian hymns to the various sun gods, or even the well-known hymn to Aten. And it can be imagined that the psalmist got his inspiration from them.

Of course, nothing could be more removed from what is actually going on in this poem. The first part of the psalm is not a hymn to nature. It does not deify creation. It is a hymn of praise to God, who has revealed himself in the glories of the universe. It is the most natural thing in the world for the psalm to turn from the revelation in nature, which all human beings possess, to that special revelation of God in Scripture, specifically given to the Jews.

This second, specific revelation is so superior to the first or general revelation that the style of the poem quite naturally changes.

The name used for God changes. In the first half, the name is *el.* It occurs only once, and that is in verse 1, which says, "The heavens declare the glory of God." *El* (not even *Elohim*) is the most generic of all names for God. It is an appropriate name for One made known by the general revelation. In the second half of the psalm the name used for God is *Jehovah.* Jehovah is the covenant name revealed to Moses at the burning bush ("I AM WHO I AM," Exod. 3:14). It is appropriate for the special and specific revelation of God in Scripture. This name occurs seven times (vv. 7, 8, 9, 14), and the frequency serves to heighten the emotional tone of the poem's second half.

The length of the lines also changes. In the first half the lines are longer, which is appropriate to the continuous, abundant, and universal witness of the heavenly bodies to God's glory. In the second half the lines are much shorter, as the poet begins to throw out descriptive epithet after descriptive epithet and adjective after adjective to capture the wonder of the written revelation. The link between the sections is the final clause of verse 6. David says of the sun, "nothing is hidden from its heat." But the same could be said of the pervasive, lifegiving law. It too embraces all of life and is as necessary for the life of the human soul as the sun is for the life of the body.

Words to Be Obeyed

It would be hard to discover in all the Bible a more perfect example of Hebrew poetic parallelism than verses 7–9. There are six parallel statements in these verses, and each contains three elements that are likewise parallel. There are six terms for the written revelation, six adjectives to describe it, and six statements of what the Bible does.

Let's look at the nouns first: law, statutes, precepts, commands, fear, and ordinances. These describe the Bible's multiple facets, just as Psalm 119 also does, though there are more terms in the longer psalm. The word *law,* literally *Torah,* is the most embracing term. It is not limited to specific legal commands, as our use of the word *law* is. The root meaning of Torah is "instruction." It has to do with everything God has revealed or says. Our best equivalent would be *Scripture* or *the Word of God. Statutes* literally is "testimony." It means an aspect of truth attested by God himself, perhaps with the idea of this being a reminder.[1] *Precepts* together with the word *commands,* which comes next, mean "orders," indicating the precision and authority with which God addresses us.[2] *Fear* is not strictly a synonym for law, though it is used as such. It describes the Scriptures by the effect they produce in those who respond to the revelation. The last verses of the psalm are an example of this godly fear or reverence. The final noun, *ordinances,* means "judgments" or "verdicts," that is, the divine evaluation of our thoughts and actions.

To my mind, the interesting thing about this list is that it is an entirely different way of dividing up the revelation of God in Scripture from what is common among us. How do we do it? We do it in various ways. One way is to divide historical from didactic material, that is, stories from teaching. We speak of narrative material, poetic material, law, and prophecy. We distinguish the Old Testament from the New Testament. We speak of Gospels and letters. Even when restricting themselves to the psalms, scholars distinguish between hymns, laments, thanksgiving psalms, psalms of confidence, psalms of remembrance, wisdom psalms, and kingship psalms.

None of these divisions are wrong, of course. In fact, each is helpful for the purposes for which it was devised. But what impresses me is how differently David goes about it. He is not dealing with style—that is, with types of literature. He is dealing with the Scripture's true nature and function. And he is lumping it all together, saying that it is always and at the same time law, statutes, precepts, commands, fear, and ordinances.

What is the one characteristic that these six terms have in common, despite the slightly different shades of meaning I have outlined? The answer is that they all portray the Bible as words to be obeyed. That is how David viewed the Bible, as the Word of God to be obeyed. Because it is the Word of God, it was to be received by him (and others) as authoritative, inerrant, and absolutely binding.

Training in Righteousness

At first glance, a person might suppose that what I have said about the way David looked at the law is not very important, at least for us today. "So what if David regarded Scripture as something to be obeyed rather than merely looking at it stylistically, as we do?" he might comment. "Different strokes for different folks." This is not an unimportant matter, however, since what is said about the law in the second half of the psalm depends upon it. In other words, it is because the Bible is God's law, statutes, precepts, commands, fear, and ordinances that it is perfect, trustworthy, right, radiant, pure, and sure, which is what David says it is. And it is because it is like this that it can do the things David also says it does do.

This is the same relationship found in Paul's well-known description of the Bible in 2 Timothy: "All Scripture is God-breathed and is useful for teaching, rebuking, correcting and training in righteousness" (2 Tim. 3:16). The combination of ideas in this verse indicates that it is because the Bible is not like other books, because it is "God-breathed," as they are not, that it is useful for teaching, rebuking, correcting, and training us.

David says the law of God does six things.

Being perfect, it revives the soul. The connection between the law's perfection and its ability to revive the soul is not easy to see at first glance, but it is found in the fact that being perfect means being so complete as to cover every aspect of life. It means that the Bible is not deficient in any way. It is an all-sufficient revelation. Therefore, no matter what our sins may have been or our problems are, the Bible is able to turn us from our sins, lead us through our problems, and both feed and enrich us so that we are able to enjoy the full benefits of spiritual life. Jesus testified to this when he told the devil, quoting from Deuteronomy 8:3, "Man does not live on bread alone, but on every word that comes from the mouth of God" (Matt. 4:4).

Being trustworthy, the law of God makes the simple wise. *Trustworthy* means worthy of trust, and the reason why the statutes of the Lord are worthy of our trust is that they correspond to reality. If we follow the directions of the Word of God, we will find salvation, contentment, joy, and eternal life. The one who is open enough to God's instructions to do that will become wise. On the other hand, the one who thinks himself too wise to adhere to God's wisdom will show himself to be a fool.

Paul elaborates upon this in Romans, saying that one result of man's abandonment of the truth of God is that he is given over to what Paul calls "a lie" (Rom. 1:25). Again, in 1 Corinthians 1 he shows that God has used the apparent foolishness of the gospel to confound the self-proclaimed wise people of this world. "For it is written: 'I will destroy the wisdom of the wise; the intelligence of the intelligent I will frustrate.' Where is the wise man? Where is the scholar? Where is the philosopher of this age? Has not God made foolish the wisdom of the world? For since in the wisdom of God the world through its wisdom did not know him, God was pleased through the foolishness of what was preached to save those who believe" (1 Cor. 1:19–21).

Being right, the law of God makes the heart rejoice. *Right* does not mean correct as opposed to being wrong; that idea is seen more in the word *trustworthy*. *Right* means straight as opposed to being crooked and is linked to the idea of righteousness. Verse 8 teaches that walking in a straight path or in an upright manner brings joy. Charles Haddon Spurgeon saw a progression in these first three statements about the law of God that highlights the meaning of this one: conversion, leading to wisdom, leading to joy. He says of the latter: "Free grace brings heart-joy. Earthborn mirth dwells on the lip, and flushes the bodily powers; but heavenly delights satisfy the inner nature, and fill the mental faculties to the brim."[3]

Being radiant, the law of God gives light to the eyes. This combination of ideas is easy for us to understand, both on the literal and metaphorical levels. Literally, an object that is radiant or gives off light makes vision possible. The sun does it; David wrote of the sun in verses 4b–6. So do candles or lamps or, in our case, light bulbs, chandeliers, or flashlights. Metaphorically, anything that illumines a right life path enables us to walk in it without stumbling. This is the idea here, though the passage probably also carries the idea of purging darkness out of us and thus enabling us to see clearly and without distortion. Psalm 119:105 embraces these ideas when it says, "Your word is a lamp to my feet and a light for my path."

Being pure, the law of God endures forever. P. C. Craigie thinks the nuance shifts at this point and that it is proper fear or reverence for God that is said to endure forever.[4] But if "fear of the LORD" actually denotes the Scriptures, the effect being substituted for the cause, then it is the Word itself that is described as being pure and, because it is pure, enduring. This is the way most commentators take it.

Corrupt things decay. That which is pure endures. Since the Word of God is entirely pure, being without any deficiency, error, fault, or inadequacy, it along with the God who spoke it is the most enduring of all things. Jesus said, "until heaven and earth disappear, not the smallest letter, not the least stroke of a pen, will by any means disappear from the Law until everything is accomplished" (Matt. 5:18). He also said, "Heaven and earth will pass away, but my words will never pass away" (Matt. 24:35). People have a relative idea of truth today, believing that truth changes from generation to generation and from one individual's perception to another individual's perception. Nothing is certain. But by contrast, the Bible teaches that truth is absolute and unchanging and that it is grounded in the character of God, who is likewise unchanging. Therefore a wise person will build his or her life upon it.

Being sure and altogether righteous, the law of God warns the servant of God against sin and provides him with great reward. The last of these six statements does not follow the precise parallelism of the other five. Where we expect to read another statement of what the Bible does we find instead the words "and altogether righteous." The parallelism is still there, however. It is just delayed. In a departure from the established pattern, which enhances the poem and makes it more interesting, the psalmist introduces a personal evaluation of the ordinances of God, saying,

> They are more precious than gold,
>   than much pure gold;
> they are sweeter than honey,
>   than honey from the comb (v. 10).

Only after this evaluation do we find the completion of the parallelism in a statement of two things the Scriptures do: "By them is your servant warned" and "in keeping them there is great reward" (v. 11). In other words, because the words of God are sure and righteous, the servants of God are warned by them and the keepers of them are rewarded.

Those two benefits are worth pursuing.

First, the one who knows the law is warned by it. Against what? Against sin and its harmful effects. And against the lies and errors of this world. We need such warnings, because the world about us is clever and pervasive, and there is nothing except the Bible to stand against its deceptions. John Bunyan had it right when he said of the Bible, "This Book will keep you from sin, or sin will keep you from this Book."[5]

Second, the keeper of the law is rewarded. But notice how this is said. The text does not say that the one who obeys God's commands *will be* rewarded, though that is certainly true too. It says rather, "*in keeping them there is great reward*" (italics added). Saint Augustine once said that sin is its own punishment. He could also have said that virtue is its own reward. Though the ungodly do not think so, the upright are actually blessed in their uprightness. Goodness is itself joyous. To be holy is to be content.

Heart to Heart

In the introduction to the last chapter I called the final three verses of this psalm a concluding section or coda, but they are actually more than that. They are a climax. For in them the psalmist applies what he has been learning to himself. They show that he has been learning.

His response to God's self-revelation falls into two categories.

The first is *prayer* that God will forgive his sin and deliver him from additional transgressions. Sometimes we treat forgiveness lightly, asking God to forgive us but not really thinking that we are sinners, at least not serious sinners, and treating forgiveness almost as a basic human right. It is clear that David does not do this. He is aware of sin's subtle nature and complexity, dividing it into categories: errors, which are wrongs innocently committed; hidden faults, that is, faults unknown to himself because so deeply ingrained in his personality, certainly not hidden to God; and willful sins, which are sins of deliberate presumption. The latter are probably equivalent to "great transgression" in verse 13. The psalmist also knows that he can never be fully aware of these sins in order to seek forgiveness unless God reveals their presence to him by the written law.

We remember the prayer of the tax collector in Jesus' well-known parable, for although it is less detailed it contains the same essential elements. The tax collector prayed, "God, have mercy on me, a sinner" (Luke 18:13). We know this man was coming to know God and was really praying to God, because he saw himself to be a sinner, as David also did. The Pharisee did not.

The second part of David's response to God's revelation of himself is an *appeal* to God as his Rock and Redeemer. We are not only led to see ourselves as sinners when we study the Bible. The Bible also leads us to the One who is our only deliverer from sin. And, wonder of wonders, he is the same one who has revealed himself gloriously in the heavens. The heavens tell us that he exists and that he is all-powerful. The Bible shows that he is our Redeemer from sin, that is, the one who is able to break sin's bonds and set us free, and that he is the Rock upon which the redeemed man or woman can build and be kept from transgressions.

Psalm 20

God Save the King

May the LORD answer you when you are in distress;
*   may the name of the God of Jacob protect you.*
May he send you help from the sanctuary
*   and grant you support from Zion.*
May he remember all your sacrifices
*   and accept your burnt offerings.*   Selah
May he give you the desire of your heart
*   and make all your plans succeed.*
We will shout for joy when you are victorious
*   and will lift up our banners in the name of our God.*
May the LORD grant all your requests.

Now I know that the LORD saves his anointed;
*   he answers him from his holy heaven*
*   with the saving power of his right hand.*
Some trust in chariots and some in horses,
*   but we trust in the name of the LORD our God.*
They are brought to their knees and fall,
*   but we rise up and stand firm.*

O LORD, save the king!
*   Answer us when we call!*

verses 1–9

The twentieth and twenty-first psalms are different from the psalms we have studied thus far, in that they were designed to be sung by the Jewish people on behalf of their king and nation. The first is a prayer for the king's victory in a day of battle. The second is a prayer of thanksgiving for that deliverance.

There are several stylistic details to be noted. For one thing, the psalms are tied together by the final lines of the first and the first lines of the second. Psalm 20 ends with a prayer that God will answer the people's intercession and save the king. Psalm 21 starts by acknowledging that God has done so. They are tied together in other ways, as well. Psalm 20 begins with the words LORD, *answer*, and *day*, although the latter is hidden by the English translation. The opening line actually speaks of a "*day* of distress." The psalm ends with the same three words: LORD, *answer*, and the "*day* of our calling" (author's translation). Psalm 21 begins and ends with the words LORD and *strength*. In scholarly language this is called *inclusio*. It is like a front and back door to a house. One striking example of it is Psalm 8, which begins and ends with the words, "O LORD, our Lord, how majestic is your name in all the earth!"

Another important feature is that the two psalms seem to be more explicitly liturgical than any we have studied thus far. Why? There are two reasons. First, they are written (for the most part) in the first person plural, that is, using the word *we* rather than *I* or *me*. Compare them with the psalms immediately before and after. Psalm 19 ends, "May the words of *my* mouth and the meditation of *my* heart be pleasing in your sight, O LORD, *my* Rock and *my* Redeemer." That is a personal prayer uttered by an individual. Psalm 22 begins, "*My* God, *my* God, why have you forsaken *me*?" It is also personal. Psalms 20 and 21 say, "*We* will shout" (Ps. 20:5), "*we* call" (Ps. 20:9), and "*we* will sing" (Ps. 21:13, italics added throughout). In these psalms many worshipers seem to be involved.

The second reason is a variation on what I have just said. In Psalm 20 the dominant voice is the first person plural, but that is at the beginning and ending only. In between there is a stanza introduced by the words "Now *I* know." It would seem, therefore, that the first stanza (vv. 1–5) was to be uttered by the people on the king's behalf; the second stanza (vv. 6–8) was to be spoken by an individual, probably a priest, assuring the people that their prayers are answered; and the final verse or stanza (v. 9) again was to be spoken by the entire people as a summary and farewell petition, probably as the king marched off to battle.[1]

Perowne summarizes this in a balanced way in his introduction, saying, "I think it to be a kind of general litany for magistrates and those who are placed in high office, for whom the apostle also (1 Tim. 2) bids us first of all pray, that we may lead a quiet and peaceable life."[2] Perowne means that the prayer is a model for what we should seek in our political leaders and how we should pray for them.

Prayer for the King

I have said that the first five verses are a prayer for Israel's king. Yet strictly speaking, they are not a prayer to God so much as words directed to the king himself, assuring him that the people believe in him and want God to answer his petitions.

The key word here is *may*. It occurs six times, introducing six fervent desires of the people: "*May* the LORD answer you when you are in distress" (v. 1); "*May* the name of the God of Jacob protect you" (v. 1); "*May* he send you help from the sanctuary" (v. 2); "*May* he remember all your sacrifices" (v. 3); "*May* he give you the desire of your heart" (v. 4); and "*May* the LORD grant all your requests" (v. 5, italics added throughout). As I say, these words are directed to the king more than to God. Yet they really are prayers in spite of their form, since the people clearly want God to deliver, protect, and bless their monarch and are obviously echoing his prayers for these things.

Something else is striking about these verses, and that is the picture of the king that emerges. For one thing, he himself is a man of prayer. We do not know the circumstances of the original composition of this psalm, but it seems to have a setting in which the king is praying before the tabernacle or temple prior to going out to battle and the people are standing about him at a slight distance, joining in his petitions. In other words, he is leading them in prayer. If this is a psalm of David, as the title says it is, we have no difficulty believing that David would have done this.

Second, the king is religiously devout, for he is offering sacrifices. It is possible for both sacrifices and prayers to be mere form, of course, but there is nothing in the psalm that would make us think that of this situation. A nation is blessed if it is favored with such godly leaders.

A Nation under God

What about our country? America had many such people at one time. Today it is fashionable, even among evangelicals, to decry the religious foundations of our nation, pointing out that many of our founding fathers were deists, skeptics, or outright unbelievers. Many were. But in our desire to correct a dishonest national mythology we have frequently forgotten the genuine open faith of many of our country's leading figures.

John Winthrop, the first governor of Massachusetts Bay Colony, wrote at the age of twenty-four, "I desire to make it one of my chief petitions to have that grace to be poor in spirit. I will ever walk humbly before my God, and meekly, mildly and gently towards all men. . . . I do resolve first to give myself—my life, my wits, my health, my wealth—to the service of my God and Savior who, by giving himself for me and to me, deserves whatsoever I am or can be, to be at his commandment and for his glory."[3]

George Washington, a devout Anglican, wrote in his youth, "O God, who art rich in mercy and plenteous in redemption, mark not, I beseech thee, what I have done amiss; remember that I am but dust, and remit my transgressions, negligences and ignorances, and cover them all with the absolute obedience of thy dear Son, that those sacrifices (of sin, praise and thanksgiving) which I have offered may be accepted by thee, in and for the sacrifice of Jesus Christ offered upon the cross for me. . . . Direct my thoughts, words and work, wash away my sins in the immaculate blood of the Lamb, and purge my heart by thy Holy Spirit."[4]

In Philadelphia, when the vote for American independence was taken on July 4, 1776, there was a moment of solemn silence after which Samuel Adams spoke. He voiced what many were thinking: "We have this day restored the Sovereign to whom alone men ought to be obedient. He reigns in heaven and . . . from the rising to the setting sun. May his kingdom come."[5]

Even Benjamin Franklin, who was not a Christian but who had deep respect for many who were, broke a serious deadlock in the debate over the American Constitution in 1787 by calling for daily prayer. He was eighty-one years old at the time.

In the beginning of the contest with Britain, when we were sensible of danger, we had daily prayers in this room for divine protection. Our prayers, sir, were heard, and they were graciously answered. All of us who were engaged in the struggle must have observed frequent instances of a superintending Providence in our favor. . . . And have we now forgotten this powerful Friend? Or do we imagine we no longer need his assistance?

I have lived, sir, a long time, and the longer I live, the more convincing proofs I see of this truth: "that God governs in the affairs of man." And if a sparrow cannot fall to the ground without his notice, is it probable that an empire can rise without his aid?

We have been assured, sir, in the sacred writings that except the Lord build the house, they labor in vain that build it. I firmly believe this. I also believe that, without his concurring aid, we shall succeed in this political building no better than the builders of Babel; we shall be divided by our little, partial local interests; our projects will be confounded; and we ourselves shall become a reproach and a byword down to future ages. And what is worse, mankind may hereafter, from this unfortunate instance, despair of establishing government by human wisdom and leave it to chance, war or conquest.[6]

The delegates to the Constitutional Convention did pray, and God again did answer. The result was the first written constitution in history in which representatives of a people sat down to devise the principles and laws by which they would be governed. Our constitution became a monument to freedom and an inspiration for millions who yearn for it.

We have fallen a long way from those early days of divine blessing, have we not? Today it is difficult to point to many contemporary leaders who are genuinely prayerful or devout or who openly seek God's blessing and guidance for our national affairs.

Assurance of the King's Success

The second stanza of Psalm 20 is the section spoken in the first person singular, perhaps by the king himself, as some scholars think,[7] or, more likely, by one of the nation's priests.[8] It is an assurance that God hears and will answer the king's (and the people's) prayers.

The heart of this section is verse 7, which compares Israel's trust in God to the confidence the pagan nations surrounding them had in their arms: "Some trust in chariots and some in horses, but we trust in the name of the LORD our God." Later in her history, particularly under Solomon who raised extensive cavalry units and built large forts to garrison them, Israel became very much like her neighbors. But Deuteronomy 17:16 had said that the kings of Israel were not to trust in or even acquire great numbers of horses, and at the beginning they did not do so.[9] Their faith was in God, and the God they trusted gave victories.

The history of Israel had been a long experience of God's powerful and timely intervention to save the people from hostile adversaries. Abraham was no warrior. He was a Bedouin chief with no army at all, only loyal servants. Yet when four kings from the east attacked Sodom and the other cities of the Dead Sea plain, carrying off Abraham's nephew Lot and his family, the patriarch pursued their armies with 318 of his men, fell on them by night, and routed them, recovering Lot, his family, and the spoil. It was a brave move, but it was not Abraham's courage that gave victory. It was God himself, as Melchizedek, God's priest, reminded Abraham when he returned from the battle (Gen. 14:20).

The deliverance of the people from Egypt was a spectacular example of God's strong intervention. The Jews were only a mixed rabble of slaves at the time. The Egyptians were the mightiest oppressors of their day. Yet God delivered Israel through ten great plagues and destroyed the pursuing armies of the pharaoh. Moses composed a song about it, which starts,

> I will sing to the LORD,
>   for he is highly exalted.
> The horse and its rider
>   he has hurled into the sea.

> The LORD is my strength and my song;
> he has become my salvation (Exod. 15:1–2).

Joshua's experience at Jericho, when the walls of the city fell by God's will, and the subsequent conquest of the promised land fit the same pattern. So do Gideon's defeat of the Midianites with just a handful of soldiers, and young David's killing of Goliath. It was no empty boast or groundless hope for the future when the psalmist wrote these lines.

Have other nations ever experienced something of this nature? Indeed, they have, though not every human claim to a divine intervention is genuine. The history of England has what seems to be some genuine examples of special divine intervention. There is the victory over the Spanish Armada in the days of Queen Elizabeth I. The fate of the English Reformation was at stake in that battle, as well as the English throne. The Spanish ships outnumbered the English. They were mightier. People all over England were praying. As a result, the English navy achieved a stunning victory, and the work begun in the southern portion of the channel was completed by a sudden and unexpected storm which drove the escaping Spanish ships northward and wrecked most on rocks off the coast of Scotland.

A contrasting deliverance occurred at Dunkirk when God sent unseasonably calm weather, allowing England to evacuate its European Expeditionary Force in the face of what seemed to be certain destruction by Adolf Hitler's encircling panzer divisions. On that day many in England were praying the very words of this psalm. "O Lord, save the king!" they prayed. And God did.

In 1989–90 Westerners were astounded by the radical political changes in Eastern Europe. Country after country repudiated its seventy-two-year communist heritage, replaced its leaders with democratically elected officials, and provided new personal freedoms. It was amazing and impressive. But the changes in the Eastern Bloc came about less by the will of one person, Mikhail Gorbachev or any other, than by a spiritual hunger and genuine trust in God by the long-oppressed people.

The strength of the Solidarity movement in Poland, where the breakthrough first came, was that of the Roman Catholic Church. Pope John Paul II had been a strong supporter of the people's faith and dreams.

Spiritual strength also lay behind the victories in East Germany. Conventional wisdom in Germany has it that the turning point was on October 9, when seventy thousand demonstrators marched in Leipzig. The army was placed on full alert, and under normal circumstances it would have attacked the demonstrators violently. But the protesters cried, "Let them shoot, we will still march." It was a spiritual statement. The army did not attack, and after that the protests grew until the government itself was overthrown.

In Romania, where President Nicolae Ceausescu just weeks before had declared that apple trees would bear pears before socialism would be endangered in Romania, the end began in the house of a Protestant pastor. His parishioners surrounded him, declaring that they were willing to die rather than let him be arrested by the state police.[10]

Joseph Tson, the founder and president of the Romanian Missionary Society, was in Romania just after the death of Ceausescu and reported the details of the story. The pastor was a Reformed minister in the city of Timisoara. His name was Laszlo Tokes. The secret police wanted to evict him from the town to eliminate his influence, but the members of the church took up a vigil around his house to prevent it. On Saturday, December 16, 1989, hundreds and then thousands of people joined these brave parishioners. One was a twenty-four-year-old Baptist church worker who got the idea of distributing candles to the ever-growing multitude. He lit his candle, and then the others lit theirs. This transformed the protective strategy into a contagious demonstration, the beginning of the revolution. The next day, when the secret police opened fire on the people, the young man was shot in the leg. The doctors had to amputate his leg. But on his hospital bed this young man told his pastor, "I lost a leg, but I am happy. I lit the first light."

Many Romanians do not call the events of December 1989 a national revolution. They say rather, "Call it God's miracle."[11]

If "every good and perfect gift" comes from the Lord, as the Bible says it does (James 1:17), then freedom also comes from him, and the nation that seeks it will receive it in God's time. On the other hand, a country that forgets God will be overwhelmed by tyranny. Our country, in spite of its genuinely religious roots, seems hell-bent on doing just that.

A Summary Petition

Psalm 20 closes with a summary petition in verse 9: "O LORD, save the king! Answer us when we call!" Here is an Old Testament text telling us to pray for the men and women God sets over us, just as the New Testament also instructs, saying, "I urge, then, first of all, that requests, prayers, intercession and thanksgiving be made for everyone—for kings and all those in authority, that we may live peaceful and quiet lives in all godliness and holiness. This is good, and pleases God our Savior" (1 Tim. 2:1–3).

So let us be faithful to do it. Let us pray for all leaders. And as we do, let us also pray that God will give us godly leaders. Let us pray that he will make us into the kind of people who can produce such leaders, who are willing to elect them to office, and then who follow them as they faithfully urge us to follow after God and his righteousness.

Psalm 21

A Day of
National Thanksgiving

O LORD, the king rejoices in your strength.
How great is his joy in the victories you give!
You have granted him the desire of his heart
and have not withheld the request of his lips. Selah
You welcomed him with rich blessings
and placed a crown of pure gold on his head.
He asked you for life, and you gave it to him—
length of days, for ever and ever.
Through the victories you gave, his glory is great;
you have bestowed on him splendor and majesty.
Surely you have granted him eternal blessings
and made him glad with the joy of your presence.
For the king trusts in the LORD;
through the unfailing love of the Most High
he will not be shaken.

Your hand will lay hold on all your enemies;
your right hand will seize your foes.
At the time of your appearing
you will make them like a fiery furnace.
In his wrath the LORD will swallow them up,
and his fire will consume them.

You will destroy their descendants from the earth,
   their posterity from mankind.
Though they plot evil against you
   and devise wicked schemes, they cannot succeed;
for you will make them turn their backs
   when you aim at them with drawn bow.

Be exalted, O LORD, in your strength;
   we will sing and praise your might.

                                              verses 1–13

I t is not always easy to show connec-
tions between the psalms, and often, perhaps usually, no connections exist.
This is not true of Psalms 20 and 21. As I showed at the beginning of the
last chapter, Psalm 20 is a prayer for God's deliverance of Israel's king on
the occasion of an impending battle. It is a prayer for victory. The twenty-
first psalm is a prayer of national thanksgiving for that deliverance.

It is not just the subject matter that links these two psalms, however. They
are linked by deliberately repeated words and by the psalms' form. In the
last chapter I pointed out how the closing words of Psalm 20 are picked up
at the start of Psalm 21. The earlier psalm says, "O LORD, save the king!
Answer us when we call!" (v. 9). The following psalm begins "O LORD, the
king . . . ," after which it tells how God answered the earlier petitions (v. 1).
There are other echoes of the first psalm in the second. Psalm 20:4 asked
God to give David the desire of his heart. Psalm 21:2 says, "You have granted
him the desire of his heart." Psalm 20:5 says, "May the LORD grant all your
requests." Psalm 21:2 answers, "You . . . have not withheld the request of his
lips." Psalm 20:7 says, "Some trust in chariots and some in horses, but we
trust in the name of the LORD our God." The twenty-first psalm declares,
"the king trusts in the LORD." Therefore, "he will not be shaken" (v. 7).

Even the structures of the two psalms show a linking similarity. Each consists of two longer stanzas in which words are addressed either to the Lord
or the king, followed by a concluding couplet of one verse in which the
people either call upon or praise God. It is hard to find a more deliberately
matched pair of psalms in all the Psalter.

The Importance of Giving Thanks

There is something to be learned by the mere existence of this psalm,
even before we begin to study it in detail, and that is the importance for us
of giving thanks. Generally we do not find it particularly hard to pray when
we are in trouble. Even unbelievers will pray in times of sickness, danger,
financial loss, or other hardship. "O God, what am I going to do?" they will

say. We do the same, though with a greater knowledge of who God is and what he has promised to do for his children. It is much harder to pray after God intervenes to help, rescue, or save us, as he often does. The fact that Psalms 20 and 21 were written together and are carefully linked shows that the Jews of this far-off day realized the importance and necessity of being thankful always.

Jesus did too. He also recognized how we easily neglect thanking God after he intervenes for us. We remember that on one occasion, when Jesus was traveling to Jerusalem along the border between Samaria and Galilee, he was met by ten lepers. They asked him to have pity on them, which he did. He told them to show themselves to the priests, which they would be required to do eventually in order to receive formal certification that they had been cleansed of this normally fatal disease, and as they went on their way they were healed. All were delighted, of course. It was a literal reprieve from death. But only one was thankful. He was a Samaritan. He returned to Jesus, fell at his feet, and thanked him profusely.

Jesus then asked those who were standing by, "Were not all ten cleansed? Where are the other nine? Was no one found to return and give praise to God except this foreigner?" (Luke 17:11–19).

Since Psalm 21 is a prayer of *national* thanksgiving, it suggests another illustration. The great poet Rudyard Kipling was asked to write a poem to celebrate the sixtieth anniversary of the reign of Queen Victoria in 1897. It had been a splendid occasion. High government officials and soldiers from all over the empire had assembled in London, along with nearly two hundred ships of the Royal Navy. They had come through a great century, and everyone was now praising England and her queen. But Kipling wrote,

> God of our fathers, known of old,
> Lord of our far-flung battle line,
> Beneath whose awful hand we hold
> Dominion over palm and pine—
> Lord God of hosts, be with us yet,
> Lest we forget—lest we forget!

> Far-called, our navies melt away;
> On dune and headland sinks the fire:
> Lo, all our pomp of yesterday
> Is one with Nineveh and Tyre!
> Judge of the Nations, spare us yet,
> Lest we forget—lest we forget![1]

Kipling understood that nations, like individuals, forget God and need always to be reminded to thank him. But he was not liked for having said so. In fact, popular opinion had it that Kipling was passed by in the search for a new poet laureate because of this "Recessional."

Thanksgiving for Past Victories

The first section of Psalm 21 (vv. 1–7) corresponds to the first section of Psalm 20. In the earlier psalm the people were addressing themselves to their king but were in effect asking God to hear the king's prayers and grant victory in the battle that was coming. The first section of Psalm 21 is an explicit prayer, directed to God to give thanks for the victory. That is why verse 5 is written in the past tense, referring to "the victories you gave."

Who is speaking in this section? This is not so easy to determine. It could be the king himself, speaking in the third person, as kings do. Derek Kidner thinks it is the king.[2] It could be someone speaking for the king, a priest, for example. P. C. Craigie suggests this possibility.[3] It could also be the people themselves, the congregation. The majority of commentators probably incline this way, and in fact, there is nothing in the psalm that could not have been spoken by the worshiping congregation. The fact that the people are speaking at the start of Psalm 20 suggests that they may also be speaking at the start of this one. It *is* reasonably clear that they are the ones speaking at the end, since the last verse uses the first person plural pronoun: "*we* will sing and praise your might" (italics added).

What are the specific blessings for which the people (or king) give thanks in this section? There are six of them, one in each of the first six verses.

Victory through God's strength (v. 1). The previous psalm had asked for victory, not through chariots and horses in which the heathen trust but in the name and by the power of God. This is precisely the blessing God gave.

It is not wrong to emphasize victory above the other items also listed, items 2–6, since victory is what was fervently prayed for earlier and since it is mentioned in this psalm, not only in verse 1 ("How great is his [the king's] joy in the victories you give!") but also in verse 5 ("Through the victories you gave, his glory is great"). Craigie says, "The military victory which the king appeared to win in battle was in reality the victory which God, in his might, had granted."[4]

Answered prayer (v. 2). The king had been praying for victory. But here, in addition to thanking God for the victory itself, Psalm 21:2 also thanks God simply for answering prayer. Thus, the specific answer of granting victory becomes merely one example of the many answers God gives in response to his people's earnest petitions. This broadens the psalm to include the kind of prayer answers you or I may have received from God.

Rich blessings associated with the crown (v. 3). The welcome of verse 3 must be the welcome David received upon returning from battle with Israel's enemies, if the context is to be taken into account. But if it is, then, since the crown is mentioned in the parallel half of the couplet, the "rich blessings" would be those associated with the king's rule over his kingdom. Our equivalent would be whatever blessings come to us as benefits of the work God has given us to do for him: good income from a good job, the appreciation of fellow workers, friends, and other such things. Are we grateful for these things? Do we thank God for them?

Length of days (v. 4). That the king should thank God for length of days is not surprising. This is something anyone might pray for, and David did indeed have a long life. He lived to be seventy. The surprising thing is the phrase "for ever and ever." How is a phrase like that to be understood? There are three possibilities.

First, it might be simple court hyperbole: "O king, live forever!" (cf. Dan. 2:4). The problem with this explanation is that it is more suited to a pagan environment than to the court of a king of Israel. Also, the verse is not a wish that the king might live forever, however exaggerated that might be, but a statement that God *has* in fact granted him "length of days, for ever and ever."

Second, it might be a reference to the watershed promise of 2 Samuel 7 in which God promised David that his house would last forever: "Your house and your kingdom will endure forever before me; your throne will be established forever" (v. 16). The "length of days" would be fulfilled not merely in David's long life but in the duration of his dynasty.

Third, it may be a reference to the messiah. The promise of God to David in 2 Samuel 7 would itself bear this out, for even there the perpetuity of David's throne is to be established ultimately, not by any mere man but by David's divine descendant, Jesus Christ. But in addition, the twenty-first psalm has other messianic elements. Like many of the psalms containing strong statements about the character or future victories of Israel's king, this one contains statements that can only have their true fulfillment in the Messiah.

Besides, consider this interesting fact. The ancient Jewish Targum (the Chaldean paraphrase of the Old Testament) and Talmud render the word *king* in verse 1 by *melek mashiach* (King Messiah), which means that the Jews in an early period understood these words to be spoken of the Messiah. A change came in the Middle Ages as a result of a judgment by Rabbi Solomon Isaaci, known as Rashi (b. A.D. 1040). He endorsed the early view but suggested it be dropped, saying, "Our old doctors interpreted this psalm of King Messiah, but in order to meet the Schismatics [that is, the Christians] it is better to understand it of David himself."[5]

In my judgment, this is merely another case in which we find ideas in the psalms that go beyond any imagined contemporary context. Though they may not always have been recognized as such, they are prophetic of the one who was to come. The next psalm, Psalm 22, is about Jesus entirely.

Glory, splendor, and majesty (v. 5). The fifth blessing for which the people (or king) thank God is that glory, splendor, and majesty have come to David as a result of his victories. In light of the previous verse, it is hard not to think of this in terms of the superlative glory given to Jesus Christ because of his victories over sin on the cross and over death by his resurrection.

The joy of God's presence (v. 6). The last of these blessings is a partial present enjoyment of the blessings of the future age, described as the joy of God's presence.

The Covenant-Keeping God

The New International Version is probably right to place verse 7 at the end of the first stanza of this psalm since it, like the preceding verses, speaks of the king in the third person (i.e., "he will not be shaken"). But verse 7 breaks the pattern somewhat and is clearly also a transition verse. Verse 7 is a bridge from the past victory or victories celebrated in verses 1–6 to the future victories anticipated in verses 8–12. It bridges these two sections by referring to the covenant relationship that had been established by God with the people.

Verse 7 is rich with covenant language, particularly the two words *hesed* (translated "unfailing love" or, in other versions, "lovingkindness") and *botah,* meaning "trust." The first describes God's part in the covenant. It is eternal and unchangeable. The second describes the king's and the people's parts. It is something that needs to be renewed constantly.[6]

We cannot read these words without again being made to think of Jesus Christ. He alone can be said utterly to have trusted God and thus never to have been shaken. Alexander Maclaren summarizes this well:

> These daring anticipations are too exuberant to be realized in any but One, whose victory was achieved in the hour of apparent defeat; whose conquest was both his salvation and God's; who prays knowing that he is always heard; who is King of men because he endured the cross—and wears the crown of pure gold because he did not refuse the crown of thorns; who liveth for evermore, having been given by the Father to have life in himself; who is the outshining of the Father's glory, and has all power granted unto him; who is the source of all blessing to all, who dwells in the joy to which he will welcome his servants; and who himself lived and conquered by the life of faith, and so became the first leader of the long line of those who have trusted and have therefore stood fast.[7]

Thanksgiving for Future Victories

The second stanza of Psalm 21 also corresponds to the second stanza of Psalm 20, though there are some differences. In Psalm 20 the speaker is apparently an individual, and while this could be the case in Psalm 21, it is not made explicit. In Psalm 20 the speaker uses the present tense, anticipating the victory that has been prayed for and is expected to be given. In Psalm 21 the tense is future, anticipating the victories yet to come.[8] Yet in spite of these differences, the tone of the two sections is very much alike. Both express confidence that God will protect the king and people in coming days as he has done in the past. In Psalm 21 this confidence follows naturally on the reference to the covenant in verse 7.

The only real problem with this section is the identity of the person being addressed ("you" and "your"), but it is not important. The person could be the king, in which case the stanza would mean that God would give him power over his enemies so they might be completely overthrown. Future victories would complete the work begun. Or the person could be God himself, in which case the stanza means that God will achieve this final victory. In the final analysis, the debate involves a distinction without a difference, because in any case it is God who works through the king.

Whatever the proper identity of the person addressed in verses 8–12 may be, there is no doubt at all about the one addressed in the final verse, which is where the psalm ends. He is God alone, all attention now being directed upward from man and anything man can do to God and God's strength.

> Be exalted, O LORD, in your strength;
> we will sing and praise your might.

We need to learn from this as Christians, particularly in respect to our prayers for political and church leaders. Usually, we make one of two errors in regard to them. Either we have little or no respect for them and do not value them, which we show by failing to pray for them. Or else we think too highly of them and are therefore disillusioned or crushed when we discover in time that they are only mere sinful human beings, as we are.

We would not do either if we would follow the pattern set by Psalms 20 and 21. Psalm 20 is a prayer for the leader God has given. The people value him and want his plans to succeed. They know that his success is their success, his victory is their victory. Since no one can succeed without God's help and intervention, they are faithful in their prayers for him. Psalm 21 thanks God for this intervention, and it rightly focuses on him, not the king. In both the intercession and the thanksgiving the people see their leader in the proper light and do what they should do in the exercise of their own spiritual and civic responsibility.

"O LORD, save the king!" Bless our leaders. Prosper them. Give success to their projects. But also, "Be exalted, O LORD, in your strength." This means that ultimately only God will be exalted and that the successes of our leaders and of us as a people will only come when we are all faithfully and consistently serving him.

Psalm 22

The Psalm of
the Cross: Part 1

The Suffering Savior

My God, my God, why have you forsaken me?
 Why are you so far from saving me,
  so far from the words of my groaning?
O my God, I cry out by day, but you do not answer,
 by night, and am not silent.

Yet you are enthroned as the Holy One;
 you are the praise of Israel.
In you our fathers put their trust;
 they trusted and you delivered them.
They cried to you and were saved;
 in you they trusted and were not disappointed.

But I am a worm and not a man,
 scorned by men and despised by the people.

All who see me mock me;
*   they hurl insults, shaking their heads:*
"He trusts in the LORD;
*   let the LORD rescue him.*
Let him deliver him,
*   since he delights in him."*

verses 1–8

But you, O LORD, be not far off;
*   O my Strength, come quickly to help me.*

verse 19

The Lord Jesus Christ is described as his people's shepherd in three ways. In John 10:11 and 14 he is "the good shepherd," who gives his life for his sheep. In Hebrews 13:20 he is "that great Shepherd," who has risen from the dead and lives now to direct his people in every good work. In 1 Peter 5:4 he is "the Chief Shepherd," who has ascended into heaven from whence he will one day return to reward the undershepherds of the church who have been faithful to him. It has been pointed out that Psalms 22, 23, and 24 show a progression similar to those passages. Psalm 22 is the song of the dying Shepherd, crying out to the Father from the cross. Psalm 23 is the song of the risen Shepherd, guiding his sheep through life's dark wilderness. Psalm 24 is the song of the ascended Shepherd who will reward those who have served faithfully.

It is possible that some may find this pattern a bit forced, of course, particularly in regard to the last two psalms. But there can be no doubt that it applies strikingly to the twenty-second psalm. For Psalm 22 is the "Psalm of the Cross," the best description in all the Bible of Jesus Christ's crucifixion.

Most modern writers on the psalms try to find a setting for them either in the life of David, if they believe David was their author, or in the experience of some later writer or group of persons. But it is impossible to do this with this psalm. Some psalms are written out of illness. But Psalm 22 is not a description of an illness. It is a description of an execution, particularly a crucifixion. Crucifixion was not practiced in the time of David or for many long centuries afterward. So this is not an account of suffering endured by any ancient person but a prophetic picture of the suffering to be endured by Jesus when he died to pay the penalty for our sins. In other words, it is prophetic and entirely messianic.

Derek Kidner, who is usually cautious in such matters, nevertheless writes, correctly, "No incident recorded of David can begin to account for this. . . . The language of the psalm defies a naturalistic explanation; the best account is in the terms used by Peter concerning another psalm of

David: 'Being therefore a prophet, . . . he foresaw and spoke of . . . the Christ' (Acts 2:30f.)."[1]

The Hours of Darkness

But it is not only that David, being a prophet, foresaw and spoke in this psalm of Jesus' sufferings. This is also the psalm upon which Jesus seems to have meditated as he hung on the cross.

We can best profit from our study if we have the main events in mind. Jesus had been arrested the previous night and had been kept under guard in the house of the high priest in order to be tried formally by the Sanhedrin in the morning. When day dawned he was quickly tried, convicted of blasphemy, and then taken to Pilate's Jerusalem residence for sentencing, since the Jewish court was unable to carry out the death penalty while Rome ruled Palestine. There were unexpected delays with Pilate. But at last his judgment was secured, and Jesus was led through the streets of the city to Golgotha bearing his cross.

What was he thinking of? He seems to have been thinking of other people. When Jesus saw the women weeping after him he said, "Do not weep for me; weep for yourselves and for your children," and he prophesied of the terrible days to come (Luke 23:28–31). When the soldiers drove the nails through his hands and feet to affix him to the rough wooden cross he prayed, "Father, forgive them, for they do not know what they are doing" (Luke 23:34). He had words for the dying thief: "I tell you the truth, today you will be with me in paradise" (Luke 23:43). He entrusted his mother to John's safekeeping, saying, "Dear woman, here is your son," and to John, "Here is your mother" (John 19:26–27). In none of these sentences did Jesus seem to be thinking of himself at all. He was thinking entirely of others.

This changed at noon. At noon a great darkness came over the land which lasted until three o'clock. The darkness was sent by the Father to shield Jesus during the hours he was made sin for us. These were private hours. It is as if God had shut the bronze doors of heaven upon Jesus so that what transpired during those hours happened between himself and Jesus alone.

What was Jesus thinking of during these three hours? There is no reason why we should have to know this, of course. God could have kept silent about it. But there are three important clues in the New Testament accounts.

First, at the beginning of this period Jesus suddenly cried out, "*Eloi, Eloi, lama sabachthani,*" which means, "My God, my God, why have you forsaken me?" (Matt. 27:46; Mark 15:34). It was a direct, explicit, and completely appropriate quotation from the first verse of Psalm 22. Second, John tells us that Jesus, "knowing that all was now completed, and so that the Scripture would be fulfilled . . . said, 'I am thirsty,'" as a result of which the soldiers offered him wine vinegar on a sponge (John 19:28). The only Old Testament

Scripture this could possibly refer to is Psalm 69:21, a psalm very similar to Psalm 22, which shows that Jesus was apparently thinking through these Old Testament texts. Moreover, since John says this was "so that the Scripture would be fulfilled," Jesus seems to have been deliberately reviewing these passages in his mind to be sure that he had fulfilled them completely. Third, at the end of the period of darkness, just before he died, Jesus called out, "It is finished" (John 19:30). This is a quotation from the last verse of Psalm 22. In our text that verse reads, "he has done it," referring to God as subject. But there is no object for the verb in Hebrew, and it can equally well be translated, "It is finished."

Putting these clues together, we can be fairly certain that Jesus was meditating on the Old Testament during the hours of his suffering and that he saw his crucifixion as a fulfillment of Psalm 22 particularly.

Psalm 22 begins with a description of Christ's alienation from the Father, as he was made sin for us. It continues with a vivid description of the crucifixion itself. It ends with triumph, as the suffering One tells how his prayer was heard and affirms that he will declare the name of God and praise God before his brethren and in the great assembly. Since Jesus ended his earthly life by quoting the last verse of this psalm, it means that he did not die in despair, as some, like Albert Schweitzer, have supposed he did. Rather, he died in triumph, knowing that the atonement was perfect and fully accepted by God and therefore that countless future generations of sinful people would be saved because of it.

Charles Haddon Spurgeon tells of a book, *Christ on the Cross*, by a man named J. Stevenson. It is a study of Psalm 22 and contains a sermon for every verse, thirty-one in all. I will not follow his example. However, because there is a turning point at the end of verse 21, I will divide this study into two chapters, one on each of the psalm's two sections.

The Suffering Savior

The most important (and most noticeable) feature of verses 1–21 is the alternating pattern of thought in the six sections. I identify these as verses 1–2, 3–5, 6–8, 9–11, 12–18, and 19–21. The first, third, and fifth sections describe the author's suffering. The second, fourth, and sixth are prayers to God. As the pattern progresses, the intensity of the anguish decreases (at least, it becomes only physical rather than spiritual and psychological), and the author's confidence in God moves upward or intensifies. Notice how it works out.

Christ's Cry of Dereliction (vv. 1–2)

The most poignant verse in the entire psalm is the first, and this is also the most disturbing section. For here the suffering One cries out to God, believing that he has been forsaken by him, asking why he has been forsaken, and asserting that God is silent. He receives no answer.

The idea that Jesus could be forsaken by God has been so disturbing to so many people that various theories have been invented to explain it. Some have supposed that Jesus was referring to the psalm only to call attention to it, as if to say that what he was suffering was what the psalm describes. Others have argued that Jesus felt forsaken, when in fact he was not. In the final outcome, of course, Jesus was not forsaken. This is what the psalm as a whole shows. Besides, we know that the crucifixion was followed by the resurrection. All this aside, however, I do not hesitate to say that, according to the teaching of the New Testament, Jesus was indeed forsaken by God while he bore the sin of his people on the cross. This is the very essence of the atonement—Jesus bearing our hell in order that we might share his heaven. To be forsaken means to have the light of God's countenance and the sense of his presence eclipsed, which is what happened to Jesus as he bore the wrath of God against sin for us.

How could this happen? How could one member of the eternal Trinity turn his back on another member of the Trinity? I do not know. I cannot explain it. But I believe that this is what the Bible teaches, so great was the love of God for us and so great was the price Jesus willingly paid to save us from our iniquities.

Memory of the Past, Part One (vv. 3–5)

There are two ways of looking at the second section. Since it calls attention to God's deliverance of the fathers, who trusted him in past days, it could be viewed as a bitter irony, that is, "You delivered them, but you have not delivered me; I am forsaken." However, the verses can also be seen as a desperate grasping for encouragement by a recollection of God's true character. God is utterly holy or righteous, says the psalmist. He is "the Holy One" (v. 3). Because of this quality, God has always shown himself faithful to those in the past who trusted him. "Will he not therefore also be faithful to me and deliver me, even though I am forsaken now?" the psalmist seems to be asking. In my judgment, the flow of the psalm suggests the second of these possibilities as the right one.

The Mockery of the Crucifixion (vv. 6–8)

The third of these six sections moves from the earlier sense of having been abandoned by God to the scorn of the people, who mock him on this basis: "He trusts in the LORD; let the LORD rescue him. Let him deliver him, since he delights in him" (v. 8). These words, as well as the gestures that accompanied them, were reproduced precisely at the crucifixion: "Those who passed by hurled insults at him, shaking their heads and saying, 'You who are going to destroy the temple and build it in three days, save yourself! Come down from the cross, if you are the Son of God!' In the same way the chief priests, the teachers of the law and the elders mocked him. 'He saved others,' they said, 'but he can't save himself! He's the King of Israel!

Let him come down now from the cross, and we will believe in him. He trusts in God. Let God rescue him now if he wants him, for he said, "I am the Son of God""" (Matt. 27:39–43).

Memory of the Past, Part Two (vv. 9–11)

The second stanza was a memory of God's past faithfulness to and deliverance of the fathers, just as the fourth stanza is also a memory. But here the sufferer has moved forward a notch in his thinking, since his memory now is not of God's faithfulness to those others only but of God's former faithfulness to himself. "From my mother's womb you have been my God," says the psalmist (v. 10). Will God not continue to be faithful to me now?

The Physical Suffering (vv. 12–18)

In some ways the most striking section of all is this one, in which the crucifixion seems to be remarkably portrayed. It is worth quoting the note on this in the well-known Scofield Reference Bible, prepared by C. I. Scofield.

> Psalm 22 is a graphic picture of death by crucifixion. The bones (of the hands, arms, shoulders, and pelvis) out of joint (v. 14); the profuse perspiration caused by intense suffering (v. 14); the action of the heart affected (v. 14); strength exhausted, and extreme thirst (v. 15); the hands and feet pierced (see v. 16 . . .); partial nudity with the hurt to modesty (v. 17), are all associated with that mode of death. The accompanying circumstances are precisely those fulfilled in the crucifixion of Christ. The desolate cry of v. 1 (Mt. 27:46); the periods of light and darkness of v. 2 (Mt. 27:45); the contemptuous and humiliating treatment of vv. 6–8, 12–13 (Mt. 27:39–44); the casting lots of v. 18 (Mt. 27:35), were all literally fulfilled. When it is remembered that crucifixion was a Roman, not Jewish, form of execution, the proof of inspiration is irresistible.[2]

Not only the physical aspects of crucifixion are described in these verses, however. The section also depicts those abusing the sufferer as "strong bulls of Bashan," "roaring lions," and "dogs," and suggests (although obliquely) why people do such things to one another. Derek Kidner lists the reasons: "resentment at those who make high claims (v. 8); the compulsion of crowd mentality (vv. 12, 16a; cf. Exod. 23:2); greed, even for trivial gains (v. 18); and perverted tastes—enjoying a harrowing spectacle (v. 17) simply because sin is murderous, and sinners have hatred in them (cf. John 8:44)."[3]

A special word should be said about verse 16, which is translated, "they have pierced my hands and my feet." The word *pierced* is the most striking indication of a crucifixion in the entire psalm, but it is well known that the Masoretic (or vowel-pointed) text of the Middle Ages does not actually read "pierced." As it stands, the word in the text should be rendered "as a lion."

A translator must always be careful how he or she disagrees with the Masoretic text, particularly when there is no explicit textual variant to base an alternative translation on. Yet in this case there seems to be good reason for doing so. For one thing, the Septuagint (Greek) translation of the Old Testament, produced a century or two before the Christian era and therefore an unbiased witness, rendered the word "pierced." Second, the other major versions also translate the Hebrew this way. Third, the meaning "as a lion" has little sense in the context and leaves the phrase in question without an explicit verb (it would have to be supplied from the preceding line). This suggests that the Masoretic text with its vowel pointing is just wrong and that alternative vowels should be supplied.

It may even suggest that the Masoretic text was deliberately pointed in the way it was by later Jewish scholars to avoid what otherwise would be a nearly inescapable prophecy of Jesus' crucifixion.[4]

The Turning Point (vv. 19–21)

The climax of the first part of Psalm 22 and the turning point between part one and part two comes in verses 19–21, as the suffering Savior finds his communion with God restored.

Yet the change is abrupt in spite of the steady progress from despair to renewed trust. Strangely, the New International Version does not capture this well. It ends the section with the words "save me from the horns of the wild oxen." But the verb translated "save me" literally means "you have heard" (see NIV note), and it is held to the end so that the final couplet should actually read:

> Rescue me from the mouth of the lions,
>   from the horns of the wild oxen. You have heard me!

This is a cry of triumph, not despair. It marks the moment at which the period of darkness passes and Jesus, having suffered a true alienation from the Father as punishment for our sins, becomes aware of God's presence and favor once again.

Died He for Me?

At this point the psalm takes on an entirely different tone, as it begins to celebrate the great victory of the cross. That victory is so great and its effects so extensive that it deserves to be explored by itself in the next chapter. But we cannot go on to that discussion without first asking if the atonement described in part one was for you.

In what is probably the greatest of all of Charles Wesley's hymns, that great evangelist and poet of the Methodist church asks:

> And can it be that I should gain
>   An interest in the Savior's blood?

> Died he for me, who caused his pain?
> For me, who him to death pursued?

That possibility was so wonderful to Wesley that he composed the entire hymn around it, describing such love as "amazing" and the death itself as a "mystery" beyond the ability even of angels to fathom. But though he could not exhaust its meaning or ever cease to marvel at such love, Wesley knew that it was indeed for him that Christ died and that his only hope of salvation lay in that atonement.

> 'Tis mercy all, immense and free;
> For, O my God, it found out me.

The question is whether it has found out you. It is a wonderful thing to know that Jesus died for sinners. It is amazing to study a prophetic picture of Christ's suffering and death, as we have done. But that can happen, and yet the person who hears can still perish because he or she has not trusted in Jesus personally. Have you? Will you do it?

All you have to do is tell him that you trust him, saying, "Thank you, Jesus, for dying for me. I am ready to follow you as my Lord and Savior." If you will pray that prayer, you will find that Jesus has indeed made atonement for your sins. He was forsaken so you might never be forsaken. He bore your sins so that you might not have to suffer for them.

Psalm 22

The Psalm of
the Cross: Part 2

"It Is Finished"

I will declare your name to my brothers;
  in the congregation I will praise you.
You who fear the LORD, praise him!
  All you descendants of Jacob, honor him!
  Revere him, all you descendants of Israel!
For he has not despised or disdained
  the suffering of the afflicted one;
he has not hidden his face from him
  but has listened to his cry for help.

From you comes the theme of my praise in the great assembly;
  before those who fear you will I fulfill my vows.
The poor will eat and be satisfied;
  they who seek the LORD will praise him—
  may your hearts live forever!
All the ends of the earth
  will remember and turn to the LORD,

and all the families of the nations
  will bow down before him,
for dominion belongs to the LORD
  and he rules over the nations.

All the rich of the earth will feast and worship;
  all who go down to the dust will kneel before him—
  those who cannot keep themselves alive.
Posterity will serve him;
  future generations will be told about the Lord.
They will proclaim his righteousness
  to a people yet unborn—
  for he has done it.

  verses 22–31

 One of the fascinating features of careful Bible study is that we so often come upon statements that are tantalizing but that we cannot fully understand. An example is the well-known statement of Jesus to the Emmaus disciples recorded in Luke 24:27.

The two disciples had been in Jerusalem over the weekend in which Jesus had been arrested, tried, crucified, and resurrected. But although they had received reports from the women who had been to the tomb and seen angels and from Peter and John who had later raced to the tomb and found it empty, they did not believe in the resurrection. So they were on their way home, convinced that their dream that the Messiah had come was over. While they were talking about all that had happened, Jesus drew alongside of them and asked what they were discussing. They replied by telling him about himself, how the leaders of the people had handed him over to be crucified, but how they had hoped that he was the one whom God had appointed to redeem Israel. That is what he had been doing, of course, but they had not understood it.

At this point Jesus could have identified himself, saying, "Look, it's me, Jesus!" But he did not do this. Instead, we are told that "beginning with Moses and all the Prophets, he explained to them what was said in all the Scriptures concerning himself" (v. 27). This was the first Bible study of the Christian era, and it was conducted by Jesus himself on the critical subject of his death and resurrection.

What a fascinating statement! "Beginning with Moses and all the Prophets, he explained to them what was said in all the Scriptures concerning himself." What do you suppose those Scriptures were? Don't you wish you could have been there to have heard him select those texts and provide their explanations?

I find this verse stimulating because it sets me thinking about the Old Testament as prophesying Christ's death and resurrection, which is certainly the most profound of all ways to understand it. Yet it is not an easy train of thought. Some passages are obvious prophecies: Isaiah 53, for example. Others are less obvious. One passage that is clearly a prophecy of the Lord's death and resurrection is Psalm 22. It is so clearly a picture of death by crucifixion and a triumph to follow that it is not possible to explain it by anything any mere human being in the Old Testament period may have suffered. David suffered through many hard times, but he never experienced anything like this. Therefore, Psalm 22 is a portrait of the death and triumph of Jesus Christ alone, and it must have been one of the texts Jesus picked out and explained to his two disciples on the famous walk from Jerusalem to Emmaus on Easter Sunday morning.

One older commentator says, "Unnatural as I cannot help thinking that interpretation is which assumes that the psalmist himself never felt the sorrows which he describes, nor the thankfulness which he utters, but only put himself into the place of the Messiah who was to come—I hold that to be a far worse error which sees here no foreshadowing of Christ at all. Indeed, the coincidence between the sufferings of the psalmist and the sufferings of Christ is so remarkable, that it is very surprising that anyone should deny or question the relation[ship]."[1]

Jesus and His Brothers

But it is not only by a process of reasoning that we must identify Psalm 22 as a prophecy of Jesus' death and resurrection. As we study the New Testament, we also find that this is its explicit teaching.

Hebrews 2:12 quotes Psalm 22:22, referring the verse to Jesus. In this important chapter of Hebrews the author is teaching the superiority of Jesus to the angels, a theme begun in chapter 1. Jesus is superior because he is God's Son and not merely a servant, as an angel is. He is superior because he has been appointed ruler of an everlasting kingdom. All things have been subjected to him. Now, however, having stressed his superiority to all other created beings in those ways, the author of Hebrews shows that Jesus has also become the Savior of his people by becoming like them and making them members of his own family. This is the point at which he quotes Psalm 22:22. "Both the one who makes men holy and those who are made holy are of the same family. So Jesus is not ashamed to call them brothers. He says,

'I will declare your name to my brothers;
   in the presence of the congregation I will sing
     your praises'" (Heb. 2:11–12).

The quotation tells us how to interpret the psalm. It tells us that Jesus is the speaker, not just in this verse but throughout. And it tells us that the "brothers" (and sisters) of the psalm's second half are those for whom he died and rose again.

An Expanding Congregation

At the beginning of the last chapter I pointed out how, during the early phases of the crucifixion, the attention of the Lord was on other people: the women who had followed him to Golgotha weeping, the soldiers who nailed him to the cross, the believing thief who was crucified with him, his mother, Mary, who was present at the cross, and John, the beloved disciple. I showed how this changed as the three hours of darkness in which Jesus was made sin for us and was punished for our sin settled over the land. These were private hours in which Jesus agonized over his abandonment by his Father and cried out to be heard.

But Jesus was heard. The very last phrase of verse 21 declares it: "you have heard (or answered)."[2] This verse marks a great turning point in the psalm, a turning point which must be associated with the passing of the period of darkness. In the context of the crucifixion, Jesus has not yet died. That comes after the final sentence of the psalm, where Jesus said, "It is finished," which is what verse 31 means. At that point the curtain of the temple that separated the Holy Place from the Most Holy Place was torn in two from top to bottom, signifying that full atonement for sin had been made; Jesus cried out, "Father, into your hands I commit my spirit" (Luke 23:46); and Jesus died. But before this Jesus was already assured that his Father had heard him, that his atonement was accepted, and that untold generations of people would be saved and would become his brothers and sisters because of what he suffered.

The second half of Psalm 22 is thus a throbbing, soaring anticipation of the expanding proclamation of the gospel and of the growing and triumphant Christian church. It is represented in three phases.

My brothers (vv. 22–24). The first phase concerns the Jewish people. In themselves the words "my brothers" could be understood of all who should come to believe in Jesus Christ, both Jew and Gentile. But the parallel phrases in verse 23 ("you descendants of Jacob" and "you descendants of Israel") make clear that in this stanza they have a more restricted meaning. They refer to Jews. If that is so, then "the congregation" of verse 22 must also be the assembly of the Jewish people. It is appropriate that Jesus' words should focus on this body of people first, of course, because the gospel was proclaimed to them first. The principle is: "first for the Jew, then for the Gentile" (Rom. 1:16). Similarly, in Acts 1 the missionary plan for the geographic expansion of the church was unfolded in these stages: "You will be my witnesses in Jerusalem, and in all Judea and Samaria, and to the ends of the earth" (v. 8).

Jesus wanted his Jewish brothers to know that, although he was despised by them, he was not despised or ultimately forsaken by God but was heard

by him. It follows from this that he was not the blasphemer he was accused
of being but rather was who he said he was, namely, the unique Son of God
and the Messiah. Moreover, he accomplished what he said he had come
into the world to achieve, which was an atonement for sins.

The great assembly (vv. 25–29). In verse 22 the psalmist speaks of the "congregation." In verse 25 he speaks of the "great assembly." Actually the words
congregation and *assembly* are the same Hebrew word *(qahal)*, so there is an
expansion of the idea of the assembly from the earlier reference to the second. It expands from Jews alone, who were to be the first target of the missionary endeavor and who would become the first Christians and the
nucleus of the church, to the Gentiles, who were the second missionary target. The parallel phrases in verse 27, "the ends of the earth" and "the families of the nations," make this progression clear.

This was a strong element in the thinking of Jesus Christ. During the
days of his itinerant teaching Jesus often spoke of a great banquet to which
the close friends of a king were invited. But when the day of the feast came
the friends made excuses and refused to come. As a result, the king sent servants to call in other people, some of whom were despised as outcasts (cf.
Matt. 22:1–14; Luke 14:15–24). It was a prophecy of the salvation of the
Gentiles after an initial period of Jewish rejection. The story of the workers
in the vineyard also has the salvation of Gentiles in mind (Matt. 20:1–16).
They are the ones hired last, paid equally, and therefore resented by those
who had labored throughout the day as the Jews had. Most striking perhaps
is Christ's great prayer of John 17, in which he prays for his disciples and for
all "who will believe in me through their message" (v. 20). It is clear from
the rest of the prayer that these new believers would be drawn from the
entire world and would be witnesses to it.

Future generations (v. 30). In the final phase of this prophesied expansion
of the number of those who would come to praise God because of what
Jesus accomplished on the cross, there is a reference to "future generations"
and to "a people yet unborn." In these last verses the psalmist bursts all
bounds, so intent is he on stressing the universal value and world-embracing
proclamation of the gospel. He has spoken of Jew and Gentile, those who
are near and those who are far off. He has embraced the poor (v. 26) and
the rich (v. 29). Now he is thinking of untold generations of people down
to the very end of time.

You and I are included in that number, if we have truly trusted in Jesus
and his death for us. Since this is what Jesus seems to have been thinking of
while he hung on the cross during the three hours of darkness, it means
that he was thinking of you and me just before he committed his spirit to
the Father.

I think that is an absolutely wonderful thought and one that should
move us to the most intent love for and devotion to Jesus Christ. You and I

were in Jesus' thoughts at the very moment of his death. It was for you and me explicitly and for our salvation from sin that he was dying.

"It Is Finished"

The last verse of the psalm contains the words "he has done it" or, as Jesus seems to have understood the sentence in his quotation of these words from the cross, "it is finished" (John 19:30). In Psalm 22 the words are linked to the proclamation of "his [that is, God's] righteousness to a people yet unborn," so we know they concern the gospel. Therefore, what was finished was the atonement by which the righteous demands of God for sin's punishment had been fully satisfied and the righteousness of God was now able to be freely offered to all who would believe on Jesus.

This is an aspect of the atonement that has always figured prominently in Protestant presentations of the meaning of the death of Christ. The Roman Catholic Church (and many unsound Protestant churches, too) maintains that the death of Christ does not relieve the believer from making satisfaction for sins which he or she has committed. More precisely, it distinguishes between sins committed before and after baptism, and between temporal and eternal punishment for those sins. So far as sins committed before baptism are concerned, both the temporal and eternal punishments are blotted out through the application of Christ's death to the individual through baptism. So far as sins committed after baptism are concerned, eternal punishment is blotted out. But the temporal punishments require the making of satisfaction by the individual himself either in this life (through a faithful use of the sacraments and by living a meritorious life) or else in purgatory. Although this system of salvation allows the greater part of the work to be God's and even acknowledges that the faith and merit of the believer are attained by the prevenient grace of God, it nevertheless requires the believer to contribute to his own salvation in some measure. More must be added. The importance of the Mass, in which the sacrifice of Christ is constantly reenacted, is evidence of this outlook.

But this is not right. Consequently, Protestant thought has always contended rightly that "the satisfaction of Christ is the only satisfaction for sin and is so perfect and final that it leaves no penal liability for any sin of the believer."[3]

It is true that Christians often experience chastisement for sins done in this life, though never in full measure for what they deserve. But this is not satisfaction. It is discipline only. It is given that we might grow by it. Even in times of severe chastisement it is still true that "there is now no condemnation for those who are in Christ Jesus" (Rom. 8:1). Similarly, it is also true that the believer is to do good works. We have been ordained to do them (Eph. 2:10). But these are done *because* we are saved, not in order to be saved. Good works flow out of the salvation already accomplished for us by Jesus and as a response to it.

How could it be otherwise? We are not the God-man. Jesus alone is that. We are not saviors. Jesus alone is the Savior. He alone shed his blood on the cross in order that we might be saved from sin. Having done it, he has set his seal upon that perfect and completed work by the declaration: "It is finished." No wonder we sing,

> Jesus paid it all, all to him I owe;
> Sin had left a crimson stain;
> He washed it white as snow.

"But what, then, is left for us to do?" asks someone. Nothing, except to believe in God's word and trust Jesus. Jesus himself said this. When some of the Galileans asked him on the occasion of his multiplication of the loaves and fish, "What must we do to do the works God requires?" Jesus replied, "The work of God is this: to believe in the one he has sent" (John 6:28–29).

Arthur W. Pink tells a story that is helpful at this point. A Christian farmer was concerned about an unsaved neighbor who was a carpenter. The farmer had been trying to explain the gospel to his friend, particularly that the death of Jesus had accomplished everything that was needed for him to be saved. But the carpenter kept insisting that he had to do something for himself.

"Jesus did it all," said the farmer.

"I must have to do something," said the carpenter.

One day the farmer asked his friend to make a gate for him, and when it was finished he came for it and carried it away in his wagon. He hung it on a fence in his field and then arranged for the carpenter to stop by to see that it was hung properly. The carpenter came at the time arranged. But when he arrived he was surprised to see the farmer standing by with a sharp axe in his hand. "What is that for?" he asked.

"I'm going to add a few cuts to your work," was the answer.

"But there's no need to do that," the carpenter protested. "The gate is perfect as it is. There is no need to do anything to it." Nevertheless, the farmer took the axe and began to strike the gate with it. He kept at it until, within a very short time, the gate was ruined. "Look what you've done," said the carpenter. "You've ruined my work."

"Yes," said his friend. "And that is exactly what you are trying to do. You are trying to ruin the work of Christ by your own miserable additions to it." According to Pink, God used the lesson to show the man his mistake, and he was led to trust Christ who had died for him.[4]

"You Shall Be My Witnesses"

The final section of Psalm 22 describes the attitudes of those who enter into this salvation. It is for all types of people—Jew and Gentile, near and far, rich and poor, living and yet to be born. But it is nevertheless also only for those who humble themselves and trust Jesus. The psalm shows that it is for those who "fear [that is, reverence] the LORD" (vv. 23, 25), "seek the LORD" (v. 26), "remember and turn to the LORD" (v. 27), and "bow down [or kneel] before him" (vv. 27, 29). The problem is not the sufficiency of the atonement. Christ's work is utterly sufficient. The problem is our own stiff necks and hard hearts.

But there is this element too: those who believe will also be witnesses. At the start of this section Jesus said that he would declare the name of God to his brothers. But here, as the psalm closes, it is the future generations who will come to Christ who have become his witnesses: "They will proclaim his righteousness to a people yet unborn." That is our task. To trust and tell others—until Jesus comes again.

Psalm 23

The Shepherd's Psalm

*The L*ORD *is my shepherd, I shall not be in want.*
He makes me lie down in green pastures,
he leads me beside quiet waters,
he restores my soul.
He guides me in paths of righteousness
for his name's sake.
Even though I walk
through the valley of the shadow of death,
I will fear no evil,
for you are with me;
your rod and your staff,
they comfort me.

You prepare a table before me
in the presence of my enemies.
You anoint my head with oil;
my cup overflows.
Surely goodness and love will follow me
all the days of my life,
*and I will dwell in the house of the L*ORD
forever.

verses 1–6

T he twenty-third psalm is the most beloved of the 150 psalms in the Psalter and possibly the best-loved (and best-known) chapter in the entire Bible. The great Baptist preacher Charles Haddon Spurgeon called it "the pearl of psalms."[1] Nineteenth-century preacher and commentator J. J. Stewart Perowne observed that "there is no psalm in which the absence of all doubt, misgiving, fear [and] anxiety is so remarkable."[2] Alexander Maclaren said that "the world could spare many a large book better than this sunny little psalm. It has dried many tears and supplied the mould into which many hearts have poured their peaceful faith."[3]

Millions of people have memorized this psalm, even those who have learned few other Scripture portions. Ministers have used it to comfort people who are going through severe personal trials, suffering illness, or dying. For some, the words of this psalm have been the last they have uttered in life.

"The Lord Is My Shepherd"

The psalm is a masterpiece throughout. But if ever a psalm could stand almost on a single line, it is this one, and the line it can stand on is the first. In fact, it can stand on only part of a line, the part which says, "The LORD is my shepherd."

What an amazing juxtaposition of ideas! The word *LORD* is the English translation of the great Old Testament personal name for God, first disclosed to Moses at the burning bush, as told in Exodus 3, and then repeated more than four thousand times in the pages of the Old Testament. The name literally means "I am who I am." It is an inexhaustible name, like its bearer. Chiefly, it refers to God's timelessness, on the one hand, and to his self-sufficiency, on the other. Self-sufficiency means that God needs nothing. He needs no wisdom from anyone else; he has all wisdom in himself. He needs no power; he is all-powerful. He does not need to be worshiped or helped or served. Nor is he accountable to anyone. He answers only to himself.

Timelessness means that God is always the same in these eternal traits or attributes. He was like this yesterday; he will be like this tomorrow. He will be unchanged and unchangeable forever.

He is the great "I am."

On the other side of this amazing combination of ideas is the word *shepherd*. In Israel, as in other ancient societies, a shepherd's work was considered the lowest of all works. If a family needed a shepherd, it was always the youngest son, like David, who got this unpleasant assignment. Shepherds had to live with the sheep twenty-four hours a day, and the task of caring for them was unending. Day and night, summer and winter, in fair weather and foul, they labored to nourish, guide, and protect the sheep. Who in his right mind would choose to be a shepherd?

Yet Jehovah has chosen to be our shepherd, David says. The great God of the universe has stooped to take just such care of you and me. This is an Old Testament statement, of course. But Christians can hardly forget that the metaphor was also taken up by Jesus and applied to himself, thus identifying himself with Jehovah, on the one hand, and assuming the task of being the shepherd of his people, on the other.

In Luke 15 Jesus defended mingling with tax collectors and "sinners," by saying, "Suppose one of you has a hundred sheep and loses one of them. Does he not leave the ninety-nine in the open country and go after the lost sheep until he finds it? And when he finds it, he joyfully puts it on his shoulders and goes home. Then he calls his friends and neighbors together and says, 'Rejoice with me; I have found my lost sheep.' I tell you that in the same way there will be more rejoicing in heaven over one sinner who repents than over ninety-nine righteous persons who do not need to repent" (Luke 15:4–7).

Even more remarkable is Jesus' teaching about himself as a shepherd in John 10.

> The man who enters by the gate is the shepherd of his sheep. The watchman opens the gate for him, and the sheep listen to his voice. He calls his own sheep by name and leads them out. When he has brought out all his own, he goes on ahead of them, and his sheep follow him because they know his voice. . . . I am the good shepherd. The good shepherd lays down his life for the sheep. The hired hand is not the shepherd who owns the sheep. So when he sees the wolf coming, he abandons the sheep and runs away. Then the wolf attacks the flock and scatters it. . . . I am the good shepherd; I know my sheep and my sheep know me—just as the Father knows me and I know the Father—and I lay down my life for the sheep. I have other sheep that are not of this sheep pen. I must bring them also. They too will listen to my voice, and there shall be one flock and one shepherd (vv. 2–4, 11–12, 14–16).

We are part of that "one flock" composed of believing Jews and Gentiles. So we are not stretching the twenty-third psalm to see Jesus as our shepherd and to apply the lines of the psalm carefully and in detail to ourselves.

"I Shall Not Be in Want"

It is not only the first half of the first line that is important, however. The second half is important too. It says, "I shall not be in want," that is, I shall lack nothing. This statement goes with the first half. Left to themselves, sheep lack everything. They are the most helpless animals. But if we belong to the one who is self-sufficient, inexhaustible, and utterly unchanged by time, we will lack nothing. He is sufficient for all things and will provide for us.

What is it that those in the care of the good shepherd shall not lack? Verses 2–6 are an answer to that question.

I Shall Not Lack Rest

This is because "He makes me lie down in green pastures, he leads me beside quiet waters" (v. 2).

Phillip Keller is a pastor and author who for eight years was himself a shepherd. Out of that experience he has written *A Shepherd Looks at Psalm 23*. It throws light on this and other statements. Sheep do not lie down easily, Keller says. In fact, "It is almost impossible for them to be made to lie down unless four requirements are met. Owing to their timidity they refuse to lie down unless they are free of all fear. Because of the social behavior within a flock sheep will not lie down unless they are free from friction with others of their kind. If tormented by flies or parasites, sheep will not lie down. Only when free of these pests can they relax. Lastly, sheep will not lie down as long as they feel in need of finding food. They must be free from hunger."[4]

Fear. Friction. Flies. Famine. Sheep must be free from each of these to be contented. And as Keller notes, only the shepherd can provide the trust, peace, deliverance, and pasture that is needed to free the sheep from them.

It is interesting that the psalm begins at this point. We might expect it to begin with motion, with some kind of activity either by the shepherd or the sheep. But strikingly, it begins with rest. It is a reminder that the Christian life also begins with resting in God or Christ. Along the way there will in time be many things for us to do. But we begin by resting in him who has done everything for us. Are you resting in Christ? Have you found Jesus to be the perfect provider of all your many needs?

Jesus said, "Come to me, all you who are weary and burdened, and I will give you rest" (Matt. 11:28).

He also declared, "I am the bread of life. He who comes to me will never go hungry, and he who believes in me will never be thirsty" (John 6:35).

Before he was crucified he told his disciples, "Peace I leave with you; my peace I give you. I do not give to you as the world gives. Do not let your hearts be troubled and do not be afraid" (John 14:27).

I Shall Not Lack Life

This is because "he restores my soul" (v. 3). In Hebrew idiom the words "restores my soul" can mean "brings me to repentance" (or conversion).[5] But since the word translated "soul" is actually "life," and since the metaphor here is that of shepherding, the words probably mean "the LORD restores me to physical health (or salvation)."

Phillip Keller explains this by the situation known to shepherds as a "cast (or cast down) sheep." What happens is this. "A heavy, fat or long-fleeced sheep will lie down comfortably in some little hollow or depression in the ground. It may roll on its side slightly to stretch out or relax. Suddenly the center of gravity in the body shifts so that it turns on its back far enough that the feet no longer touch the ground. It may feel a sense of panic and start to paw frantically. Frequently this only makes things worse. It rolls over even further. Now it is quite impossible for it to regain its feet."[6] In this position gases build up in the body, cutting off circulation to the legs, and often it is only a matter of a few hours before the sheep dies. The only one who can restore the sheep to health is the shepherd.

Sometimes we are like cast sheep. We are spiritually on our backs, quite helpless. But Jesus comes to us when we are in this condition, as he did to Peter after Peter had denied him even with oaths and cursing (Matt. 26:72, 74), and he restores us. Jesus restored Peter. He gets us up on our feet and going again.

I Shall Not Lack Guidance

This is because the Lord "guides me in paths of righteousness for his name's sake" (v. 3).

Sheep are foolish creatures. In fact, they are probably the most stupid animals on earth. One aspect of their stupidity is seen in the fact that they so easily wander away. They can have a good shepherd who can have brought them to the best grazing lands near an abundant supply of water, and they will still wander away to where the fields are barren and the water undrinkable. They are creatures of habit. They may be brought to good grazing land by their shepherd, but, having found it, they may keep on grazing until every blade of grass and every root is eaten; the fields are ruined, and they themselves are impoverished. No other class of livestock requires more careful handling than do sheep. Therefore, a shepherd who will move them from field to field yet always keep them near an abundant supply of water is essential for their welfare.

In his translation of this psalm Martin Luther rendered the phrase "paths of righteousness" by *auf rechter Strasse*. The connotation is not just of a straight way, but of a right way: a righteous way. We stray by sinning, but God leads us into upright moral paths. Isaiah said,

> We all, like sheep, have gone astray,
>   each of us has turned to his own way;
> and the LORD has laid on him
>   the iniquity of us all (Isa. 53:6).

I Shall Not Lack Safety

This is because "Even though I walk through the valley of the shadow of death, I will fear no evil, for you are with me; your rod and your staff, they comfort me" (v. 4).

This verse is often used to comfort those who are dying, and it is not wrongly used in this way. God is certainly a source of comfort in a person's dying moments. However, this verse primarily speaks of the shepherd's ability to protect his sheep in moments of danger. The picture, as Keller points out, is of the seasonal passage from the lowlands, where sheep spend the winter, through the valleys to the high pastures, where they go in summer. The valleys are places of rich pasture and much water, but they are also places of danger. Wild animals lurk in the broken canyon walls. Sudden storms may sweep along the valley floors. There may be floods. Since the sun does not shine into the valley very well, there really are shadows which at any moment may become shadows of death.

It is important to note that "the valley of the shadow of death" is as much God's right path for us as the "green pastures" which lie beside "quiet waters." That is, the Christian life is not always tranquil nor, as we say, a mountain-top experience. God gives us valleys also. It is in the valleys with their trials and dangers that we develop character.

Yet the valley has its own unique problem. The problem is fear. What is the answer to it? Clearly, the answer is the shepherd's close presence, for he is the only one who can protect the sheep and calm their anxieties. Many commentators on Psalm 23 have noticed that the second person pronoun "you" replaces the third person pronoun "he" at this point. Earlier we read, "*He* makes me lie down . . . *he* leads me beside quiet waters . . . *he* guides me." But now, "I will fear no evil, for *you* are with me; *your* rod and *your* staff, they comfort me" (italics added). We are never so conscious of the presence of God as when we pass through life's valleys.

I Shall Not Lack Provision

The twenty-third psalm also mentions the shepherd's provision for the physical needs of the flock, saying, "You prepare a table before me in the presence of my enemies. You anoint my head with oil; my cup overflows" (v. 5).

Some commentators think this represents a change in the psalm's basic image, passing now from that of a shepherd guiding his sheep to that of a householder welcoming a guest to his table.[7] This may be, particularly since the poem ends with the psalmist dwelling "in the house of the LORD forever." But on the other hand, Keller may be right when he sees this as the shepherd's preparation of the high tablelands or mesas where the sheep graze in summer. A good shepherd will prepare these before the sheep arrive, removing physical hazards, destroying poisonous plants, and driving predators away. Keller also has a chapter in which he describes how ancient shepherds used a mixture of olive oil, sulfur, and spices to protect their sheep from insects and promote the healing of infectious skin diseases.

In biblical imagery oil and wine also speak of joy and prosperity, since olives and grapes take time to grow and oil and wine require time to prepare. In periods of domestic turmoil or war these tasks were not performed.

Moreover, oil and wine were highly valued in the dry, barren lands of the Near East. In Palestine, where the sun shines fiercely most of the year and the temperatures continually soar up into the hundreds, the skin becomes cracked and broken and throats become parched. Oil soothes the skin, particularly the face. Wine clears the throat. When a guest arrived at the home of a friend, hospitality demanded the provision of oil and wine so the ravages of travel might be overcome. David spoke of this, though somewhat differently, when he prayed, "O Lord, . . . let your face shine on your servant" (Ps. 31:14, 16). A shining face was the face of a friend. In another passage David thanks God for "wine that gladdens the heart of man" and "oil [that makes] his face shine" (Ps. 104:15).

If we will allow God to lead us where he will, we will find that a table has been prepared for us, our heads have been anointed with purest oil, and our cups have been filled to overflowing with the wine of true joy.

I Shall Not Lack a Heavenly Home

The twenty-third psalm portrays life as a pilgrimage, and in the final verse the psalmist rightly comes to life's goal, which is God's house. "Surely goodness and love will follow me all the days of my life, and I will dwell in the house of the Lord forever."

To have a sure home was always a desire of the nomadic people who occupied the area of the Near East bordered by the Mediterranean Sea, the Red Sea, and the great Arabian desert. T. E. Lawrence, who gained fame as Lawrence of Arabia during the First World War, wrote of this in his classic volume *Seven Pillars of Wisdom*. He tells how, because of the geography of this area, one tribe after another came out of the desert to fight for the lush Judean highlands which contained the best trees, crops, and pastures. Under Joshua, the Israelites were one of these peoples. When a group like this succeeded, the conquered people generally moved just a bit south into the Negev, which was also good land, though not so good as the highlands. They in turn displaced others, and those still others, until the last of these people were pushed out into the desert with nothing before them but Damascus. Thus, for most of them Damascus, with its ample rivers and fertile fields, thereby became a symbol for the happy end of life's long passage.

We too long for such a home. Only our home is not Damascus. It is the place the Lord himself, our Good Shepherd, has gone to prepare for us. "I am going . . . to prepare a place for you," he said. "And if I go and prepare a place for you, I will come back and take you to be with me that you also may be where I am" (John 14:2–3).

Psalm 24

Letting the King Come In

The earth is the LORD's, and everything in it,
  the world, and all who live in it;
for he founded it upon the seas
  and established it upon the waters.

Who may ascend the hill of the LORD?
  Who may stand in his holy place?
He who has clean hands and a pure heart,
  who does not lift up his soul to an idol
  or swear by what is false.
He will receive blessing from the LORD
  and vindication from God his Savior.
Such is the generation of those who seek him,
  who seek your face, O God of Jacob. Selah

Lift up your heads, O you gates;
  be lifted up, you ancient doors,
  that the King of glory may come in.
Who is this King of glory?
  The LORD strong and mighty,
  the LORD mighty in battle.

Lift up your heads, O you gates;
   lift them up, you ancient doors,
   that the King of glory may come in.
Who is he, this King of glory?
   The LORD Almighty—
   he is the King of glory.   Selah
                              verses 1–10

I do not know if Psalm 24 has a setting in any event we know of from the Old Testament. But if there is a historical setting, I suppose it is the occasion on which David brought the Ark of the Covenant to Jerusalem from its temporary resting place in the house of Obed-Edom the Gittite (2 Sam. 6). Symbolically, the God of Israel was understood to dwell between the outstretched wings of the two cherubim mounted on the lid of the ark. So when the ark was taken to Jerusalem, it would have been appropriate to have composed a hymn like Psalm 24 for the occasion. Twice over it intones,

> Lift up your heads, O you gates . . .
> that the King of glory may come in (vv. 7, 9).

The title of Psalm 24 identifies it as a psalm "Of David," which also means that David may himself have composed it for the ceremony.

Yet I am not entirely happy with this explanation. At least I am not willing to stop with it. The reason is that, however important and moving the transport of the Ark of the Covenant to Jerusalem by David may have been, it is not nearly as significant as the single occasion on which, much later, the true "King of glory" actually did enter the holy city. I am referring, of course, to the entry of Jesus into Jerusalem on the day we call Palm Sunday.

Interestingly, the ancient rabbinical sources tell us that, in the Jewish liturgy, Psalm 24 was always used in worship on the first day of the week.[1] The first day of the week is our Sunday. So, putting these facts together, we may assume that these were the words being recited by the temple priests at the very time the Lord Jesus Christ mounted a donkey and ascended the rocky approach to Jerusalem. The people who were outside the walls, who were approaching Jerusalem with him, exclaimed:

> Hosanna to the Son of David!
> Blessed is he who comes in the name of the Lord!
> Hosanna in the highest! (Matt. 21:9).

Inside the priests were intoning:

> Lift up your heads, O you gates;
>> lift them up, you ancient doors,
>> that the King of glory may come in.
> Who is he, this King of glory?
>> The LORD Almighty—
>> he is the King of glory. *Selah* (Ps. 24:9–10).

But the priests were not joining in the cries of acclamation for Jesus, and within days they would conspire to have him executed as a blasphemer. As far as the common people were concerned, even though some of them hailed him as the Lord's Anointed on Palm Sunday, they would be crying, "Crucify him! Crucify him!" before the week was out.

A Clearly Messianic Psalm

I have pointed out in dealing with earlier psalms that it is not always easy to tell which psalms are messianic, that is, which psalms actually prophesy something about the Messiah to come. This is because they are often couched in images based on natural situations or events. For example, they may speak of a king. But we wonder: Are we to think of the king as King David (or one of the human descendants of King David), or is this rather a veiled reference to the King of Kings, that is, to Jesus? Since it is not always easy to tell which is the case, we have to be cautious when we draw Christian allusions or teachings from these essentially Jewish poems.

But we do not have such a problem with this psalm. Some psalms may be ambiguous. But how can a psalm be ambiguous that speaks of opening the gates of Jerusalem to "the LORD" (that is, Jehovah), to "the King of glory," or to "the LORD Almighty"? Here there is no ambiguity at all.

Some psalms take a human condition and build it to describe a situation that may involve God. This psalm is the reverse. It forthrightly describes the entrance of God into his holy city of Jerusalem, though in terms of an earthly king returning to his capital after a military victory.

The psalm is not simple. It is more complex even than this introductory description makes it sound. To begin with, two entries are described. The first, which occupies verses 3–6, is about God's people coming to God's city. It asks the question: Who is able to come? This part sounds very much like Psalm 15, which asks, "LORD, who may dwell in your sanctuary?" (v. 1), or one of the Psalms of Ascent (Pss. 120–34). The second part, verses 7–10, describes the coming of God to his people. These two sections are preceded by a statement that the earth and all that is in it are God's (vv. 1–2).

Part One: The Earth Is God's

At first glance, the opening verses of Psalm 24 may seem inappropriate. For what is the point of a declaration that God owns the world and everything in it in a psalm that describes the coming of the ark of God (or Jesus) to Jerusalem? Not a few scholars have felt the difficulty and have proposed that the psalm is actually a combination of three formerly unrelated compositions: verses 1–2, verses 3–6, and verses 7–10. However, even if they are right, we still have no explanation why an editor should have made such an unwise and inappropriate combination, if this is what he did.

Actually, the opening is not strange as long as we understand it as a warning not to think of God in exclusive or nationalistic terms. As such it is appropriate. The bulk of the psalm describes God and the people of God coming to Jerusalem—we must assume that the people are largely Jews. It would be easy for them to conclude from this description that God is a Jewish God exclusively, that is, that he is for Jews only or somehow loves Jews more than other people. We know how strong that idea later became, because even in the days of Jesus Christ the disciples seemed unable to think of a worldwide kingdom and thought instead of an exclusively Jewish one. Thus, even after the resurrection they were asking Jesus, "Lord, are you at this time going to restore the kingdom to Israel?" (Acts 1:6). Their understanding of the kingdom was restricted ethnically (it was for "Israel"), politically (it was a "restoration" of the earlier kingdom of David), and geographically (it was to be centered in Jerusalem). Jesus had to teach them that his was to be a spiritual kingdom which would extend throughout the world: "You will receive power when the Holy Spirit comes on you; and you will be my witnesses in Jerusalem, and in all Judea and Samaria, and to the ends of the earth" (v. 8).

The opening verses of Psalm 24 are an Old Testament expression of this truth. They tell us that, although for a time God did in a way tie his earthly presence to Jerusalem, God nevertheless is God of all the earth. "The world, and all who live in it" belong to him. This means that if you are a part of this world, as you are, you owe God allegiance as your true and rightful King. You have a great responsibility. But from responsibility there also flows a great blessing.

Part Two: Who May Come to God?

Who may come to such a great king to pay homage? This is no mere earthly monarch, whose presence would be awe-inspiring enough, but rather the thrice-holy God. Who dares come into his holy presence? The answer to this question is in verses 3–6, and it is both wonderfully complete and profound. It deals with two concerns.

The heart of the worshiper. Verse 4 answers the important question of verse 3 in terms of the worshiper's inner character and outward actions. It also answers it in terms of his relationships to God and to other people. The one who may approach God is

> He who has clean hands and a pure heart,
>> who does not lift up his soul to an idol
>> or swear by what is false.

To have a "pure heart" refers to inward holiness. It is what Jesus was speaking of in the Sermon on the Mount when he said, "Blessed are the pure in heart, for they will see God" (Matt. 5:8).

"Clean hands" designate one who is holy in deed, that is, in outward actions as well as inwardly. Such a person is the exact opposite of Pilate, for although he washed his hands publicly, saying, "I am innocent of this man's blood" (Matt. 27:24), nevertheless he was guilty. He was guilty of violating the laws of Rome as well as of his conscience by agreeing to the crucifixion of one he had three times declared innocent (cf. John 18:38; 19:4, 6).

The second line of verse 4 refers to one who has a right relationship to God; he worships the true God, not idols.

The third line describes one who has a right relationship to others. He is an honest person; he has not sworn falsely.

These requirements are a shortened version of those mentioned earlier, in Psalm 15. Indeed, they are so similar that either the author of the one psalm knew or copied from the other or else, which is what is claimed and is most likely, both were written by the same man, namely, King David. Psalm 15 asks the question: "LORD, who may dwell in your sanctuary? Who may live on your holy hill?" It answers:

> He whose walk is blameless
>   and who does what is righteous,
> who speaks the truth from his heart
>   and has no slander on his tongue,
> who does his neighbor no wrong
>   and casts no slur on his fellowman,
> who despises a vile man
>   but honors those who fear the LORD,
> who keeps his oath
>   even when it hurts,
> who lends his money without usury
>   and does not accept a bribe against the innocent (vv. 2–5).

This is the inner character of those who please God, whom God approves.

Vindication from God. What will such a person find when he or she comes to God? The answer is in the second part of the description of the worshiper in Psalm 24:5. First, he or she will find "blessing from the LORD"; second, "vindication from God his Savior."

This is a most remarkable verse, for it is an Old Testament expression of what we speak of as the doctrine of justification by faith. It tells us that the one who approaches God sincerely and trustingly will find salvation in him. This is not salvation by works, of course. It is similar to the case of the tax collector in Jesus' story. Jesus compared him to the Pharisee who approached the temple self-righteously, saying: "God, I thank you that I am not like other men—robbers, evildoers, adulterers—or even like this tax collector. I fast twice a week and give a tenth of all I get."

The tax collector stood at a distance. He was conscious of his sin and would not even look up to heaven, but beat his breast and said, "God, have mercy on me, a sinner." Jesus said that it was this man, rather than the Pharisee, who "went home justified before God" (Luke 18:9–14).

David Dickson, a seventeenth-century Scottish divine who finished his career as a professor of divinity first at Glasgow and then at Edinburgh Universities, wrote of these verses: "The holy life of the true believer is not the cause of his justification before God, . . . but he shall receive justification and eternal life, as a free gift from God, by virtue of the covenant of grace: therefore it is said here that *he shall receive righteousness from the God of his salvation.*"[2]

I suggest that in order to understand verses 4 and 5, it is best to take the phrases in an inverse order. In other words, although it is true that we must approach God sincerely and trustingly to find salvation, it is better to say that these characteristics are provided for us by God as a result of justification. That is, they are part of the blessing verse 5 promises. I would make the order like this:

1. Vindication (or justification) from God our Savior (v. 5b),
2. Blessing from the Lord (v. 5a), and then
3. Clean hands and a pure heart, resulting in a life which does not lift itself up to idols or swear falsely (v. 4).

This is a way of saying that justification precedes sanctification. It means that only those who are born again can seek, find, and know God. I suppose this is what Charles Haddon Spurgeon was thinking about when he wrote wittily of verse 6: "These are the *re*generation [of them that seek him]."[3]

Part Three: The Coming of the King

The final section of Psalm 24 describes the entrance of the king into Jerusalem. It is the obvious climax. In verses 1 and 2 the earth is prepared for his coming. In verses 3–6 his people, the inhabitants of the earth, are prepared for him. In the third section, verses 7–10, the king comes. Who is he? He is "the great representative man, who answered to the full character laid down, and therefore by his own right ascended the holy hill of Zion."[4] He is Jesus, who entered the city on Palm Sunday in order to die for us. It is because he ascended the approach to Jerusalem, entered it, and died there that we can enter heaven.

Many of the psalms seem to have been arranged for antiphonal singing, one voice or one choir asking a question and another choir or chorus answering it. Psalm 24 is quite obviously like this. Verses 3, 8, and 10 ask

questions. They could have been sung solo. The other parts are either introductions or responses. They could be (and probably were) sung by massed
choirs. The psalm is arranged for antiphonal response in a number of com-
mentaries.[5] I do not see how it is possible to get the true effect of its last section without approaching it in this way. It goes like this:

> *The chorus approaching with the king:*
> Lift up your heads, O you gates;
> > be lifted up, you ancient doors,
> > that the King of glory may come in.

> *A voice from within the walls:*
> Who is this King of glory?

> *A spokesman for the king:*
> > The LORD strong and mighty,
> > the LORD mighty in battle.

> *The original approaching chorus:*
> Lift up your heads, O you gates;
> > lift them up, you ancient doors,
> > that the King of glory may come in.

> *The voice from within, repeating the former question:*
> Who is he, this King of glory?

> *Everyone:*
> > The LORD Almighty—
> > he is the King of glory.

It is easy to get excited about something as beautiful and moving as this
liturgy. But we need to remember that the priests and people of Jesus' day,
though they sang it, did not really do what they were singing. In a sense
they did; they let Jesus into the city and then into the temple area, where he
threw out the moneychangers. But although they let him in, they did not
actually let him in. That is, they did not let him into their hearts and lives.

That is the way he really wants to come in, of course. He wants to come
into your life to save you and change you. The way for you to respond is to
let the King come in. Will you do it?

Spurgeon wrote,

It is possible that you are saying, "I shall never enter into the heaven
of God, for I have neither clean hands nor a pure heart." Look then
to Christ, who has already climbed the holy hill. He has entered as

the forerunner of those who trust him. Follow in his footsteps, and repose upon his merit. He rides triumphantly into heaven, and you shall ride there too if you trust him. "But how can I get the character described?" say you. The Spirit of God will give you that. He will create in you a new heart and a right spirit. Faith in Jesus is the work of the Holy Spirit, and has all virtues wrapped up in it.[6]

What a blessing it would be to come thus to him who came to his own on Palm Sunday. It is a blessing God holds out for you.

Psalm 25

A Bible Acrostic

To you, O LORD, I lift up my soul;
in you I trust, O my God.
Do not let me be put to shame,
nor let my enemies triumph over me.
No one whose hope is in you
will ever be put to shame,
but they will be put to shame
who are treacherous without excuse.

Show me your ways, O LORD,
teach me your paths;
guide me in your truth and teach me,
for you are God my Savior,
and my hope is in you all day long.
Remember, O LORD, your great mercy and love,
for they are from of old.
Remember not the sins of my youth
and my rebellious ways;
according to your love remember me,
for you are good, O LORD.

Good and upright is the LORD;
therefore he instructs sinners in his ways.

He guides the humble in what is right
and teaches them his way.
All the ways of the LORD are loving and faithful
for those who keep the demands of his covenant.

verses 1–10

Redeem Israel, O God,
from all their troubles!

verse 22

There is a tendency among commentators to exaggerate the greatness, depth, or pathos of any portion of Scripture they are expounding. For example, some have called Psalm 25 "a sob of great sorrow"[1] or "the deep soul exercise of the godly remnant of Israel in the time of trouble and distress."[2] I think the tendency is misleading in this case. Psalm 25 is great, but it is great in its calm and quiet maturity, not as some deep or powerful cry of anguish. It is a thoughtful prayer by one who knows that the only adequate foundation for any worthwhile life is God.

The psalm is in the form of an acrostic, the third such poem we have encountered. That is, with a few slight variations, each of the verses of the psalm begins with a successive letter of the Hebrew alphabet—the first word of the first verse beginning with *aleph,* the first word of the second verse beginning with *beth,* and so on. This is not an uncommon device in the Psalter. Altogether there are nine such psalms, though the first two make up one full acrostic together. The psalms are 9–10, 25, 34, 37, 111, 112, 119, and 145. The most polished example is Psalm 119. It has 22 stanzas of eight verses each, each stanza featuring one alphabet letter. In Psalm 119 each verse of each stanza begins with the featured letter. The first eight verses of the psalm begin with *aleph,* each of the next eight verses begins with *beth,* and so on throughout the whole psalm to the last eight verses (vv. 169–76), each of which begins with *taw.* The other acrostic psalms are not so elaborate. Nor in every case is the sequence of alphabet letters even complete.

Psalm 25 is not complete. As the text stands, the second rather than the first word of verse 2 begins with *beth; waw* and *qoph* are omitted (or are at least questionable); *resh* is repeated (in vv. 18–19); and the final verse, which does not fit the pattern and seems instead simply to have been added on, begins with *pe.*[3]

Why did the psalmists follow an acrostic pattern? We can think of several reasons. (1) It may be an artistic device used to add a certain beauty to the psalm, as rhyme does in our poetry. (2) It may indicate that the subject is being covered completely, from A to Z, as we might say. This is a particularly attractive possibility in regard to Psalm 119, which explores the nature and value of the written Word of God exhaustively. (3) The acrostic may have been a mnemonic device designed to assist the young in learning the psalms. That is probably why many Old Testament passages are poetry rather than prose. Poetry is easier than prose to memorize.

Yet, in this case at least, there may be an additional factor. As soon as we look at the psalm we discover that the theme that ties it together is "learning." If that is the emphasis, then an alphabetical or schoolhouse device is particularly appropriate. Notice verses 4 and 5. In them David, who is identified in the title as the psalmist, asks God to "teach" him right paths in which to walk and to "teach" him truth. Other verses contain the same idea but use different words. Then, in verses 8–15, the author confesses that this is precisely what God does. God "instructs sinners in his ways" (v. 8), "teaches [the humble] his way" (v. 9), and "will instruct [the one who fears God] in the way chosen for him" (v. 12).

Each of these verses also has to do with guidance. So we could rightly say that the psalm is a school-book lesson on how to live so as to please God and be blessed by him.

Trusting to the End

Since Psalm 25 is not a highly dramatic or emotionally charged psalm but rather a quietly mature one, it presents its theme in a way most of us can easily identify with. We see it at the beginning. The entry point or door of the psalm is *shame,* a word that occurs three times in the opening verses (once in verse 2 and twice in verse 3). Since the word also occurs in verse 20, near the end of the psalm, the thought of shame provides a context or background for what is said.

To understand what David is talking about we have to realize that the Bible uses the words *shame* and *ashamed* differently than we do. In fact, the primary biblical use is not even in most of our dictionaries. When we speak of being ashamed we usually mean being embarrassed or feeling foolish. *Webster's New Collegiate Dictionary* defines shame this way: a "painful emotion excited by a consciousness of guilt, disgrace or dishonor." This idea is found in the Bible, particularly in appeals to us not to be ashamed of God or of spiritual things. Jesus was speaking along these lines when he said, "If anyone is ashamed of me and my words, the Son of Man will be ashamed of him when he comes in his glory" (Luke 9:26). In a similar vein, Paul wrote, "I am not ashamed of the gospel, because it is the power of God for the salvation of everyone who believes" (Rom. 1:16). We are warned against shame because we all *are* often embarrassed of Jesus or the gospel, though we should actually be embarrassed to be embarrassed.

Yet this is not the chief biblical idea connected with shame, as I said. The unique biblical idea is that of being let down or disappointed or of having trusted in something that in the end proves unworthy of our trust.

There are a few places where this important meaning is unmistakable. In Romans 5:5 Paul writes about the Christian's hope, saying, as the older King James Version of the Bible has it, "hope maketh not ashamed." This means that the Christian's hope will never be seen to be illusory. It will never be exposed as being vain. Recognizing this meaning, the New International Version has altered the King James reading to say, "hope does not disappoint us." Another verse that requires this translation is Isaiah 49:23 (also Isa. 28:16, a parallel), which Paul quotes twice further on in Romans (Rom. 9:33; 10:11). The King James Version says, "They shall not be ashamed that wait for me." The New International Version rightly reads, "those who hope in me will not be disappointed" (or, in Isa. 18:16, "the one who trusts will never be dismayed"). These verses all mean that those who have staked their all on God will not be abandoned by him in the end. This is the way David uses *shame* in this psalm.

But why should there even be the thought of his being abandoned by God, particularly if he is writing as a mature believer, as I have suggested he is? There are two reasons, and this is where the psalm comes around to where we can easily understand it. First, David is surrounded by enemies. He mentions them explicitly in verses 2 and 19 ("Do not . . . let my enemies triumph over me," and "See how my enemies have increased"); he refers to them indirectly elsewhere by mentioning the threat they pose ("only he [God] will release my feet from the snare," v. 15). Second, David is conscious of his sins, particularly the sins of his youth, which he asks God to forget (v. 7). He speaks of these as "iniquity" in verse 11 and as being many ("all my sins") in verse 18.

It is easy to identify with these two problems, especially as we grow older and come to know ourselves better than we did when we were young. When we were young we considered ourselves equal to almost anything. We did not fear anyone, and we were not aware of the sins we committed or of which we now know ourselves to be capable.

Now we know that we do have formidable enemies. The world is our enemy. It is opposed to every good and godly thing. The devil is our enemy. The Bible tells us that he is "a murderer from the beginning" (John 8:44) and that he "prowls around like a roaring lion looking for someone to devour" (1 Peter 5:8). Then, as if that were not enough, we have an enemy within, even our own sinful natures together with the memory of the sins we have committed. What if our enemies should prove to be too strong for us? What if they should succeed in drawing us down to their level or causing us to abandon our former trust in God? Or what if God, remembering our past sins, should in the end be unwilling to save and help us?

Haven't you ever felt like that? If that should be the case, then in the end we would be put to shame. We would be abandoned.

In God's School

David knows that is not going to happen, however, because this is a psalm not of anguish but of mature trust in God and instruction for others. From the beginning David's assertion is that he will *not* be put to shame ("No one whose hope is in you will ever be put to shame," v. 3). His treacherous enemies will be put to shame instead.

But there is another side to this confidence, valid as it may be, and that is that if this is to happen—if David is to remain firm to the end—then he must be taught of God so that he will be enabled to walk in God's way and be found always to be a person of integrity and uprightness (v. 21). In other words, although it is true that God will not let us down, abandon us, or disappoint us, this blessed truth of perseverance is not something that merely works itself out automatically or mechanically. Rather, it is something that requires responsible learning, obedience, faithfulness, trust, and deep reverence on our part.

Verses 4 and 5 show that what is needed is to know the truth, that is, the truth found in the Bible, and thereby also to know the ways in which we must walk if we are to be pleasing to and be preserved by God. This is a very practical matter. It is not a question of abstract ideas but of true obedience.

One of the most helpful contemporary commentators on the psalms is P. C. Craigie, who taught at the University of Calgary, Alberta, until his early death in 1985. He made this point by comparing Psalm 25 with the well-known opening psalm of the Psalter. He writes,

> The prayer of Psalm 25 complements the wisdom of Psalm 1. The latter, in the more didactic tradition of wisdom, established the two ways, that of the righteous and that of the wicked. But taken alone the dispassionate wisdom of Psalm 1 could be misleading; it might be taken to imply that the essence of life was simply choosing the right road—once the choice had been made, all would be well. But in Psalm 25 . . . the prayer is that of a person who has made the choice [presented in Psalm 1] and is walking the road of the righteous; but the dispassionate wisdom has been transformed to passionate petition, for the right road is not an easy one on which to walk. It is lined with enemies who would like nothing better than to put the walker to shame; and the traveler on the road is also plagued with internal doubts, as he calls to mind previous wanderings from the path and former sins. The essence of the road of the righteous is this: it is a road too difficult to walk without the companionship and friendship of God.[4]

How, then, does the psalmist arrive at his settled confidence that God will instruct him and lead him unerringly on this road? The answer is that this very instruction teaches him this, because it teaches him about God's character.

Here are the things David has learned about God as he has studied the revelation God has given.

1. God is *faithful,* because "No one whose hope is in you will ever be put to shame" (v. 3).
2. God is characterized by *truth,* because his paths are paths of truth (vv. 4–5).
3. God is his *Savior* (v. 5).
4. God is *merciful* and *loving* and has been "from of old" (v. 6).
5. God is *good* and *upright* (v. 8).
6. Again, God is *loving* and *faithful* in all his ways (v. 10).
7. God is *forgiving* (v. 11).
8. God is open with his people and freely *confides* in them (v. 14).
9. God is *gracious* (v. 16).
10. God is *powerful* to rescue his people; therefore he is one in whom they can take *refuge* (vv. 15, 20).

When Mercy and Justice Meet

Two of these characteristics deserve special mention, since they are brought together strikingly in verse 8. They are "goodness" and "uprightness" or, as we would more naturally say, "mercy" and "justice." It is a significant combination, because without God's special revelation to us in this area we cannot see how God can be both good and upright at the same time, at least for us. We can understand how God can be good or merciful and therefore want to save us from our sins. That is why we can be bold to appeal to him. But how can God be just while doing it? Doesn't justice require that he condemn us for our manifold transgressions?

The only adequate answer to this dilemma is Jesus Christ, who satisfied the justice of God by bearing our punishment in our place on the cross. His death satisfied the justice of God completely, allowing him to forget about our sins and thus reach out to save us graciously.

In his commentary on the psalms Harry Ironside tells of visiting a very old Christian. The man was about ninety years old, and he had lived a godly life. However, in his last days he sent for Ironside because, as he expressed it, "Everything seems so dark."

"Whatever do you mean?" asked Ironside. "You have known the Lord for nearly seventy years. You have lived for him a long, long time. You have helped others. Whatever do you mean 'dark'?"

The man replied, "In my illness, since I have been lying here so weak, my memory keeps bringing up the sins of my youth, and I cannot get them out of my mind. They keep crowding in upon me, and I cannot help thinking of them. They make me feel miserable and wretched."

Ironside turned to this psalm and read the verse in which David prays,

> Remember not the sins of my youth
>   and my rebellious ways;
> according to your love remember me,
>   for you are good, O LORD (Ps. 25:7).

After he had read the words he said, "When you came to God seventy years ago you confessed your sin and put your trust in Jesus Christ. Do you remember what happened then?" The old man couldn't remember. Ironside said, "Don't you remember that when you confessed your sins God said, 'Your sins and iniquities I will remember no more.' If God has forgotten them, why should you think about them?"

The man relaxed and replied, "I am an old fool remembering what God has forgotten." He found peace because he had been instructed in the nature of God and God's ways.[5]

How to Receive God's Blessing

There is one more thing that we need to understand about this psalm, however. It presents a problem; it suggests a solution; it expresses confidence that God will provide the solution needed. But, finally, it also shows the attitude of heart that will enable the psalmist to receive the anticipated blessing. This attitude has several parts.

Humility (v. 9). Verse 8 says that God will instruct sinners in his ways because he is good and upright. But that implies that sinners know themselves to be sinners and that they come before God humbly, as the next verse makes clear: "He guides the *humble* in what is right and teaches them his way" (v. 9, italics added). There is no promise in the Bible that God will teach an arrogant mind or a haughty spirit. On the contrary, "God opposes the proud but gives grace to the humble" (James 4:6; cf. Prov. 3:34).

Obedience (v. 10). The reason why many of us do not learn much about God or God's ways is that we are not ready to obey him when he makes the way plain. We want to know what the way is before we will obey it; that is, we want to keep the options for sin open. David tells us that this will not work, since "the ways of the LORD are loving and faithful for those who keep the demands of his covenant" (v. 10). We must be committed to obedience before God unfolds his loving and faithful ways to us.

Reverence (vv. 12, 14). Some of us are brash in approaching God, regarding him more or less as some celestial buddy, rather than as the great, holy, awesome God he truly is. Verses 12 and 14 remind us that reverence is necessary if we would know him: "Who, then, is the man that fears the LORD? He will instruct him in the way chosen for him," and "The LORD confides in those who fear him; he makes his covenant known to them."

Expectation (v. 15). Finally, God desires a spirit of believing expectation, for, as David says in verse 15, "My eyes are ever on the LORD." He is telling us that if we want to be taught and led by God, we must get into the habit of looking to him regularly.

Each of these characteristics we need to possess and practice. In fact, this is the note on which the psalm ends. You will recall from my original analysis of the acrostic pattern of this psalm that the final verse does not fit the pattern. It begins with the letter *pe,* for one thing. But even more noticeably, it suddenly refers to Israel when the earlier material seems to have been a personal prayer of King David. This is no accident. On the contrary, it has the effect of broadening what has been said to include all Israel and therefore also to include us. It is a serious invitation to us to put our own name into the final couplet.

If we will come to God Almighty as David came to him, then we can say expectantly, "Redeem *me,* O God, from all my troubles!" and we can know that he will answer us.

Psalm 26

Standing on Level Ground

Vindicate me, O LORD,
  for I have led a blameless life;
I have trusted in the LORD
  without wavering.
Test me, O LORD, and try me,
  examine my heart and my mind;
for your love is ever before me,
  and I walk continually in your truth.
I do not sit with deceitful men,
  nor do I consort with hypocrites;
I abhor the assembly of evildoers
  and refuse to sit with the wicked.
I wash my hands in innocence,
  and go about your altar, O LORD,
proclaiming aloud your praise
  and telling of all your wonderful deeds.
I love the house where you live, O LORD,
  the place where your glory dwells.

Do not take away my soul along with sinners,
  my life with bloodthirsty men,

in whose hands are wicked schemes,
   whose right hands are full of bribes.
But I lead a blameless life;
   redeem me and be merciful to me.

My feet stand on level ground;
   in the great assembly I will praise the LORD.
                                        verses 1–12

There are two phrases in the English translation of Psalm 26 that I would like to place together, except that they occur in different translations. The first phrase is from the New International Version and is the one from which I derived the title for this chapter: "on level ground." It is found in verse 12. The other is from verse 1 of the King James Version: "therefore I shall not slide." I would like to put them together, because they unify the psalm, teaching that the one who trusts God will have a level foundation on which to build a life, while the one who does not trust God is on steep, slippery terrain.

To my mind the most memorable line in the psalm is in the last verse—the one about standing on level ground. The others do not command a great deal of special attention, though they do link the psalm to other important psalms in the Psalter.

Let me show how this is so. There are similarities between Psalm 26 and Psalm 25, the one immediately preceding. Both express a quiet confidence in God (cf. 25:2 and 26:1). Both claim personal integrity for the psalmist (cf. 25:21 and 26:1, 11). Both pray for deliverance (cf. 25:16–22 and 26:9–11). There are also echoes of Psalm 1 in Psalm 26, particularly verses 4 and 5, which remind us of Psalm 1:1. And there are connections between this psalm and Psalms 15 and 24, which have to do with the moral character necessary for a human being to approach God. Psalm 15 asks, "LORD, who may dwell in your sanctuary?" (v. 1). Psalm 24 inquires, "Who may ascend the hill of the LORD? Who may stand in his holy place?" (v. 3). Psalm 26 seems to give answers, since in it David claims to be exactly such a person.

Here is another introductory matter. Some scholars link Psalms 26, 27, and 28, since all mention the temple in some way.[1] Similarly, Harry Ironside saw a pattern linking the block of fifteen psalms from Psalm 25 to Psalm 39. "The first five of them, Psalms 25–29, deal largely with the basis or the ground of the soul's confidence [before God]. . . . In the second section, Psalms 30–34, we seem to move on a step and find these psalms occupied with the heart's appropriation of God's salvation. . . . In the third section, Psalms 35–39, . . . [we] are occupied largely with the question of personal holiness."[2]

Nothing to Hide

In my judgment there is a natural connection between Psalm 25 and this one, but it is not to be found in verbal similarities so much as in a natural development of themes. What was the theme of Psalm 25? In that psalm David was afraid that he would be put to shame or be shown to have built upon a bad foundation in the day of testing. He asks God to teach him his ways so he will be able to walk in them and so that his fears will not be realized. In Psalm 26 he tells us that this is exactly what God and he have done. God has taught him, and he has walked in God's ways. He has led a blameless life. Therefore, he stands (and expects to continue standing) on level ground.

I think that is the way we have to take the appeal of the opening two verses of Psalm 26, which set its tone. David pleads for vindication in verse 1 ("Vindicate me, O Lord"), adding in verse 2,

> Test me, O Lord, and try me,
> examine my heart and my mind.

At first glance the word *vindicate* suggests a desire to be shown to be right over against other people: "I have been falsely accused; show everybody that I am really innocent." But as I read this psalm I sense that it is not David's reputation in the eyes of other people that concerns him but rather God's vindication of the rightness of a devout and moral life. In other words, it is not his own reputation but God's reputation that he covets. He has been trying to obey God. He is surrounded by many who think that he is foolish, just as we are surrounded by similar mockers of righteousness today. What he is asking is that God will show by the quality and steadiness of his life that a moral life is always best—for the sake of God's own honor and for the good of those who may be looking on.

This is how the three major themes of the prayer come together. They are a plea for vindication, the claim that the psalmist has led an upright life, and confidence that in the end he will be found standing on level ground when the bad moral choices of others have caused them to be swept away.

We need a lot more of this kind of thinking today. Many of today's Christians think that all that is needed for an effective Christian witness before the world is a proper presentation of gospel facts and doctrine. In other words, all we need is words. I believe in words. I also believe that the element that is most missing in our day is sound teaching. We need teaching, teaching, and then more teaching. That is what David was asking for in Psalm 25 ("teach me your paths; guide me in your truth and teach me"). But what I am saying here is that we need something in addition. We need people who have been taught and who then also walk in that way so that they demonstrate to unbelievers that the path of faith and morality is the

happy and successful way to live. The goal is that, when other peoples' immorality leads them to disaster, as sin always does, they might be able to look around, see those whose lives are working well, and be directed to God by those available examples.

So here is a question. You who profess to be believers in Jesus Christ, are you following in God's ways so closely that the way of life you profess with your lips is vindicated? Is it clear to an impartial observer that your way of life is better than those of the ungodly?

If that is not the case, then you need to become more serious about the Bible's teaching and begin to walk in God's ways more closely. If you are a true Christian, you know that the problem does not lie in God or the teachings of the Bible but in your own lack of faith, devotion, and obedience. And you should pray for God's testing, trying, and examination, with the goal of a godly life, as David expressed it in another of his great psalms, Psalm 139:

> Search me, O God, and know my heart;
>   test me and know my anxious thoughts.
> See if there is any offensive way in me,
>   and *lead me in the way everlasting* (vv. 23–24, italics added).

If that is the goal of the testing, then the confidence that results will be without presumption since you will be reminded of your abiding need to obey and depend on God.

The Way of the Righteous

The way of the righteous, which David claims to have been following, is outlined in verses 3–8. But verse 2 has something important to contribute to it. In that verse David asks God to examine both his "heart" and his "mind." In other words, in order to walk in a right way David must be both instructed in God's truth and born again, which is the only way anyone ever acquires a heart that desires to go in God's paths. He needs to know the way, but he also needs to want to follow it. These two ideas carry over into verse 3, for the idea of heart desire is preserved in the word *love*, and the idea of mind instruction is echoed in the word *truth*.

> for your love is ever before me,
>   and I walk continually in your truth.

But now we must go a step further and ask for some specifics. What are the marks of the "blameless" or righteous life? What will the godly person do if he or she is actually walking in God's "truth"? There are several important considerations.

Separation from Wicked People (vv. 4–5)

The first specific David offers is also the most fully developed and the one that reminds us of Psalm 1. Psalm 1 describes the happy person as one "who does not walk in the counsel of the wicked or stand in the way of sinners or sit in the seat of mockers" (v. 1). In Psalm 26 David says,

> I do not *sit* with deceitful men,
>   nor do I consort with hypocrites;
> I abhor the assembly of evildoers
>   and refuse to *sit* with the *wicked* (italics added).

This is a far more difficult and delicate matter than we may at first be aware of. For, of course, it goes beyond merely doing evil ourselves. It is a matter of becoming involved and even associating with evildoers.

Why is it difficult? It is difficult because it is almost impossible to avoid evil people. We are constantly surrounded, not merely by sinners (we are all sinners), but by people who actually delight in doing evil. I do not necessarily mean people who murder other people and chop up their bodies for weekend fun. I mean people who merely think nothing of cheating other people in business if they can get away with it, or people who deliberately circulate lies about a political or business rival to defeat him, or people who practice open sexual immorality, flaunting the laws both of God and man. We are surrounded all the time by such people, and it is difficult to know how to disassociate ourselves from them, or even if we can.

Again, the matter is delicate, because honest attempts to put a distance between ourselves and "evil" people quite easily slide over into pharisaism, the outlook that assumes that we are inherently better than other people and that loves to be thought so.

Clearly we seem to be caught between the horns of a dilemma. If we are often in the company of the unrighteous, we will be dragged down by them. If we work at disassociation, we incline to the equally damaging sin of pride.

The problem may be both difficult and delicate, but it is obviously not unsolvable since there is a kind of separation recommended in this psalm. What is it? Like every other similar passage in Scripture, it is a separation based, not on a sense of our being better than others but of not being good enough to survive in such company. Jesus had no trouble in his associations with sinners, because he was not one of them. We are and do. So, although we will be in the world and will associate with sinners daily for the gospel's sake (we can hardly avoid it), we will not "consort with" or otherwise appear to condone those whose lives are openly opposed to God's truth or morality.

C. S. Lewis has an excellent chapter on this problem in *Reflections on the Psalms*. It is on what he calls "connivance." He writes wisely, "Many people have a very strong desire to meet celebrated or 'important' people, including those whom they disapprove. . . . But I am inclined to think a Christian would be wise to avoid, where he decently can, any meeting with people who are bullies, lascivious, cruel, dishonest, spiteful and so forth. Not because we are 'too good' for them. In a sense because we are not good enough. We are not good enough to cope with all the temptations, nor clever enough to cope with all the problems, which an evening spent in such society produces."[3]

Many Christians can trace a lost youth or fruitless middle years to the bad influence of evil persons, whom they looked up to and even envied at one time.

Personal Innocence (v. 6)

We must not think that all the problems we face in trying to live a blameless life are due to other people, however. That is exactly opposite to the solution I proposed for dealing with people who are blatantly evil. On the contrary, we must know that we are sinners, inclined constantly to wrong ourselves, and therefore in continual need of confession, forgiveness, and cleansing. What David says is that we need to be able to "wash [our] hands in innocence" (v. 6), a well-known symbolic gesture for being free of personal guilt in some matter.

We are reminded of Psalm 24, which asks,

> Who may ascend the hill of the LORD?
> Who may stand in his holy place?

and answers,

> *He who has clean hands and a pure heart,*
> who does not lift up his soul to an idol
> or swear by what is false (vv. 3–4, italics added).

Audible Testimony to God's Nature and Deeds (vv. 6–7)

Verses 6–8 have been overemphasized by those who see them as a ritual followed by Jewish pilgrims as they stood before the temple gates. They would undergo a symbolic purification and then proceed into the courts of God with praise, according to this interpretation.[4] Psalm 26 may have been used that way, of course. We do not have any evidence either for or against the idea. But it is not necessary to restrict the meaning of verses 6 and 7 in this fashion. David would have expressed his praise of God at the temple naturally. However, the point is not the need for some ritual but rather for audible praise, which we and every one of God's people can (and should) voice everywhere.

What is the point of such praise? It is a natural expression of our delight in God, of course. It is pleasing to God. But in the context of this psalm David's thought is probably that vocalized testimony identifies him with God and thus helps to hold him to that side.

During World War II a young soldier from a very wealthy and sophisticated Philadelphia family became a Christian. When his time of service was over and he was about to go home, he expressed concern that his old acquaintances would soon draw him back into the immoral life he had led before entering the army. His pastor advised him to give a testimony concerning his conversion to the first ten of his old friends he should meet. "If you speak about Jesus, either they will become converted themselves or they will drop you; you will not have to drop them," he was told. This is what the young man did. "The most wonderful thing has happened to me," he said to the first and then to the second and third of his old friends. "I have received Jesus Christ as my Savior." It was not long before word got around that he was "strange" since he had come back from fighting, and his friends began to stay away from him. He testified that it was a joyful and strengthening experience to be thus firmly identified with the Lord Jesus Christ and his righteousness.

Love for God's House (v. 8)

The final practical element in David's prescription for how to walk in God's ways and live a blameless life is to love God's house which, I presume, also has to do with loving to be with God's people. David states this in verse 8, which says, "I love the house where you live, O LORD, the place where your glory dwells." Putting this against what we have already seen to have been David's heart desires, we find him choosing the company of God's people rather than the company of sinners and choosing the glory of God rather than the way of wickedness. Remember the saying: "Bad company corrupts good character." It is true. But it is equally true that good company develops it. If you want to grow in righteousness, you need to spend time with God and with those who are striving to model morality.

Final Separation

If we have had any doubts about the possible self-righteousness of the psalmist, they should be dispelled by the prayer's closing stanza. For in it David pleads for redemption and a mercy that will spare him from the fate of sinners at the final judgment.

It is an interesting way of speaking. David has separated himself from those who are wicked in this life; now he wants God to separate him from them also in the judgment. "Do not take away my soul along with sinners, my life with bloodthirsty men; . . . redeem me and be merciful to me," he says (vv. 9–11). Will God do it? Of course, he will, which is why David comes to the level ground of confidence he occupies in the concluding couplet. It is why you and I can have confidence too, if we are trusting in God.

Here is the way that great prince of preachers, Charles Haddon Spurgeon, put it.

If you have prayed this prayer, if your character be rightly described in the psalm before us, be not afraid that you ever shall be gathered with sinners. Have you the two things that David had—the outward walking in integrity and the inward trusting in the Lord? Do you endeavor to make your outward conduct and conversation conformable to the example of Christ? Would you scorn to be dishonest toward men or to be undevout toward God? At the same time, are you resting upon Jesus Christ's sacrifice and can you compass the altar of God with humble hope? If so, then rest assured, with the wicked you never shall be gathered. . . . but [your] feet shall stand in the congregation of the righteous in the day when the wicked are cast away for ever.[5]

That is a great confidence. It was the confidence of the psalmist, and it should be the confidence of each of us too.

Psalm 27

My Light and My Salvation

The LORD is my light and my salvation—
  whom shall I fear?
The LORD is the stronghold of my life—
  of whom shall I be afraid?
When evil men advance against me
  to devour my flesh,
when my enemies and my foes attack me,
  they will stumble and fall.
Though an army besiege me,
  my heart will not fear;
though war break out against me,
  even then will I be confident.

One thing I ask of the LORD,
  this is what I seek:
that I may dwell in the house of the LORD
  all the days of my life,
to gaze upon the beauty of the LORD
  and to seek him in his temple.
For in the day of trouble
  he will keep me safe in his dwelling;

> *he will hide me in the shelter of his tabernacle*
> *and set me high upon a rock.*
>
> > *verses 1–5*

> *Wait for the LORD;*
> *be strong and take heart*
> *and wait for the LORD.*
>
> > *verse 14*

P salm 27 is one of the best-known and most comforting psalms in the Psalter. But it is hard to know whether it is chiefly a psalm of confidence, written against the dark background of David's many enemies, or chiefly a lament in which David cries out for help against implacable foes. The reason for the confusion is obvious. The first half of the psalm (vv. 1–6) exudes confidence. The second half (vv. 7–14) is a very moving prayer.

It is no surprise to anyone acquainted with critical scholarship to learn that these two moods, reflected in the two parts of the psalm, have led some writers to argue that these are actually two psalms awkwardly put together. They point to the change in mood, plus some corresponding differences in structure. In the first part God is referred to in the third person. In the second he is addressed directly. But there is another side to this argument, since there are links between the psalm's two halves. The enemies whom David fears in part two are also present in part one (vv. 2–3), and the desire to dwell in God's house in order to "gaze upon the beauty of the LORD" in the first half (v. 4) finds a natural sequel in the later determination to seek God's face (v. 8). What is even more significant, the two chief themes of part one, confidence in God before enemies and the desire to seek God's face, are also the two chief themes of part two, though they occur there in inverse order: first the desire to seek God's face, then confidence. An arrangement like this points not only to both parts having been composed by the same author but to both halves being parts of a single composition.

What we have here is an unfolding of two closely related moods by the same inspired author, put together like two movements of a symphony.[1] And the point is that these two apparently opposing moods are also often in us, frequently at the same time or at nearly the same time. Don't you find that you are often both confident and anxious, trusting and fearful, or at least that your mood swings easily from one to the other? I do. It is part of what it means to be a weak human being.

Since that is true of us, it should be a comfort to realize that it was also true of David. We can be instructed by what he did at such times.

The Soul's Confidence

The first three verses of Psalm 27 express the soul's confidence in God on the basis of the psalmist's previous experience of him. David says that God has been three things to him: his light, his salvation, and his stronghold.

My Light

When any of us think of God, perhaps trying to visualize him, the best we can do is to think of light, remembering Paul's teaching that God "lives in unapproachable light" (1 Tim. 6:16). For this reason, it is a bit of a surprise to learn that, although God is often associated with light in the Bible, this verse is the only direct application of the name *light* to God in the Old Testament. Job speaks of heaven as the "abode of light" (Job 38:19). Psalm 104 says that God "wraps himself in light as with a garment" (v. 2). Several verses affirm that "the LORD turns my darkness into light" (2 Sam. 22:29; cf. Ps. 18:28). Psalm 36:9 declares, "In your light we see light." However, Psalm 27:1 is the only Old Testament text in which God is actually called *light*.

We have to go to the New Testament to find a good parallel, and when we do, we find that there *light* is a name for Jesus Christ: "The light shines in the darkness, but the darkness has not understood it. . . . The true light that gives light to every man was coming into the world" (John 1:5, 9). John, who makes this identification, also says, "God is light; in him there is no darkness at all" (1 John 1:5).

What is this image supposed to mean? In the gospel of John it has to do with understanding, which is why it is applied to Jesus. It is in him that we see or understand what God the Father is like. In the first letter of John light has to do with God's purity or sinlessness, because it is opposed to the darkness of sinful behavior (v. 7). What about Psalm 27? Here the term is not specifically explained. It could suggest illumination, purity, joy, life, and hope, among other things. But since David is thinking about his enemies and is seeking deliverance from them, Craigie is probably right when he says, "The psalmist is affirming that even in the darkness of the terrible threat of war, he has no fear, for God is the light that can dispel such fearful darkness."[2]

My Salvation

The Hebrew word for salvation means "deliverance" explicitly, and again this probably has to do with deliverance from the king's immediate enemies. The very next psalm expresses the same idea when it says, "The LORD is the strength of his people, a fortress of salvation for his anointed one" (Ps. 28:8).

The Stronghold of My Life

The military images and the concerns they represent continue in the third of these great images for God, namely, that he is a refuge or stronghold. David clearly needed a refuge from his foes. He had had it in the past. Therefore, he will not fear any future dangers. Even if his foes should attack, an army should besiege him, or war should break out against the nation, David will not fear as long as God is his stronghold.

Proverbs 18:10 expresses the same idea saying,

> The name of the LORD is a strong tower;
> the righteous run to it and are safe.

On the other hand, we have to say that, although in this setting these three images for God all probably have to do with military deliverance and protection, they also rightly suggest even greater meanings to us. Light speaks of spiritual understanding. Salvation points to the greatest of all deliverances, namely, deliverance from sin by the death of Jesus Christ. Stronghold refers to that spiritual refuge from the pains and buffetings of life which God himself is for his people. For us this is a well-rounded statement of God's manifold spiritual blessings, and it has generally been so understood. John Stott puts our understanding well when he says, "The Lord is my light, to guide me; my salvation, to deliver me; and the stronghold of my life, in whom I take refuge."[3]

The Soul's Desire

The second stanza of the psalm expresses David's one great desire, which is to "dwell in the house of the LORD all the days of [his] life" (v. 4). This sounds a great deal like Psalm 23, which ends with David dwelling "in the house of the LORD forever." But there it has to do with heaven, while here, in Psalm 27, the reference is to the earthly tabernacle. Indeed, David seems to be ransacking the Hebrew language for nouns to describe it: "the house of the LORD" (v. 4), "his temple" (v. 4), "his dwelling" (v. 5), "his tabernacle" (vv. 5–6).

Why, we might ask, does David have this single and obsessive longing for God's house, particularly when we remember that the glorious temple of Solomon was yet many years in the future? At this point God's house was still a tent, the tent David erected for the ark when he brought it from Kiriath Jearim to Mount Zion (cf. 2 Sam. 6:17).

The answer, of course, is that it was not the earthly temple itself that charmed David but rather the beauty of the Lord that was to be found at the temple in a special way. When we were studying Psalm 26 and found a similar desire (in v. 8) I suggested that David's longing for the house of God had something to do with his being with God's people, who would be found there. But that is not the case here. Here the reason is solely that the psalmist might "gaze upon the beauty of the LORD." It is the Lord himself that he is seeking.

And yet, he seeks it in the temple. Quite a few commentators seem to fall all over themselves trying to prove that this was not a literal desire for God's house but rather a matter of spiritual fellowship.[4] I would argue to the contrary that, although there is some truth in this, basically it is an anachronistic and misleading distinction.

C. S. Lewis has unusual sensitivity for what is going on in statements like this (about David's desire to "gaze upon the beauty of the LORD . . . in his temple"), born of his own long and perceptive study of literature; I appeal to him here. He begins by acknowledging the way we naturally distinguish between the forms of religion and the spiritual reality behind it. We think of an awareness of God or of God's qualities entirely apart from the tangible elements of worship. But, says Lewis, for the ancients, including the ancient Jews, religion was not like that. The tangible and the intangible were not separated for them but rather were joined. They actually seemed to experience God *in* the temple. Thus their appetite for God was something to be satisfied almost physically. "Their longing to go up to Jerusalem and 'appear before the presence of God' is like a physical thirst (Ps. 42). From Jerusalem His presence flashes out 'in perfect beauty' (Ps. 50:2). Lacking that encounter with Him, their souls are parched like a waterless countryside (Ps. 63:2). They crave to be 'satisfied with the pleasures' of His house (Ps. 65:4). Only there can they be at ease, like a bird in the nest (Ps. 84:3). One day of those 'pleasures' is better than a lifetime spent elsewhere (Ps. 10)."[5]

I am aware, as was Lewis, that we live in a different time and are ourselves very different. We remember how Jesus said, "Yet a time is coming and has now come when the true worshipers will worship the Father in spirit and truth" (John 4:23). But still, I believe Lewis is also right when he reminds us that we have probably swung too far to the other extreme and would do well to recover something of this robust Old Testament worship.

Let me put it like this. There is something to be experienced of God in church that it is not quite so easy to experience elsewhere. Otherwise, why have churches? If it is only instruction we need, we can get that as well by an audio tape or a book. If it is only fellowship, we can find that equally well, perhaps better, in a small home gathering. There is something to be said for the sheer physical singing of the hymns, the sitting in the pews, the actual looking to the pulpit and gazing on the pulpit Bible as it is expounded, the tasting of the sacrament, and the very atmosphere of the place set apart for the worship of God that is spiritually beneficial. Isn't that true? Haven't you found a sense of God's presence simply by being in God's house? I do not mean to deny that God can (and should) be worshiped elsewhere. But I am suggesting that the actual physical worship of God in the company of other believers can be almost sacramental.

For what it is worth, let me state that the Puritans were not as hesitant as we are on this point, since they easily linked the Old Testament temple to specific churches. Richard Sibbes said boldly, "Particular visible churches under visible pastors . . . now are God's tabernacle."[6]

The Soul's Prayer

The latter half of Psalm 27 begins with verse 7, as I pointed out earlier, and it is here that we find the abrupt change of language, structure, and tone I also mentioned. The verbs change from the first or third person to the second. The earlier affirmations become prayers. The mood changes from confidence to earnest entreaty.

> Hear my voice when I call, O LORD;
>   be merciful to me and answer me.
> My heart says of you, "Seek his face!"
>   Your face, LORD, I will seek.
> Do not hide your face from me,
>   do not turn your servant away in anger;
>   you have been my helper.
> Do not reject me or forsake me,
>   O God my Savior (vv. 7–9).

In this section of the psalm most people's attention is directed to verse 10 which says, "Though my father and mother forsake me, the LORD will receive me." This is partially because being forsaken by a parent is so poignant and partially because so many people have experienced disappointment from a parent to some degree. One of my friends, a clinical psychiatrist, tells me that she uses this psalm often in her counseling because so many of her patients speak of being abandoned emotionally and often physically by their parents. Indeed, an increasing number seem to have been abused by them. She uses the psalm to teach her patients that God does not abandon us like our earthly, sinful parents or friends.

There is another reason why we are naturally drawn to verse 10, however, and that is because the idea of a rightly functioning parent is ideally suited to everything David notes in this section that he is seeking from God. What do we seek from a parent after all? We look to a parent to receive, listen to, guide, and protect us, don't we? Well, that is exactly what David is seeking from God in these verses.

We seek acceptance. In the world, we experience much rejection. Parents reject children; children reject parents. Husbands reject wives, and wives, husbands. We are rejected by erstwhile friends, potential employers, people we are courting, and others in dozens of diverse situations. Most of us experience rejection from someone almost every day. But God does not refuse us. David prays, "Do not hide your face from me, do not turn your servant away in anger. . . . Do not reject me or forsake me" (v. 9), and he knows, even as he prays, that God will not forsake him. God has accepted him in the past. He will continue to accept him.

"Though my father and mother forsake me, the LORD will receive me," he writes (v. 10).[7]

Spurgeon said, "These dear relations will be the last to desert me, but if the milk of human kindness should dry up even from their breasts, there is a Father who never forgets." He added, "Some of the greatest of saints have been cast out by their families."[8]

We seek to be heard. Sometimes children talk to us only because they want to be listened to, not really caring what we say in response, and unfortunately many parents are too busy to listen. Is God ever too busy to listen when we speak to him? Never! Why don't we do it more often then? The reason is that we are too busy, not God. Or perhaps the reason is our sin or unbelief. Perhaps we do not really believe that God is a true, listening parent, a parent who says: "Ask and it will be given to you; seek and you will find; knock and the door will be opened to you" (Matt. 7:7).

We seek guidance. Which of us knows the way to walk so we will be kept out of sin and make progress in the way of righteousness? No one! We no more know how to live our lives for God than children know how to avoid danger and care for themselves and others. They need to be taught, as do we. In God we have one who can be turned to for guidance. David prays, "Teach me your way, O LORD; lead me in a straight path because of my oppressors" (v. 11). He prays confidently because he knows that God will do it.

We seek protection. The fourth thing a child looks for in a parent is protection, and David is certainly seeking this of the Lord because of his many enemies. They are the background of the psalm, being mentioned as early as verse 2 and being suggested even in verse 1 ("whom shall I fear? . . . of whom shall I be afraid?"). They are the bullies of the neighborhood, and David needs the protecting presence of God just as a small child needs his father in such circumstances.

The Soul's Prescription

Does David have the acceptance, answers, guidance, and protection he needs from God? Yes, because the psalm ends on this note, returning to the tone of quiet confidence with which it began: "I am confident of this: I will see the goodness of the LORD in the land of the living" (v. 13). David is not speaking about the afterlife here. He is speaking about "the land of the living," here and now.

But there is this warning, which I call a prescription. The things he is praying for (and for which we pray) do not always come to us at once. God has his timings, which are not ours, and therefore what we pray for and need is sometimes delayed. What then? Are we to despair of having answers, to lose confidence? Not at all! We simply need to wait. "Wait for the LORD; be strong and take heart and wait for the LORD" (v. 14). If some wealthy person promised to give you an expensive gift, wouldn't you wait for it expectantly? If you were in trouble and a king were coming to your aid, wouldn't you be alert for his appearance? God is just such a generous benefactor and powerful king. He is well worth waiting for. It is a privilege to wait for him.

Yet how little true waiting most of us really do.

Psalm 28

Hope in God Alone

To you I call, O LORD my Rock;
    do not turn a deaf ear to me.
For if you remain silent,
    I will be like those who have gone down to the pit.
Hear my cry for mercy
    as I call to you for help,
as I lift up my hands
    toward your Most Holy Place.

Do not drag me away with the wicked,
    with those who do evil,
who speak cordially with their neighbors
    but harbor malice in their hearts.
Repay them for their deeds
    and for their evil work;
repay them for what their hands have done
    and bring back upon them what they deserve.
Since they show no regard for the works of the LORD
    and what his hands have done,
he will tear them down
    and never build them up again.

Praise be to the LORD,
   for he has heard my cry for mercy.
The LORD is my strength and my shield;
   my heart trusts in him, and I am helped.
My heart leaps for joy
   and I will give thanks to him in song.

The LORD is the strength of his people,
   a fortress of salvation for his anointed one.
Save your people and bless your inheritance;
   be their shepherd and carry them forever.
                                                        verses 1–9

At the end of the last chapter I wrote about waiting for the Lord, which is where Psalm 27 ends. This is something we must learn to do better, since God does not usually respond to prayer according to our timetable. We do not expect to have to wait for God forever, of course. But what should we do while we are waiting? The answer is that we need to keep praying, to persevere in prayer. Significantly, this is the point to which Psalm 28, the next psalm in the Psalter, takes us. It is about importunity.

This reminds us of a story Jesus told, introduced by the words: "Then Jesus told his disciples a parable to show them that they should always pray and not give up" (Luke 18:1). He said that there was once a judge who cared nothing for God, the law, or other people. There was a widow in his town who had a case that needed to be heard. The judge wasn't interested. She had nothing to bribe him with. But she kept coming, and finally the judge said to himself, "Even though I don't fear God or care about men, yet because this widow keeps bothering me, I will see that she gets justice, so that she won't eventually wear me out with her coming!" (vv. 4–5).

Jesus' comment was: "And will not God bring about justice for his chosen ones, who cry out to him day and night? Will he keep putting them off? I tell you, he will see that they get justice, and quickly" (vv. 7–8).

Jesus was not teaching that God is an unjust judge, of course, or even that he is indifferent to the cries of his people. On the contrary, his point was that God is the exact opposite of the indifferent magistrate of the story and that, for this reason alone, you and I should be bold and persistent in praying. We need to be persistent, because God's answers do not always come at once, which is why the story is introduced as showing that we should always pray "and not give up."

An Appeal to Be Heard

The structure of Psalm 28 is a common one. It is called *dipodia*, which means stanzas of two verses. Each of the four stanzas has two verses (of four lines each), except the second or central one, which has three. The first stanza is an appeal to God to hear the psalm's prayer, a prayer the psalmist had apparently been making for quite a long time.

Why do I say this?

I say this because David appeals to God to no longer "remain silent." If he is appealing to God not to *remain* silent, it must be because God has been silent for awhile. He has not been answering, and David is appealing to him to break silence and speak to him at last.

He has a good argument, too. For he reminds the Lord that if he remains silent, David "will be like those who have gone down to the pit" (v. 1). This is worth thinking about on several levels.

First, the pit is Sheol or the abode of the dead. Because of the way the sentence is written, however, we are probably not to think that David is saying that he will die or be killed if God fails to intervene. That might be an appropriate thing for him to have said in other psalms where he is being threatened by hostile armies. But here his plea is for justice, particularly a vindicating judgment upon the wicked who surround him with hypocritical smiles and schemes (vv. 3–5). What David seems to be saying is not that he will be killed or die but that spiritually speaking he will be as good as dead unless God speaks to him. If God refuses to answer his prayers, how will David differ from the dying godless who have no relationship with God whatever?

A moment ago I referred to a parable that has bearing on this psalm. At this point it is hard not to think of another thing Jesus said. At the beginning of his ministry he was led into the wilderness to be tempted by the devil. He spent forty days fasting and praying, and at the end of that time he was hungry. Satan came to him with the suggestion that he use his divine powers to turn some of the stones that were lying around him into bread. "If you are the Son of God, tell these stones to become bread," Satan said (Matt. 4:3).

Jesus' reply was a citation from the book of Deuteronomy: "It is written: 'Man does not live on bread alone, but on every word that comes from the mouth of God'" (v. 4; cf. Deut. 8:3).

I wonder if you have ever thought about your life in those terms. All Christians speak about spiritual life and how much more important it is than mere physical life. We quote Jesus' words: "What good will it be for a man if he gains the whole world, yet forfeits his soul?" (Matt. 16:26). But if the only way life is received, sustained, and preserved is by hearing the words of God, shouldn't we be profoundly serious about developing our relationship with him—indeed, much more serious than we are? If we really believed that we were perishing apart from hearing the voice of God, as David apparently did, wouldn't we study the Bible more? And wouldn't we pray more? Wouldn't we be always crying out to him in prayer and seeking his face regularly through diligent Bible study?

Or let me put it another way. Since David speaks of "the pit," imagine yourself standing on the edge of a tremendous pit, about to topple into it to certain death. Wouldn't you cry out for help in such circumstances? And if you knew someone was near who could help you, wouldn't you keep calling out to him or her until you were helped?

There are two more things we need to see about David's appeal to God in this stanza.

First, *his attitude.* David is not praying arrogantly or belligerently, as if God owed him anything. God is no man's debtor. Rather, the psalmist is asking for mercy. Later, in Psalm 34, he will report on God's answer in corresponding terms, saying, "This poor man called, and the LORD heard him; he saved him out of all his troubles" (v. 6).

Second, *the basis of his appeal.* The last line of the first stanza describes David lifting up his hands toward God's "Most Holy Place." This refers to the innermost part of the tabernacle or temple enclosure, where the Ark of the Covenant rested. It was there where the blood sacrifices were offered for the nation's sin on the annual Day of Atonement. So when David addresses his appeal toward God's Most Holy Place he is telling God that he is coming on the basis of the shed blood, a sinner who knows that his sin must be atoned for before he can approach the Almighty.

This is the way the tax collector approached God in Jesus' parable, praying, "God, have mercy on me, a sinner" (Luke 18:13). In that prayer the words "have mercy on" are actually a reference to the mercy seat of the Ark of the Covenant; they mean the same thing as David's invocation. That is, "Receive me on the basis of the blood atonement." The tax collector was thinking of the Day of Atonement. Today we know that the actual atonement was made for us by the Lord Jesus Christ.

Charles Spurgeon captured something of this model approach to God when he wrote, "We stretch out empty hands, for we are beggars; we lift them up, for we seek heavenly supplies; we lift them towards the mercy seat of Jesus, for there our expectation dwells."[1]

The Psalm's Petition

The central stanza of this psalm, the one that contains three verses rather than two, is the second. It carries David's actual petition (vv. 3–5).

> Do not drag me away with the wicked,
>   with those who do evil,
> who speak cordially with their neighbors
>   but harbor malice in their hearts.
> Repay them for their deeds
>   and for their evil work;

repay them for what their hands have done
    and bring back upon them what they deserve.
Since they show no regard for the works of the LORD
    and what his hands have done,
he will tear them down
    and never build them up again.

This is an example of the many places in the psalms in which David or another writer asks God to judge the wicked, a feature of the psalms that troubles many people. At the very least, it is opposed to the more accepting spirit of our times. But, more than that, it is a problem for Christians who have been taught by Jesus not to judge others, lest we be judged (Matt. 7:1–5), and to pray, "Father, forgive them, for they do not know what they are doing" (Luke 23:34). We looked at this problem briefly when studying Psalms 5 and 7, and we will be looking at it again as these studies continue.

But a few things need to be said about this problem here.

David is not self-righteous in these statements. That is the problem we feel in statements asking God to judge others. It is what Jesus was warning about in the command not to judge, since he went on to speak about trying to take a speck out of another's eye when we have a beam in our own. That is a real difficulty for us, and a common one. But it is not a problem David has here. David has already approached God on the basis of his mercy, that is, acknowledging his own sinfulness. But even more to the point, he begins his petition (in vv. 3–5), not with an appeal to God to judge the wicked but with the request that God keep him from being dragged along into their evil stratagems. In other words, David is aware that in himself he is able to behave exactly like the wicked. He knows that anything any other sinner is capable of doing, he too is capable of doing.

That is why he is so anxious to hear God's voice and to receive answers to his prayers. Apart from the lifegiving, sustaining power of God's words, he will be swept along with the wicked and will perish with them.

David is never able to speak merely as a private citizen, but speaks instead as God's appointed king, Israel's judge. A private citizen may choose to forgive another who has done him a personal wrong. It happens all the time, particularly among Christians. But this is not a valid option for a judge, which is what David was. A judge must dispense justice, not waive it. David was responsible for seeing that justice was done, and here he is praying rightly that it might be. This may be why there is a sudden reference to him as God's "anointed one" in verse 8.

Evil should not prosper. Regardless of how we may feel about those who do evil—and we should certainly try to save them and redirect them if we can—evil itself is not good. We should pray that all evil plans might be frustrated and that all who persist in evil should be stopped and in the end be judged. If we do not feel this way, it is probably an indication that we are not very sensitive to sinful acts and have little concern for those who are victimized by them. There are many who feel—I am one—that our criminal justice system is floundering because it has erred in exactly this way. It has placed concern for the criminal or wrongdoer ahead of compassion for his victim and thereby fails to provide justice for either one.

It is important for the sake of all who are watching that right be vindicated. This is the other side of what we were looking at in Psalm 25, where David prayed that he might not be put to shame (vv. 2–3, 20). He said there that he was trying to live an upright moral life while those about him were doing the opposite, and his appeal was for God to vindicate the right way. If David should be overcome and perish in spite of having lived for God, people would say that righteousness does not pay, that the only way to survive in a wicked world like ours is to do evil. David wanted those who observed him to say, "No, the way of the righteous is the right way. The way may be hard, but in the end it is better to have obeyed and served God."

In Psalm 28 we have the other side of that concern, as I said. For here David wants God to prove that the way of the ungodly does not succeed. Notice, for instance, that he is not praying for the final judgment of the wicked by which they are to be consigned to hell but rather that he is praying for a proper present recompense to them for the evil they are doing. In our terms, what he is praying for is that those who are looking on will see that "crime does not pay." David is so confident that in a moral universe this must be the case that he ends with a prediction:

> Since they show no regard for the works of the LORD
>   and what his hands have done,
> he will tear them down
>   and never build them up again (v. 5).

This is a lesson that many people have learned the hard way. They have spent lifetimes building without regard for God, only to see what they have built melt away like castles of sand. We have a bit of doggerel which says truthfully: "Only one life, 'twill soon be past; only what's done for Christ will last."

Where Are the Nine?

David's prediction of the fate of evildoers is so strong that he immediately passes into thanksgiving for what God has done or will be doing, which is what the third stanza is about (vv. 6–7). It is a joyous response to God for having answered him, and it is expressed in three tenses: "he *has heard* my cry for mercy," "I *am helped*," and "I *will give thanks* to him in song" (italics added). It is difficult to read this without feeling something of David's strong joy and nearly wild thanksgiving.

But the important thing for us is probably merely that he remembers to give thanks, which we do not always do. Throughout this study I have been relating the psalmist's words to Jesus' teaching about prayer. What I am reminded of here is a story I had occasion to refer to in an earlier chapter. We are told in Luke's Gospel that on one occasion Jesus was met by ten lepers, whom he healed, sending them to the priests for formal certification of their cure in accordance with Old Testament law. After a short while, one of them, a Samaritan, came back and threw himself at Jesus' feet, thanking him. Jesus responded by asking, "Were not all ten cleansed? Where are the other nine? Was no one found to return and give praise to God except this foreigner?" (Luke 17:17–18).

It is worth remembering that story in our prayer times, because although we are sometimes (though infrequently) persistent in prayer when we really want something, not many of us are equally careful to thank God afterward.

A Final Broadening Stanza

Up to this point the twenty-eighth psalm has been intensely personal, a true psalm of David the individual. But now it suddenly broadens to include all the Lord's people (vv. 8–9). A verse earlier, David called the Lord *his* strength and shield (v. 7). Now he claims the same thing for others.

> The LORD is the strength of his people,
> a fortress of salvation for his anointed one.

He closes by praying, "Save your people and bless your inheritance; be their shepherd and carry them forever."

From a literary point of view this last stanza seems to be tacked on, naturally leading some scholars to see the hand of a later liturgist or editor. But it is a perfectly natural addition if the author was Israel's great king, as the title claims. As Alexander Maclaren says, ". . . if the singer were king over Israel, and if the dangers threatening him were public perils, . . . it is most natural that God's 'anointed,' who has been asking deliverance for himself, should widen his petitions to take in the flock of which he was but the under-shepherd, and should devolve the shepherding and carrying of it on the Divine Shepherd-King, of whom he was [but] the shadowy representative."[2]

This ought to be a pattern for us. When we pray to God earnestly and get answers, we should do two things. First, we should thank God. This is what verses 6 and 7 model. Second, we should expand our prayers to request that others receive the same benefits. This is the burden of the psalm's final stanza. We remember that the petitions of the Lord's Prayer are spoken, not with first person singular pronouns ("*My* Father" or "Give *me my* daily bread") but with plural pronouns:

> Give *us* today *our* daily bread.
> Forgive *us our* debts, . . .
> And lead *us* not into temptation (Matt. 6:11–13, italics added).

This leads to one final observation on the teaching of Jesus about the right way to pray, though this one comes not from his direct teaching but from his example. It is the example he provides in the great final prayer before his crucifixion, recorded in John 17. It is similar to Psalm 28 in that it begins with Jesus' petitions for himself (vv. 1–5) but then quickly passes over into prayers on behalf of his people: for his disciples (vv. 6–19) and for the untold millions who were to believe on him because of their message (vv. 20–26). If Jesus prayed for his people, we should pray too. We should pray as David prayed, looking to God for answers to all proper requests. And we should pray knowing that, apart from hearing God's voice, we shall be as those who are spiritually dead. Regardless of where others may turn, our help will be in God alone.

Psalm 29

The Lord,
the Lord Almighty

Ascribe to the LORD, O mighty ones,
  ascribe to the LORD glory and strength.
Ascribe to the LORD the glory due his name;
  worship the LORD in the splendor of his holiness.

The voice of the LORD is over the waters;
  the God of glory thunders,
  the LORD thunders over the mighty waters.
The voice of the LORD is powerful;
  the voice of the LORD is majestic.
The voice of the LORD breaks the cedars;
  the LORD breaks in pieces the cedars of Lebanon.
He makes Lebanon skip like a calf,
  Sirion like a young wild ox.
The voice of the LORD strikes
  with flashes of lightning.
The voice of the LORD shakes the desert;
  the LORD shakes the Desert of Kadesh.
The voice of the LORD twists the oaks
  and strips the forests bare.
And in his temple all cry, "Glory!"

> *The LORD sits enthroned over the flood;*
>   *the LORD is enthroned as King forever.*
> *The LORD gives strength to his people;*
>   *the LORD blesses his people with peace.*
>   *verses 1–11*

I do not know of any book of the Bible that requires more knowledge, more experience of life, and more skill of interpretation to understand it well than the Book of Psalms. It is because the psalms are so diverse. They cover the vast range of biblical theology and the full scope of human experience—from doubt to faith, suffering to jubilation, defeat to victory—and they do so in an amazing variety of poetic forms. The psalms are so deep, so diverse, so challenging that I do not believe anyone can ever really master them.

Moreover, as soon as the student begins to get hold of one type of psalm and thinks he understands it, he is suddenly confronted with another that is quite different.

An Extraordinary Poem

That is what happens as we come to Psalm 29. This psalm is unlike any we have seen before. To begin with, it consists entirely of praise to God. Other psalms praise God, of course. But almost all mix praise with something else, frequently with appeals to God to help the psalmist or applications from the greatness of God to how we should live now. This psalm has no other elements. It is pure praise. It does not call upon us to do anything, because the psalm is itself doing the only thing it is concerned about. It is praising God.[1]

Second, the psalm is pure poetry. To be sure, all psalms are poetry. But this psalm reaches new poetic heights. You will recall that the chief elements in Hebrew poetry are repetition and parallelism. We have seen these to some degree in every psalm thus far. This entire psalm is built upon them.

The most striking example of repetition is the name of the Lord, Jehovah. The poem only has eleven verses, but "the LORD" (or Jehovah) occurs eighteen times, in some parts of the poem appearing in every line (vv. 1, 2, 4, 5, 8, 10, 11). In the middle portion (vv. 3–9) the name is found in the phrase "the voice of the LORD," and this occurs seven times.

The poem's parallelism is equally pronounced. It begins with three parallel appeals to the angels to give glory to God, followed by a fourth line that says the same thing, though in slightly different words (vv. 1–2).

> Ascribe to the LORD, O mighty ones,
>   ascribe to the LORD glory and strength.

> Ascribe to the LORD the glory due his name;
>   worship the LORD in the splendor of his holiness.

The middle portion (vv. 3–9) describes a thunderstorm in which the constant repetition of words evokes the echoing of thunder. In verse 3 the ideas of the first two lines of the stanza (the voice of God being "over the waters" and God thundering) are combined in the third: "the LORD thunders over the mighty waters." All the other verses of the middle section are simple parallels in which the second line repeats the idea of the first, usually intensifying it, except for verse 7 which appropriately breaks the pattern with two short lines describing flashes of lightning, and verse 9 which has an additional sentence added on.

The final section (vv. 10–11) returns to simple parallelism with two couplets in which "the LORD" occurs four times and "enthroned" and "his people" twice.

> The LORD sits enthroned over the flood;
>   the LORD is enthroned as King forever.
> The LORD gives strength to his people;
>   the LORD blesses his people with peace.

We might think that a poem this narrowly focused would be dull, but the psalm avoids dullness by two forms of motion. One is the passing of the storm which is described as sweeping over the entire country from north to south (vv. 3–9). The other is the movement from heaven where the psalm begins (vv. 1–2) to earth where it ends (vv. 10–11).

Psalm 29 is not particularly well known or appreciated. But the more I study it, the less surprised I am that Harry Ironside called Psalm 29 probably the finest poem in the Bible and "one of the loveliest poems I have ever seen."[2]

If you do not have a poetic spirit, you will never appreciate this psalm. For this is not a poem to be critically analyzed, above all not in a scientific frame of mind. If you keep telling yourself that the voice of God is not in thunder, that thunder is only the clashing of differently charged electronic particles, you will miss it all. To appreciate this psalm we have to get out in the fields, watch the majesty of some ferocious storm, and recall that God is in the storm, directing it, as he is in all other natural and historical phenomena.

Charles Haddon Spurgeon has a great poetic soul, and here is what he advised: "Just as the eighth psalm is to be read by moonlight, when the stars are bright, as the nineteenth needs the rays of the rising sun to bring out its beauty, so this can be best rehearsed beneath the black wing of tempest, by the glare of the lightning, or amid that dubious dusk which heralds the war of elements. The verses march to the tune of thunderbolts. God is everywhere conspicuous, and all the earth is hushed by the majesty of his presence."[3]

The commentators tell us that in the early church this psalm was often read to children or to an entire congregation during storms.

Glory in the Highest

The psalm opens with a two-verse introduction in which heavenly beings or angels are called upon to praise God.[4] This will seem strange to us if we are approaching the psalm in a rationalistic rather than a poetic frame of mind, for, of course, praising God is what the angels of God are employed in doing constantly. Strictly speaking, it is human beings, not angels, who need to be urged to praise God. Hearing a mere human being do the urging only seems to make the situation bizarre.

Why does David call on the angels, then? As soon as we think of this poetically the reason is obvious. It is because he feels that his praise and that of other mere human beings is not adequate. David is overwhelmed with the majesty of God revealed in the storm that he has witnessed and is now going to describe. He feels that he needs help to praise God properly. To praise God adequately the entire created order must join in, and even then sufficient praise will be lacking.

David's appeal to the angels does indicate something significant about worship, however, something we must keep in mind. (The angels already know it.) The appeal describes the praise of God as consisting of two things: *ascribing* glory to him, that is, acknowledging his supreme worth with our minds, and *worshiping* or bowing down to him (the Hebrew word means "to bow down"), which means a subordination of our wills and minds to his. The two belong together, and each is essential. So what the angels do naturally, we also must learn to do if the glory of God is to make its proper impact upon us and we are to worship him properly.

The Passing of the Storm

The second stanza of the psalm (vv. 3–9) contains the description of the storm. What a description it is! It is hard to read it without thinking of great storms one has witnessed.

One summer, when my family was young, my wife and I and our children were privileged to spend nearly two months at a chalet partway around the southern edge of Lake Brienz, not far from Interlaken, Switzerland. We were fairly high up the mountainside, so we had a wonderful view over most of the lake and could even see the edge of Interlaken to our left. The second of two lakes that meet at Interlaken, the Thunersee, was beyond the city further down the valley. One August afternoon we saw a storm come up the valley from the west. It was unlike anything we had seen before. We were mesmerized by it. It was dark and glowering and was preceded by sheets of driving rain and hail. Yet we were in bright sunshine. We watched the storm from our balcony, not understanding how strong it was until suddenly it reached us, blowing things about, pelting us with hail followed by a fierce rain. We barely made it indoors, where in safety we watched it pass on up Lake Brienz. The next day we learned how terrible it had been. It had done extensive damage in Interlaken, among other things uprooting some of the massive trees that for centuries had surrounded and adorned the central park.

That is the kind of experience the central part of Psalm 29 describes, a storm arising over the Mediterranean Sea to the north, sweeping down the entire length of Canaan, and then disappearing out over the desert to the south. Some interpreters divide the middle stanza into three parts to mark each of those movements.

Verses 3 and 4 seem to portray the storm as it gathers power out over the Mediterranean Sea, before coming ashore in full fury, though this is not certain. I take the phrases "over the waters" and "over the mighty waters" to refer to the Mediterranean, but the words can also refer to the water collected in the atmosphere in the dark thunderclouds of the storm soon to fall as rain. *Water* is used this way in Genesis 1, where God creates an "expanse," later called "sky," to separate water from water, that is, the water in the atmosphere from the collected water of the rivers, lakes, and seas. Whatever the meaning, the emphasis is on the "voice of the LORD," the thunder, which is "over the waters" and is heard by the psalmist on land.

In verses 5–7 the storm strikes, moving down from Lebanon. The place name Lebanon is used twice, once in verse 5 and again in verse 6. Verse 6 also mentions Sirion, which is an ancient Sidonian name for Mount Hermon. These verses describe the damage done to the great cedars of Lebanon, which were an important symbol for strength in the ancient Mediterranean world and yet are as nothing before the storm and the voice of God accompanying it. The storm is so fierce it seems to make even the mountains tremble. Verse 7 describes the flashing of the lightning which, quite accurately, is linked to the voice of the Lord or thunder.

Finally, in verses 8 and 9 the storm passes away over the southern Desert of Kadesh, where the people had spent time during the wilderness journey under Moses. Yet it does not pass away before it "twists the oaks and strips the forests bare."

What are the people doing who have witnessed the storm? They are in the temple praising God. David says with an economy of words and to great effect, "And in his temple all cry, 'Glory!'" (v. 9). This could refer to the praise of the angels taking place in heaven, which the psalmist has solicited in the opening stanza. But without some specific indication that this is what he intends or is thinking, it is most natural to think of the temple as the literal temple in Jerusalem and thus of those who are crying, "Glory!" as human beings.[5] If this is the right meaning, then the praise already begun in heaven (vv. 1–2) is echoed by the people of God who have seen his glory in the storm (v. 9).

In looking back over this description of the storm, we notice that its chief feature is "the voice of the LORD," a phrase that occurs seven times. This is not to be overlooked. It indicates that, although David is describing the majesty of God as revealed in a storm, what he is chiefly concerned with is the power of God's voice—and not just thunder! The thunder is only a poetic image for a reality, the actual voice of God, which is infinitely beyond it.

This is an important biblical theme. For example, we think of the power of the voice of God *in creation*. The Bible begins with God speaking. As a result of his voice, the created order springs into being. God said, "Let there be . . . ," and it was so.

The power of the voice of God is also revealed as he calls *in grace to draw sinners to himself.* Spurgeon liked this application and linked it to each phase of the storm's description. He read about the voice of God breaking the mighty cedars of Lebanon and wrote, "The gospel of Jesus has . . . dominion over the most inaccessible of mortals, and when the LORD sends the word, it breaks hearts far stouter than the cedars." He read about the storm's effect on the mountains and wrote, "The glorious gospel of the blessed God has more than equal power over the rocky obduracy and mountainous pride of man." He read about the lightning and observed that "flames of fire attend the voice of God in the gospel, illuminating and melting the hearts of men; by these he consumes our lusts and kindles in us a holy flame of ever-inspiring love and devotion." He observed the progression of the storm to the desert and noted, "Low lying plains must hear the voice of God as well as lofty mountains; the poor as well as the mighty must acknowledge the glory of the Lord."[6]

We may also think of the power of the voice of God *in judgment*. This is probably explicit in the psalm's final stanza, as we will see.

Peace on Earth

In the final two verses the storm has passed but God remains as the enthroned King of the universe. The earth may have been shaken as well as the people who live on it, but God is not shaken. He remains as calmly in control as ever, and there is peace for those who are his.

The tone of these final verses reminds us of God's appearance to Elijah after he had fled into the desert out of fear of Ahab and Jezebel who had threatened to kill him. Elijah was emotionally drained and exhausted. But God told him, "Go out and stand on the mountain in the presence of the LORD, for the LORD is about to pass by." Elijah did, sheltering himself in a cave. The story continues: "Then a great and powerful wind tore the mountains apart and shattered the rocks before the LORD, but the LORD was not in the wind. After the wind there was an earthquake, but the LORD was not in the earthquake. After the earthquake came a fire, but the LORD was not in the fire. And after the fire came a gentle whisper."

When Elijah heard the gentle whisper he pulled his cloak over his face and went out from the cave where he had been hiding and met with God (see 1 Kings 19:11–13).

This is what it is like as we come to the end of Psalm 29. The storm has passed by. What remains is God himself, as peaceful and as much in control of things as he has always been.

There are two more points that should be made, however.

First, God is said to sit "enthroned over the flood" (v. 10). That is a natural thing to say in this final stanza, for the normal aftermath of a storm of this scope would be localized flooding as the rains coursed down the hillsides and filled the valley bottoms. It was just such flooding Jesus was thinking of when he described the falling rains, rising streams, and destruction of the house of the man who built on sand without an adequate foundation (Matt. 7:26–27).

Yet there may be more than this to the use of flood imagery here. Psalm 29:10 is the only place in the Old Testament where this particular Hebrew word for flood occurs except in the classic flood narrative of Genesis 6–9. It is as if the word should appear in our English translations as "deluge" or "*the* flood." Every Jew would know the flood story. So the use of this word for flood would immediately remind them all of that great judgment and would associate the storm that has just been described with it. In fact, the tenses of verse 10 seem to call for this association, since the word *sits* is actually *sat* (past tense); the contrast is perhaps between the Genesis flood as a past event over which God presided and the storm as a present experience. The verse probably means: "The Lord sat enthroned over the Genesis flood, continues to be enthroned, and will be enthroned forever."

This is what I referred to when I said that the last stanza speaks explicitly of the voice of God in judgment. It is telling us that a final storm of judgment is coming. It warns people to get ready, using the thunderstorm as a powerful image. The only ones who will be ready for that judgment are God's people, to whom the Lord "gives strength" and "blesses . . . with peace" (v. 11).

Do you remember the words of the angels to the shepherds at the midnight announcement of the birth of Jesus in Luke 2:14? The words were:

> Glory to God in the highest,
>   and on earth peace to men on whom his favor rests.

This is the very pattern of Psalm 29, as Franz Delitzsch noted more than a hundred years ago. It begins with the angels singing praise to God in heaven: *Gloria in excelsis.* And it ends with the blessing *et in terra pax,* that is, "peace" to those on whom his favor rests.[7]

Psalm 30

A Litany of
Uplifting Contrasts

I will exalt you, O LORD,
for you lifted me out of the depths
and did not let my enemies gloat over me.
O LORD my God, I called to you for help
and you healed me.
O LORD, you brought me up from the grave;
you spared me from going down into the pit.

Sing to the LORD, you saints of his;
praise his holy name.
For his anger lasts only a moment,
but his favor lasts a lifetime;
weeping may remain for a night,
but rejoicing comes in the morning.

When I felt secure, I said,
"I will never be shaken."
O LORD, when you favored me,
you made my mountain stand firm;
but when you hid your face,
I was dismayed.

To you, O LORD, I called;
  to the Lord I cried for mercy:
"What gain is there in my destruction,
  to my going down into the pit?
Will the dust praise you?
  Will it proclaim your faithfulness?
Hear, O LORD, and be merciful to me;
  O LORD, be my help."

You turned my wailing into dancing;
  you removed my sackcloth and clothed me with joy,
that my heart may sing to you and not be silent.
  O LORD my God, I will give you thanks forever.
                                                    verses 1–12

From time to time in these studies I have pointed out that there are various types of psalms—the scholars call them genres—and that it is often helpful to remember the type one is dealing with in a specific psalm. Psalm 30 is a thanksgiving psalm. However, thanksgiving psalms are closely related to psalms of lament, since thanksgiving psalms are usually expressions of praise to God for having heard a lament. In this psalm, some of the words of the prior and presupposed lament are preserved in verses 9 and 10. Thanksgiving psalms are also related to hymns, another genre, since the psalmist's thanksgiving usually takes the form of sung praise.

The title of this psalm identifies it as being "for the dedication of the temple" (actually, "for the house"). This does not help us understand it very much, although there has been a great deal of speculation as to what "house" might refer to.[1]

What is helpful is to realize that this is a psalm of thanksgiving for deliverance from a great sickness, which becomes evident as we read through it. Sometimes language like this occurs in less explicit psalms, and we find ourselves asking whether the psalm is talking about real sickness or sickness that is somehow symbolic. We wonder whether it is referring to spiritual sickness, depression, or even danger from enemies. There is no such question here. It is clear that David had been sick enough to die. But God had rescued him, bringing him up from what he describes as "the depths," "the grave," or "the pit." Now, having been rescued, he not only praises God himself but also calls on others of the Lord's people to join him, on the ground that his experience is common to God's saints. This leads to the best-known and most frequently quoted verse of the psalm, verse 5:

> For his anger lasts only a moment,
>   but his favor lasts a lifetime;
> weeping may remain for a night,
>   but rejoicing comes in the morning.

From a literary point of view, the most striking feature of Psalm 30 is its remarkable sets of contrasts, which is also probably the most helpful way to approach it. I highlight the four main ones in this study, but each of these contains further contrasts within as elaborations of the central idea. I count more than a dozen in all.

Serious Sickness and Renewed Health

When we were studying Psalm 28 I pointed out that, although David speaks of "the pit" in that psalm, meaning Sheol or the abode of the dead, he does not say that he has fallen into it. On the contrary, he pictured himself as tottering on the edge, crying out for help before he falls and is gone forever. In this psalm David says he had already fallen into the depths or the grave, though he is careful not to use the word *pit* (Sheol), since that would imply that he had died. What he is saying is that he had fallen into what was apparently his final illness and that he was on the very brink of death. We speak of a man being so old or so sick that he has one foot in the grave. But David is saying that he was so sick that his enemies had actually, in their minds at least, laid him out in his coffin. It is from this that God delivered him.

Verse 1 contains a nice image for what happened, for when David says "you lifted me out of the depths" he chooses a verb which was used of drawing a bucket up out of a well. He is saying that it is as if God reached down and pulled him up out of death's pit when, apart from God, there was no hope for him at all. The image introduces the first set of uplifting contrasts:

- lifted "up" versus "going down"
- God who helped versus enemies who gloated
- serious sickness versus renewed health
- threat of the "grave" versus life
- physical suffering versus praise and thankfulness to God

P. C. Craigie says rightly of this section, "The occasion for the present act of worship is not merely the assurance that God would answer, but the experience of actual healing because God had answered."[2]

The important point, of course, is that God was responsible for the healing, which is why David is thanking him. It leads to this question: Do we adequately think of sickness and recovery in these terms? Generally speaking, we do not, though as Christians we do tend to think of God and call to him when we are actually sick. We live in a scientific age, which has had the bad effect of removing us from a sense of God's presence and intervention in our lives. It makes us substitute secondary causes for the first Cause. We speak of "the miracles of modern medicine" much more easily than we speak of God's miracles or miraculous intervention. But strictly speaking, as thankful as we should be for medical knowledge, skills, personnel, and resources, medicine is no "miracle." It is a technology. The "miracle" even in contemporary medical healing is God's.

So when you are sick, pray. Ask God for healing.

And when you are well again, remember that it is God who has healed you, and thank him for it, as the psalmist does.

God's Anger and God's Favor

After expressing thanks to God for his healing the psalmist quite naturally turns to God's people, whom he calls "you saints of his," and asks them to join in praising God too. It would be right for David to have asked them merely to thank God that their king had been spared. But he does something much finer than that in this section (vv. 4–5). He asks them to praise God, not merely because God had been gracious to himself but because it is God's nature to be gracious. In other words, David was calling on the people to realize that this is how God is and that, because he is like this, it is how he has also been treating them.

To understand the principle David develops in this section we need to recognize that it is a spiritual statement regarding God's character and not just a detached observation on life. Without the first half of verse 5, the second half might suggest the latter:

> weeping may remain for a night,
> but rejoicing comes in the morning.

By itself, this passage could mean, merely, "into each life a little rain must fall" or "every cloud has a silver lining" or "you've got to take the bad with the good" or "cheer up, things will get better." But, of course, that is not the idea at all. It is true that there are good and bad things in life and that we do not always have to see a specific judgment or blessing of God in each one. But what David is talking about is God's disfavor versus his favor, expressed in the experiences of life. His conviction is that the favor always outweighs the disfavor for God's people.

The point is this. God is indeed displeased with sin and can never be indifferent to it. He judges sin with a holy anger, even in Christians. But for his people God's judgments and anger are short-lived. They pass quickly. What remains is his favor, which lasts for our lifetimes and indeed forever.

We know that this was no mere theory for David, because there is an incident from his later life in which he put his convictions regarding this aspect of God's character into practice. Second Samuel 24 and 1 Chronicles 21 tell how David decided to number the fighting men of Israel. He sent Joab and the other commanders throughout the kingdom to do it, despite their protest that it was a vain request and would displease God. The act did displease God, with the result that a man named Gad, David's prophet at court, came to him with a choice of judgments. He could experience three years of famine, three months of being swept away before his enemies, or three days of plague in the land, with the angel of the Lord ravaging every part of the kingdom. David chose the latter because, he said, "Let me fall into the hands of the LORD, for his mercy is very great; but do not let me fall into the hands of men" (1 Chron. 21:13; cf. 2 Sam. 24:14).

David's choice reflected the conviction we have seen in Psalm 30, and it proved to be a wise choice. The plague did fall on Israel, and seventy thousand men died the first day. But when the angel of death came to Jerusalem and was about to attack it, the Lord was grieved for the people and told the angel to withhold his hand and withdraw. So the plague was arrested.

The place the plague stopped was the threshing floor of Araunah, which David then bought and appointed appropriately to be the future site of the temple and of the altar of burnt offering where atonement for sin by sacrifice should thereafter be made.[3]

I wrote that David is thinking of the character of God in our text and not merely of a balancing out of good and bad times with the weight being on the side of the good. He is thinking of God's favor and disfavor. But it is also true, isn't it, that God's favor (forget his disfavor for a moment) also controls those otherwise simply good and bad experiences. We do experience hard times. They are part of life. But God is gracious in those things too, so that we generally experience far more of the good than the bad. Haven't you found it to be so? Can't you look back on your life as a Christian and confess that God has been very good to you, that he has kept the bad days to a minimum and multiplied the good? It is a rare Christian who cannot say that.

I acknowledge that some Christians do suffer a great deal, and sometimes their suffering is so intense that it seems longer than it truly is. What do we say of such circumstances? In the face of such suffering, we need to see our experiences not only in the light of this world but of eternity.

Harry Ironside tells that when his father was dying he was suffering a great deal. A friend visited him and, leaning over, said, "John, you are suffering terribly, aren't you?"

The father did not deny it. "I am suffering more than I thought it was possible for anyone to suffer and still live," he said. "But," he added, "one sight of his blessed face will make up for it all."[4] That is the true Christian's ultimate perspective. It is the faith that triumphs strongly over everything.

So here is an additional and rich set of contrasts:

- God's "anger" versus God's "favor"
- "weeping" versus "rejoicing"
- "night" versus "morning"
- "a moment" versus "a lifetime"

I must add a warning before I go on. It is true that for the people of God the sufferings of this life are minimized; even if their miseries should be great here, for reasons known only to God, they will be more than compensated for hereafter. This is not true for unbelievers. For them it is exactly the opposite. For those who go their own way now, there may be many times of temporary rejoicing. The world has its pleasures. Even the very wicked may have an occasional moment of "heaven" here on earth. But their portion hereafter will be hell. In fact, even if they go through "hell" now, as they sometimes say they do, that hell will be heaven compared with the judgment yet to come. And it will come. It is true to say that for them the anger of the Lord will last, not only a lifetime but forever.

The time to discover God's favor through Jesus Christ is now, while it is still the day of God's grace.

The Psalmist's Sin and His Repentance

At first glance the psalm seems to take an unexpected turn at verse 6, for suddenly the writer is revealing a former sin of self-confidence or pride and is apparently linking it to his illness. He recalls the time God turned his face away from him because of that sin, how dismayed he was, and even the words he prayed as he sought mercy from the one he had offended:

> "What gain is there in my destruction,
>   in my going down into the pit?
> Will the dust praise you?
>   Will it proclaim your faithfulness?
> Hear, O LORD, and be merciful to me;
>   O LORD, be my help."

This is not so surprising, however, when we remember the principle the psalmist has just explained. He has been speaking of the Lord's anger lasting only for a moment and of his favor lasting a lifetime. The Lord's anger presupposes the sin against which it is directed. So here David confesses that the sin that led to his sickness was that of saying, "I will never be shaken" (v. 6), forgetting that we are only secure when God upholds us. If there is a connection between Psalm 30 and the incident in which David sinned in numbering the people, as H. C. Leupold (and some others) have argued,[5] the psalm is confessing that self-confidence is what lay behind the numbering. In other words, David had fallen into the trap of trusting in the numbers of his army rather than in the Lord.

The contrasts here are:

- feeling "secure" versus being "dismayed"
- enjoying God's "favor" versus God hiding his face

Self-confidence rather than God-confidence is a common failure among us, blessed as many of us have been with abundant wealth, enviable education, and technical skills. As a people we think we can prosper by our hustle. As a church we think we can manage our affairs and advance our work by secular skills and fund-raising techniques without relying on God. As a nation we think we can survive on the strength of our military might and industrial production. What a shaking there will have to be! What calamities before we again humble ourselves under the hand of God and look to him to exalt us in his way and time!

Personal Grief and Great Joy

The last set of uplifting contrasts is found in verses 11 and 12, but the wailing and sackcloth of those verses recall the time David has already described in verses 8–10. Wailing describes the words themselves, reflecting the anguished tone of David's utterance. Sackcloth describes the attitude in which his words were uttered, since sackcloth was the accepted attire of one who was demonstrating personal repentance from sin.

These contrasts are:

- "wailing" versus "dancing"
- "sackcloth" versus being "clothed . . . with joy"

There is one more important contrast, however. It is in the last verse, a contrast between singing to God (which means praising him openly) and being silent. It reminds us how silent many of us are in spite of having received many abundant blessings and deliverances from God.

Do you recall the hymn written by Charles Wesley in which we sing: "O for a thousand tongues to sing my great Redeemer's praise"? It is a pious thought but a vain one. For what would be the advantage of possessing a thousand tongues to sing God's praise when the one tongue we do have is so silent? Jesus told us, "Out of the overflow of his heart his mouth speaks" (Luke 6:45). So if we are not speaking God's praise, it is because our hearts are not full of him. Instead they are filled with the things of this world, things that will perish with the world and pass away. What a sad exchange! The things of this world for the glories of the eternal God.

I counsel you to fill your heart and mind with God. Think about him for what he is in himself and for what he has done. And then, when your heart is overflowing with his praise, speak about him to others, as David is doing in this psalm. You will find two things. First, you will find that God delights in such praise; you will be drawn to him even more than you are now. Second, you will find that God uses your praise to attract others and win them to faith, as a result of which you will have even more cause for rejoicing than you do now.

Psalm 31

Rock of Refuge

In you, O LORD, I have taken refuge;
let me never be put to shame;
deliver me in your righteousness.
Turn your ear to me,
come quickly to my rescue;
be my rock of refuge,
a strong fortress to save me.
Since you are my rock and my fortress,
for the sake of your name lead and guide me.
Free me from the trap that is set for me,
for you are my refuge.
Into your hands I commit my spirit;
redeem me, O LORD, the God of truth.

verses 1–5

Be strong and take heart,
all you who hope in the LORD.

verse 24

P salm 31 is longer than most of those immediately preceding it. Only Psalms 18 and 22 are longer. But Psalm 31 has this interesting distinction. As a psalm of trust growing out of an individual lament—"a magnificent psalm of confidence"—it has appealed to many Bible characters.

For example, the phrase "terror on every side," from verse 13, seems to have appealed to Jeremiah as a description of the dangers of his day, since he borrowed it no less than six times in his writings, sometimes picking up other echoes of the psalm along with it (Jer. 6:25; 20:3–4, 10; 46:5; 49:29; Lam. 2:22). In his prayer of repentance from inside the great fish, Jonah, the minor prophet, quoted the words "those who cling to worthless idols," from verse 6 (Jonah 2:8). The author of Psalm 71, possibly David himself, quotes the first verses of Psalm 31 as his opening. Most striking of all, verse 5 of the psalm seems to have provided Jesus' words for his last moving utterance from the cross: "Father, into your hands I commit my spirit" (Luke 23:46).

In spite of the apparent popularity of this psalm, it is a hard psalm to outline. In fact, no two writers agree on an outline. Some divide the psalm into three parts, some into two. But even among those who agree about how many parts to divide it into, there is no agreement about where the divisions come. Most even disagree about the flow of thought within the sections.

In this study it seems best to me to follow the stanza divisions of the New International Version, describing them this way:

First, there are two main parts to the psalm: (1) the body of the psalm (vv. 1–20) and (2) a brief concluding application (vv. 21–24). Second, the body or main part of the psalm has five parts: a *prayer* for help in trouble (vv. 1–5); an expression of *trust* in God (vv. 6–8); a *lament* arising from the psalmist's physical sickness or distress (vv. 9–13); a further expression of *trust* in God (vv. 14–18); and *praise* to God for his help in trouble (vv. 19–20). As we will see in our study, these five parts move from an emotional peak to an emotional valley and then back to an emotional peak again. It is as if David is riding an emotional roller coaster. Or, as if he is riding a wave from one high crest to a trough and then back to another high crest in closing.

Prayer for Help in Trouble

The first five verses of this psalm are a prayer for help in trouble. They are a confident prayer since they, like all the sections of the psalm, express a very strong trust in God.

These verses have a theme. It is that God is the psalmist's "rock of refuge." The phrase itself occurs in verse 2, but the two nouns are also repeated separately. *Refuge* is found in verses 1 and 4. *Rock* is used again in verse 3. In addition, the nearly synonymous term *fortress* is used twice (in vv. 2 and 3). This was a popular metaphor with David, being found in Psalms 18, 19, 28, 61, 62, and 71, for example. Unquestionably it comes from the years when he was fleeing from King Saul and so often found safety in the high rocks of the Judean wilderness. On the plain, David's warrior band was no match for the numerically superior and better-equipped troops of his enemy. But he was safe if he fled to the mountains. In the same way, David saw God as his true "rock of refuge" when his later enemies encircled him and set traps for his soul.

David says two things about God as his rock that have been described as illogical by some who know little of the life of faith. He says that God *is* his rock in verse 3 ("since you are my rock and my fortress") and yet asks God to *be* his rock in verse 2 ("be my rock of refuge"). How, such critics ask, can God be and yet be asked to be a refuge all at the same time?

How little such critics know! Charles Haddon Spurgeon understood that this is a logic not of words but of the heart, writing that it teaches us to ask God that we may "enjoy in experience what we grasp by faith."[1] We know by faith that God is many things, because the Bible tells us he is. But this is a very different thing from proving God to be those things in our personal experience. Do you believe that God is all powerful? Of course, you do. Then pray that he will prove himself strong in your weakness. Do you believe that God is wise. Of course! Then ask him to display his wisdom in the ordering of your life. In the same way, you can ask him to be to you loving and gracious and merciful and everything else the Bible says he is.

"You are . . . then be . . . ," should be the prayer of every Christian.

Particularly in death. When David spoke the words we find in the first half of verse 5, he was asking God to save his life from enemies. But ever since Jesus used these words on the cross, saints everywhere have echoed him in asking God to receive their souls in death and so bear them safely to his presence. In other words, they have asked God to be to them in death what they have known him to be in life. One of the great commentators on this psalm, J. J. Stewart Perowne, points out that these were the last words of Saint Bernard, John Huss, Jerome of Prague, Martin Luther, Philip Melanchthon, and many others. He quotes Luther as saying, "Blessed are they who die not only *for* the Lord, as martyrs; not only *in* the Lord, as all believers; but likewise *with* the Lord, as breathing forth their lives in these words: 'Into thy hands I commend my spirit.'"[2]

When John Huss was condemned to be burned at the stake, the bishop who conducted the ceremony ended with the chilling words: "And now we commit thy soul to the devil." Huss replied calmly, "I commit my spirit into thy hands, Lord Jesus Christ; unto thee I commend my spirit, which thou has redeemed."

An Expression of Trust

The second section of the psalm expresses *trust* in God (vv. 6–8). This trust has been anticipated in part one, but it comes to a fuller expression here, David saying explicitly, "I trust in the LORD" (v. 6).

This trust is not something "off the wall," as we say. It is not without reasons, since David gives his reasons in the various phrases of this section. He was in trouble, and the Lord did four things. First, God "knew the anguish of [his] soul." That is, God took note of his trouble and identified with him in it. Second, God "saw [his] affliction." This means more than that God merely took note of it. It means that God did something about it, that he came to David's rescue. Third, God did not hand him "over to [his] enemy." He protected him and kept him from the destruction the enemy wanted to bring upon him. Finally, God "set [his] feet in a spacious place." In other words, God was faithful to deliver David from affliction. Since God did that in the past, David is determined to trust him now.

The memory of past deliverance bears fruit in present confidence.

A Lament

The emotional heart of the psalm is the lament found in verses 9–13, in which David tells the Lord of his present distress and danger. In studying an earlier psalm I pointed out that language expressing physical affliction sometimes refers to actual sickness and sometimes not. In Psalm 30 it does. There David was so sick he was on the point of dying. In Psalm 31 the problem does not seem to be illness, though the language sounds like it, but rather the danger created by David's enemies. For that reason the language used to describe bodily affliction should be seen primarily as metaphorical or at least as poetically exaggerated.

The best way to read the stanza is backwards. David starts with his personal distress and works outward to its cause. We do better if we begin with the cause and work inward to the effect it had on David.

The chief problem (v. 13) is that his enemies had surrounded him on all sides and were conspiring together to take his life. This was literally true during much of David's reign. The kingdom was surrounded by hostile neighbors, just as the present nation of Israel is surrounded by hostile Arab neighbors. But David may also be thinking of plots within his kingdom by Jewish enemies or of the days he had to flee from King Saul.

Because of the enormity of this danger and of his own apparent weakness, David was scorned by his neighbors and was even deserted by his friends (vv. 11–12). Many people have experienced this. As long as we are successful or influential or rich, everyone wants to know us and be considered our friend. But as soon as we lose these advantages, people desert us. This is the way of the world. We should not be surprised at it. We should only be thankful that God is quite different.

Finally, because of his precarious position and of being deserted by his friends, David was affected physically. His strength seemed to fail, his bones and eyes grew weak, and his body filled with grief. These words may be poetic exaggeration, but they describe real affliction. They describe the weakness, sorrow, and grief of many.

A Further Expression of Trust

Earlier in this study I said that the body of the psalm moves from the emotional crest of praying to God down into a trough of sorrow and then back upward to a crest of praise again. In the last section we were in the trough. In this section (vv. 14–18) we are starting up the other side.

To many people the most striking sentence in these verses is the first sentence in verse 15, which says, "My times are in your hands." What times are these? Well, all times. The times of our *youth* are in God's hands, times when others make decisions for us. Some of those decisions are good decisions, some are bad. But God holds both the good and bad in his hands and works all things out for the good of those who love him. The times of our *maturity* are in God's hands, that is, days in which we are (or should be) about our Father's business. In such days we probably have successes, but we also have defeats. Even in spiritual work everything does not always go well. Does that mean that God has abandoned us? Not at all. The times of defeat as well as the times of victory are controlled by God. Finally, the times of our *old age* are in God's hand, days in which the strength of youth has faded away and the opportunities for starting new work are past. God cares for us also in old age, and he is able to bless those days as much as any others.

> Even down to old age thy saints shall prove
> Thine own inestimable, unchangeable love.
> And when hoary hairs shall their temples adorn
> Like lambs they shall to thy bosom be borne.

In brief this means that God is present in all the circumstances of your life. Nothing ever comes into your life to surprise him. Indeed, nothing can come into your life that has not first of all passed through the filter of his "good, pleasing and perfect will" (Rom. 12:2).

"In all things God works for the good of those who love him," Paul says (Rom. 8:28). Therefore, like Paul, we can also say, "I have learned to be content whatever the circumstances" (Phil. 4:11).

Praise to God for His Help

In verses 19 and 20 we reach the crest of the wave again. But I want you to notice something interesting. Up to this point the psalm has followed a regular and therefore a nearly predictable pattern. It began with a prayer; that was the first section. It expressed personal trust in God, section two. Section three was the lament. Section four once again expressed trust in God, a section almost identical in tone and meaning to section two. With that pattern established, what should we expect in this last section? The answer is: the same thing we had in section one, a prayer. But here is the interesting thing. Although section five is a kind of prayer, what it is more specifically is an expression of praise to God. In other words, as a result of working through the content of the first four sections of the psalm, the last section is changed from a prayer of petition in which God is asked to do something to a prayer in which he is praised for what he has done and will continue to do.

Have you ever experienced that in your times of prayer? You should. It is normal to begin with some great need and to express great requests but then come away from prayer with the assurance that God has heard you and will help you, and so be praising him for it.

The theme of the last section of this main body of the psalm is God's goodness. It has appealed to many preachers because of the distinction David makes between the goodness God has "stored up for those who fear [him]" and the goodness he has bestowed "in the sight of men." The one is hidden. The other is manifest. The distinction suggests the following contrasts.

The goodness of God to us that other people see and the even greater goodness to us that they cannot see. When God blesses his people with happy and prosperous lives, stable families, and the joy that comes from knowing that what we do has usefulness and meaning, other people can see this whether or not they acknowledge God to be the source.

Some years ago George Gallup of the Gallup Poll organization pointed out quite objectively that people who are "highly religiously motivated" are happier than other people, have fewer divorces, are less prejudiced, and are more active in helping others in areas of social need. That is the goodness of God bestowed "in the sight of men." But it is nothing compared to the goodness of God to us that others cannot see at all. They cannot see the comfort that God alone gives. They cannot see those moments of quiet rapture when the soul of the believer is conscious of the very presence of God and rejoices in it. They cannot see the goodness of God revealed in response to believing prayer.

The goodness of God that other people see because it has already been given and the goodness that is yet to be given which they will see later. In an objective way, others may consider us blessed now because of God's goodness to us. But present experience of God's goodness is only a sample of greater and more varied goodness yet to come. Therefore, in the future even we will look back on more abundant evidences of God's goodness than we see now. That was David's experience, for in the well-known twenty-third psalm he looked both backward and forward, saying,

> You prepare a table before me
>   in the presence of my enemies.
> You anoint my head with oil;
>   my cup overflows.

> Surely goodness and love will follow me
>   all the days of my life,
> and I will dwell in the house of the LORD
>   forever (vv. 5–6).

The goodness that is experienced and at least partially seen in this life and the superlative goodness yet to be experienced in heaven. God's goodness will certainly follow us all the days of our lives. But it will not stop there. It will follow us even into heaven, where it will be disclosed in a measure not even imaginable now.

Alexander Maclaren's commentary has a section on this contrast that is so eloquent it deserves to be quoted at length.

> Here we see, sometimes, the messengers coming with the one cluster of grapes on the pole. There we shall live in the vineyard. Here we drink from the river as it flows; there we shall be at the fountain head. Here we are in the vestibule of the King's house; there we shall be in the throne room, and each chamber as we pass through it [will be] richer and fairer than the one preceding. . . . When God begins to compare his adjectives he does not stop till he gets to the superlative degree. . . . *Good* begets *better,* and the better of earth ensures the *best* of heaven.
>
> So out of our poor little experience here, we may gather grounds of confidence that will carry our thoughts peacefully even into the great darkness, and we may say, "What thou didst work is much, what thou hast laid up is more." And the contrast will continue for ever and ever; for all through that strange Eternity, that which is wrought will be less than that which is laid up, and we shall never get to the end of God, nor to the end of his goodness.[3]

Those who know God know that this is true and so say a hearty "Amen."

Part Two: The Application

We have already applied what we have seen in the body of Psalm 31 in a variety of ways. But David has his own application, which comes in the last two stanzas, each of two verses. They are a sort of coda to the psalm in which David turns to others (his earlier words had been directed to God) and advises them to praise and love God also.

The first two verses call for *praise.* They are much like verses 4 and 5 of the preceding psalm, in which David calls on others to praise God for his goodness since they, as well as he, have learned that "his anger lasts only a moment, but his favor . . . a lifetime." These verses are not so explicit as those in Psalm 30 in basing the call for praise on an aspect of God's character which these others should also have experienced. That is probably because their experience was one with David's. What I mean is that in Psalm 31 David is praising God because he delivered him when he was in "a besieged city," which is probably to be taken as a literal historical moment. If that is the case, then his deliverance was the deliverance of his friends and followers also.[4] They could praise God for exactly the same thing as David did.

The second short stanza and the last two verses call upon these same people to *love* God as well as praise him. It is significant that the psalm should end this way. For although love has not been mentioned before this, it is nevertheless true that love and trust go together. It is true in regard to human relations. It is true in our relationships with God too.

The very last lines encourage the saints of God to "be strong and take heart," which is a way of saying "keep trusting." The point is that we will do this only as long as we keep close to God and thus continue to grow in our love for him. H. C. Leupold puts it like this: "The practical application . . . amounts to this: Don't ever lose faith in him." Then he adds, wisely, "Faith will not be lost if love keeps burning."[5] You can never love God too much, and you can never trust God too much. But you will do both well whenever you reflect deeply on the degree to which he has loved you.

Psalm 32

A Great Man's Great Testimony

Blessed is he
whose transgressions are forgiven,
whose sins are covered.
Blessed is the man
whose sin the LORD does not count against him
and in whose spirit there is no deceit.

When I kept silent,
my bones wasted away
through my groaning all day long.
For day and night
your hand was heavy upon me;
my strength was sapped
as in the heat of summer.   Selah
Then I acknowledged my sin to you
and did not cover up my iniquity.
I said, "I will confess
my transgressions to the LORD"—
and you forgave
the guilt of my sin.   Selah

Therefore let everyone who is godly pray to you
while you may be found.

verses 1–6

P salm 32 is the second of the so-called penitential psalms. The others are Psalms 6, 38, 51, 102, 130, and 143. But the psalm might better be called "a psalm of instruction" from the title word *maskil,* which seems to mean "the giving of instruction."[1] Psalm 32 is the first of twelve psalms that bear this title.[2]

The psalm should probably be interpreted in connection with Psalm 51, which is David's great psalm of repentance. David had sinned in committing adultery with Bathsheba and had then manipulated the plan of battle to have her husband, Uriah, who was a soldier, killed. He had tried to ignore or hide the sin for some time. But when the prophet Nathan came to him to expose the transgression, David confessed it and was restored. Psalm 51 is the immediate expression of that confession and restoration. It breathes with the emotion of the moment. Psalm 32 seems to have been written later than Psalm 51, after some reflection, and may therefore, as Leupold suggests, be "the fulfillment of the vow contained in Psalm 51:13: 'Then will I teach transgressors thy ways, and sinners shall be converted unto thee.'"[3] That "teaching" may be the *maskil* which is Psalm 32.

The psalm certainly functioned as instruction, because Paul later quoted its first two verses in Romans 4 to add David's testimony to his own proof that justification is by grace through faith alone. It seems significant for our understanding of Psalm 32 that, of all David's recorded words and all the many writings that bear his name, it is the first two verses of this psalm rather than something else that Paul chose as Old Testament support for that important doctrine. He linked David's testimony to the experience of Abraham recorded in Genesis 15:6.

This was Saint Augustine's favorite psalm. Augustine had it inscribed on the wall next to his bed before he died in order to meditate on it better. He liked it because, as he said: *intelligentia prima est ut te noris peccatorem* (the beginning of knowledge is to know oneself to be a sinner).

A Great Beatitude

The first stanza (vv. 1–2) begins on a jubilant note, expressing the joy of the person whose sin has been forgiven. This is only the second time in the Psalter that a psalm has begun with the word *blessed* (literally, "blessed-nesses," plural). The first was in Psalm 1. But the happiness of the man speaking here is greater even than that of the man in Psalm 1. In Psalm 1 he is described as blessed who walks in God's way, which none of us do; in Psalm 32 the word is reserved for the person who has not walked in God's way, has sinned, but has repented of his or her sin and now knows the joy of restoration.

These verses are another example of Hebrew poetic parallelism, for there are three side-by-side terms for sin and three corresponding terms for how God deals with sin. As in the best of parallel constructions, these are not mere synonyms but are words chosen to cover the entire spectrum of sin and the wide scope of God's salvation from it.

Three Words for Sin

The first word for sin is "transgression" (Hebrew, *peshah*), which literally means "a going away" or "departure" or, in this case, "a rebellion" against God and his authority. This is what makes sin so dreadful, of course—that it is transgression not only against other people, whom we hurt by our sin, but at its root also against God. It is why Psalm 51 contains the words "Against you, you only, have I sinned and done what is evil in your sight" (v. 4). It is not that David had not sinned against others. He had. He had sinned against Uriah and also against the nation, which suffered for his sin. But in light of the enormity of his sin against God these other matters faded into the background. Alexander Maclaren captures the force of this word when he writes, "You do not understand the gravity of the most trivial wrong act when you think of it as a sin against the order of Nature, or against the law written on your heart, or as the breach of the constitution of your own nature, or as a crime against your fellows. You have not got to the bottom of the blackness until you see that it is a flat rebellion against God himself."[4]

The second word for sin is *chattath* (Hebrew, translated "sin" in verse 1). It is a nearly exact equivalent of the Greek word *hamartia*. Both mean "coming short" or "falling short" of a mark. In the ancient world the term was used in archery to describe a person who shoots at a target but whose arrow falls short. The target is God's law, and the sin described by this word is a failure to measure up to it.

The third word for sin is "iniquity" (Hebrew, *hawon*), which the New International Version also translates as "sin" (v. 2). It means "corrupt," "twisted," or "crooked." It rounds out the other terms in this way: The first describes sin in view of our relationship to God. It pictures us as being in rebellion against him. The second word describes sin in relation to the divine law. We fall short of it and are condemned by it. The third word describes sin in relation to ourselves. It is a corruption or twisting of right standards as well as of our own beings. That is, to the degree that we indulge in sin we become both twisted and twisting creatures.

Three Words for What God Does with Sin

The three words for sin that I have just explained are matched in the opening stanza by a second set of three terms describing what God does with the sin of those who confess it to him. He forgives it, covers it over, and refuses to count (or impute) it against the sinful person.

The first of these words is *forgiven,* and it literally means to have our sin "lifted off." Before the sin is confessed we bear it like some great burden, but when we confess it to God he lifts it from our shoulders. John Bunyan captured this well in *Pilgrim's Progress* where he describes Pilgrim coming to the cross, at which point "his burden loosed from off his shoulders and fell from off his back and began to tumble, and so continued to do so, till it came to the mouth of the sepulchre, where it fell in" and was seen no more.[5] This is what happens to all Christians. When we confess our sin God removes it "as far as the east is from the west" (Ps. 103:12) and no longer "remembers" it against us (Isa. 43:25).

> My sin—O the bliss of this glorious thought!—
> My sin, not in part, but the whole,
> Is nailed to the cross, and I bear it no more.
> Praise the Lord, praise the Lord, O my soul!

The second word that describes what God does with our sin is *covered*. It is a strong religious term taken from the imagery of the Day of Atonement. On the Day of Atonement the high priest of Israel took blood from an animal that had been sacrificed in the courtyard of the temple and carried it into the Most Holy Place, where it was sprinkled on the mercy seat of the Ark of the Covenant. The mercy seat was the lid or "covering" of the ark, and the blood was sprinkled there because it thereby came between the presence of the holy God, symbolized as dwelling in the space between the wings of the cherubim above the ark, and the broken law of God that was contained in the ark itself. It thus covered the broken law, shielding the sinner from God's judgment.

In Greek the word for mercy seat means "propitiation," which is the act of turning God's wrath aside. In Hebrew the word is "covering," the term used by David in our psalm.

The third word for what God does with sin is negative; that is, it describes what God does not do. He "does not count" the sin against us. The word *count* is elsewhere translated "impute," and it is a bookkeeping term, as "count" especially suggests. It is the word used by Paul in Romans to explain how God writes our sin into Christ's ledger and punishes it in him while, at the same time, writing the righteousness of Christ into our ledger and counting us as justified because of his merit. That is why Paul quotes these particular verses rather than others in Romans 4:7–8.

There is much more of Psalm 32 to come, but I have taken half of this chapter to deal with its first two verses because there is no greater blessedness than to know that our sin has been forgiven and covered over by the blood of Christ and it is no longer counted against us. Do you know that blessedness? If so, testify to it. If not, come to Jesus where alone that forgiveness may be found. It does not matter what you may have done. David had committed murder to cover up adultery. You may have stolen money, cheated your friends or business partners, and lied about nearly everything. You may even have cursed God. It does not matter. God will forgive and

restore you. The forgiveness of God is for all and for all sins, and the blessing that follows forgiveness is the greatest of all joys.

A Great Testimony

The second stanza of this psalm (vv. 3–5) is a recollection of David's
experience of unconfessed sin and of the immediate result of confessing it.
It is the heart of this very great man's great testimony.

Verses 3 and 4 recount the effect of his sin on David. We do not need to
spend much time on them except to say that they aptly describe the malaise
of any believer who is trying to ignore his or her sin. David says that his very
bones seemed to be wasting away and that his strength was drawn out of
him as if he were exposed to the heat of the summer sun. The reason, of
course, is that the Lord's hand was upon him heavily in judgment, as it will
be with anyone who tries to do as David did. When we sin we wish God
would ignore our transgression. But God cannot ignore sin and will not. He
brings pressure upon us, often very acute pressure, until we acknowledge
the sin, confess it, and return to him.

What is really striking about this second stanza is verse 5, in which David
explains how God forgave his sin once he had confessed it. God forgave it
completely and immediately. It was not brought up again.

Notice a few things about this verse. First, it is the longest verse of the
psalm, which is a way of saying that it is the most important verse or that it is
the very heart of the psalm. If this psalm is David's testimony, then this verse
is the heart of that testimony. In the same way, our experience of the forgiveness of God in Christ should be the heart of our spiritual experience
and the very center of what we try to convey to others when we speak of
spiritual things.

Second, verse 5 contains each of the three words for sin introduced in
verses 1 and 2: "transgressions," "sin," and "iniquity" (NIV "sin"). At the
beginning of the psalm the words were chosen to cover the scope of sin in
all its diverse aspects. Here the words recur to show that all David's sin was
confessed—he did not hold back from confession in any area—and thus
that all his sin was forgiven. David confessed it all, and God forgave it all.
The slate was wiped clean.

Third, the forgiveness was immediate. I think this is the best thing of all,
and probably David did too because of how he writes. Notice how the words
follow one another. David said, "I will confess my transgressions to the
Lord." Then immediately: "and you forgave the guilt of my sin."

At the right margin of the text are three occurrences of the word *selah*,
which probably means "pause and take notice." One occurrence of the word
is immediately before verse 5, after David's description of the debilitating
effect of unconfessed sin on him. The next occurrence is immediately after
verse 5, after the words "and you forgave the guilt of my sin." We are to pause
and reflect on that. But notice this important thing: there is no "pause" within

the verse, no hesitation whatever between the confession of sin and God's forgiveness of it. In fact, David does not even say that he voiced the confession. What he says is that he determined to do it, saying, "I *will* confess my transgressions . . . ," and that, as soon as he did, God forgave him.

I cannot read this without thinking of the nearly identical sequence in Jesus' story of the prodigal son. The son had sinned against God and against his father, as he acknowledges in the story (Luke 15:18). He says, "I *will* . . . go back." He plans to confess his sin to his father, asking to be received merely as one of his father's hired men. But the son does not actually get to say this. He starts his confession. But before he finishes it the father is already calling out to the servants, "Quick! Bring the best robe and put it on him. Put a ring on his finger and sandals on his feet. Bring the fattened calf and kill it. Let's have a feast and celebrate. For this son of mine was dead and is alive again; he was lost and is found" (vv. 22–24).

That is an insight into God's nature by him who is himself God, and it should be the greatest possible encouragement to each of us, for we are all sinners. God is ready and even yearning to forgive and restore us fully—if only we will confess our sin and come to him believing in Jesus Christ, who has made atonement for it. And he will do it right away.

A Great Admonition

In Psalm 51, after David has confessed his sin and asked God to forgive him, he says, "Then I will teach transgressors your ways, and sinners will turn back to you" (v. 13). We find the same thing in the third stanza of Psalm 32 (vv. 6–7), because, having experienced the forgiveness of God, David next and naturally turns to others, exclaiming, "Therefore let everyone who is godly pray to you while you may be found" (v. 6). He wants everyone to experience the joy he has found as the result of his confession.

David gives two reasons why we should do as he did.

First, today is a day of opportunity, a time when God "may be found." It is as Isaiah also wrote.

> Seek the LORD while he may be found;
>   call on him while he is near.
> Let the wicked forsake his way
>   and the evil man his thoughts.
> Let him turn to the LORD, and he will have mercy on him,
>   and to our God, for he will freely pardon (Isa. 55:6–7).

It is a great thing to be living in a day of grace, in a time when God "is not far from each one of us" (Acts 17:27). "Now is the time of God's favor, now is the day of salvation" (2 Cor. 6:2). But implied in David's words is the sobering teaching that the day of God's grace will not last forever. The day of judgment is coming, and on that day it will be too late to repent and find forgiveness. Do not wait until then. Come to Christ now.

Second, we should do as David did, because God will protect the penitent: "You are my hiding place; you will protect me from trouble and surround me with songs of deliverance" (v. 7). Charles Wesley thought of these troubles as the troubles of life, and the waters of verse 6 as our afflictions.

> Jesus, lover of my soul,
> Let me to thy bosom fly,
> While the nearer waters roll,
> While the tempest still is high:
> Hide me, O my Savior, hide,
> Till the storm of life is past;
> Safe into thy haven guide,
> O receive my soul at last!

But it is equally if not more likely that David is thinking of the waters of God's final judgment. In verses 3 and 4 David was seen hiding *from* God, but in verse 7 he is hiding *in* God and is eternally secure. J. J. Stewart Perowne interprets this verse as saying, "He who thus seeks Jehovah when he may be found shall not be swept away when his judgments are let loose like a flood of waters upon the earth."[6]

> Rock of Ages, cleft for me,
> Let me hide myself in thee.

A Great Promise

From a poetic standpoint Psalm 32 might have stopped with verse 7. But David adds a fourth stanza (vv. 8–10) on spiritual and moral guidance. To this is appended a final verse calling on those who have experienced forgiveness and guidance to rejoice in God and praise him.

Verse 8 (and possibly the entire stanza) is written as if God is speaking directly to the restored individual, promising to "instruct," "teach," "counsel," and "watch over" him. In the King James Version of the Bible this often-quoted text seems to suggest that God promises he will guide us "with mine eye." But, as attractive as this idea is, the true meaning seems to be that God will continually watch over us. The idea is of one who is offering direction to another so he can follow a certain path and reach a certain place. This one promises as well to keep an eye on him as he travels so he will not get lost and go wrong.

I am glad God promises to do that for us. For great as forgiveness is, the one who has sinned and been forgiven does not want to repeat the sin or again fall into error but rather wants to go on walking in the right way and so please our heavenly Father. How are we to do that unless God continues to keep his eye on us? If we ignore that care and refuse that counsel, we will be like brute beasts that have no understanding (v. 9). If we persist in our folly, we will be like the wicked who experience many woes (v. 10). But if we listen to God, obey him, and so walk in his right way, we will be able to rejoice in God. And we will be able to teach others also, which is what David has been doing in the psalm.

Psalm 33

A Praise Psalm
for Everyone

Sing joyfully to the LORD, you righteous;
it is fitting for the upright to praise him.
Praise the LORD with the harp;
make music to him on the ten-stringed lyre.
Sing to him a new song;
play skillfully, and shout for joy.

For the word of the LORD is right and true;
he is faithful in all he does.
The LORD loves righteousness and justice;
the earth is full of his unfailing love.

By the word of the LORD were the heavens made,
their starry host by the breath of his mouth.
He gathers the waters of the sea into jars;
he puts the deep into storehouses.
Let all the earth fear the LORD;
let all the people of the world revere him.

verses 1–8

We wait in hope for the LORD;
he is our help and our shield.

verse 20

May your unfailing love rest upon us, O LORD,
even as we put our hope in you.

verse 22

$\mathbf{T}$he Psalter has been called "Israel's Hymnbook" because so many of its psalms are nationalistic or individualistic. That is, they are written from the perspective of Israel's experience as a nation, or they express the personal defeats, victories, or longings of some individual Jewish writer such as David. Psalm 33 follows a somewhat different pattern. It looks to all nations and to all generations and calls on all people everywhere to praise God and thank him for his universal blessings.

It is a praise psalm for everyone.

In spite of the obviously new direction of this composition, it has a verbal link with Psalm 32, which precedes it. Psalm 32 ended by calling on the righteous to sing praises to God. This note is picked up in Psalm 33, almost as if its first three verses were written as an elaboration of Psalm 32:11. In particular, the words *sing, upright,* and *righteous* are repeated.

There is also another possible link. Psalm 33 is one of the few psalms in Book 1 of the Psalter without a title. The last time that occurred was at Psalm 10. I suggested there, as others also have, that Psalm 10 may originally have come under the heading of Psalm 9 and that the two belonged therefore together. They are actually printed as one psalm in eight Hebrew manuscripts[1] as well as in the Septuagint (Greek) and Vulgate (Latin) versions of the Old Testament. As a result, the numbering of the psalms is different in those translations and in Roman Catholic Bibles, which are based on the Vulgate.

The content and tone of Psalm 33, however, are so different from Psalm 32 that no one today seriously suggests that they were once one psalm. The second may not even be by David. Nevertheless, the fact that they are placed together as they are suggests that the arrangers of the Psalter saw some connection between them. Consider this possibility: Psalm 32 describes the joy of the person who has confessed his or her sin and has been restored. For such a person, it is now natural to praise and thank God, which is what Psalm 33 does. Any person who has experienced God's forgiveness should be thankful.

Moreover, I think this explains something else that is interesting. The psalm praises God for his word and his works, focusing on creation and God's deliverance of the people from enemies. But underlying this is praise of God's attributes, particularly his "unfailing love," mentioned in verses 5, 18, and 22. The one who has been forgiven by God will be particularly overtaken by this quality.

A Call to Worship

The psalm has a straightforward outline. The first three verses are a call to worship. The last three verses (vv. 20–22) are a conclusion in which the worshipers declare their intention of waiting trustingly on God. In between is the body of the psalm (vv. 4–19), in which the Lord is praised for his word and works, as I have indicated.

Not only is the outline straightforward. The opening call to worship is straightforward too. It contains six imperatives in which the righteous are called upon to "sing joyfully," "praise," "make music," "sing," "play," and "shout" their thanks to God. They are to do it loudly, which the last verb specifically commands. And they are to do it with instruments, as if the human voice by itself is not enough. This is the first time in the Psalter that musical instruments are mentioned as being employed in worship, and it shows that the Jews played instruments. In the time of Nehemiah they even had the ancient equivalent of an orchestra (Neh. 12:27). In light of this fact it is hard to believe, as some nevertheless do, that it is improper to use musical instruments in worship. This psalm is actually an endorsement of them.

Verse 3 encourages us to sing a "new song" to God. This is an unusual thing to say, and there have been various explanations of what the author meant by "new." At one point Alexander Maclaren suggested that it might be a reference to this being the first psalm like this in the Psalter.[2] Others suggest that the psalm is a new telling of Genesis 1 and Exodus 15, which are echoed in the psalm's main section. It is more likely, however, that "new song" simply means that every praise song should emerge from a fresh awareness of God's grace. H. C. Leupold says that a new song is "one which springs freshly from a thankful and rejoicing heart."[3] P. C. Craigie calls it "the ever-new freshness of the praise of God."[4] Alexander Maclaren adds, "There is always room for a fresh voice to praise the old gospel, the old creation, the old providence."[5]

So here are three important qualities of worship: freshness, skill (because of the instruments), and fervor. We need to make use of all three.

God's Word and Works

The body of the psalm (vv. 4–19) expresses the psalmist's praise to God. The two opening verses of this section establish the theme. They tell us that God is to be praised for his *word* and his *works*.

> For the word of the LORD is right and true;
>   he is faithful in all he does.
> The LORD loves righteousness and justice;
>   the earth is full of his unfailing love.

The "word of the LORD" leads off the stanza. "All he does" refers to God's works. (The King James Version says, "all his works are done in truth.") In verse 5, the "righteousness" and "justice" God loves are not the practice of these virtues by human beings, though God does love the pursuit of justice and righteousness by men and women. Rather they are the righteousness and justice that God demonstrates in his dealings with mankind.

There are six qualities of God in these verses—rightness and truth (which describe his word) and faithfulness, righteousness, justice, and unfailing love (which describe his actions). However, each of these is seen in all God's words and all God's works. God's words and God's works always go together.

How different it is with us. We say one thing and do another, so that we are inconsistent at best and hypocritical or blatantly dishonest at our worst. God is utterly consistent, always upright, and consistently good. Thus he is always to be praised for everything he says and for everything he does. There are no areas of his speech or actions for which he can be faulted.

Creation and Providence

The next stanza contains two subjects that are closely related: creation and providence. Both are examples of the way the word and the works of God go together.

Creation (vv. 6–9). The first and most obvious example of the unity of God's word and works is the creation of the heavens and the earth, and the psalmist turns to it naturally. Genesis 1, which these verses echo, says that God created the heavens and earth by speaking. The words "and [or then] God said" occur eight times in that chapter in regard to God's creating something. This emphasis is picked up in verses 6 and 9 of our psalm, where the psalmist notes that it was by "the word of the LORD" and by "the breath of his mouth" that the heavens were created, adding,

> For he spoke, and it came to be;
> he commanded, and it stood firm.

This is *fiat* creation, creation by the naked word of God, and it is entirely different from and infinitely superior to anything mere human beings can do. It is no wonder the writer interjects at this point: "Let all the earth fear the LORD; let all the people of the world revere him" (v. 8).

Providence (vv. 10–11). The second example of the unbreakable link between God's word and God's work is providence, the ordering of all things according to the secret counsels of God. The author's statement of this is a longer expression of the better-known words in Proverbs 19:21.

> Many are the plans in a man's heart,
> but it is the LORD's purpose that prevails.

We should be glad it is so, because "the word of the LORD is right and true; he is faithful in all he does" (Ps. 33:4), while our words are inconsistent or false, our plans frequently wrong, and ourselves unfaithful.

Responding to this from a New Testament perspective, as we do, it is hard to think of God's unfailing purposes in Psalm 33 without also reflecting on God's stated purposes for us, as expressed in Romans 8:28–30: "And we know that in all things God works for the good of those who love him, who have been called according to his purpose. For those God foreknew he also predestined to be conformed to the likeness of his Son, that he might be the firstborn among many brothers. And those he predestined, he also called; those he called, he also justified; those he justified, he also glorified." The passage tells us that God's purpose is to make us like Jesus Christ by the path of foreknowledge, predestination, effectual calling, justification, and glorification, and that in everything God works good for those who are on that path. This means that we can thank him for anything and should thank him for everything, even hardships and suffering.

This is a uniquely biblical approach to thanksgiving, one which very few persons practice.

The Nation Whose God Is the Lord

Having spoken of God's providence in thwarting the hostile plans of the surrounding nations and of firmly establishing his own good purposes for his people, the writer naturally turns to God's special care of these people, which is what the next stanza (vv. 12–19) describes.

The author is thinking of Israel as this special people when he writes, "Blessed is the nation whose God is the LORD, the people he chose for his inheritance" (v. 12). That cannot be said strictly of any nation but Israel. But it is said elsewhere in the Bible that righteousness exalts a nation and that even an ungodly nation can be blessed because of the godly in it.

How shall we think of our own nation? Our nation has never been a pure Christian nation, any more than Israel was ever entirely godly. But our nation certainly had strong Christian roots, and God, truth, the Bible, and morality were revered even if not consistently obeyed or practiced in those early days. The Puritans, who were an unusually strong force in our nation's founding, looked upon America as a new Israel and regarded their venture as an "errand into the wilderness," much like the Jews' desert journey toward the Promised Land. Isn't it right to say that America was blessed in its early history because in a large measure its God was the Lord? I think that is obvious. Large numbers of our people sought God fervently, and God heard them and blessed them with peace and prosperity.

But now? Now we have a remnant of believing people and have no doubt been spared many great tragedies because of them. But our country is not Christian anymore. It is militantly secular. God is not sought out, nor is his word honored. I fear to think what is coming for the United States of America, whose god no longer is the Lord. America's real god is money.

And yet, the blessings of God surround his people, even in a godless or fiercely secular environment, and it is right to remember them. What are these blessings? The psalm lists them in three categories.

God's watchfulness over us. The thought of God looking down on us and watching over us is so strong in this section that a number of scholars have titled it "God's eye," just as the previous stanza could be titled "God's word." The verses stress that God's eye is upon everyone, the just and the unjust alike: the Lord "sees *all* mankind" (v. 13), he "watches *all* who live on earth" (v. 14), "he who forms the hearts of *all,* who considers everything they do" (v. 15, italics added). This is a good portrayal of omniscience over all of humanity. But it is not this kind of watchfulness that the writer is particularly concerned about. What he cares about is that God's eye is upon his people and that he watches over them, as verse 18 makes clear.

> But the eyes of the LORD are on those who fear him,
>   on those whose hope is in his unfailing love.

In other words, this is precisely the kind of watchfulness mentioned in the preceding psalm, where David quotes God as saying: "I will counsel you and watch over you" (Ps. 32:8). It means that God is keeping an eye on us so he can intervene in a timely way to counsel, help, and redirect us and thus keep us from wandering off the right path and doing wrong.

Aren't you glad that the watchful eye of God is on you? If a person is not in Christ, the thought of God's watching eye is terrifying. It is frightening to know that "all hearts are open, all desires known" by him with whom we have to do. But to those who are in Christ, those whose sins are covered by his blood, the thought of God's watchful care is comforting.

God's protection. The second blessing in these verses is that God protects his people, foiling the plans of their enemies and turning back their enemies' attempts to harm them.

It occurs to me, as I think about these words, that many deliverances are probably unknown to us because they are turned back before they even come within our vision. I think this is important. In our prayers we usually remember the many tangible blessings God has given to us: families, homes, health, work, friends, special things that are important just to us, and the privileges we have as citizens of a democratic nation. We also think of less personal but nevertheless tangible blessings worldwide: that the world is more or less at peace, that other peoples are currently achieving or rediscovering their freedoms, that the gospel is widely proclaimed in our days. But while we remember these things, let us not forget to thank God for the things we do not have, the things we are spared because of his faithful and effective care. We do not know what these are specifically, but we can think of the categories.

Have we been spared severe sickness during the past year? We should be thankful for that. Not everyone has been. If we have been spared, we should thank God for it.

Have we been kept from serious accidents? That should be a cause of our most grateful thanksgiving.

Have we been delivered from people who would harm us at work? In our homes? On the streets? If you have been preserved from harm by such enemies, it is the Lord's doing and you should acknowledge it.

And what about temptations? The Bible tells us that "God . . . will not let [us] be tempted beyond what [we] can bear" (1 Cor. 10:13). This implies that there are temptations that God turns aside before they can reach us. If he did not, we would certainly have fallen into them. That we continue on the path of discipleship and righteousness is a result of God's care of those who are his people.

God's preserving care. This leads to the third area of blessing highlighted by Psalm 33: God's preserving of his people in this uncertain and tenuous life. The author covers a lot of ground when he speaks of God "deliver[ing] his people] from death and keep[ing] them alive in famine" (v. 19). Among other things, he covers the positive elements I mentioned earlier, including food, health, good homes, and other necessities for our physical survival.

Hope in the Lord

The conclusion of the psalm (vv. 20–22) strikes an entirely different note than was heard at the start. The opening verses call for joyful and loud praise to God. At the end the tone is quiet, as God's people, who have now reflected on his power and goodness to them, declare their intention to "wait in hope for the LORD" and "trust in his holy name." That is the natural thing to do. For if God is powerful and good, as he is declared to be, it is foolish not to trust him.

In Charles Haddon Spurgeon's *Treasury of David* there is a story credited to Edward Calamy about a young boy who was at sea during a dangerous storm. The passengers were frightened and at their wits' end, but he was not disturbed at all. In fact, he was even cheerful. The others asked how he could be cheerful when they seemed in danger of losing their lives. He replied that the pilot of the ship was his father, and he knew his father would take care of him.[6]

In this life a confidence such as that might be misplaced. For, however loving and skillful a human father might be, there are always dangers in life that are beyond us, and no one is able to guarantee the physical, much less the spiritual safety of another. Yet with God there can be no misplacing of confidence, no error of trust. How could there be? God has made the entire universe by his mere word and by the breath of his mouth. He foils the evil plans, not merely of individuals but of nations. God's purposes prevail. His plans prosper. Besides, he constantly looks upon the affairs of this world to care for his people—to bless, defend, preserve, and prosper them. No one who trusts in this God is ever disappointed. No one who waits in trusting hope will be let down. Alexander Maclaren said rightly, "Hands, lifted empty to heaven in longing trust, will never drop empty back and hang listless, without a blessing in their grasp."[7] Let God's people say,

> May your unfailing love rest upon us, O LORD,
>   even as we put our hope in you (v. 22).

Psalm 34

A Poor Man's Rich Legacy

I sought the LORD, and he answered me;
he delivered me from all my fears.
Those who look to him are radiant;
their faces are never covered with shame.
This poor man called, and the LORD heard him;
he saved him out of all his troubles.
The angel of the LORD encamps around those who fear him,
and he delivers them.

Taste and see that the LORD is good;
blessed is the man who takes refuge in him.

verses 4–8

A righteous man may have many troubles,
but the LORD delivers him from them all;
he protects all his bones,
not one of them will be broken.

verses 19–20

The Psalter contains fourteen psalms introduced by words linking them to incidents in the life of King David.[1] These introductions are not always helpful for understanding the psalms they introduce, but sometimes they are, and that is undoubtedly the situation here. The title to Psalm 34 says that it was written of the time when David "pretended to be insane before Abimelech, who drove him away, and he left."

The incident to which this refers is recorded in 1 Samuel 21:10–15. David was fleeing from his great enemy, King Saul, and his circumstances seemed to be so desperate that he left his own land and went to the coastal area of the Philistines to seek asylum with Achish, the king of Gath.[2] David must have felt extremely desperate, because Gath had been the home of Goliath, the Philistine champion whom he had killed years before. Just before going to Gath he had received Goliath's sword from Ahimelech, one of the priests of Nob. We can suppose that the very sight of the sword must have been an offense to the Philistines. Moreover, David seems to have been in danger, because the story says that he was so much afraid of Achish that he pretended to be a madman in his presence, making meaningless marks on the gates of the city and letting the saliva run down his beard. Achish took his acting at face value. Instead of arresting or killing him he simply drove him away, saying, "Am I so short of madmen that you have to bring this fellow here to carry on like this in front of me?" (v. 15).

Most commentators believe that this was a sad episode in David's life, since he obviously had failed to trust God to protect him from Saul and was relying on his own cunning instead. Whether that is true or not, David nevertheless did cry out for help and was delivered, as Psalm 34 makes clear. In 1 Samuel we are told that he escaped from Gath and fled to the cave of Adullam, where the psalm may have been written.

Psalm 34 is the third acrostic psalm in the Psalter, each of the verses (with the exception of the last) beginning with a successive letter of the Hebrew alphabet. The only variation is the omission of a verse for *waw*, which is also true of the second of the acrostic psalms, Psalm 25.[3]

Psalm 34 is quoted twice in the New Testament and may be alluded to in other passages. Verses 12–16 are quoted by Peter as a promise of God's blessing for those who live a godly life (1 Peter 3:10–12). Verse 20 is quoted by John as having been fulfilled at the time of Jesus' crucifixion: "he protects all his bones, not one of them will be broken" (see John 19:36, "These things happened so that the scripture would be fulfilled: 'Not one of his bones will be broken'").

The psalm is divided into two clear parts: (1) a testimony coupled with encouragement to praise and trust God, and (2) a set of wise observations based on the psalmist's experiences. Appropriately, Charles Haddon Spurgeon called the first ten verses a "hymn" and the last twelve verses a "sermon."[4]

An Invitation to Praise

The first half of the psalm has three parts, however, and the first of these (vv. 1–3) is similar to the introductory call to worship of Psalm 33. Yet there is a difference. The introduction to Psalm 33 is a forthright call to the

upright to praise God; it contains six imperatives. The introduction to
Psalm 34, which is a testimony by David to God's goodness, begins with
David himself praising God and only then invites others to join him as they
exalt God's name together.

The person who has experienced God's mercy naturally looks to others
to praise God with him. Corporate worship is one of the natural instincts of
the new life of Christ in God's people.

One of the arguments of critics against the validity of the psalm's title is
that Psalm 34 has nothing to do with the incident at Gath. But the very first
line is enriched if we take the setting literally. David says that he will extol
the Lord "at all times," and this must mean therefore even in times like
those of 1 Samuel 21. You and I usually find it easy to praise God in good
times, when everything seems to be going our way, but hard to boast in the
Lord when our circumstances are difficult. Yet David was prepared to praise
God even when he was in fear for his life, had gone down to Gath where he
had been forced to play the part of a madman, or was now in hiding in the
cave of Adullam.

He may have acted like a fool, but he was not so foolish as to neglect
praise of him who was his only true wisdom. He may have been hiding in a
dismal cave, but his psalm tells us that in his heart he was hiding in the
Lord.

This Poor Man

The second part of the psalm's first half (vv. 4–7) contains David's own
testimony. It is a good testimony, especially in light of his circumstances.
Here again the background provided by the title is instructive.

If we read the appropriate chapters of 1 Samuel carefully, we discover
that this was the lowest point of David's life thus far. In the previous chapter
he had had to part from Jonathan, his friend, after Jonathan had confirmed
that his father, King Saul, had determined to kill him. David was alone. He
had no bodyguard. He had no armor or weapons. In fact, he was even without food. The first verses of chapter 21 tell how he came to the priests at
Nob in order to get food. Ahimelech, the chief priest, gave him consecrated
bread after David had explained that it was right to do so. Then Ahimelech
gave him Goliath's sword, which I referred to earlier. When David went to
Gath this was all he had. And when he escaped from Achish and hid in the
cave of Adullam, he was still utterly alone. It was only later that his brothers
and his father's household heard where he was and went to him as the first
of the four hundred men that eventually became the core of his army and
his most trusted followers.

No wonder David described himself as "this poor man." He had nothing.
He was not even certain that he would escape alive.

So this is a psalm for *poor* men—and poor women too. It is a psalm for all
who are alone or destitute—for you, if you have nothing at all or are not

even sure that you will live long. It is for people who find themselves at the absolute low point in life, which is where David was. Or find themselves between a rock, which in this case was King Saul, and a hard place, which was King Achish. It is for you when everything seems against you.

If David were here in person and you were able to explain your situation to him, here is what he would say. Note the emphasis.

> *I* sought the LORD, and he answered *me;*
>   he delivered *me* from all *my* fears.
> Those who look to him are radiant;
>   their faces are never covered with shame.
> *This poor man* called, and the LORD heard *him;*
>   he saved *him* out of all *his* troubles.
> The angel of the LORD encamps around those who fear him,
>   and he delivers them (vv. 4–7, italics added).

What a great testimony this is! And what a helpful set of instructions! It gives a sequence. First, there is trouble. David speaks of his many "fears" (v. 4) and "all his troubles" (v. 6). Second, there is prayer. He says, "I sought the LORD" (v. 4) and I "called" upon him (v. 6). Third, there is deliverance, the answer to his prayers. He says, "The LORD . . . answered me; he delivered me" (v. 4). Again, "The LORD heard [me]; he saved [me] out of all [my] troubles" (v. 6). Fourth, his life became radiant with the joy of being in the care of such a good God: "Those who look to him are radiant; their faces are never covered with shame" (v. 5).

I notice, because the end of the psalm points in this direction, that David's circumstances did not immediately change. He was still a fugitive. He was still in danger. For a time at least he was still alone. But God did deliver him from Achish; that is, he preserved his life. And his grim circumstances did begin to change. The future leaders of his kingdom began to come to him.

That is important. The promise of prayer does not mean that God will change every difficult thing in your life. But he will preserve you for as long as he has work for you to do, and he will transform even the difficult circumstances by his presence and perhaps by the presence of others whom he sends to be with you.

Moreover, he will do this even if you are unable to see it for a time. I say this because of the superb illustration of verse 7 in an event that occurred somewhat later in Israel's history. Verse 7 says, "The angel of the LORD encamps around those who fear him, and he delivers them." What do you think of when you read that? I think of God's deliverance of the prophet Elisha and his servant recorded in 2 Kings 6.

Elisha and his servant were in Dothan. The king of Aram had sent his armies to surround the city because God had been revealing the military plans of the king to Elisha, Elisha had been passing them on to Israel's king, and the Jewish armies had then been able to avoid and outwit the Arameans. The king of Aram thought that if he could capture Elisha, he could shut off this information leak and begin to win battles. As the story tells it, the armies of the Arameans surrounded Dothan by night so that they were there in the morning when Elisha's servant went out of the city to draw water for his master. I can see him suddenly noticing the shining hosts of the enemy, rubbing his eyes in disbelief, and then hurrying back inside the safety of the city's walls to tell Elisha, "Oh, my lord, what shall we do?" (v. 15).

"Don't be afraid," Elisha answered. "Those who are with us are more than those who are with them" (v. 7). Then he prayed for God to open the young man's eyes, and when God did, "he looked and saw the hills full of horses and chariots of fire all around Elisha" (v. 17).

That was David's situation in the cave of Adullam, even though he could not see the divine hosts. It is your situation too, since the text speaks universally when it says, "The angel of the LORD encamps around those who fear him, and he delivers them." Deliverance is an important theme in this psalm, occurring four times. In verse 4 we are told that the Lord delivers us from our *fears*. In verse 7 the Lord is said to deliver us from our *enemies*. In verses 17 and 19 the Lord is seen delivering the righteous from their many *troubles*. The psalm does not say that we will not have fears, enemies, and troubles. But it does promise deliverance from them (sometimes in them) by God's power.

The angel of the Lord is the commander of the Lord's hosts who appeared to Joshua before the conquest of Canaan (cf. Josh. 5:13–15), possibly a preincarnate manifestation of the second person of the Trinity, Jesus Christ. This figure is mentioned in the Psalter only here and in Psalm 35:5–6.

Try It and See

When I was living in Switzerland in the mid-1960s, I had a friend for whom the first half of verse 8 was probably her favorite passage in the Bible: "Taste and see that the LORD is good." She liked the strong physical quality of it and probably, because she was liturgically inclined, viewed its best fulfillment as being in the communion service.

I do not think this verse is about communion, though that is not an inappropriate application of the principle. But my friend was certainly right in this, that the verse encourages us to try God out, almost physically, just as we would some great treat or delicacy. Does that seem indelicate or impious to say? To compare God to good food? Maybe. But although God is more than this image suggests, he is certainly not less. Our problem is not that we think of him too literally but that we do not think of him literally enough. Moreover, as far as the communion service goes, the eating of the broken bread and the drinking of wine is to teach us that God becomes as literally a part of us by faith as food becomes a part of our bodies by the eating of it.

How does God become a part of you, a part of your thinking, of what you really are? It is by faith, and faith means believing God and acting upon that belief. In other words, it is exactly what David is speaking of in this stanza, though in other words. He wants us to act on what we know of God and his goodness, for only then will we actually experience for ourselves how good God truly is.

"I found him to be good," says David. "He delivered me from all my fears and enemies, and provided for me too. I want you to experience his provision as I have."

The Fear of the Lord

With verse 11 we begin the second half of the psalm. This half has its greatest biblical parallels in the wisdom material that opens the Book of Proverbs (chaps. 1–9). In fact, its theme is the theme of Proverbs, namely, "The fear of the LORD is the beginning of wisdom, and knowledge of the Holy One is understanding" (Prov. 9:10). Earlier the psalmist said, "The angel of the LORD encamps around those who fear him" (v. 7). Now he is going to teach us what that right fear is.

There are two parts to this last half of the psalm. Part one provides instruction (vv. 11–14). Part two is a summary of what has been said in the earlier verses (vv. 15–22).

What is "the fear of the Lord"? Most writers make a distinction between what we mean by fear and what we call reverence. This is correct, of course. It is even one of several dictionary meanings of fear: "awe, profound reverence, especially for the Supreme Being" *(Webster's New Collegiate Dictionary)*. But this is not how David defines the fear of the Lord in this section. He defines it, not by an emotion or attitude but by action, using words later picked up by the apostle Peter to describe the essentials of a moral life.

> Whoever of you loves life
> > and desires to see many good days,
> keep your tongue from evil
> > and your lips from speaking lies.
> Turn from evil and do good;
> > seek peace and pursue it.
> The eyes of the LORD are on the righteous
> > and his ears are attentive to their cry;
> the face of the LORD is against those who do evil.
> > (Ps. 34:12–16a; cf. 1 Peter 3:10–12)

David is saying that the fear of the Lord is doing right, that is, that it involves obedience. Moreover, since the fear of the Lord is the enjoyment of the Lord, the way to enjoy the Lord, to "taste and see that [he] is good," is to obey him. One commentator explains this by saying, "The good you *enjoy* (v. 12) goes hand in hand with the good you *do* (v. 14). It is an emphasis which answers the suspicion (first aroused in Eden) that outside the will of God, rather than within it, lies enrichment."[5]

A Summary

The very last section of the psalm is a summary, extending (in the New International Version) over four short stanzas (vv. 15–22). These verses introduce a contrast, not yet mentioned, between those who are righteous and turn to the Lord and those who do evil. We are told that the "eyes" and "ears" of the Lord are toward the righteous, to see their distress and hear their cries, but that the "face" of the Lord is against evildoers.

The earlier parts of this psalm are so well known that it is easy to pass over these last verses. But they are profound in two ways and so deserve at least equal notice.

First, they present a mature and very balanced view of life, pointing to the deliverance God provides for those who fear him but not overlooking the fact that, in spite of God's favor, the righteous nevertheless do frequently suffer in this life. David himself had troubles; the psalm is a hymn of praise to God for delivering him out of them. So becoming a Christian does not mean a trouble-free existence. P. C. Craigie writes, "The fear of the Lord is indeed the foundation of life, the key to joy in life and long and happy days. But it is not a guarantee that life will be always easy. . . . It may mend the broken heart, but it does not prevent the heart from being broken; it may restore the spiritually crushed, but it does not crush the forces that may create oppression."[6] Deliverance is one thing. Exemption from trouble is another.

Second, in the last stanza the psalm moves beyond mere deliverance or blessing in this life to speak of death and, by implication, also of life beyond the grave. In this context it speaks of redemption and deliverance from God's final condemnation or judgment (vv. 21–22).

This points us to the ultimate fulfillment of these promises in the gospel. Deliverance here is good. But what is essential is deliverance from the eternal punishment due us for our sins, and for that deliverance we must look to Jesus Christ. The first part of verse 22 says, "The LORD redeems his servants." How? By the death and resurrection of Christ. The second half says, no one will be condemned who takes refuge in him." Why not? Because Jesus has taken that condemnation in our place.

Psalm 35

No One Like You!

May those who seek my life
be disgraced and put to shame;
may those who plot my ruin
be turned back in dismay.
May they be like chaff before the wind,
with the angel of the LORD driving them away;
may their path be dark and slippery,
with the angel of the LORD pursuing them.
Since they hid their net for me without cause
and without cause dug a pit for me,
may ruin overtake them by surprise—
may the net they hid entangle them,
may they fall into the pit, to their ruin.
Then my soul will rejoice in the LORD
and delight in his salvation.
My whole being will exclaim,
"Who is like you, O LORD?
You rescue the poor from those too strong for them,
the poor and needy from those who rob them."
verses 4–10

May those who delight in my vindication
shout for joy and gladness;

may they always say, "The LORD be exalted,
who delights in the well-being of his servant."
My tongue will speak of your righteousness
and of your praises all day long.

verses 27–28

When I was preaching through the psalms on Sunday evenings at Tenth Presbyterian Church it was my pattern to close each service with a hymn based on the psalm we were studying. I was surprised at how many such hymns there were. Most psalms have at least one hymn based on them, and some have several, sometimes as many as six or eight.

But there was no hymn for Psalm 35.

There is an easy explanation for that, of course. Psalm 35 is one of the so-called imprecatory psalms, psalms in which the writer asks God to pour out judgment on his enemies. Psalms that do that do not seem to have been written in a right spirit to be sung by Christians. Here David says, "May those who seek my life be disgraced and put to shame; may those who plot my ruin be turned back in dismay. May they be like chaff before the wind, with the angel of the LORD driving them away" (vv. 4–5). We have been taught by Jesus to pray, "Father, forgive them, for they do not know what they are doing" (Luke 23:34). Indeed, we remember that Jesus said, "I tell you: Love your enemies and pray for those who persecute you, that you may be sons of your Father in heaven" (Matt. 5:44–45).

We find these prayers for God's judgment on the psalmist's enemies in four psalms especially, Psalms 7, 35, 69, and 109, though imprecations like these are also found elsewhere. They seem to grow in vehemence as we read through the Psalter. Psalm 7 is the mildest. Psalm 109 is the worst; commentators have counted at least thirty anathemas in that one psalm alone.[1]

A Balanced Appraisal

How are Christians to think about these imprecations? It is usual for commentators to say that there is a difference between the spirit of the Old Testament and the spirit of the New, to say that a whole new attitude of forgiveness and patient endurance was introduced by Jesus Christ. There is something to that, of course. Jesus did tell us to forgive our enemies, and there is nothing exactly like his teaching in the Old Testament. That is true of some of his other teachings too. Yet I am not satisfied with this somewhat easy explanation, if for no other reason than that the Bible is a whole, given by God himself; we should not therefore easily set one part of it against another. Consider this:

First, the author of each of the imprecatory psalms is said in its title to be David. Yet in spite of the tone of these psalms, David was known personally, not for exacting vengeance on his enemies, but rather for forgiving them. His treatment of Saul was exemplary and is probably the best Old Testament parallel to Jesus' attitude toward his enemies at the time of his arrest and crucifixion.

Second, in the imprecatory passages David claims to be innocent of that for which he is being attacked or charged. He was not always innocent, and when he was not the psalms written under those circumstances have an entirely different tone. They confess the sin and ask for forgiveness.

Third, although the tone of the New Testament is somewhat different from that of the Old Testament, the rejoicing of the righteous at the fall of the wicked is nevertheless not entirely absent from it. The chief example is the joy of the righteous at the fall of mystical Babylon, recorded in Revelation 18 and 19. The text says, "Rejoice over her, O heaven! Rejoice, saints and apostles and prophets! God has judged her for the way she treated you" (Rev. 18:20). The hosts of heaven actually rejoice that "the smoke from her goes up for ever and ever" (Rev. 19:3). As far as Jesus himself is concerned, we must remember that the One who said, "Father, forgive them," also pronounced a terrible catalogue of woes upon the teachers of the law and the Pharisees, recorded in Matthew 23.

So what is the solution? I suggest that what we need is a balanced view of this subject, tempered by knowledge of our own sin and frequent hypocrisy.

In my judgment the chief thing to note is that, in Psalms 7, 35, 69, and 109, David is not writing as a private citizen but as the king and judge of Israel. The judgment he calls for is a righteous judgment upon those who, by opposing him, oppose God and godliness. It is one thing to forgive a wrong done against us personally. To do so is commendable. But it is quite another thing to overlook a wrong done by an evil person to another party, especially if you are the one chiefly responsible for administering law or justice in that circumstance. A policeman, judge, governor, or president must deal with violent people differently from how you or I might deal with them.

I also suggest that there is a place for private citizens, especially Christians, to oppose evil vigorously. We can pray for the conversion of the very wicked, but if they are not going to be converted (and many are not), we can certainly pray for their overthrow and destruction. It was right for all good people to pray for and rejoice at the fall of Adolf Hitler. It is right to pray for the overthrow of Saddam Hussein.

We must pray, however, with awareness of our own sins and with confession and requests for forgiveness for the sins of the United States of America. That is what I mean by a balanced view. On the one hand, it recognizes evil for what it is and prays for its defeat. On the other hand, it acknowledges the sin that is always also in us and prays for forgiveness.

David has that balance in these psalms.

It is only God's people, those who know something of their own sin as well as something of the holiness of God, who can achieve it.

A Three-Part Psalm

I have sometimes pointed out in our studies how difficult many of these psalms are to outline, with the result that the suggestions of commentators frequently differ widely. Strikingly, almost all agree on the outline of this psalm. It is in three parts, each of which begins with a prayer and ends on a note of confident hope in God's just intervention or deliverance. The first part embraces verses 1–10. The second part covers verses 11–18. The third part comprises verses 19–28.[2] However, the first three verses and the last three verses stand somewhat apart and can be considered as an introduction and conclusion.

In the introductory stanza (vv. 1–3) David introduces two images for what he wants God to do on his behalf. The first image is of a court of law. A suit is in progress. David is being attacked by ruthless witnesses. He wants God to be his advocate. He says, "Contend, O LORD, with those who contend with me." Although we miss this in English, the word *contend* refers to an attorney's pleas for his client. The second image is of a battlefield. David's enemies are waging war against him, and he wants God to be his champion.

> Take up shield and buckler;
>   arise and come to my aid.
> Brandish spear and javelin
>   against those who pursue me.

The last words apply to both the lawsuit and the battle: "Say to my soul, 'I am your salvation.'"

Champion and Advocate

These images fit well into the outline of the psalm. Part one (vv. 1–10) develops the second of the two, the image of the battle. Part two (vv. 11–18) develops the first, the image of a lawsuit. At the end, in part three, both come together (vv. 19–28).

Part One: A Battle

I have said that David develops two "images" in the psalm's introduction and that these are then worked out in the following three sections of the psalm. That might suggest that the battle described in this section (vv. 4–10) or the lawsuit described in the next (vv. 11–18) are not real but are only suggestive of something else. That could be the case, but knowing who David was, as we do, it probably is not. David was surrounded by hostile military forces most of his life, and it is not hard to imagine other enemies spreading false accusations against him, particularly during the times he was fleeing from King Saul or from his rebellious son Absalom.

Two things stand out in David's description of this military threat. First, his enemies have been scheming against him, plotting to take his life. Using an illustration of how a person might go about capturing a wild animal, David says that they have hidden a net for him or dug a pit (v. 7). Less poetically, he says that they are plotting his ruin and seeking his life (v. 4).

Second, he insists that they have done this "without cause." That claim appears twice in verse 7, and it reappears again in verse 19. It is not the same thing as David claiming to be innocent. All it means is that he had done nothing to merit the hostility of these enemies. To give a more modern example, we do not have to claim that the people of Poland, Austria, Holland, and France were innocent of all wrongdoing to say that they did not deserve the destruction brought by the German army in World War II.

David's basic prayer is that his enemies will be caught in their own devices, which is not an inappropriate thing to say. It would be a case of what we call poetic justice. May the violent meet a violent end, he says. May the crafty be deceived, cheaters be cheated, liars be lied to.

The unusual thing is that David calls on "the angel of the LORD" to pursue these enemies or drive them away. This figure was mentioned in the previous psalm (in v. 7), but these are the only psalms in the entire psalm collection that do mention him. Who is he? He could be just any angel, of course. But he seems to be a special being, otherwise unidentified, who appears at irregular intervals in the Bible to help selected individuals.

He is first mentioned as coming to Hagar, when she was about to perish in the desert after having run away from Sarah, Abraham's wife. Hagar called the angel of the Lord who appeared to her to help her "the God who sees me" (Gen. 16:13), thereby identifying him as more than an angel. This same figure appeared to Abraham to stop him from sacrificing his son on Mount Moriah (Gen. 22:11) and probably appeared to him earlier to announce the destruction of Sodom and Gomorrah, though the precise phrase "angel of the LORD" is not used (Gen. 18). There are three heavenly beings in that story; two are called "angels," but the third is repeatedly referred to as "the LORD" (Gen. 18:1, 10, 13, 17, 20, 22, 26, 33). This figure is probably the same one who appeared to Hagar. Later he appeared to Joshua before the battle of Jericho to take charge of the Jewish armies, though he is identified there as the "commander of the army of the LORD" rather than an angel (Josh. 5:14–15). He is probably also the one who was with Shadrach, Meshach, and Abednego in the blazing furnace, recorded in Daniel 3.

In my judgment this figure was a preincarnate manifestation of the second person of the Trinity, the Lord Jesus Christ, which is why he is regularly called "the LORD." It is also why he does not appear in the New Testament as "the angel." Instead, Paul on the road to Damascus, Stephen at his death, and John on Patmos saw Jesus.

What does David have in mind in this psalm? Since he is writing about a military threat, he is probably thinking of the "commander of the army of the LORD" and is looking to him and the heavenly legions to overcome his enemies. He is sure they will, because the first section of the psalm ends with praise to the Lord who will do it (vv. 9–10).

Part Two: A Lawsuit

In the second part of the psalm (vv. 11–18) the image changes to that of a lawsuit, and the problem here is that David's enemies are slandering him, just as, in the previous section, they had been scheming against his life. Is this literal? Probably! For even if there was no actual lawsuit—we have no record of anyone being able literally to bring a suit against the king—the slander was no doubt real, and David is pleading to the Lord to be his advocate.

What chiefly bothered David is that he was being slandered by people to whom he had behaved without reproach. More than that, he had gone out of his way to be kind to them. When they were sick, David interceded for them with "sackcloth," a sign of mourning, and with "fasting." When his prayers on their behalf were not immediately answered, he assumed the role of a mourner (vv. 13–14). He did good to these people (v. 12). What about them? For their part, they returned "evil for good" (v. 12). They accused him of things he knew nothing about (v. 11). And when he got into some unspecified trouble, they gathered around him gleefully to mock at his sad misfortune (vv. 15–16).

In verse 17 David calls on God to rescue him from "these lions," and in verse 18 he says that he is going to thank God for doing so.

Part Three: Deliverance

In the last of these three sections (vv. 19–28) the images of a military threat and a lawsuit come together, which makes us think that the two might have been parts of a single complex plot to unseat him. With some success apparently! His enemies were already gloating in section two (vv. 15–16). Now the word *gloat* appears three times (in vv. 19, 24, and 26) to describe their vicious actions.

Nothing hurts quite so much as this. Defeat we can usually handle. But when people rejoice in our failures or mock us in our defeats the wounds are more than doubled. It is almost more than we can bear.

Our only defense in such times is the Lord, who sees what is happening and can be counted on to vindicate us in due time. There is an interesting way of stating this in verses 21 and 22. In verse 21 David's enemies are speaking gleefully, saying, "Aha! Aha! With our own eyes we have seen it." This refers to the "false accusations" of the previous verse. It means that they are claiming to have seen a wrong that never happened. But notice verse 22. Here David appeals to God's omniscience, saying, "O LORD, you have seen this." In other words, God has seen the facts of the case, and these include not only David's innocence but also that he is being falsely accused and slandered. Surely the Judge of all the universe will do right. God will rise to his defense and contend for him (v. 23).

In the last three verses David wraps the psalm up, asking that those who have gloated over him might be put to confusion, while those who delight in his eventual vindication should be present to join him in singing God's praise. As for himself,

> My tongue will speak of your righteousness
> and of your praises all day long (v. 28).

Our Great Adversary

I have saved the application of this psalm to the end of the chapter, because it is difficult to apply and because I wanted to get the whole of the psalm before us first. How should we apply it? Is it right to ask God to judge our enemies, as David did? Can we pray part of what he prayed, eliminating other parts? If so, how do we distinguish between the parts? Or should we reject the imprecatory psalms entirely?

Let me suggest the following.

First, we need to remember what I said at the beginning about David not writing as a private citizen but as the king and chief justice of Israel. We are not in that role, of course. We are private citizens, although some of us might serve as judges or high political figures. The bearing for us of David's position as king is that, while we must be very careful about asking God to judge those who have offended us personally, there is nothing wrong with asking for justice on behalf of others who have been wronged. In fact, we should be vigorous in the pursuit of such justice. Usually, our problem is not that we are too vindictive at this point, but rather that we do not care about justice for other people much at all.

Second, in a more subdued way there is also a sense in which we can pray along these lines for ourselves. This is because we *are* sometimes unjustly slandered, and it is right for truth to triumph.

But we have to be extremely cautious how we do this. For one thing, we are seldom entirely innocent of wrong ourselves, though we may not see it at the time we are slandered. We must therefore always pray with a humble and contrite heart, asking God to reveal whatever fault may lie in us and so lead us in the way of righteousness. Again, while we properly appeal to God for justice, we are not authorized to take matters into our own hands and so try to do to the other person what he or she has done to us. Judgment is a prerogative of God. "It is mine to avenge; I will repay" (Deut. 32:35). The apostle Paul quotes this verse in Romans with this application: "Do not take revenge, my friends, but leave room for God's wrath, for it is written: 'It is mine to avenge; I will repay,' says the Lord. On the contrary:

> 'If your enemy is hungry, feed him;
>   if he is thirsty, give him something to drink.
> In doing this, you will heap burning coals on his head.'

Do not be overcome by evil, but overcome evil with good" (Rom. 12:19–21).

Still further, although our enemies may be vicious now, it is true that God may convert them. We should never despair of their conversion. The apostle was himself a fierce persecutor of the early Christians, but after his conversion he became the church's greatest missionary.

Third and last, we can apply the words of this psalm to the devil, for he is described in Scripture precisely as David describes his enemies. He is our great foe, "a roaring lion looking for someone to devour" (1 Peter 5:8) and a slanderous "accuser of our brothers" (Rev. 12:10). We are like helpless sheep before this powerful enemy. But, thank God, we have a powerful champion and advocate in King Jesus. It is not wrong for us to pray for his help for the confounding of Satan's devices and to rejoice in anticipation of the devil's ultimate and certain fall.

Psalm 36

An Oracle

An oracle is within my heart
    concerning the sinfulness of the wicked:
There is no fear of God
    before his eyes.
For in his own eyes he flatters himself
    too much to detect or hate his sin.
The words of his mouth are wicked and deceitful;
    he has ceased to be wise and to do good.
Even on his bed he plots evil;
    he commits himself to a sinful course
    and does not reject what is wrong.

Your love, O LORD, reaches to the heavens,
    your faithfulness to the skies.
Your righteousness is like the mighty mountains,
    your justice like the great deep.
O LORD, you preserve both man and beast.
    How priceless is your unfailing love!
Both high and low among men
    find refuge in the shadow of your wings.
They feast on the abundance of your house;
    you give them drink from your river of delights.

For with you is the fountain of life;
in your light we see light.

Continue your love to those who know you,
your righteousness to the upright in heart.
May the foot of the proud not come against me,
nor the hand of the wicked drive me away.
See how the evildoers lie fallen—
thrown down, not able to rise!

verses 1–12

Psalm 36 is a lot like Psalm 1 in contrasting the ways of the righteous with those of the wicked, showing their natures, paths of life, and ends. But there are two differences. First, the order is reversed. In Psalm 1, the righteous are described (vv. 1–3), then the wicked (v. 4), then the ends of each are compared (vv. 5–6). In Psalm 36 the order is: first, the wicked (vv. 1–4), then the righteous (vv. 5–9), then the contrast (vv. 10–12). The other difference is that in Psalm 36 the section on the righteous is not focused on these persons so much as on God, whose steadfast love and faithfulness they alone appreciate and trust.

The psalm is introduced as "an oracle." *Oracle* is a common word in the Old Testament, being used literally hundreds of times. However, it is nearly always joined to the name Jehovah or its equivalent, meaning "an oracle (or word) of the Lord." What is surprising about its use in Psalm 36 is that, in the psalm's phrase, *Jehovah* is replaced by the word for "wickedness" or "transgression," so the phrase reads literally "an oracle of wickedness." This led the King James translators to render the verse, "The transgression of the wicked saith within my heart, that there is no fear of God before his eyes." They suggested thereby that the psalm is an oracle somehow spoken by wickedness personified rather than by God. This would be a strange idea, however, and the older commentators seem to have struggled with this obviously difficult rendering.[1]

There is another possibility, however, and that is that the word *transgression* is an objective rather than a subjective genitive. This is the meaning adopted by the New International Version, indicating that the oracle is not spoken *by* transgression but rather is *about* it. That is, it is a word from God about the nature of evil and evil persons.[2] The New International Version says,

An oracle is within my heart
concerning the sinfulness of the wicked.

The verses that follow (through v. 4) fit that description, which suggests that this is the best and right way to handle the problem.

The Way of the Wicked

The insight given to David, "the servant of the LORD," in this psalm is not a trivial one. On the contrary, it is as profound in its way as the apostle Paul's magnificent analysis of the same matter in Romans 1. In fact, it is likely that Paul had this psalm in mind as he composed the opening chapters of his great letter, since he quotes verse 1 ("There is no fear of God before his eyes") in Romans 3:18. In Romans Paul analyzes the fundamental problem of human beings in their opposition to God (that they "suppress" the truth about God because of their wickedness, 1:18). He also traces their inevitable decline ("God gave them over," 1:24, 26, 28) and shows their true end ("Although they know God's righteous decree that those who do such things deserve death, they not only continue to do these very things but also approve of those who practice them," 1:32).

This is exactly what we have in Psalm 36:1–4.

David's great insight is that wickedness begins with the rejection of God: "There is no fear of God before his eyes" (v. 1). Fear usually means "reverence" in Scripture, and that is probably the case here. But even if fear only means being afraid, which is what we usually mean by it, the analysis is still profound. For David is saying that the wicked person is characterized above all else by the fact that he does not take God into account. Like the fool of Psalm 14, the wicked person lives as if God were nonexistent, refusing to believe that he or she will need to give an accounting to God and be judged by him one day.

This denial has a profound impact on how the wicked person lives, which is what the next verses are about. As Arno Gaebelein says, "Loving darkness more than light, he calls evil good and good evil and is self-righteous and has an excuse for everything."[3]

David sees five steps in the decline of the wicked.

Having displaced God, the wicked person becomes the center of his or her own universe and is therefore self-deceived. Nothing is more deceiving than to think ourselves the center of the universe, but this deception leads to others.

Jonathan Edwards in his majestic and comprehensive manner writes of eight such deceptions:

1. Some flatter themselves with a secret hope that there is no such thing as another world. 2. Some flatter themselves that death is a great way off. . . . 3. Some flatter themselves that they lead moral and orderly lives and therefore think that they shall not be damned. 4. Some make the advantages under which they live an occasion of self-flattery. . . . 5. Some flatter themselves with their own intentions. . . . 6. There are some who flatter themselves that they do, and have

done, a great deal for their salvation. . . . 7. Some hope by their striv-
ings to obtain salvation of themselves. . . . 8. Some sinners flatter
themselves that they are already converted.[4]

Most of these deceptions have to do with those who will at least accept
God's existence. But what of those who banish thoughts of God entirely?
Clearly their self-deception is the greatest of all.

Having lost the necessary reference point for determining what is good or evil, the
wicked person is unable to "detect or hate" sin. It is bad enough to recognize sin
and be unable to reject it, but it is obviously much worse not even to be able
to detect it as sin or be repulsed by it. This deplorable state comes inevitably
if we dabble in sin enough. Alexander Pope, the eighteenth-century English
poet, captured it well when he wrote:

> Vice is a monster of so frightful mien
> As, to be hated, needs but to be seen;
> Yet, seen too oft, familiar with her face,
> We first endure, then pity, then embrace.

That is the problem with sinning "just a bit." We cannot sin just a bit,
because the little bit becomes a little bit more and that a bit more still until,
in the end, we cannot even distinguish right from wrong or understand
what we are doing. In Romans Paul says that the downward path of sin
brings us to the point where we eventually call the wrong right and the right
wrong, that is, not only practicing sin but approving of those who practice it
(cf. Rom. 1:32).

Since he or she is unable to detect or hate sin, the wicked person is also unable to
speak truth, be wise, or do good. Sins of the mind inevitably express themselves
in conduct, in this case speech, judgments, and actions. Here is the exact
opposite of the wise man of Proverbs, who does good precisely because he
has the fear of God before his eyes. "The fear of the LORD is the beginning
of wisdom, and knowledge of the Holy One is understanding" (Prov. 9:10).

Without any restraining influence from what is good, the wicked person becomes so
abandoned to evil that he or she plots it by night as well as by day and becomes thor-
oughly committed to an evil course. At this stage of his or her fall the evil person
is not merely drifting into evil ways. He is inventing ways to do it, in contrast
to the godly who spend the wakeful night hours meditating on God and his
commandments. Psalm 1:2 says of the righteous man, "His delight is in the
law of the LORD, and on his law he meditates day and night." David wrote of
himself in Psalm 63:6, "On my bed I remember you; I think of you through
the watches of the night."

In the end the wicked person cannot reject what is wrong, even when it is apparent to
everyone that it is wrong. This is the closest equivalent to the point Paul reaches
at the end of Romans 1, where he shows that the person who has been aban-

doned to a "depraved mind" (v. 28) comes at last to approve only evil. This means that in his depraved thinking the good becomes evil and the evil good. Black is white, good is evil, truth is error, peace is turmoil, joy is misery. Our word for a person whose thinking is twisted like that is *crazy*. It is correct to say that such a person is out of his or her mind. He is spiritually insane.

Progression into increasing abandonment to evil is marked by the verbs used in Psalm 36 to describe the wicked person's actions. First, he "flatters" himself. Second, he "cease[s]" to do good. Third, he "plots" evil. Fourth, he "commits" himself to a wicked course. J. J. Stewart Perowne traces this flow similarly, concluding that the wicked person's "very conscience is hardened, so that he does evil without repugnance or misgiving."[5]

The Lovingkindness of God

Abruptly, so abruptly that liberal scholars speak of two independent compositions awkwardly put together, the psalmist turns to contemplating the attributes of God and the blessedness of those who find refuge in him (vv. 5–9). He lists four attributes of God, followed by four blessings of the godly. In between he indicates how the goodness of God embraces everyone.

First, the attributes.

Lovingkindness. The most important of the attributes from the perspective of this psalm is *hesed,* usually translated "unfailing love" or "lovingkindness." It is important because it begins the list of attributes (in v. 5) and closes it (in v. 7). It also reappears in the closing prayer (in v. 10). Alexander Maclaren has a sermon on this psalm in which he unfolds the meaning of the term, calling it goodness, mercy, and grace. "All his goodness is forbearance, and his love is mercy, because of the weakness, the lowliness, and the ill desert of us on whom the love falls. . . . The first and last, the Alpha and Omega of God, beginning and crowning and summing up all his being and his work, is his mercy, his lovingkindness."[6]

Faithfulness. The second attribute is faithfulness. Maclaren rightly argues that this has to do with God's verbal revelation, for only a God who has spoken promises to mankind can be thought of as faithful. This God has done. He has given numerous revelations and promises, and he has adhered unwaveringly to each one. Charles Haddon Spurgeon wrote, "He never fails, nor forgets, nor falters, nor forfeits his word. . . . To every word of threat or promise, prophecy or covenant, the Lord has exactly adhered, for he is not a man that he should lie, nor the son of man that he should repent."[7]

Saying that God's faithfulness is "to the skies" does not mean that it is to be found in heaven rather than on earth but that it is without any limits. It means that God is utterly and entirely faithful.

Righteousness. The third attribute is righteousness. By it David teaches that God is upright in all his ways. As Abraham before him well knew, "The Judge of all the earth [does] do right" (Gen. 18:25).

Justice. Justice concludes David's four-item list of attributes. He is not thinking here of the final judgment, when the wicked will be punished for their sins and the righteous will be vindicated on the basis of God's righteousness, which we now know is provided for us in Jesus Christ. He is thinking of God's justice in human affairs.

The wonderful thing about these attributes of God, says David, is that they are shown to all God's creation. This does not mean that there is no distinction between the measure of love shown to the godly in their salvation and that shown to the wicked who are not saved. There is a discriminating love which we refer to by the terms *election* and *reprobation.* But what David does want to say is that even the wicked, in spite of their rejection of God and his ways, experience a measure of love, faithfulness, righteousness, and justice. These things are for both the "high and low" among men (v. 7). In fact, God's love is so broad as to include "both man and beast" (v. 6). The scope of such grace only renders the rebellion of the wicked even more odious.

The Blessings of the Righteous

The wicked know nothing of the lovingkindness of the God they reject, but those who find refuge in God experience this goodness personally. As he has listed four of God's attributes, so now David lists four ways in which the righteous are blessed.

Satisfaction. David does not use the word satisfaction, but this is what he means when he speaks of the righteous feasting on the "abundance" of God's house. What is "God's house" in this psalm? Some writers see the phrase as a reference to the temple, which can indeed be called the house of God. But there is nothing in the context to suggest this. Others suppose it to be a reference to heaven, in line with Jesus' saying, "In my Father's house are many rooms" (John 14:2) or his stories about guests feasting in the king's great hall. In my judgment, the "house" David speaks of here is the world in which we live and in which God's blessings are poured out. The reason I say so is that a present feasting is spoken of, not a future one. These verses describe a present and continuous enjoyment of God's bounties.

Spurgeon has a wonderful little story at this point, telling of a father who moved his family from a rather small house to a large one. His youngest child was only a toddler and was so overwhelmed with the new home that he ran from room to room, exclaiming about everything he saw, "Is this ours, Father? Is this ours?" He had no trouble appropriating the father's provision and was obviously fully satisfied by it.[8]

Joy. Our word for the second blessing is joy, though the word David uses here is *delights.* The interesting thing about David's word is that it is the plural of the word *Eden* and undoubtedly looks backward to the joys of our first parents before the fall.[9]

Life. Verse 9 adds two more blessings of the righteous—life and light. It does so, as Perowne says, by "some of the most wonderful words in the Old Testament."[10] Their fullness begins to be hinted at by the apostle John in the prologue to his gospel, when he writes of Jesus, "In him was life, and that life was the light of men" (John 1:4). The prologue makes clear that the life spoken of is both physical (since "without him nothing was made that has been made," v. 3) and spiritual (since "to all who received him, to those who believed in his name, he gave the right to become children of God—children born not of natural descent, nor of human decision or a husband's will, but born of God," vv. 12–13).

It is hard to doubt that John was thinking of Psalm 36:9 as he composed the prelude.

Light. "In your light we see light" (v. 9). Where is the light of God to be found so that we might walk in light and grow as children of light? A glimmer is seen in nature. It is what the heathen have but reject, according to Romans 1. A steady beam is seen in the Old Testament, pointing onward to him who is himself the Light. The full glory of God's light is in the gospel we proclaim. Yet the fullest revelation awaits the day when we shall see God in his glory and be like Jesus, whom we will encounter face to face (2 Cor. 3:7–18).

Under His Wings

The conclusion of the psalm is a prayer in which David prays for others who know God and are upright (v. 10) and for himself that he may be preserved from evildoers (v. 11). So confident is he of this final deliverance that the psalm closes with a prophetic glimpse of the wicked who, in his vision, already "lie fallen—thrown down, not able to rise" (v. 12).

What is the final application of the psalm? It is what we have already seen in verse 7. What distinguishes the righteous from the wicked are not the good deeds of the godly (though they inevitably express their right relationship to God by good deeds), but rather that they, in distinction from the wicked, have taken refuge under the shadow of God's wings. The words "find refuge" mean to flee for refuge, like a man guilty of manslaughter fleeing from the avenger of blood. They mean to flee with haste and intensity, stopping for nothing, until by the full thrust of our entire natures we find safety and deliverance beneath the wings and in the unfailing mercy of Almighty God.

That mercy is to be found in Jesus Christ. He said of Jerusalem, "O Jerusalem, Jerusalem, . . . how often I have longed to gather your children together, as a hen gathers her chicks under her wings, but you were not willing!" (Luke 13:34). The masses of Jesus' day missed that great blessing and perished. The masses miss them today. Do not be one of them. Come to Jesus now.

Psalm 37

Not to Worry: Part 1

Blessed Are the Meek

Do not fret because of evil men
*   or be envious of those who do wrong;*
for like the grass they will soon wither,
*   like green plants they will soon die away.*

Trust in the LORD and do good;
*   dwell in the land and enjoy safe pasture.*
Delight yourself in the LORD
*   and he will give you the desires of your heart.*
verses 1–4

A little while, and the wicked will be no more;
*   though you look for them, they will not be found.*
But the meek will inherit the land
*   and enjoy great peace.*
verses 10–11

An important principle of Bible interpretation is progressive revelation. Progressive revelation means that a doctrine that is introduced in an early portion of the Bible is unfolded more fully in later sections. A good example is the Bible's doctrine of what lies beyond death. Ideas of the afterlife are rudimentary and scarce in the Old Testament, but they are developed at length in the New Testament after the resurrection of Jesus Christ. The same is true of the doctrine of the atonement. Salvation by substitution is taught in the Old Testament, but it is only explained fully after Jesus accomplished it by dying for his people.

Yet it sometimes works the other way. An Old Testament passage sometimes expounds a New Testament verse more fully.

Psalm 37 is a case in point. The eleventh verse of this psalm has to do with meekness and is quoted by Jesus in the Sermon on the Mount (Matt. 5–7). He used it as one of the beatitudes: "Blessed are the meek, for they will inherit the earth" (Matt. 5:5). That teaching is not explained by Jesus, certainly not in the Sermon on the Mount. But it is what Psalm 37 is all about. So it is right to say that Psalm 37 is an exposition of the third beatitude, even though it was written a thousand years before Jesus began his public ministry.[1] It unfolds the character of the meek or trusting person in the face of the apparent prosperity of the wicked.

Psalm 37 is another acrostic psalm. That is, each of its stanzas of double verses begins with a successive letter of the Hebrew alphabet. The acrostic psalms are Psalms 9–10, 25, 34, 37, 111, 112, 119, and 145.

Some of the best-loved verses in the Old Testament come from this psalm. Here are some examples:

> Delight yourself in the LORD
> and he will give you the desires of your heart (v. 4).
> Commit your way to the LORD;
> trust in him and he will do this . . . (v. 5).

> Better the little that the righteous have
> than the wealth of many wicked (v. 16).

> I was young and now I am old,
> yet I have never seen the righteous forsaken
> or their children begging bread (v. 25).

That last verse establishes the psalm as a psalm of mature wisdom. If it was written by David, as the title says it was, it was apparently composed by him in his old age after a lifetime of reflection on the ways of the righteous and the wicked and of God's dealings with each.

316   **Psalms—Volume 1**

Like most acrostic psalms, this one is fairly hard to outline. Mostly it seems to be a string of aphoristic sayings, like portions of Proverbs. Yet certain themes dominate various sections of the psalm as one moves through it, and these give a framework for study. I suggest the following five sections: the quiet spirit (vv. 1–11), the way of the wicked (vv. 12–20), the ways of the righteous and the wicked contrasted (vv. 21–26), an old man's counsel to the young (vv. 27–33), and taking the long view (vv. 34–40).

We will look at the first two of these sections in this chapter and the last three sections in the next.

The Quiet Spirit

The first eleven verses are the most direct exposition we have of the third beatitude, which is where they end. They describe the quiet spirit of one who trusts in God and does not fret because of evil men.

The note is struck at the very beginning, in verses 1 and 2: "Do not fret because of evil men or be envious of those who do wrong; for like the grass they will soon wither, like green plants they will soon die away."[2] The words "do not fret" literally mean "do not get heated," which is also how we might express it. Or we might say, "Don't get all worked up." Or even "Be cool." This is what the psalm chiefly wants to say to us. So in case we might miss it, the words "do not fret" are repeated three times, being found in verses 1, 7, and 8. They are the recurring theme of this section.

But how are we to do it? How are we to remain cool when we see evil men prospering? Especially when they prosper at the expense of truly righteous persons, as is often the case?

The beatitude says, "the meek . . . will inherit the earth." But it seems to us that it is the ungodly who get it.

Nice guys finish last!

How can we not fret when we see that happening?

Verses 3–11 give two answers to those questions: We are to look up, and we are to look ahead.

The most important answer is to get our eyes off the wicked and even off ourselves and on the Lord. More than that, we are to trust him and commit our way to him. I suppose there is hardly a place in all the Bible better suited than these verses to teach us how to live godly lives and grow in the love and knowledge of God, which is what the godly life is about. They tell us to do five things.

"*Trust in the LORD*" (v. 3). Trust is faith. It is the proper starting point for all right relationships with God. Yet as always, faith is not merely passive but active too, and not merely God-related but related to others. This is why the verse adds the words "and do good." It means that the person who is quietly trusting God will experience the life and power of God in his or her life and that this new life will express itself by doing good to others. I often say when I am teaching about faith as the channel of justification that there is never any justification without regeneration and that the one who is regenerated will necessarily lead a new life. In other words, although we are not saved by works but rather are saved by the grace of God through faith, faith will inevitably express itself in right conduct.

Faith (trust) has three elements: *notitia* or "content," *assensus*, which is personal "consent to" or "agreement with" that content, and *fiducia* or "trust." The last point involves personal commitment to God, just as marriage involves a personal commitment of each marriage partner to the other. God has committed himself to us. We must commit ourselves to him if we are to be Christians.

"*Delight . . . in the LORD*" (v. 4). Before people are converted, they resist a relationship to God, because they do not think that God is desirable. They suppose him to be moralistic and harsh, establishing rules intended only to keep people from fulfilling themselves or having fun.

The truth is entirely different, for the God we come to know in salvation is entirely delightful. He is holy, to be sure. He is also the sovereign, exalted, awesome God the Bible everywhere pictures him to be. We cannot trifle with him. He cannot be taken lightly. But in addition to understanding those incontrovertible truths, the one who trusts God also finds him to be a source of exquisite delight. For he is the perfection of grace, compassion, mercy, kindness, patience, and love. He is, in other words, like Jesus Christ, and the better we know him the more we inevitably delight in him. The reason many apparent Christians do not delight in God is that they do not know him very well, and the reason they do not know him well is that they do not spend time with him.

The promise attached to this verse is that if we delight in God, God will give us the desires of our hearts. This does not mean that God will give us any foolish thing we may long for. It means that if we are delighting in God and longing for God, God will give us himself.

"*Commit your way to the LORD*" (v. 5). The command to "commit" our ways to God is not a redundancy, something that has already been covered in what it means to trust God (assent and commitment to a specific content), but actually carries us further in showing what it means to live with God whom we trust and in whom we delight. The word actually means "to roll one's way onto God," the figure being, as H. C. Leupold says, to "dislodge the burden from your shoulders and lay it on God."[3] This is what the apostle Peter was thinking about in 1 Peter 5:7—in fact, he was probably referring to Psalm 37:5 explicitly—when he wrote, "Cast all your anxiety on him because he cares for you." He meant that we do not need to worry about things, because God cares for us, is equal to all circumstances, and will manage anything that can possibly come into our lives.

"*Be still before the LORD*" (v. 7). One of my favorite quotes is from Blaise Pascal who said that the basic thing that is wrong with the world is that man "does not know how to stay quietly in his own room."[4] It is a good thought, expressed in humorous and therefore memorable language. But this fourth step in the life of godly trust in God goes beyond simply sitting quietly. It tells us to be still "before the LORD," that is, to "wait patiently for him," as the verse goes on to say. In other words, mere stillness is not enough. What is needed is a quiet waiting upon God. As we go on in our study of this psalm we are going to see how important waiting is. This is because the psalmist's ultimate answer to the problem of the prosperity of the wicked is that the end is not yet; the wicked will be brought down and the godly will be lifted up, but only in God's time.

"*Refrain from anger*" (v. 8). P. C. Craigie says that "almost certainly" this is anger against God.[5] But whether it is against God or only against those who are doing wrong, particularly against ourselves, it is a mark of the godly person that he or she is able to maintain a settled and calm frame of mind because of trusting God.

Look Ahead

The second answer to how we are to remain calm when the wicked prosper is part of what I have already been saying. We are to look ahead as well as looking up, because if we do, we will see that those who do evil only flourish for a time and then are thrown down, while the people of God are preserved in the meantime and rewarded at last. Verses 9–11 develop this second idea, saying,

> For evil men will be cut off,
>   but those who hope in the LORD will inherit the land.
>
> A little while, and the wicked will be no more;
>   though you look for them, they will not be found.
> But the meek will inherit the land
>   and enjoy great peace (vv. 9–11).

It is hard for most of us to take the long view, because we are consumed by the present. But we need to do it if we are to grow in grace and begin to understand something of what God is doing in this world.

The Meekest Man

Before we go further I want to introduce an example of what it means to be meek. I do this because we usually think of meekness as weakness, and that is not the idea at all. The example I have in mind is from the life of Moses as recorded in Numbers 12. I refer to it because of a verse in the story that says that Moses was an illustriously meek man. The New International Version uses the word *humble*. The King James Version says *meek*. But both express the same idea. The verse says, "Moses was a very

humble [meek, KJV] man, more humble [meeker] than anyone else on the
face of the earth" (Num. 12:3).

This is the story. When Moses had to escape from Egypt he went to Midian
where he settled and married Zipporah, the daughter of a priest of Midian.
Zipporah was of the same stock as the Jewish people. But she had died by the
time of the events told in Numbers 12, and Moses had married a Cushite
woman. The point of the story lies in the fact that Cush was the ancient name
for Ethiopia and that this second wife was therefore apparently black.

This was an offense to Moses' brother Aaron and his sister Miriam, and
Miriam in particular launched a rebellion. She said, "Has the LORD spoken
only through Moses? Hasn't he also spoken through us?" (v. 2).

God was displeased, of course. So he called Miriam and Aaron to meet
with him before the tent of meeting. God reiterated his choice of Moses to
be the leader of the people, rebuked Moses' offended siblings, and then
pronounced a judgment on Miriam frighteningly appropriate to her preju-
dice. The text says, "The anger of the LORD burned against them, and . . .
when the cloud lifted from above the Tent, there stood Miriam—leprous,
like snow" (vv. 9–10). In other words, God said to Miriam, "You're offended
because your brother married a black woman. You're brown, and you think
light is better than dark. Why not be white, then? See how you like that."
The judgment was so horrible that Aaron pleaded for Miriam with Moses,
Moses interceded with the Lord, and Miriam was healed.

What was Moses' conduct throughout this incident?

His wife was insulted and despised. His authority was challenged. Did he
fight back against this injustice? Did he try to vindicate himself, as we might
have done? Not at all. That is why he is called a meek man. Moses did
exactly what we find in Psalm 37. He trusted God, delighted himself in God,
committed his way to God, was still, and refrained from anger. Thus God
protected him and vindicated him in time.

This is not weakness but strength, because the same man who committed
his way to God on this occasion had also been able to stand before Pharaoh
and demand that the powerful king of Egypt let the Jews go. Moses was not
weak; he was strong, because he trusted God. This same is true of Jesus
Christ. Meekness was one of the great characteristics of Jesus. Peter writes:
"When they hurled their insults at him, he did not retaliate; when he suffered, he made no threats. Instead he entrusted himself to him who judges
justly" (1 Peter 2:23).

Meekness will take off its shoes before the burning bush, but in the
power of God it will also always be able to stand tall before the powerful of
this world.

The Way of the Wicked

The second section of this psalm (vv. 12–20) describes the way of the
wicked, much like Psalms 1, 36, and others do. In fact, from here to the end

of the psalm nearly every verse mentions either the wicked or the righteous or both. Later, in section three, there is a series of contrasts between the righteous and the wicked. In this section there are also contrasts, but they concern the wicked more directly. Here are four of them.

The wicked plot against the righteous, but the Lord laughs at them (vv. 12–13). We do not often think of the Lord laughing, especially at wickedness, and it is right we do not since to us laughter usually means that someone is taking a matter lightly. The laughter in verse 13 is like that of Psalm 2, which says that the Lord "scoffs" at those who think they are able to overthrow him and thus determine their own rebellious destinies. God laughs at the wicked scornfully, because he knows their appointed ends. He knows they will be brought low and be judged by him.

If God can laugh at the wicked, shouldn't we be able at least to refrain from being agitated by them? Shouldn't we be able to trust God and commit our ways to him in quiet confidence?

The wicked draw weapons against the righteous, but they will fall by their own weapons (vv. 14–15). The principle expressed here is that sin carries the seeds of its destruction in itself. An evil empire can endure for a time by its own brute strength, but if it is corrupt, the corruption will weaken it from within and it will eventually fall. It is the same with individuals. People can cheat, use, or intimidate others for a time, but eventually their characters will become known and others will either refuse to deal with them or destroy them by the same tactics.

The wealth and power of the wicked will be taken away, but God will sustain the righteous (vv. 16–17). This point and the next require special faith on the part of God's people, since the fulfillment of this promise often takes considerable time. Yet those who have trusted God over a lifetime will testify to its truth. The wicked do fall, and the righteous are preserved even in the times of their severe persecution by the wicked.[6] In the next section of the psalm David expresses this as his own observation and testimony:

> I was young and now I am old,
>> yet I have never seen the righteous forsaken
>> or their children begging bread (v. 25).

The righteous will survive days of deprivation, but the wicked will perish (vv. 18–20). The text says that although the wicked flourish like "the beauty of the fields, they will vanish—vanish like smoke." We speak of "the beautiful people," meaning Hollywood entertainers, high fashion models, those with exceptional wealth or influence, and other celebrities. These people seem to flourish like field flowers after spring rains. But, like flowers, they soon vanish. Beauty fades, popularity wanes, wealth overextends itself and is lost, and influence passes to other hands.

Those who do the will of God endure—and not just for this life. They endure for eternity. As Psalm 1 says, the righteous are "like a tree planted by streams of water, which yields its fruit in season and whose leaf does not wither" (v. 3). "For the LORD watches over the way of the righteous" (v. 6).

These themes are pursued again in the psalm's second half, concluding with a section on "taking the long view." But that is already the psalm's answer to present wickedness. P. C. Craigie gives this summary: "Why should morality be adopted, when it is self-evident that wicked persons seem to get along fine in this world? . . . In the short run, the wicked seem to prosper, whereas the righteous very often seem to suffer at their hands. But it is the longer run that counts, and in the long run the only true satisfaction is to be found in the righteousness which is the hallmark of the one who lives in relationship with the living God."[7]

Psalm 37

Not to Worry: Part 2

Two Ways and Two Destinies

I was young and now I am old,
yet I have never seen the righteous forsaken
or their children begging bread.
They are always generous and lend freely;
their children will be blessed.

verses 25–26

The salvation of the righteous comes from the LORD;
he is their stronghold in time of trouble.
The LORD helps them and delivers them;
he delivers them from the wicked and saves them,
because they take refuge in him.

verses 39–40

At the beginning of the last chapter I pointed out that Psalm 37 is a good exposition of the third of Jesus' beatitudes, from the beginning of the Sermon on the Mount: "Blessed are the meek, for they will inherit the earth" (Matt. 5:5). Jesus does not explain the meaning of meekness in that sermon, but Psalm 37 does.

This does not mean that the idea of meekness is neglected in the New Testament, of course. On the contrary, it is found in several places, though in the New International Version the word *meekness* is usually translated *gentleness* or *humility*. Paul lists meekness as one of the fruits of the Spirit: "The fruit of the Spirit is love, joy, peace, patience, kindness, goodness, faithfulness, gentleness [meekness] and self-control" (Gal. 5:22–23). Likewise in Colossians: "Therefore, as God's chosen people, holy and dearly loved, clothe yourselves with compassion, kindness, humility, gentleness [meekness] and patience" (Col. 3:12). Peter writes that Christians are to witness to others in a spirit of meekness: "Always be prepared to give an answer to everyone who asks you to give the reason for the hope that you have. But do this with gentleness [meekness] and respect" (1 Peter 3:15). James says, "Get rid of all moral filth and the evil that is so prevalent and humbly [meekly] accept the word planted in you" (James 1:21).

These verses say that meekness comes into our lives by the work of the Holy Spirit and is intended to bring blessing, not only to us but to others. Still, not one of these texts really explains what meekness is or elaborates the steps by which we may attain it. In all the Bible, the place where that is done best is Psalm 37. This is what Jesus seems to be quoting in his third beatitude:

> But the meek will inherit the land
> and enjoy great peace (Ps. 37:11; cf. Matt. 5:5).

In the last chapter I also acknowledged how difficult it is to outline this psalm, probably because it is an acrostic psalm and the flow of thought merely follows the alphabetical structure. My outline (or any other outline) is therefore somewhat arbitrary. Still, there is some development of thought in the psalm, and I have highlighted it by designating the following five sections: the quiet spirit (vv. 1–11), the way of the wicked (vv. 12–20), the ways of the righteous and the wicked contrasted (vv. 21–26), an old man's counsel to the young (vv. 27–33), and taking the long view (vv. 34–40).

We looked at the first two of those sections in the last chapter and will look at the last three in this one.

Two Ways and Two Destinies

The third part of the psalm contrasts the ways of the righteous and the wicked (vv. 21–26), but we had already begun to move in this direction in the preceding section. I called that section "the way of the wicked" (vv. 12–20). It expressed four contrasts showing how the wicked plan one thing but that God causes the opposite to happen. However, the last two of those contrasts also brought the righteous into the picture:

1. The wealth of the wicked will be taken away and their power will be broken, but God will sustain the righteous (vv. 16–17).
2. The righteous will survive days of deprivation, but the wicked will perish (vv. 18–20).

In this section the psalmist continues with three more contrasts:

"The wicked borrow and do not repay, but the righteous give generously" (v. 21). There are two ways of looking at this contrast. Since the psalm is speaking of the overthrow of the wicked as opposed to blessing on the righteous, who will inherit the land, some writers think of this not as a moral failure of the wicked but rather as a failure to pay debts because they have not prospered and so are unable to repay. H. C. Leupold writes: "The one borrows and has not the wherewithal to repay, but the other is so well blessed by God that he can always repay his honest debts."[1]

The trouble with this view is that the specific words of the verse do not seem to stress ability and non-ability but rather what we would call the difference between a selfish and a generous spirit. This has inclined other commentators, including myself, to a second view, namely, that the contrast is between what P. C. Craigie calls "perpetual takers" and "constant givers."[2]

The wicked are always out for themselves. They borrow because they want to get ahead quickly and see borrowing as a short road to success. They are slow to repay because they want to keep their capital as long as possible. Often they do not repay at all, either because they think they can get away with it or because they overextend themselves and are unable to meet their obligations. With the righteous it is not a question of getting ahead or borrowing or repaying at all. For them money is a gift of God to be used to help others. Therefore, they are essentially generous rather than being essentially acquisitive. They are for others, rather than being only for themselves.

I need to say something very practical about our own culture at this point—and about Christians who are caught up in it. Our current economic system is trying to achieve short-term prosperity at the cost of long-term debt. The government is doing it, borrowing against the future. Government debt is astronomical. But the really frightening and corrupting thing is that individuals are also doing it and are being encouraged to do it more and more.

If you have a regular job or any credit at all, you know what I mean. You receive mailings from your credit card company assuring you that your credit is so good that they have raised your borrowing limit from three thousand dollars to five thousand dollars, or higher. And companies you have not even heard of try to get you to apply for their cards, giving you a pre-approved line of credit. When you put these limits together you may find that it is possible for you to borrow tens of thousands of dollars, perhaps getting a hundred thousand dollars or even more in debt.

You do not have to be a Christian to realize what is happening either. Who is foolish enough to think that he or she is so select a customer that the credit card companies have carefully sought him out or are courting her because the credit is deserved? The banks want you to borrow on time because they can make more money lending to you than they can lending to businesses. The commercial prime rate at the time of this writing is well under 10 percent, but they can get 16 to 20 percent, double, by getting you to buy on credit. As I say, you don't have to be a Christian to understand that for what it is and to know that consumer debt is a very foolish bargain.

There is only one reason why anyone ever gets caught up in our credit-debt system besides stupidity, and that is greed. It is a desire to have what we covet immediately and an unwillingness to wait and work for it.

But that is where the difference between the unbeliever and the Christian comes in, or should. Christians should not be covetous. Greed breaks the tenth commandment, which tells us not to covet (Exod. 20:17). More than that, the believer must be generous: content with what he or she has, first, then showing generosity to others. I am not saying that it is wrong for Christians to use credit cards, since it is obviously impossible to carry around the large sums of money that are necessary to do business in our culture. But here are two guidelines. I call them the first and second great economic commandments.

First, never charge more than you are able to pay off immediately when the monthly bill comes, avoiding interest entirely.

Second, never charge so much that you are unable to meet your Christian obligations first and always have some additional money left over to be able to help others.

Remember that Paul praised the poor churches of Macedonia, because "their overflowing joy and their extreme poverty welled up in rich generosity" (2 Cor. 8:2). The reason they were so generous is that "they gave themselves first to the Lord and then to us in keeping with God's will" (v. 5). That is the character of the righteous. The spirit of our age, which is trying to catch us and keep us in an ever-escalating cycle of debt, is the spirit, not of Jesus, but of the wicked.

The righteous will inherit the land, but the wicked will be cut off (v. 22). This second contrast is meant to be taken of the land of Israel literally, since inheritance of the land is one of the great Old Testament promises. It is not the same for us, since there are no promises that New Testament believers are to possess or inherit portions of the Promised (or any other) Land. Yet, there is the third beatitude: "Blessed are the meek, for they will inherit the earth" (Matt. 5:5). That is a New Testament promise, spoken to Christians. What does it mean?

There are three things it can mean. First, it can be speaking of a future day in which believers will reign with Christ on earth. Not all views of eschatology allow this, but if it is a permissible interpretation, it is significant that Jesus changes the words "inherit the land," meaning the land of Israel, to "inherit the earth," which is broader. Second, the beatitude can be speaking of prosperity in general, which would be a fair contemporary application of the psalm's teaching. It would mean that God will care for those who seek him and live for him. They will have their share of good things. Most Christians can testify to that, even those whom the world would regard as not being very well off. Riches are relative, and the little the righteous have is better than the abundance of the wicked, as the psalm has already said (v. 16). The third possible meaning of the beatitude is that the entire earth is given to the righteous to enjoy and that they can enjoy it as the wicked cannot. This is because they see it and receive it as a gift of their gracious heavenly Father.

The meek can inherit all things in this way, because they do not have to possess them exclusively or selfishly. Paul was such a man. He owned little yet could describe himself as "possessing everything" (2 Cor. 6:10). Likewise, he reminded the Corinthians, "All things are yours, whether Paul or Apollos or Cephas or the world or life or death or the present or the future—all are yours, and you are of Christ, and Christ is of God" (1 Cor. 3:21–23).

The wicked will be cut off, but although the righteous may stumble, they will not fall since the Lord upholds them (vv. 23–24). The last of these contrasts picks up from the end of the one preceding and does not use the word *but,* as the others do. Still it is a clear contrast. The wicked will be cut off, but the Lord will sustain the righteous, even though they may stumble along the way or experience hardships for a time.

Verse 23 is better known (and may even be better translated) in the King James Version of the Bible, which says, "The steps of a good man are ordered by the LORD." In his commentary on this psalm Harry Ironside tells a story about George Mueller, the founder of the great faith orphanages in England in the last century. Mueller was a man of great prayer and faith. He spent a lifetime placing the needs of his orphanages before God and saw many wonderful answers to his prayers. Ironside's story is about someone who once picked up George Mueller's Bible and was thumbing through it when he came to Psalm 37:23 and saw that next to the words "the steps" Mueller had written into the margin "and the stops." Apparently, Mueller had been meditating on this verse, and it had occurred to him that it is not only forward motion that is ordered by the Lord but also times of enforced inactivity. For the righteous, even these times have a gracious design.[3]

An Old Man's Testimony

After highlighting the seven contrasts of these two sections, David appends an old man's testimony to the truth of what he has said (vv. 25–26). He tells us that he has never seen these truths contradicted.

> I was young and now I am old,
> > yet I have never seen the righteous forsaken
> > or their children begging bread (v. 25).

Would it be possible for us to say that? The first part is all right. We can be sure that God himself never abandons the righteous. Besides, Jesus said, "I am with you always, to the very end of the age" (Matt. 28:20). But can we say that we have never seen the children of the righteous begging bread? That we have never seen the righteous without life's necessities? That question troubled Charles Haddon Spurgeon, who solved it by distinguishing between David's testimony and his own. He did not fault David, but he acknowledged that verse 25 was not his personal observation, at least as it stands. He had seen the children of the righteous begging. "I have relieved the children of undoubtedly good men, who have appealed to me as common mendicants," he reported.[4]

I suppose my testimony is somewhere in between. I have never seen the children of believers actually begging food, though I know poor Christians and do not doubt that there are places where living is so poor that the offspring of believers beg, as do others.

But the observation is still a good one even if it needs to be taken in less than an absolute sense. God does provide for the righteous and their children. Millions will testify to that. Indeed, they will testify to all that has been said here. Derek Kidner, one of the most interesting and useful commentators on the psalms, was so impressed with this that he joined phrases the apostle Paul used of his experience of God's provision (in 2 Cor. 4:9 and 6:10) with David's words in Psalm 37 to provide the following outline for verses 12–26: "persecuted but not forsaken" (Ps. 37:12–15); "as having nothing, and yet possessing all things" (Ps. 37:16–20, 25); "making many rich" (Ps. 37:21–22, 26); and "cast down, but not destroyed" (Ps. 37:23–24).

In other words, David's testimony was Paul's testimony too. And so it has been with millions of God's people.

An Old Man's Counsel

I have called the fourth part of Psalm 37 "an old man's counsel to the young" (vv. 27–33), because, having spoken of himself as an old man, David then goes on to give advice to people who have not lived as long or seen as much of God's workings as he had.

The section begins with a command, just as the next section also does. Here David says, "Turn from evil and do good" (v. 27). This is a combination similar to the words "Trust in the LORD and do good" in verse 3. It is an affirmation about faith leading to good works. We studied it earlier. Here, however, the verses go on to speak of good words, since verse 30 elaborates the earlier teaching by adding, "The mouth of the righteous man utters wisdom, and his tongue speaks what is just." Why is this? The answer is in verse 31. It is because "the law of his God is in his heart." Spurgeon calls this "the best thing in the best place, producing the best results."[5] Alexander Maclaren writes wisely, "That is the foundation on which all permanence is built. From that as center, there issue wise and just words on the one hand and stable deeds on the other. . . . [Therefore] he who orders his footsteps by God's known will is saved from much hesitancy, vacillation and stumbling, and plants a firm foot even on slippery places."[6]

Taking the Long View

Part five of Psalm 37 encourages us to take the long view (vv. 34–40). This is not a new theme in the psalm. We have seen it earlier, but it seems to dominate this last section. The ground for this teaching is that in the long run the righteous will be exalted and protected, and the wicked will be brought down. Therefore, the psalmist commands us to: "Wait for the LORD and keep his way" (v. 34).

In Psalm 1 the author used an attractive metaphor for the life of the person who lives by God's Word. He said he will be "like a tree planted by streams of water, which yields its fruit in season" (v. 3). In Psalm 37 the same metaphor reappears. But here it is used in reverse, the wicked being compared to a green tree which flourishes for a time but soon passes away and is seen no more (vv. 35–36). This is not what we would naturally expect. Earlier in the psalm the wicked were compared to pretty flowers of the field, which do not last long. That seems right. But it is hard to think of a great tree suddenly passing away, unless perhaps it is cut down, which may be what the psalmist is thinking.

Nothing in the Bible is a mistake, of course. So in this case I imagine the image of the tree to be teaching that there are times when the wicked do so well that they seem indistinguishable from the righteous. Their security seems equally assured. They flourish. But we are taught not to judge by appearances but by the Word of God. Proverbs 3:5–6 says:

> Trust in the LORD with all your heart
>   and lean not on your own understanding;
> in all your ways acknowledge him,
>   and he will make your paths straight.

That is what Psalm 37 has been encouraging us to do and what the child of God will experience if he or she trusts in the Lord, delights in the Lord, commits his or her way to the Lord, is still before the Lord, and refrains from anger. The one who does those things will end as the psalm itself does, with meek objectivity, reiterating that the Lord helps, delivers, and saves those who trust him.

"But I can never become like that," someone protests. "It is not my nature to be meek."

Perhaps not. Perhaps none of us are meek by nature. But we can become meek if we will commit our way to God and learn from him, just as the psalm advises. Or to put it in New Testament terms, we are to learn from Jesus, who said, "Come to me, all you who are weary and burdened, and I will give you rest. Take my yoke upon you and learn from me, for I am gentle [that is, meek] and humble in heart, and you will find rest for your souls" (Matt. 11:28–29).

Psalm 38

A Sick Man's Cry for Help

O Lord, do not rebuke me in your anger
or discipline me in your wrath.
For your arrows have pierced me,
and your hand has come down upon me.
Because of your wrath there is no health in my body;
my bones have no soundness because of my sin.
My guilt has overwhelmed me
like a burden too heavy to bear.

My wounds fester and are loathsome
because of my sinful folly.
I am bowed down and brought very low;
all day long I go about mourning.
My back is filled with searing pain;
there is no health in my body.
I am feeble and utterly crushed;
I groan in anguish of heart.

verses 1–8

O Lord, do not forsake me;
be not far from me, O my God.
Come quickly to help me,
O Lord my Savior.

verses 21–22

330

Psalm 38 is listed among the penitential psalms because of its confession of sin in verses 3–5 and 18. The complete list of such psalms includes Psalms 6, 32, 38, 51, 102, 130, and 143. But David, who is identified as the author in the title, does not actually name his sin in this psalm. Rather, he asks for mercy and help from God because of the terrible sickness, loneliness, and isolation he is experiencing because of it. Specifically, he says that God sent the sickness "because of [his] sinful folly" (v. 5).

The psalm is actually a lament, or simply a prayer. P. C. Craigie says, "Psalm 38 is a prayer . . . evoked by the experience of sickness and the consequent sense of alienation from both God and fellow human beings."[1]

Here are two introductory questions.

Is the psalm really by David? The only real objection to David being the author is that it describes a very poor state of physical health on the writer's part, and we do not have anything like this recorded of David in the Old Testament. But that is a very inadequate argument. It amounts to the expectation that the Bible owes us an account of every time David got sick or at least every time he got seriously sick, and there is no reason why it should do this. I have argued that serious illness was certainly more frequent in ancient societies than today, when we have wonder drugs and modern medicine. That would make sickness so commonplace that there would be no reason to mention it unless it had bearing on an important historical event. David was certainly sick many times in his life. So the only thing unusual about this description is that he sees his illness as a punishment by God for his sin.

What is the psalm's outline? It can be handled in a variety of ways. The psalm begins and ends with prayers for God's mercy and help. In between it describes the psalmist's experience, which in turn can be divided into a description of the illness, followed by a description of the isolation it produced. The latter part also speaks about enemies.

But there is another way of looking at the psalm, which Charles Haddon Spurgeon suggests and which I have found helpful. That is, in addition to the opening and closing prayers, there are also prayers in verses 9 and 15. So the psalm is actually one in which David alternately describes his condition and prays to God, asking relief from it. Altogether there are seven of these alternating sections. Spurgeon says, "The psalm opens with a prayer (v. 1), continues in a long complaint (vv. 2–8), pauses to dart an eye to heaven (v. 9), proceeds with a second tale of sorrow (vv. 10–14), interjects another word of hopeful address to God (v. 15), a third time pours out a flood of griefs (vv. 16–20), and then closes as it opened, with renewed petitioning (vv. 21–22)."[2] I like this outline because it emphasizes the way David seems to take a step forward in faith and increased calmness of spirit with each glance in God's direction.

The Opening Prayer

One thing immediately strikes us about the opening prayer: It is identical (in the Hebrew, *almost* identical) to the first verse of Psalm 6, which is the first of the penitential psalms. In fact, the two psalms bear very close resemblances. True, Psalm 6 is shorter, only ten verses as opposed to twenty-two. Psalm 38 describes the illness at greater length as well as elaborating upon the desertion by the psalmist's friends and the scheming of his enemies. But each of these elements is present in the earlier psalm too, which makes me think that they were probably written by David at about the same time and in connection with the same situation or condition. If a chronological order can be determined, it is probably that Psalm 38 comes first, because at the end of it David is praying for God to hear him and help him, while at the end of Psalm 6 he declares that God has.

In each psalm David's specific prayer is that God will not rebuke him in anger or discipline him in wrath. Does this mean that David does not want to be rebuked or that he is rejecting discipline? Not at all! The emphasis is not upon the discipline but upon the words *anger* and *wrath.*

What David is asking is that God not discipline him *in anger.* And the reason he is asking this is that the severity of his illness suggests that this is precisely what God is doing.

Psalm 6 gives us the right direction at this point. For immediately after his appeal to God not to rebuke him in anger or discipline him in wrath, David cries, "Be merciful to me, LORD, for I am faint" (v. 2). And later in the psalm he adds, "The LORD has heard my cry for mercy" (v. 9). David is not suggesting that he does not deserve the sickness that has come on him. He is not faulting God for a second. He deserves the anger, but he is asking God to show mercy instead. This is always a proper way to appeal to God. It is always right to ask for mercy. We cannot demand it. We have no claim to it. But God is a merciful God, and no one who has cried to God for mercy has ever gone away empty-handed. God has never turned a deaf ear to any honest cry.

A Sickness Described

The next section (vv. 2–8) describes the psalmist's physical and mental anguish. Physical, because he is suffering. Mental, because he is suffering for sin. The words "because of," repeated three times in verses 3 and 5, leave no doubt that in David's mind this was a judicial illness. He was being punished for a serious transgression.

Not all sickness is punishment, however. In fact, most sickness is not. It is important to say this, because physical suffering often depresses us mentally, and in such depressions we are inclined to see connections between our past sins and our present sickness that do not necessarily exist. We need to remember Job, who was a righteous man and yet suffered. God described

Job as "blameless and upright, a man who fears God and shuns evil" (Job 1:8). Job's suffering was a demonstration before Satan that a human being will love God for who God is and not just for what the person can get out of him. Job proved God's point when he said,

> Naked I came from my mother's womb,
>   and naked I will depart.
> The LORD gave and the LORD has taken away;
>   may the name of the LORD be praised (1:21).

Another purpose of suffering is explained in the case of the man who had been blind from birth, recorded in John 9. The disciples of Jesus wanted to make an easy link between sin and suffering, asking, "Rabbi, who sinned, this man or his parents, that he was born blind?" (v. 2). But Jesus replied, "Neither this man nor his parents sinned, . . . but this happened so that the work of God might be displayed in his life" (v. 3). In other words, God had chosen to glorify himself through the man's suffering, in this case by having Jesus heal his blindness.

But neither of these is an explanation of David's suffering. David was suffering for sin. As long as we are sinners, you and I have to recognize this as a possibility. I suggest the following when we undergo some great calamity or sickness. Ask:

"Have I sinned or gotten off the track of obedience to what I know I should be doing, and is this setback God's way of getting me back on track and into fellowship with him?" I do not think we need to be too introspective in the way we ask this question. We certainly do not need to be morbid in digging up a catalogue of past failures which we can then exaggerate in our confessions. If God is using sickness to stop us short and bring us back to him, he will make clear that this is what he is doing. Otherwise it would be a futile exercise. If God is doing this with you, you will know it, just as David did.

"Is God using this to trim off some rough edges of my personality and develop a more Christ-like character in me?" We may not like hard times, but they do produce character. If nothing else, God may be developing a sensitivity in us to others who are going through similar times of suffering, so we will be able to help them.

"Is God using my suffering as a stage upon which his name and wisdom may be glorified? Is it a place for me to show that I love him for who he is, entirely apart from whatever material and physical benefits he may have given me?" This is the hardest of God's purposes for us to see and accept. It is why Job is such an outstanding Old Testament example in his suffering. Still, there should be an element of this in anything we suffer, simply because we are told to glorify God in everything we do, suffering included. This theme is also in Psalm 38. For although David confesses that he is being judged for his sin—God has made this clear to him—he is nevertheless glorifying God in the way he deals with

it. Primarily, he is not faulting God, but is instead praising God as the source of mercy and salvation.

A Second Prayer

I wrote earlier that whenever David turns his eyes from his suffering to God, he seems to move a step forward spiritually and experience a calmer frame of mind. We see this in his second prayer (v. 9). In the earlier verses he has been describing his sickness. He has no health in his body (v. 3). His bones are affected (v. 3). Loathsome wounds cover his flesh (v. 5). His back is filled with searing pain (v. 7). Besides, he is overwhelmed with guilt (v. 4), so that his very spirit is crushed and he groans in anguish (v. 8). Now he reminds himself that this is known to God already. All his longings, sighs, and sufferings are plain to God's eyes.

Sometimes we refer to the collect that contains the words "before whom all hearts are open, all desires known." It is a collect of confession, and the words are a sobering reminder that all sins are known to God.

But it is also true that our suffering is all likewise known to God. Nothing that comes into our lives escapes his watchful eye, and he is concerned for us in everything that happens. So when David says, "All my longings lie open before you, O Lord; my sighing is not hidden from you," this is a truly comforting reassurance. Others may not know about us, or care. But God does both and does both perfectly. When we see this, our natural anxieties begin to lessen and our trust grows.

All Alone

Psychiatrists tell us that people do not like to be around those who are suffering because they imagine themselves being in the same condition and do not like to think along those lines. So they stay away. This is probably true and undoubtedly also explains why people make cruel jokes about retarded people, people who are crippled, and others who have suffered physical misfortunes. But even if people do not do that, they at least prefer the company of those who are prospering and having a good time.

This is what David experienced. This section of the psalm describes his sense of isolation (vv. 10–14).

I do not think it is necessary to elaborate on the attitude of David's friends, companions, neighbors, and enemies, which are described in turn. The neglect of the former and the taunts of the latter left David speechless. He could not defend himself. Who can? All he could do was leave his case with God. What I do need to say is that the sense of isolation and alienation those who are seriously ill experience should encourage Christians to behave toward them in exactly the opposite way. Instead of avoiding those who are suffering, we should go to them—to help them, serve them, comfort them. And Christians do. In fact, this is one mark distinguishing the sheep from the goats, according to Jesus' parable in Matthew 25. Among other things, the sheep looked after the sick and were rewarded for it.

If even King David, with all his many friends and courtiers, felt abandoned in his sickness, certainly you and I know someone who feels the same way. Perhaps it is someone in a nursing home or hospital or someone recovering at home from an illness. Make it a point to visit that person and do so on a regular basis, daily or weekly. If you do, you will have a reward both here and in heaven.

A Third Prayer

The third time David looks up from his state of physical and emotional suffering he tells the Lord that he will wait patiently for the answer to his prayer for deliverance.

> I wait for you, O LORD;
> you will answer, O Lord my God (v. 15).

Usually it is impossible to say why one psalm follows another in the Psalter, but in this case verse 15 may be the reason why Psalm 38 follows Psalm 37. The whole message of Psalm 37 is to trust God and wait for his deliverance, even though the wicked seem to prosper for a time. In Psalm 37 "wait for the LORD" is advice (cf. v. 34). In Psalm 38 waiting is practiced, and by the very person who gave the advice in Psalm 37.

Waiting is hard to do, especially for us. We live in an impatient age. Someone has said that a hundred years ago, if someone was taking a trip and missed the stagecoach, well, that was all right. He would get it next month. Today we get impatient if we miss one turn of the revolving door.

We can learn what it is to wait upon God from David, for David was a master and model of waiting. When Samuel first approached him, when he was just a youth, he was told that he would be the king of Israel. Yet this did not happen for several decades, and during many of those years David was a fugitive hunted by his enemy King Saul. Even after Saul's death in battle against the Philistines, David remained a king in Hebron for seven years before being asked to rule over the entire nation. And even later, when his son Absalom revolted against him, David was content to wait for God to rescue him and vindicate his cause. Derek Kidner says, "His fugitive years, his Hebron period and his attitude to Absalom's revolt, all proved the sincerity of his prayer in 15f., and of his advice in Psalm 37."[3]

David was not utterly inactive, of course. He was praying. In fact, he was composing his prayers, which is why we have Psalms 6 and 38 and probably some others. The very fact that he was praying meant that he was leaving the outcome of his sickness and trial with God.

A Good Man Badly Treated

The last section of this psalm (vv. 16–20), before the final prayer, concerns David's unjust treatment by his enemies, picking up on a theme he introduced earlier in verse 12. In this respect the psalm moves from: (1) his wretched physical condition to, (2) his abandonment by his friends to, (3) his treatment by his enemies. But this is only part of what we find in this last section. Actually, everything found here has been mentioned or suggested earlier. It is brought in again, in my judgment, as an argument why God should hear his prayer. Twice, the reasons are actually introduced by the word *for*, meaning "for this reason."

I see five arguments, one in each verse.

It is not right that his enemies should be allowed to gloat over his misfortune or boast when his foot slips (v. 16). They may be his enemies, but their conduct toward him is nevertheless not right. They should sympathize with him, rather than gloat, and pray for him rather than boast over his sins and missteps.

His condition is desperate. He has already slipped, and now he is about to fall (v. 17). It would be bad enough if David had merely slipped for a moment. But the situation is worse than this. David is about to fall completely. If Psalm 6 was written at this time, as I suggested above, *fall* means die (cf. Ps. 6:5). So this is a prayer *in extremis*. He is in danger of death. God must help him now or never. Later it will be too late.

He has confessed (and is confessing) his sin. He is troubled by it (v. 18). The purpose of discipline is to bring honest confession followed by a corresponding change of life. That purpose has been accomplished. David has confessed his sin. Therefore, it is time for the heavy hand of God that is upon him to be lifted.

His enemies are numerous, and he is just one person (v. 19). What hope does one person have against many, especially if they are enemies and in such circumstances? If God abandons him, his enemies will overwhelm him. His only hope is if God is by his side.

He has been good to his enemies, even though they are now doing evil to him. Therefore, their words about him are slanderous (v. 20). At first glance it may seem strange that David claims to have done good in a psalm containing a confession of his sin. But it is not strange. In fact, it is an accurate description of all who are God's people. God's people sin, but if they are truly God's people, their real (or renewed) natures are nevertheless set on doing good and have done it. Therefore, it is not right that those committed to evil should triumph over them ultimately. At the very least, the evil of wicked people should be frustrated and ultimately judged.

A Closing Petition

With all this description and pleading behind him, David now makes his final prayer (vv. 21–22). It is that God will not abandon him or be far from him in his sickness, as his friends and companions have been, but will instead come to him quickly to help him.

Will God do it? Of course he will, for God is his Savior. This last line, like similar statements elsewhere, is the very theme of the Bible. We can never stress it enough. "Salvation comes from the LORD" (Jonah 2:9). And, "you are to give him the name Jesus, because he will save his people from their sins" (Matt. 1:21). Nobody else brings salvation. We cannot achieve it for ourselves. But it exists, and it is provided for all who, like David, confess their sins and wait upon God for his sure help and deliverance.

Psalm 39

Creature of a Day

I said, "I will watch my ways
    and keep my tongue from sin;
I will put a muzzle on my mouth
    as long as the wicked are in my presence."
But when I was silent and still,
    not even saying anything good,
    my anguish increased.
My heart grew hot within me,
    and as I meditated, the fire burned;
    then I spoke with my tongue:

"Show me, O LORD, my life's end
    and the number of my days;
    let me know how fleeting is my life.
You have made my days a mere handbreadth;
    the span of my years is as nothing before you.
    Each man's life is but a breath.   Selah
Man is a mere phantom as he goes to and fro:
    He bustles about, but only in vain;
    he heaps up wealth, not knowing who will get it.
                    verses 1–6

"Hear my prayer, O LORD,
    listen to my cry for help;
    be not deaf to my weeping.

For I dwell with you as an alien,
*   a stranger, as all my fathers were.*
Look away from me, that I may rejoice again
*   before I depart and am no more."*

verses 12–13

Psalm 39 asks us to think about the brevity of life. The world, by contrast, does not like us to think much at all, especially about such things as life, death, and eternity. Thinking about them spoils the world's fun and makes us harder to manipulate. The flesh is unable to think about eternal matters, at least on a spiritual level. It cannot understand them because "they are spiritually discerned" (1 Cor. 2:14). The devil hates us to think and does everything he can to keep us from thinking, especially about the meaning of life and the fact that we must spend an eternity either with God in heaven or without him in hell. Therefore, the world, the flesh, and the devil conspire to keep us amused or entertained.

That is what the word *amusement* means, of course. It is a compound word of two main parts. The heart of the word is "muse," which means to "ponder," "meditate," or "think." The prefix is the negative "a," which means "no" or "not." So "a-muse-ment" means "not thinking." It is what most people do as they drift through life and inevitably pass through the dark doors of death into eternity. Psalm 39 is a rebuke to such folly, as I said. It wants us to think about the brevity of life, so we may apply our hearts to wisdom and use the time we do have well.

In his study of these verses Arno Gaebelein says, "Read this psalm frequently; it will bring blessing to heart and life."[1]

Psalm 39 is a good psalm to follow Psalm 38. In the preceding psalm David is seriously ill and is facing the prospect of imminent death. In this psalm, as might be expected following such sickness, he is contemplating life's brevity. In Psalm 38 the author is silent before other people: "I am like a deaf man, who cannot hear, like a mute, who cannot open his mouth, . . . whose mouth can offer no reply" (vv. 13–14). This theme is picked up in the opening verses of Psalm 39 (vv. 1–3). In fact, there are several Hebrew words that are repeated, though the English translation sometimes hides this fact. "My hope" (v. 7) is similar to "wait" in Psalm 38:15. "Your scourge" in verse 10 is the same as "my wounds" in Psalm 38:11.[2]

Jeduthun, in the psalm's title, is the first personal name other than David or a name that is part of a historical reference (Absalom in the title to Ps. 3, Cush in the title to Ps. 7, Abimelech in the title to Ps. 34) to appear in these headings. This man, along with Asaph and Heman, was one of the musicians appointed by David to lead public worship (1 Chron. 16:37–42; 25:1–8; 2 Chron. 5:12; 35:15).[3] His name also appears in the titles to Psalms

62 and 77. Interestingly, the subject matter of Psalm 62 is similar to that of
Psalm 39, though this may be coincidental.

The four-point outline of Psalm 39 is marked well by the stanzas in the
New International Version.

A Preface: Compelled to Speak

The first three verses are a preface explaining the circumstances of the
psalm's composition. They explain how the psalmist had been trying hard
to keep quiet and not express what was troubling him, but how at last the
fire burning within him burst out. Undoubtedly, this expresses a real situation. David was troubled. If not, we have to suppose that such depths of feeling, here and in other psalms, are mere literary compositions. Nevertheless,
from a literary perspective, the preface plays an effective role in heightening our interest in what is coming.

"What is bothering David?" we want to ask. "Why is he so troubled? Why
is he not saying anything?"

In the next stanza we are going to learn that David is troubled about the
brevity and corresponding vanity of life. But what he tells us here is why he
was keeping silent. It was because of "the wicked" who were around him.
Why should that be a problem? The answer is that he knew how his words
would be misunderstood and misused by such persons. To them his words
would seem to be a criticism of God and his ways. Therefore, although
David was troubled to the point of boiling over inside, he refused to express
himself in their presence. In fact, when he finally does speak, it is not men
or women at all, whether wicked or righteous, but God to whom he
expresses his anguish and from whom he seeks wisdom.

We should learn a number of things from David's conduct. (1) What we
say is vitally important; we can sin with our mouths as well as with other parts
of our bodies. (2) It is better to be silent than to say things that can be used
against God by wicked persons. (3) We should not be anxious to share such
grief even with godly persons. (4) We should bring our troubles to God.

If we follow David's example at this point, we will be doing what Paul recommended to the Philippians and we will receive the corresponding blessing: "Do not be anxious about anything, but in everything, by prayer and
petition, with thanksgiving, present your requests to God. And the peace of
God, which transcends all understanding, will guard your hearts and your
minds in Christ Jesus" (Phil. 4:6–7).

Out, Out, Brief Candle!

The problem bothering David finally emerges in verse 4 and is developed in the psalm's second stanza (vv. 4–6). It is the brevity of life and the
corresponding emptiness or meaninglessness of human existence, as I have
been pointing out.

The key word in this stanza, as well as in the next, is *hebel*, which is translated: "a breath" (vv. 5, 11) and "in vain" (v. 6). It is the word rendered "vanity" or "meaningless" in Ecclesiastes, the ideas of which are obviously echoed in this psalm. Ecclesiastes begins with the well-known and often-quoted lines: "'Meaningless! Meaningless!' says the Teacher. 'Utterly meaningless! Everything is meaningless'" (Eccles. 1:2).

The apostle James, who was a great student of the wisdom literature, also seems to echo these ideas in the New Testament, where he gives an exposition of how Christians are to handle the problem. "Now listen, you who say, 'Today or tomorrow we will go to this or that city, spend a year there, carry on business and make money.' Why, you do not even know what will happen tomorrow. What is your life? You are a mist that appears for a little while and then vanishes. Instead, you ought to say, 'If it is the Lord's will, we will live and do this or that.' As it is, you boast and brag. All such boasting is evil" (James 4:13–16).

I notice that after two of the three uses of *hebel* in Psalm 39 (in vv. 5 and 11) the sentence in which it occurs is followed by *selah,* which means stop, pause, and consider. It is good advice! It is a reminder to think about the brevity of life so you may apply your heart to wisdom.

The brevity of life is a thought that troubles everyone, or should. I do not know whether William Shakespeare knew this psalm or had these words in mind when he penned Macbeth's despairing speech from act 5 of the play by that name, but he expressed the idea well:

> Tomorrow, and tomorrow, and tomorrow,
> Creeps in this petty pace from day to day,
> To the last syllable of recorded time;
> And all our yesterdays have lighted fools
> The way to dusty death. Out, out, brief candle!
> Life's but a walking shadow, a poor player
> That struts and frets his hour upon the stage,
> And then is heard no more; it is a tale
> Told by an idiot, full of sound and fury,
> Signifying nothing (act 5, scene 5).

But King David is not King Macbeth. So although he frets over the same problem, the brevity and apparent vanity of life, he does not do it in the same way. What he does do is unburden himself to God and seek wisdom from God, as we have seen.

This is the meaning of verse 4. Verse 4 does not mean: "I am weary of this suffering; tell me when I am going to die so this will end," or "Life is too short for all I have been given to do; this is unfair." Instead, it means, as J. J. Stewart Perowne expressed it, "Make me rightly to know and estimate the shortness and uncertainty of human life, that so, instead of suffering myself to be perplexed with all that I see around me, I may cast myself the more entirely upon thee."[4] This is exactly what David does in the verse immediately following this stanza, in verse 7.

It is also what we find in classic language in Psalm 90:12. Psalm 90 was written by Moses, but it raises the same issues as Psalm 39, though in a much calmer and more trusting frame of mind. It is often read at funerals.

> Teach us to number our days aright,
>   that we may gain a heart of wisdom.

Does David learn by turning to God? Yes, he does. The first thing he learns is that, puzzling as the brevity of life may be, it is nevertheless something that God has willed. God has fixed the span of human years. Verse 5 says, "*You* have made my days a mere handbreadth." Therefore, the brevity of human life is no accident; it has meaning. And this meaning must be good, because God, the author of this puzzling reality is a good God.

There is a second thing that David learns. He learns that, since life is short, the only real meaning of a man or woman's existence must be in his relationship to God, for God is eternal. David therefore turns to God, which is where we begin the next stanza. Verse 7 expresses his determination. It is the turning point of the psalm.

Disciplined for Sin

The third stanza (vv. 7–11) also introduces a second, additional problem which intensifies the first one, namely, God's heavy-handed treatment of so insubstantial and fleeting a creature as man. Stanza 2 protests the brevity and apparent vanity of life. This stanza talks about transgressions, sin, rebuke, and discipline. Why does God bother to discipline men and women, particularly when they are such insubstantial creatures? This was Job's plaintive and piercing question when he was made to endure so much suffering at God's hand.

> What is man that you make so much of him,
>   that you give him so much attention,
> that you examine him every morning
>   and test him every moment?
> Will you never look away from me,
>   or let me alone even for an instant?
> If I have sinned, what have I done to you,
>   O watcher of men?
> Why have you made me your target?
>   Have I become a burden to you?
> Why do you not pardon my offenses
>   and forgive my sins?

> For I will soon lie down in the dust;
>   you will search for me, but I will be no more (Job 7:17–21).

Do you understand that? Can you see how David and Job are saying the same thing, asking the same question? Can you perceive how the question arises precisely from the fact that we are so small and that God is so great, that we are creatures of a day and he is of eternity? If you do understand that, I am sure you also realize that you have asked the same the question yourself many times in one way or another. I have counseled many people who have asked it.

"What does God want with me?"

"Why does he care what I do? Nothing I do can possibly affect him or hurt him. I don't have anything to contribute to him."

"Why doesn't God just forget about me and leave me alone?"

The answer, of course, is the very paradox of human existence, namely, that although man is a passing creature who often does merely strut and fret his short hour upon life's stage, he is also more than a passing creature of an earthly day—for he is made for eternity, for God himself. Therefore, what happens to him and in him, as well as what is done by him, though of short temporal duration, has eternal value. This is the point of God's rebukes and discipline. What God is making of men and women now is forever. What we do here matters.

So I go back to verse 7, which I called the turning point of the psalm: "My hope is in you." Now we can understand it. It does not mean, "You are my last hope, and I am not very hopeful even of you." It means, "You are the one who gives meaning to life. Nothing else does, because everything else is passing. You alone are eternal, and you have made me for lasting fellowship with yourself. I am restless until I find my rest in you."

Alexander Maclaren, who also regards this verse as the turning point of the psalm, finds the same sentiments in verses 8–13 as in verses 1–6. But he thinks that in the second half they are considered in an entirely different light since the psalmist is now looking to God rather than being consumed by life's sorrows.[5]

This World Is Not My Home

The fourth stanza (vv. 12–13) contains the psalm's final petition, which is also the climax. By this point the psalmist has come a long way in his thinking, recognizing that life does have meaning, though it is not in the possession of wealth or other vanities (v. 6). David sees that he is an "alien" or "stranger" in the land. In the Old Testament these are terms for foreign residents in Israel, the first probably of short duration, the second longer. Such people were to be treated well, but they were prohibited from owning land. They were not permanent residents. They were pilgrims.

This has both an Old Testament history and a New Testament perspective.

Abraham is the great Old Testament example of a pilgrim since, although God had given him the entire land of Israel from the borders of Egypt to the great river Euphrates, Abraham never possessed any of it—with one exception. This exception highlights the poignancy of his pilgrim status. For when his wife Sarah died and he had no ground in which to bury her he had to negotiate the purchase of a burial plot from the Hittites. Abraham mourned for Sarah. Then, as the text says, "Abraham rose from beside his dead wife and spoke to the Hittites. He said, 'I am an *alien* and a *stranger* among you. Sell me some property for a burial site here so I can bury my dead'" (Gen. 23:4, italics added).[6]

The New Testament perspective is found in several places. For example, 1 Peter 2:11. "Dear friends, I urge you, as *aliens* and *strangers* in the world, to abstain from sinful desires, which war against your soul" (italics added). The passage is an appeal to live like citizens of the heavenly country to which we belong and to which we are going and not as citizens of this earth.

Again, there are the examples of Hebrews 11, described in verse 13: "All these people were still living by faith when they died. They did not receive the things promised; they only saw them and welcomed them from a distance. And they admitted that they were *aliens* and *strangers* on earth" (italics added). In the next chapter, having listed the Old Testament saints as examples, the author of Hebrews applies the pilgrim principle to those of his day, much as Peter did in the verse to which I have just referred: "Therefore, since we are surrounded by such a great cloud of witnesses, let us throw off everything that hinders and the sin that so easily entangles, and let us run with perseverance the race marked out for us. Let us fix our eyes on Jesus, the author and perfecter of our faith, who for the joy set before him endured the cross, scorning its shame, and sat down at the right hand of the throne of God. Consider him who endured such opposition from sinful men, so that you will not grow weary and lose heart" (Heb. 12:1–3).

Jesus had a short life of only thirty-three years. Yet his was the most significant ever lived. If we live for him, our lives will be significant too, however short or long they may be. As Alexander Maclaren says, "The lives that are lived before God cannot be trifles."[7]

The last request in this psalm is not a particularly edifying one, though it is understandable: "Look away from me, that I may rejoice again before I depart and am no more" (v. 13). This is asking God to lift his heavy hand of judgment so the psalmist may be happy once again before he dies. It is what Job meant in the verses I quoted earlier: "Will you never look away from me, or let me alone even for an instant?" (Job 7:19). Or even more directly later, "Turn away from me so I can have a moment's joy before I go to the place of no return, to the land of gloom and deep shadow" (Job 10:20–21).

This is quite understandable, as I said. Most of us have probably had times when we have thought along these lines. But there is a better way. Instead of worrying about where God has fixed his eyes, we should be concerned about where our eyes are fixed and should fix them on God himself, on the Lord Jesus Christ, and on that eternal city yet to come (Heb. 11:10). That is what it means rightly to number our days and to apply our hearts to true wisdom.

Psalm 40

Up from the Pit

I waited patiently for the LORD;
  he turned to me and heard my cry.
He lifted me out of the slimy pit,
  out of the mud and mire;
he set my feet on a rock
  and gave me a firm place to stand.
He put a new song in my mouth,
  a hymn of praise to our God.
Many will see and fear
  and put their trust in the LORD.

Blessed is the man
  who makes the LORD his trust.
                              verses 1–4

Yet I am poor and needy;
  may the LORD think of me.
You are my help and my deliverer;
  O my God, do not delay.
                              verse 17

There are portions of Scripture that need substantial introductions, because they are not well known; and there are sections that need very little introduction, because they are. Psalm 40 is in the second category. It tells of a man who was stuck in a slimy pit, bogged down in mud and mire, but then was rescued by God, who set his feet on a rock and gave him a firm place to stand. That man was King David.

Perhaps that is the most important thing to say at the beginning of this study. I remind you that David was the beloved king of Israel, who reigned powerfully and well for forty years. He was installed, blessed, and approved by God, who called him "a man after his own heart" (1 Sam. 13:14). David was nearly always in close fellowship with God, and he wrote almost half of the psalms. By his writings and by his common speech he regularly and faithfully proclaimed the grace of God to others. Yet in Psalm 40 he describes himself as having been mired down in a pit from which he was unable to escape.

So I begin with the truth that muddy times may be the experience even of the greatest saints and slimy pits the lot even of kings and preachers.

Is this a messianic psalm? Saint Augustine, Charles Haddon Spurgeon, William L. Pettingill, and Harry A. Ironside thought so, in large part because verses 6 and 7 are applied to Jesus Christ in the New Testament.[1] But this is an unnecessary and misleading assumption for the psalm as a whole. The mere fact that the psalmist confesses his sin in verse 12 warns us against applying everything in the psalm to Jesus Christ.

A more interesting question concerns the relation of this psalm to Psalm 70, which is an almost exact repetition of verses 13–17. A number of scholars, particularly those of the critical school, think that Psalm 40 was originally two psalms, verses 1–12 being the first and verses 13–17 being the second, and that they were put together somewhat awkwardly by an unknown editor. They think it awkward, because the first part speaks of deliverance from the pit and the second part is still seeking a deliverance. Such a combination of apparently diverse ideas is not strange to the psalms, however. It is equally possible—I believe this is actually the case—that Psalm 70 was detached from the longer psalm in order to salvage it for general use in a later period. The placing of the two psalms in the Psalter, the first in an early section among the many psalms of David and the second in a later, somewhat more eclectic section, may point in this direction.[2]

Psalm 40 has three clear sections: an opening joyful testimony of God's past deliverance (vv. 1–3); a present reflection on God's goodness (vv. 4–10); and a prayer for God's deliverance in the future (vv. 11–17). The tone is established in the last verse, which is presented to us as a poor man's cry to God for God's help.

A Joyful Testimony

In the thirty-eighth chapter of Jeremiah there is a well-known incident in which Jeremiah is thrown into a cistern because of his unpopular prophecies about the fall of Jerusalem to the Babylonians. It is a grim story. The cistern was empty of water, or Jeremiah would have drowned. But the bottom was filled with the accumulated mud of centuries so that Jeremiah sank down into it, into the "mud and mire." He would have perished there if a foreigner from Cush named Ebed-Melech had not interceded for him with the king, who instructed the friendly Cushite to take thirty men and draw Jeremiah out of the cistern with ropes (Jer. 38:1–13).

Jeremiah was placed in the mud and mire of a pit quite literally, but there is no reason to think of the words *pit, mud,* and *mire* as anything more than metaphors in Psalm 40. We do not know what David was describing in this way, but it must picture a period in his life in which circumstances had trapped him so that he was unable, as we might say, to free himself.

It is good that we do not know the literal meaning of this pit, because we can the more easily see our own slimy pits in David's reference. What is your slimy pit? I do not know the answer to that question. You will have to answer it for yourself. But I can think of a number of possible examples.

The pit of sin. Some people are caught in the mud and mire of sin. David himself was an example of this at one point in his life, although we do not know whether this is what he was describing in Psalm 40. He began his descent into this pit by staying home from battle in the season when kings were supposed to be at war. While enjoying himself in Jerusalem, he saw a woman named Bathsheba bathing herself on the roof of a home close to the palace. He asked about her and learned that she was married to a soldier named Uriah. In spite of that, David brought her to the palace, slept with her, and then, when he learned she was pregnant, arranged to have Uriah abandoned in battle so that he was killed by enemy soldiers. David continued nearly a year in this condition. The story is in 2 Samuel 11.

Maybe you are caught in just such a sin. Perhaps one sin has led to another. You know what is happening, but you can't get out of it. That is no surprise. Sin is like that. Romans 1 describes the downward pull of sin on all people. When you are caught in this way, there is no point beyond which you may not go. You need help. Where is your help to come from if not from God?

The pit of defeat. Some people have a very different kind of pit from which they need to be lifted. It is the pit of personal defeat, whether at work or school or in the home or in some other setting or relationship. Some people would say that their entire lives have been one long and unending defeat. They have never succeeded at anything.

I do not know the answer in your specific case, of course. And I do not want to trivialize your discouragement or make light of it. But I can tell you this. God does have things he wants you to succeed at, and he will enable you to succeed at those, even though they may be different from what you are doing now. The place to begin is where David began. He began by laying his problem before the Lord. I repeat that I do not know what David was referring to by his metaphor of the pit, but there was a time early in his life when he could have spoken very graphically of his defeats. No matter what he did he was unable to please King Saul, and Saul in his hatred and jealousy of David ruthlessly hounded the young man from place to place. It was many years before the Lord intervened to remove Saul and eventually bring David to the throne. If you are defeated, bring your defeats to God. Wait on God. David "waited patiently for the LORD." That is how Psalm 40 begins (v. 1). If you wait patiently, you too will learn that God has important things for you to do, and he will give you significant victories in his own perfect time.

The pit of bad habits. Other people are stuck in a pit of bad habits. Some of these habits are terribly destructive, like addictive drugs. Others are merely harmful, like an uncontrolled temper, patterns of self-pity, laziness, or overeating. Bad habits can be broken. New habits can take their place. But where are you going to learn these new habits? The best place is from God, who has made you in his image and wants to develop you into the fullness of the character of Jesus Christ. If that is to happen, you must turn to him and seek his help.

The pit of circumstances. The last example of a slimy pit that I think of here is circumstances, like the pattern of severe trials the apostle Paul mentions in 1 and 2 Corinthians. These were not sin, or defeats necessarily, or even the result of bad habits. Just the opposite was true. Paul had been persecuted because of his stand for Jesus Christ.

Nevertheless, as he says,

> Five times I received from the Jews the forty lashes minus one. Three times I was beaten with rods, once I was stoned, three times I was shipwrecked, I spent a night and a day in the open sea, I have been constantly on the move. I have been in danger from rivers, in danger from bandits, in danger from my own countrymen, in danger from Gentiles; in danger in the city, in danger in the country, in danger at sea; and in danger from false brothers. I have labored and toiled and have often gone without sleep; I have known hunger and thirst and have often gone without food; I have been cold and naked. Besides everything else, I face daily the pressure of my concern for all the churches (2 Cor. 11:24–28; cf. 1 Cor. 4:9–13; 2 Cor. 6:4–10).

Circumstances like those could be a pit for anyone. Yet Paul sought help from God, and God answered. Though he did not change the circumstances, he did help Paul, so that he was able to say, "We are hard pressed on every side, but not crushed; perplexed, but not in despair; persecuted, but not abandoned; struck down, but not destroyed" (2 Cor. 4:8–9).

David's testimony in respect to his own difficult and seemingly hopeless circumstances is that God heard him and helped him step by step. It is what verses 1–3 are all about. He says that God did five things: God turned to him, noticing his plight, God heard his cry, God lifted him out of the pit,

God set his feet on a rock, giving him a firm place to stand, and God placed a new song of praise in his mouth.

Reflection on God's Past Goodness

It is a characteristic of the psalms, particularly those of David, that they frequently first tell of the writer's personal experience of God's goodness and then reflect on that goodness, commending it to others. This is what the second section of Psalm 40 does (vv. 4–10). There are three aspects to this reflection.

A recommendation of his own trust in God to other people (vv. 4–5). This section begins with a beatitude reminiscent of Psalm 1.

> Blessed is the man
>   who makes the LORD his trust,
> who does not look to the proud,
>   to those who turn aside to false gods.

Why is the person who trusts God a blessed person? The answer is in the next verse, which reminds us that God has done great things for his people in the past and assures us, because his character has not changed, that God has many more similarly good things planned for those who trust him today. To experience these good things you must trust him. Or, to use the metaphor that was used a few psalms earlier, you must "taste and see that the LORD is good" (Ps. 34:8). It is possible that someone could invite you to the most magnificent banquet in all the world. But you would never know how good the food was unless you tasted it. It is the same with God's goodness. Until you trust God, you will never know how good his goodness is.

A statement about the proper relationship of the trusting person to God (vv. 6–8). What is the right relationship of a person to God? It is not something that is established through mere ceremony but is rather the expression of a fully surrendered heart. In these verses David reiterates an important biblical principle: obedience takes precedence over sacrifice (cf. 1 Sam. 15:22; Isa. 1:10–17; Jer. 7:21–26; Hosea 6:6; Micah 6:6–8). The words are well known because of being applied to Jesus in Hebrews 10:5–10.

> Sacrifice and offering you did not desire,
>   but my ears you have pierced;[3]
> burnt offerings and sin offerings
>   you did not require.
> Then I said, "Here I am, I have come—
>   it is written about me in the scroll.
> I desire to do your will, O my God;
>   your law is within my heart" (Ps. 40:6–8).

Verse 6 is a puzzling verse, which may explain the paraphrase found in the Septuagint. There are various ways of translating it. The word rendered "pierced" literally means "dug." But because it can also mean "pierced," many of the older commentators understood it to refer to the ceremony by which a slave could declare his desire to remain with his master permanently, as described in Exodus 21:1–6. If a slave had a good master and wanted to remain with him even after the legal six-year term of his slavery, the master was to take him to the judges where he would declare this intention. Then one of his ears would be pierced with an awl, indicating that he had become a servant for life.

The meaning of this ceremony certainly fits the context of Psalm 40. It would be an illustration of the nature of willing obedience and service. But there is a problem. The problem is that in this ceremony only one ear was pierced, and here the word is plural, *ears* rather than *ear.* The disparity is just enough to make us question the traditional understanding of the passage.

Today almost all commentators consider the word *dug* to mean "dug (or opened) up." Obviously, this fits the context too, particularly since the passage goes on to talk about the scroll of God's law and about the fact that its message is now written not only in the scroll, but in the psalmist's heart.[4]

Is there any better way to talk about the priority of obedience over sacrifice? I do not know of any. I do know that Jeremiah prophesied the coming of a new covenant, saying, "'This is the covenant I will make with the house of Israel after that time,' declares the LORD. 'I will put my law in their minds and write it on their hearts. I will be their God, and they will be my people'" (Jer. 31:33). To Jeremiah, having the law in our hearts is a proper definition of what it means to be in a right relationship to God.

Jesus, too, had much to say about the heart, often stressing that the people's hearts were calloused (cf. Matt. 13:15; Mark 7:6, 21). In regard to the law, Jesus said that the chief commandment is to "love the Lord your God with all your heart and with all your soul and with all your mind" (Matt. 22:37).

How many people, even Christians, have plugged ears! Or to put it in other terms, how many hear with their ears only but do not hear with their hearts! They can't hear anything anyone, even God, says to them. As a result they do not know the blessing of God this psalm speaks of, nor the deliverance from the pits of sin, defeat, bad habits, or circumstances.

A faithful testimony (vv. 9–10). Jesus said something else about the heart that parallels the next point of David's testimony. He said, "For out of the overflow of the heart the mouth speaks" (Matt. 12:34). Do you ever wonder why the speech of some people is so vile? It is because their hearts are vile. They need to get their inner lives cleaned out; then their speech will follow. But it works the other way too, which is the point made here. If our hearts are open to God's Word and are being cleansed and reformed by it, then our mouths will be speaking God's words and will be praising him. This is the third part of David's reflection on God's goodness. He says,

> I proclaim righteousness in the great assembly;
>   I do not seal my lips,
>   as you know, O LORD.
> I do not hide your righteousness in my heart;
>   I speak of your faithfulness and salvation.
> I do not conceal your love and your truth
>   from the great assembly (vv. 9–10).

Have you experienced the righteousness of God toward you through faith in Jesus Christ? Have you found the Lord faithful? Is his salvation good? Have you learned that he loves you, and have you discovered his truth in Scripture? To be a Christian is to have experienced exactly those things. But how can you have experienced them "in your heart" and yet fail to speak about them? If you are really aware of them, you will speak of them often, as David did.

A Prayer for Future Deliverance

The final section of this psalm is a prayer for future deliverance (vv. 11–17), which is particularly interesting in this context. David had been in a situation so hopeless that he could only adequately describe it as being in a slimy, muddy pit. He had waited for God, and God had delivered him, lifting him out of the pit and setting his feet on a rock. Yet now, even though he has been delivered from great trouble, as recounted in verses 1–3, Israel's beloved king and poet still continues to have trouble and needs further help. In fact, as he writes about it, he knows that he is at least partly to blame since his "sins" have been part of the problem (v. 12). What poignant cries these are.

> Do not withhold your mercy from me, O LORD.
>
> For troubles without number surround me;
>   my sins have overtaken me, and I cannot see.
>
> Be pleased, O LORD, to save me;
>   O LORD, come quickly to help me.
>
> O my God, do not delay (vv. 11–13, 17).

It is a way of saying that life is one long trouble. Should we be surprised at this? Hardly! Ours is a sinful, evil world. Jesus said, "In this world you will have trouble." But he added, "Take heart! I have overcome the world" (John 16:33).

That is worth remembering, isn't it? Troubles, yes. Pessimism, no. There can be no pessimism for us, because Jesus has overcome the world and we are now destined to be more than conquerors in him. I think this is exactly what David felt as he got to the end of this psalm. He is asking God for help, but he is not discouraged. The tone is optimistic because of his former deliverance by God. And the ending ties in with the beginning in another way too. At the start he is waiting patiently for God. Here at the end he is still waiting, knowing that future deliverances will come.

"Poor and needy"? Yes, we will always be that. But we know that the Lord does think of us. We know that he is our help. We confess it: "You are my help and my deliverer." We ask, "O my God, do not delay."

Psalm 41

A Weak Man's Strong Tribute

Blessed is he who has regard for the weak;
*   the LORD delivers him in times of trouble.*
The LORD will protect him and preserve his life;
*   he will bless him in the land*
*   and not surrender him to the desire of his foes.*
The LORD will sustain him on his sickbed
*   and restore him from his bed of illness.*

I said, "O LORD, have mercy on me;
*   heal me, for I have sinned against you."*
My enemies say of me in malice,
*   "When will he die and his name perish?"*
Whenever one comes to see me,
*   he speaks falsely, while his heart gathers slander;*
*   then he goes out and spreads it abroad.*
*   verses 1–6*

Even my close friend, whom I trusted,
*   he who shared my bread,*
*   has lifted up his heel against me.*

But you, O LORD, have mercy on me;
*   raise me up, that I may repay them.*

I know that you are pleased with me,
  for my enemy does not triumph over me.
In my integrity you uphold me
  and set me in your presence forever.

verses 9–12

It is hard to understand why the Psalter has been divided into five parts or why the divisions occur where they do. But regardless of the reasons, Book 1 contains Psalms 1–41, and this means that we have come to the last psalm of Book 1 with this chapter. The other books contain Psalms 42–72 (Book 2), Psalms 73–89 (Book 3), Psalms 90–106 (Book 4), and Psalms 107–150 (Book 5).

There is a connection between Psalm 41 and Psalm 40. Psalm 40 ended with the confession that the psalmist was "poor and needy" (v. 17). Psalm 41 picks up at this point with a promise of blessing for the one who has regard for just such needy people. *Weak* is the word used. And that is what the psalmist is! He is at an extremely low point in life. He is sick, slandered by malicious enemies, surrounded by false friends, even betrayed by one of his close friends, whom he trusted. Besides, he is aware, as we should all be, that he is a sinner and is therefore not without guilt of his own. These conditions have been preying on his mind and have distressed him.

The theme of the psalm is "mercy." The word itself is found in verses 4 and 10 in an impassioned plea to God for mercy. But the idea is already present in the opening stanza in the blessing pronounced upon those who have regard for the weak, that is, upon those who show the weak mercy. It is also present by contrast in the description of the poet's enemies and false friends in the middle portion of the psalm, since his complaint is that they have not been merciful to him in his sickness, as he has been to others.

A summary of Psalm 41 is in the Sermon on the Mount: "Blessed are the merciful, for they will be shown mercy" (Matt. 5:7). Its exposition is in the Olivet Discourse: "Come, you who are blessed by my Father; take your inheritance, the kingdom prepared for you since the creation of the world. For I was hungry and you gave me something to eat, I was thirsty and you gave me something to drink, I was a stranger and you invited me in, I needed clothes and you clothed me, I was sick and you looked after me, I was in prison and you came to visit me" (Matt. 25:34–36).

Like so many of the psalms, this one falls into three easily discernible parts: a statement of the psalmist's theme (vv. 1–3), a plea for mercy in which he states his sad condition (vv. 4–10), and a final expression of his very firm confidence in God (vv. 11–13). It is an appropriate ending to the first book of Psalms.

Blessed Are the Merciful

The composition begins with the word *blessed*. This is the third psalm opening with a benediction. The others are Psalms 1 and 32. Thus Book 1 of the Psalter both opens and closes with a benediction.

There are two ways the blessing can be taken. It can be understood as an encouragement to show compassion for the weak or as an objective statement implying that the speaker is one who did so and was therefore cared for by God.[1] No doubt it is both. As the rest of the psalm will make clear, David is weak due to his illness, and he wants people to show mercy to him and to those like him, which his enemies were not doing. At the same time he is turning to God for mercy, and his chief claim on God's mercy is that he has been merciful himself. This may have been the first time in biblical history in which the issue was formulated as sharply as this, though it is certainly elaborated later. It is the meaning of Jesus' beatitude mentioned above, namely, that God will show mercy to those who show mercy. He blesses those who bless other people.

There are seven things that the psalmist says God will do for the one who shows mercy. The Lord will "deliver him in times of trouble," "protect him," "preserve his life," "bless him in the land," "not surrender him to the desire of his foes," "sustain him on his sickbed," and "restore him" to health.

It would seem that this list of things the Lord will do for the one who is merciful moves from the most general (deliver him in times of trouble) to the more specific (sustain him on his sickbed and restore him from his present, particular illness). This is worth noting. For it is not merely that the Lord cares for us in a general way, though he does do that. The wonderful thing about the Christian life is that God cares for us in specific ways. It is when we are sick that he provides comfort. It is when we are discouraged that he lifts us up. When we are not sure what decision to make, he gives clear guidance. Such is the personal interest and care provided by our God.

A Plea for Mercy

I have placed verse 10 with the section of the psalm beginning with verse 4, because the subject matter is the same in those seven verses. It is a plea for mercy in view of the merciless treatment the psalmist has been receiving from his foes and friends alike. This does not follow the stanza divisions in the New International Version. But if mine is a right division, it is noteworthy that this section both begins and ends with "mercy." It begins, "I said, 'O LORD, have mercy on me; heal me, for I have sinned against you.'" It ends, "But you, O LORD, have mercy on me; raise me up, that I may repay them."

We need to take this plea for mercy at full value and allow it to help us interpret the opening stanza. Without it we might think that the psalmist somehow thought himself deserving of God's protection and favor because he had protected and helped others. It is true that he had done this. He is also expressing the principle "God shows mercy on the merciful," which is a true principle. But this is not the same thing as claiming a right to mercy *because* one is merciful. By its very definition, mercy is undeserved. In fact, it is God's favor shown to those who deserve the precise opposite. So when David asks God for mercy, he is acknowledging that he is at best an unprofitable servant and can be blessed only if God, for his mercy's sake, chooses to be merciful. In fact, he is even worse than an unprofitable servant. He is a sinner, which he makes clear in verse 4 by confessing his sin to God.

The Hebrew words "heal me" are literally "heal my soul" and mean more than just "heal me" physically. They mean heal all of me, body and soul. The plea is for both physical and spiritual healing.

Was this psalm written by David as the title suggests? The only real objection to David being the author is that it, like Psalm 38, describes a serious illness on the writer's part, and we do not have anything like this recorded of David in the Old Testament. I showed in the chapter on Psalm 38 that this is an inadequate argument. It amounts to saying that the Bible owes us an account of every time David got seriously ill, and there is no reason why it should do this. (See p. 331.) David must have been seriously ill many times in his life.

It is possible, however, that Psalm 38 and Psalm 41 are referring to the same illness. I suggest this because in both the psalmist traces the illness at least in part to his own sin (Ps. 38:4–5, 18; Ps. 41:4). He is also concerned in both about the attitude of false friends and enemies toward him while he is sick (Ps. 38:11–12, 16, 19; Ps. 41:4–9). The difference is that in the earlier psalm David was focusing on the illness itself while in this later psalm he is focusing on the reprehensible conduct of those about him.

What were his enemies and false friends doing? The psalm specifies four things.

His enemies were hoping for his death (v. 5). It is hard for us to imagine such ill will on the part of anyone toward David, because we have such a good impression of him from the account of his life given in the Old Testament. But David did have enemies. At the beginning of his reign he had enemies from the family and house of King Saul, his predecessor. Later, even his own son Absalom turned against him, and when he did, there were many in the palace and army who followed Absalom.

Why should David have had so many enemies if he was actually a good king and a moral person? The reason is jealousy as well as a desire for power in those who were jealous. This is instructive for us, because jealousy is undoubtedly a major cause of strife within the church. Those who attack others usually cloak their intentions with pious language. They say they are merely contending for the truth. But actually they are usually just jealous of someone who has greater popularity or greater influence than they do. They hope that by toppling the other leader they will be able to acquire his influence for themselves.

His supposed friends paid proper courtesy to him while saying quite contrary things to others (v. 6). When they visited the king his courtiers said the right things: "We were so sorry to hear that you are sick. . . . We have been praying for you and will continue to pray. . . . We hope you are going to be better really soon. . . . Everything is being taken care of. . . . Is there anything we can do?" The words were sheer hypocrisy. These people were not hoping that David would get well at all. After they left him they said things like, "Didn't he look awful? . . . I don't think he's going to make it, do you? . . . Well, not to worry. He hasn't been handling things very well lately anyway, and it's time for a change." They said one thing to David and an entirely different thing once they left his presence.

Instead of sympathizing with David in his illness, some attributed the illness to God's judgment on him for some moral failure (vv. 7–8). The phrase translated "a vile disease" is literally "a thing of Belial," which suggests a moral evil. It is a vague expression, of course, which is why the translators render it in different ways: "some shocking thing" (Perowne), "an evil disease" (KJV), "a deadly thing" (RSV), "a wicked thing" (NASB), "an evil spell" (NEB), "a vile disease" (NIV). But the vagueness is exactly to the point. In slandering David there was nothing specific to point to, even though David himself was conscious of sin. His detractors were saying only that God must be punishing him for some (unknown) failure.

Christians also tend to do this with other Christians, though not always with malicious intent. We need to remember that illness and other forms of suffering come to God's people for various reasons. Some suffering is merely in the nature of what it means to be a human being. Job said, "Man is born to trouble as surely as sparks fly upward" (Job 5:7). Some suffering is sent by God to develop Christian character. Paul wrote, "suffering produces perseverance" (Rom. 5:3). Still other suffering is intended for the glory of God. This was Job's situation. Job suffered greatly, but it was to prove to Satan that a person can love God for himself alone and not merely for what he can get out of him. Only a portion of suffering is for chastisement.

So if a Christian is suffering, it is far more likely that this is a good thing given to him or her by God for God's glory rather than a punishment for some wrong done or sin committed.

The worst thing of all was that David had been betrayed by his close friend (v. 9). This may have happened more than once in David's life and no doubt did. But the situation in the psalm is adequately accounted for or at least well illustrated by the betrayal of Ahithophel, David's trusted counselor, at the time of Absalom's rebellion (2 Sam. 16:15–17:23).

Part of verse 9 was used by Jesus to explain the betrayal of Judas, saying that it was to fulfill Scripture (John 13:18). This has led some commentators to regard the entire psalm as messianic. But there is no more reason to regard the whole of Psalm 41 as messianic than there is to regard all of

Psalm 40 as messianic, just because the sixth through eighth verses of that psalm are applied to Jesus by the author of Hebrews.

The application of this verse by Jesus is useful in showing how some Old Testament citations in the New Testament should be understood. J. J. Stewart Perowne has written helpfully on the subject:

> Part of this verse is quoted by our Lord in John 13:18 as applicable to the treacherous conduct of Judas, but with the significant omission of the words "mine own familiar friend *whom I trusted*"; for our Lord knew what was in Judas from the beginning, and therefore did not trust him. Nothing can be more decisive both as to the way in which quotations were made, and also as to the proper interpretation of the apparently strong phrase "in order that the scripture might be fulfilled" with which the quotation is introduced. First, it is plain that *particular expressions* in a psalm may be applicable to events which befell our Lord, whilst the whole psalm is not in like manner applicable. And next it is evident that "the Scripture is fulfilled" not merely when a prediction receives its accomplishment, but when words descriptive of certain circumstances in the life of the Old Testament saints find a still fuller and truer realization—one not foreseen by the psalmist, yet one no less designed by God—in the circumstances of our Lord's earthly life.[2]

Verse 10 has also been a problem for some people, since David is asking to be raised up so "that I may repay them [his enemies]." The words have a vindictive ring, which is startling and seems inconsistent with David's conduct toward his enemies elsewhere as well as with the entirely different standard for Christians modeled by the Lord Jesus Christ, who prayed even for those who were crucifying him, "Father, forgive them, for they do not know what they are doing" (Luke 23:34). However, I have argued elsewhere that there is a difference between the standards binding upon David as the king of Israel and those applying to him as a private person. If the speaker is David and he is conscious of his divine appointment to be king, he might well pray to be restored to power in order to punish traitors as they deserve, while at other times, as an individual, he would leave vengeance to Jehovah (cf. 1 Sam. 25:33; 2 Sam. 3:39).

Leupold says, "It may be added that punishment of treason is among the duties of a faithful ruler. Our soft age has largely overlooked this responsibility in its overly sympathetic attitude toward all miscreants."[3]

The Psalmist's Confidence

Verses 11 and 12 express the psalmist's confidence in God even in the midst of his sickness and the taunts and ill will of his enemies. Here the tone of the psalm reverts to that of the beginning, where David expresses his persuasion that in the times of their trouble the Lord delivers those who have regard for the meek. David had lived by that standard; therefore, he is assured that the Lord will not abandon him now.

As a matter of fact, his expression is even stronger than this since it is in the present tense, saying not "you *will be* pleased with me, my enemy *will not* triumph over me, and you *will* uphold me," but rather "you *are* pleased with me," "my enemy *does not* triumph over me," and "you *uphold* me and set me in your presence forever" (italics added). This means, you are pleased with me even though my sickness causes many to think you are not. My enemy does not triumph over me even though I am sick and he is in health and working against me—you are keeping him at bay—and you are upholding me even in this low period. This is a great testimony, and it has been the testimony of the saints down through the ages, since believers maintain that they triumph not only when things go well, but in defeat also.

The saints have their share of victories. But they also triumph at other times, times that the world would call defeats. They are always victorious. As for the world, its defeats are unmitigated by any breath of triumph, and even its triumphs are tarnished by the specter of God's sure and pending judgment of sin.

Amen and Amen

Verse 13, the last verse of Book 1 of the Psalter, is a final outbreak of praise. Significantly, it is how each of the five books ends. Books 1, 2, and 3 end with the phrase "Amen and Amen." Book 4 ends with the words "Let all the people say, 'Amen!' Praise the LORD" (or "Hallelujah"). Book 5 ends with a double "Praise the LORD."

How can it be any other way?

As we have made our way through these first psalms in this great book of psalms, we have been reminded of all the Lord has done and continues to do for his people. Psalm 1 tells us that God blesses those who root themselves in his word, and he watches over them. Psalm 2 assures us of the final victory of the divine messiah, our Lord Jesus Christ. Psalms 3 and 4 teach that God is with us in the morning and evening. Because he watches over us we can lie down and sleep in peace, and we can rise up rejoicing. Psalms 6 and 32 tell us that God is willing and able to forgive sin. Psalm 7 speaks of God's justice, Psalm 8 of his majesty. Psalms 9, 20, 34, 35, and 40 speak of deliverance from enemies and of the preservation in trouble of both the king and the nation. Psalm 14 exposes the folly of spiritual fools.

The sixteenth psalm is a prophecy of the resurrection. Psalm 22 is a prophecy of the cross. Indeed, Psalms 22–24 are shepherd psalms, Psalm 22 being the psalm of the good shepherd who gives his life for the sheep, Psalm 23 the psalm of the great shepherd who guides and protects his sheep, and Psalm 24 the psalm of the chief shepherd who will return in righteous judgment to reward his sheep.

Psalm 27 teaches that God is our light and salvation. Psalm 28 tells how he answers prayer. Psalm 29 emphasizes God's glory. In Psalm 30 God is our joy. In Psalm 31 he is our refuge. Because of this, Psalm 37 affirms that we can rest secure in God in all circumstances, and Psalms 38 and 41 explain that God is our help even in sickness or in other trying moments of our lives. No wonder we say,

> Praise be to the LORD, the God of Israel,
> from everlasting to everlasting.
> Amen and Amen.

Endnotes

Psalm 1: The Fast Lane or the Right Path

1. Robert Frost, "The Road Not Taken," in *Major American Writers*, vol. 2, ed. Howard Mumford Jones, Ernest E. Leisy, and Richard M. Ludwig (New York: Harcourt, Brace and World, 1952), 1609.

2. Dante Alighieri, *The Divine Comedy: The Inferno*, trans. Dorothy L. Sayers (Harmondsworth, England: Penguin, 1951), 71.

3. See Tremper Longman III, *How to Read the Psalms* (Downers Grove, Ill.: InterVarsity, 1988), 23–35.

4. C. H. Spurgeon, *The Treasury of David*, vol. 1a, *Psalms 1–26* (Grand Rapids: Zondervan 1968), 1.

5. Longman, *How to Read the Psalms*, 45.

6. H. C. Leupold says, "It is true, these three clauses are presented in an ascending climax. But no particular importance is attached to this climax" (*Exposition of the Psalms* [Grand Rapids: Baker, 1969], 34). P. C. Craigie says, "Though the three lines, taken together, provide a full picture of what is to be avoided, it would be stretching the text beyond its natural meaning to see in these lines three distinct phases in the deterioration of a person's conduct and character" (*Psalms 1–50*, vol. 19 of the *Word Biblical Commentary* [Waco: Word, 1983], 60).

7. Spurgeon, *The Treasury of David*, 1a: 1–2.

8. C. S. Lewis, *Reflections on the Psalms* (New York: Harcourt, Brace & World, 1958), 59–60. The full discussion is on 54–65.

9. John R. W. Stott, *Favorite Psalms, Selected and Expounded* (Chicago: Moody, 1988), 8.

10. Craigie, *Psalms 1–50*, 61.

11. Arno C. Gaebelein, *The Book of Psalms: A Devotional and Prophetic Commentary* (Neptune, N.J.: Loizeaux, 1965), 18.

12. H. A. Ironside, *Studies on Book One of the Psalms* (Neptune, N.J.: Loizeaux, 1952), 9–10.

Psalm 2: The Wrong Path and Its Consequences

1. *Meshiach* is Hebrew for "anointed" or "anointed one." The Greek word is *Christos*.

2. See P. C. Craigie, *Psalms 1–50*, vol. 19 of the *Word Biblical Commentary* (Waco: Word, 1983), 59–60.

3. Arno C. Gaebelein, *The Book of Psalms: A Devotional and Prophetic Commentary* (Neptune, N.J.: Loizeaux, 1965), 21.

4. C. H. Spurgeon, *The Treasury of David*, vol. 1a, *Psalms 1–26* (Grand Rapids: Zondervan, 1968), 10.

5. Ibid. 1a: 16. The quotation from Plumer is dated 1867.

6. H. A. Ironside, *Studies on Book One of the Psalms* (Neptune, N.J.: Loizeaux, 1952), 21.

7. Ibid.

8. This phrase has been the subject of imaginative reworkings by scholars because the word translated "son" is *bar*, the Aramaic word for "son," rather than the Hebrew word *ben*, which would be expected. But use of an Aramaic loan word is not impossible and may even be appropriate since the admonition is directed, not to Jews, but to the Gentile nations. The word did not seem to bother the oldest Jewish commentators, who explained it as an attempt to avoid the dissonant sound that would result in the Hebrew sentence if *ben* were used. The sentence would read: *Nasku ben pen jenoph*. As it stands, it reads: *Nasku bar pen jenoph*. For a discussion of the debate see Craigie, *Psalms 1–50*, 64; H. C. Leupold, *Exposition of the Psalms* (Grand Rapids: Baker, 1969), 56–57; and Franz Delitzsch, *Biblical Commentary on the Psalms*, vol. 1, trans. Francis Bolton (Grand Rapids: Eerdmans, n.d.), 97–98.

Psalm 3: New Day Dawning: A Morning Psalm

1. The first book of psalms (Psalms 1–41) contains thirty-seven psalms "by," "of," or "to" David. The second book (Psalms 42–72) contains nineteen such psalms, that is, eighteen of thirty-one. The rest of the Psalter (books 3–5) has seventeen more Davidic psalms scattered throughout, for an overall total of seventy-three, that is, nearly half of the one hundred fifty in the collection. In addition to Davidic authorship, some of the psalms are also identified with: Solomon (Psalms 72, 127), Moses (Psalm 90), Asaph (twelve psalms), Heman the Ezrahite (Psalm 88), Ethan the Ezrahite (Psalm 89), the Sons of Korah (eleven psalms), and the Director of Music (more than fifty psalms). Thirty-four of the one hundred fifty psalms have no titles and are therefore explicitly anonymous.

2. Strangely, some of the best ancient commentators (e.g., Saint Augustine and Martin Luther) ignore the historical setting in favor of spiritualizing the text. Augustine and Luther view the psalm as a prophecy of the passion and resurrection of Jesus, Augustine saying, "The words . . . sound more appropriate to the Passion and Resurrection of our Lord, than to that history in which David's flight is described from the face of his rebellious son" (*Expositions of the Book of the Psalms* in *A Select Library of the Nicene and Post-Nicene Fathers of the Christian Church*, vol. 8, ed. Philip Schaff [Grand Rapids: Eerdmans, 1974], 4).

3. H. C. Leupold, *Exposition of the Psalms* (Grand Rapids: Baker, 1969), 59.

4. P. C. Craigie, *Psalms 1–50*, vol. 19 of the *Word Biblical Commentary* (Waco: Word, 1983), 71.

5. Leupold, *Exposition of the Psalms*, 59.

6. C. H. Spurgeon, *The Treasury of David*, vol. 1a, *Psalms 1–26* (Grand Rapids: Zondervan, 1968), 23.

7. There is no universal agreement about what *selah* means, though it occurs seventy-one times in the Psalter and three additional times in the psalm which ends Habakkuk. It usually occurs at the end of stanzas, but sometimes it occurs at the end of a psalm (as here, in verse 8), and it can even interrupt a stanza. One thing is certain: it is some kind of musical notation, probably indicating a pause for reflection. The great Hebrew grammarian Heinrich Gesenius believed it to have come from the Hebrew verb *salah* (to be still, silent) and thus took it to imply a pause in the singing, perhaps for an instrumental interlude. Franz Delitzsch believed it to have come from the verb *salal* (to raise, lift up). He saw it as an indication to modulate to a higher key. See Craigie, *Psalms 1–50*, 76–77; Franz Delitzsch, *Biblical Commentary on the Psalms*, vol. 1, trans. Francis Bolton (Grand Rapids: Eerdmans, n.d.), 101–4.

8. Spurgeon, *The Treasury of David*, 1a: 24.

9. Leupold, *Exposition of the Psalms*, 62.

10. Spurgeon, *The Treasury of David*, 1a: 24.

Psalm 4: An Evening Psalm

1. Spurgeon states this as a probability: "The Psalm was most probably written upon the same occasion as the preceding, and is another choice flower from the garden of affliction" (C. H. Spurgeon, *The Treasury of David*, vol. 1a, *Psalms 1–26* [Grand Rapids: Zondervan, 1968], 34). Delitzsch merely assumes it (Franz Delitzsch, *Biblical Commentary on the Psalms*, vol. 1, trans. Francis Bolton [Grand Rapids: Eerdmans, n.d.], 113. Original German edition 1859–1860. First English edition 1867).

2. H. C. Leupold, *Exposition of the Psalms* (Grand Rapids: Baker, 1969), 66.

3. See Tremper Longman III, *How to Read the Psalms* (Downers Grove, Ill.: InterVarsity, 1988), 24–35.

4. P. C. Craigie, *Psalms 1–50*, vol. 19 of the *Word Biblical Commentary* (Waco: Word, 1983), 82.

5. Ibid. 82.

6. Ibid. 80. Leupold translates the phrase as "brave men" but then has to explain that the expression must be used ironically (Leupold, *Exposition of the Psalms*, 67).

7. Leupold, *Exposition of the Psalms*, 69.

8. Craigie, *Psalms 1–50*, 82.

Psalm 5: A Prayer for Coming to God's House

1. P. C. Craigie, *Psalms 1–50*, vol. 19 of the *Word Biblical Commentary* (Waco: Word, 1983), 89.

2. C. H. Spurgeon, *The Treasury of David*, vol. 1a, *Psalms 1–26* (Grand Rapids: Zondervan, 1968), 46.

3. Ibid. 1a: 45.

4. Derek Kidner, *Psalms 1–72: An Introduction and Commentary on Books I and II of the Psalms* (London: InterVarsity, 1973), 58.

5. H. C. Leupold, *Exposition of the Psalms* (Grand Rapids: Baker, 1969), 75.

6. Since the Ark of the Covenant, the earthly center of Israel's worship, was kept in a tent during David's lifetime (2 Sam. 7:2), it is puzzling to know how David can speak of God's "house" and "temple," as he does in verse 7. This would seem to be appropriate for a later day, after the temple of Solomon had been constructed, but not earlier. There are four possible explanations. (1) The psalm was not actually written by David. This is the view of most modern commentators. (2) Although the psalm was originally written by David, David's language has been altered to fit the needs of later worshipers. (3) The terms for God's dwelling that had been used when the ark was at Shiloh lived on as traditional expressions (cf. 1 Sam. 1:7, 9, where the words *house* and *temple* both occur). This view is particularly attractive since in 2 Samuel 12:20 the word *house* is used of the very tent David erected to hold the ark after it had been brought to Jerusalem. (4) Psalm 5 is not referring to an earthly house or temple at all but to the heavenly temple where God actually dwells. For a discussion of these possibilities see Kidner, *Psalms 1–72*, 59, 121; and Leupold, *Exposition of the Psalms*, 77–78.

7. Craigie, *Psalms 1–50*, 87.

Psalm 6: A Psalm of Repentance

1. D. Martyn Lloyd-Jones, *Spiritual Depression: Its Causes and Cure* (Grand Rapids: Eerdmans, 1965).

2. Don Baker and Emery Nester, *Depression: Finding Hope and Meaning in Life's Darkest Shadow* (Portland, Oreg.: Multnomah, 1983).

3. P. C. Craigie, *Psalms 1–50*, vol. 19 of the *Word Biblical Commentary* (Waco: Word, 1983), 93–94.

4. C. H. Spurgeon, *The Treasury of David*, vol. 1a, *Psalms 1–26* (Grand Rapids: Zondervan, 1968), 57.

5. David's gloomy statement "No one remembers you when he is dead. / Who praises you from the grave?" has been taken by some commentators as proof of a lack of faith in an afterlife by the psalmist. But the conclusion does not follow from these words. Indeed, it would be strange in a psalm written by the same man who said, upon receiving news of the death of Bathsheba's child, "I will go to him, but he will not return to me" (2 Sam. 12:23). What can be said about the expectation of life beyond the grave by the Old Testament saints is that it was not strongly developed or even much in their thoughts, which is not surprising since the fullness of the believer's hope did not come until after the resurrection of Jesus Christ. But this does not mean that all hope in an afterlife was missing. In this psalm, what seems to be uppermost in David's mind is that, if he should be allowed to die as a result of his agony of soul and body, his opportunity for praising God in life would be over, and that concerned him. Spurgeon says, "Churchyards are silent places; the vaults of the sepulchre echo not with songs" (Spurgeon, *The Treasury of David*, 1a: 57). For a fuller discussion of Sheol and the ancient believers' hope of an afterlife, see the chapter on "Death in the Psalms" in C. S. Lewis, *Reflections on the Psalms* (New York: Harcourt, Brace & World, 1958), 34–43; H. C. Leupold, *Exposition of the Psalms* (Grand Rapids: Baker, 1969), 86–87; and Derek Kidner, *Psalms 1–72: An Introduction and Commentary on Books I and II of the Psalms* (London: InterVarsity, 1973), 61–62.

6. See Craigie, *Psalms 1–50*, 94, and others.

7. Kidner, *Psalms 1–72*, 62.

8. Baker and Nester, *Depression*, 101–2.

Psalm 7: Cry Justice!

1. P. C. Craigie, *Psalms 1–50*, vol. 19 of the *Word Biblical Commentary* (Waco: Word, 1983), 103.

2. H. C. Leupold, *Exposition of the Psalms* (Grand Rapids: Baker, 1969), 94.

3. Arno C. Gaebelein, *The Book of Psalms: A Devotional and Prophetic Commentary* (Neptune, N.J.: Loizeaux, 1965), 40.

4. Ibid. 39.

5. C. S. Lewis, *Reflections on the Psalms* (New York: Harcourt, Brace & World, 1958), 17–18. The chapter "'Judgement' in the Psalms" is on 9–19.

6. Craigie, *Psalms 1–50*, 104.

Psalm 8: Our God, Our Glory

1. C. S. Lewis, *Reflections on the Psalms* (New York: Harcourt, Brace & World, 1958), 132.

2. Derek Kidner, *Psalms 1–72: An Introduction and Commentary on Books I and II of the Psalms* (London: InterVarsity, 1973), 65–66.

3. See the footnote, however, in which the NIV translators also suggest the words "than God."

4. P. C. Craigie, *Psalms 1–50*, vol. 19 of the *Word Biblical Commentary* (Waco: Word, 1983), 108. So also H. C. Leupold, *Exposition of the Psalms* (Grand Rapids: Baker, 1969), 107.

Psalm 9: Praise the Lord!

1. P. C. Craigie provides the following comparative table of the Hebrew and Greek numbering.

Hebrew Text	Septuagint
1–8	1–8
9–10	9
11–113	10–112
114–15	113
116	114–15

Hebrew Text	Septuagint
117–46	116–45
147	146–47
148–50	148–50

See Craigie, *Psalms 1–50*, vol. 19 of the *Word Biblical Commentary* (Waco: Word, 1983), 42.

2. Scholars have restored two of them by making slight changes in the text, but this does not prove that the original version had these letters. See Ibid. 123.

3. When the apostle Paul was in Athens on Mars Hill, he seems to have quoted verse 8 to show that God "will judge the world with justice" at the last day (Acts 17:31). However, in the psalm David is speaking of a present, earthly justice, as the context makes clear.

4. See my discussion of the psalmist's plea for justice in Psalm 7 and C. S. Lewis's chapter on "'Judgement' in the Psalms" (*Reflections on the Psalms* [New York: Harcourt, Brace and World, 1958], 9–19), to which I refer. We, who think largely of an ultimate heavenly judgment, fear justice and seek deliverance from it through the atoning death of Jesus Christ. The Old Testament figures, who thought largely of an earthly judgment, rightly pleaded for immediate justice. Lewis argues that, without forgetting the higher Christian conception, we should all nevertheless be concerned for the other, too.

5. C. H. Spurgeon, *The Treasury of David*, vol. 1a, *Psalms 1–26* (Grand Rapids: Zondervan, 1968), 99.

Psalm 10: Practical Atheism

1. George Gallup, Jr., "Is America's Faith for Real?" in Princeton Theological Seminary's *Alumni News* 22, no. 4 (Summer 1982): 15–17.

2. P. C. Craigie, *Psalms 1–50*, vol. 19 of the *Word Biblical Commentary* (Waco: Word, 1983), 126.

3. Cited by C. H. Spurgeon, *The Treasury of David*, vol. 1a, *Psalms 1–26* (Grand Rapids: Zondervan, 1968), 115.

4. C. S. Lewis, *Reflections on the Psalms* (New York: Harcourt, Brace & World, 1958), 75.

5. Craigie, *Psalms 1–50*, 127.

Psalm 11: What Can the Righteous Do?

1. Arno C. Gaebelein, *The Book of Psalms: A Devotional and Prophetic Commentary* (Neptune, N.J.: Loizeaux, 1965), 57.

2. Later David wrote Psalm 52 about this incident.

3. *Time*, September 11, 1989, 26.

4. P. C. Craigie, *Psalms 1–50*, vol. 19 of the *Word Biblical Commentary* (Waco: Word, 1983), 134.

5. C. H. Spurgeon, *The Treasury of David*, vol. 1a, *Psalms 1–26* (Grand Rapids: Zondervan, 1968), 130.

6. H. C. Leupold, *Exposition of the Psalms* (Grand Rapids: Baker, 1969), 127.

7. Delitzsch says, "It is not possible to say that what is intended is a future vision of God; but it is just as little possible to say that it is exclusively a vision in this world. To the Old Testament conception the future . . . is certainly lost in the night of Sheol. But faith broke through this night and consoled itself with a future beholding of God" (Franz Delitzsch, *Biblical Commentary on the Psalms*, vol. 1, trans. Francis Bolton [Grand Rapids: Eerdmans, n.d.], 191).

Psalm 12: False Words or Faithful Words

1. H. C. Leupold, *Exposition of the Psalms* (Grand Rapids: Baker, 1969), 129.

2. See Derek Kidner, *Psalms 1–72: An Introduction and Commentary on Books I and II of the Psalms* (London: Inter-Varsity, 1973), 75.

3. Herbert Lockyer, *Last Words of Saints and Sinners* (Grand Rapids: Kregel, 1969), 133.

4. This summary of contemporary views of Scripture is borrowed with some changes from James Montgomery Boice, *Standing on the Rock* (Grand Rapids: Baker, 1994), 48, 49.

5. *Time,* December 30, 1974, 41.

6. C. H. Spurgeon, *The Treasury of David,* vol. 1a, *Psalms 1–26* (Grand Rapids: Zondervan, 1968), 143.

7. The last phrase of verse 8 ("when what is vile is honored among men") has been a puzzle for translators because the word rendered "vile" or "what is vile" is a *hapax legomenon,* a word occurring only once in existing Hebrew texts. Its meaning is therefore difficult to determine. The translators of the New International Version have the best possible rendering, given the accepted text. But Robert A. Coughenour suggests an attractive possibility based on a redivision (not a rearrangement) of the letters. His translation refers to the wicked "go[ing] around in circles," while "constellations [the signs of the zodiac] are misrepresented [as truth] to . . . mankind." See Coughenour, "The Generation of a Lie: A Study of Psalm 12" in *Soli Deo Gloria: Essays in Reformed Theology, Festschrift for John H. Gerstner,* ed. R. C. Sproul (Nutley, N.J.: Presbyterian and Reformed, 1976), 103–17.

8. The source of this quotation is uncertain.

Psalm 13: How Long? How Long?

1. D. Martyn Lloyd-Jones, *Spiritual Depression: Its Causes and Cure* (Grand Rapids: Eerdmans, 1965).

2. Franz Delitzsch, *Biblical Commentary on the Psalms,* vol. 1, trans. Francis Bolton (Grand Rapids: Eerdmans, n.d.), 199.

3. J. J. Stewart Perowne, *Commentary on the Psalms,* 2 vols. in 1 (Grand Rapids: Kregel, 1989), 1:181. Original edition 1878–1879.

4. Quoted by C. H. Spurgeon, *The Treasury of David,* vol. 1a, *Psalms 1–26* (Grand Rapids: Zondervan, 1968), 155.

5. Lloyd-Jones, *Spiritual Depression,* 14.

6. Ibid., 19.

7. H. C. Leupold, *Exposition of the Psalms* (Grand Rapids: Baker, 1969), 136.

Psalm 14: Ship of Fools

1. See Arno C. Gaebelein, *The Book of Psalms: A Devotional and Prophetic Commentary* (Neptune, N.J.: Loizeaux, 1965), 65.

2. H. C. Leupold, *Exposition of the Psalms* (Grand Rapids: Baker, 1969), 139.

3. P. C. Craigie, *Psalms 1–50,* vol. 19 of the *Word Biblical Commentary* (Waco: Word, 1983), 148.

4. C. H. Spurgeon, *The Treasury of David,* vol. 1a, *Psalms 1–26* (Grand Rapids: Zondervan, 1968), 162.

5. Ibid. 1a: 169. The story is from one of Addison's essays in *The Tattler.*

Psalm 15: A Man after God's Own Heart

1. The question-and-answer structure of Psalm 15 has in recent years led some commentators to identify it as an "entrance liturgy," referring to what is imagined to have happened when a worshiper approached the temple. He was to have asked the priest, "Who may dwell in the sanctuary?" and to have received the answer contained in verses 2–5. No doubt, the psalm could have been used this way from time to time, just as we might use it like this in a liturgical setting today. But like so much modern work on the psalms, the supposition of such a liturgical use is mere speculation. The Old Testament has no examples of such procedure, and there are even elements in the psalm that discourage this view, most notably the fact that it is addressed

to the "LORD" (v. 1) and not a priest. There is no reason why the psalm should have been used any differently in Israel's worship than our own (cf. P. C. Craigie, *Psalms 1–50*, vol. 19 of the *Word Biblical Commentary* [Waco: Word, 1983], 150, and H. C. Leupold, *Exposition of the Psalms* [Grand Rapids: Baker, 1969], 146).

2. Craigie traces the origin of this number to Sigmund Mowinckel (Craigie, *Psalms 1–50*, 150).

3. J. J. Stewart Perowne, *Commentary on the Psalms*, 2 vols. in 1 (Grand Rapids: Kregel, 1989), 1:187. Original edition 1878–1879.

4. There are other types of parallelism, which are not illustrated by the couplets of this psalm. For a good analysis of these see Tremper Longman III, *How to Read the Psalms* (Downers Grove, Ill.: InterVarsity, 1988), 95–106.

5. Quoted by C. H. Spurgeon, *The Treasury of David*, vol. 1a, *Psalms 1–26* (Grand Rapids: Zondervan, 1968), 183.

6. The great English churchman and martyr Hugh Latimer wrote, "I am sure this is *scala inferni*, the right way to hell, to be covetous, to take bribes, and pervert justice. If a judge should ask me the way to hell, I should show him this way: first, let him be a covetous man; let his heart be poisoned with covetousness. Then let him go a little further and take bribes; and lastly, pervert judgments" (quoted by Spurgeon, *The Treasury of David*, 1a: 189).

Psalm 16: A Prophecy of the Resurrection

1. Psalm 110:1, the Old Testament verse quoted most in the New Testament, must have been one of them. So also were probably Psalm 118:22, cited in Acts 4:11; Psalm 2:1–2, 7, quoted in Acts 4:25–26 and 13:33; Isaiah 53, which Philip expounded to the Ethiopian (Acts 8:32–35); and many others. The first chapter of Hebrews alone refers to seven Old Testament texts, and there are four more in chapter 2. To these specific texts the great themes and images of the Old Testament could also be added.

2. "Christ in Gethsemane" by James Frame. It is referred to by Charles Haddon Spurgeon in *The Treasury of David*, vol. 1a, *Psalms 1–26* (Grand Rapids: Zondervan, 1968), 198.

3. Mike Bellah, *Baby Boom Believers: Why We Think We Need It All and How to Survive When We Don't Get It* (Wheaton: Tyndale, 1988), 49.

4. H. C. Leupold, *Exposition of the Psalms* (Grand Rapids: Baker, 1969), 152.

5. Reuben A. Torrey, *The Bible and Its Christ* (New York: Revell, 1906), 107–8.

Psalm 17: The Prayer of a Righteous Man

1. For a simple modern treatment of these types see Tremper Longman III, *How to Read the Psalms* (Downers Grove, Ill.: InterVarsity, 1988), 19–36.

2. C. H. Spurgeon, *The Treasury of David*, vol. 1a, *Psalms 1–26* (Grand Rapids: Zondervan, 1968), 215.

3. Ibid. 1a: 218.

4. H. A. Ironside, *Studies on Book One of the Psalms* (Neptune, N.J.: Loizeaux, 1952), 97.

Psalm 18: My God Is My Rock: Part 1

1. I discussed the various genres of psalms in the last chapter, listing hymns, laments, thanksgiving psalms, psalms of confidence, psalms of remembrance, wisdom psalms, and kingship psalms. See Tremper Longman III, *How to Read the Psalms* (Downers Grove, Ill.: InterVarsity, 1988), 19–36.

2. Derek Kidner, *Psalms 1–72: An Introduction and Commentary on Books I and II of the Psalms* (London: InterVarsity, 1973), 96–97.

3. See E. M. Blaiklock, "New Light on Bible Imagery: The Rock," *Eternity,* June 1966, 28–29.

4. C. H. Spurgeon, *The Treasury of David,* vol. 1a, *Psalms 1–26* (Grand Rapids: Zondervan, 1968), 239.

5. D. L. Moody, "Their Rock Is Not as Our Rock," in *Great Pulpit Masters,* vol. 1, *Dwight L. Moody,* intro. Charles R. Eerdman (New York: Revell, 1949), 47–58.

Psalm 18: My God Is My Rock: Part 2

1. Arno C. Gaebelein, *The Book of Psalms: A Devotional and Prophetic Commentary* (Neptune, N.J.: Loizeaux, 1965), 81.

2. H. C. Leupold, *Exposition of the Psalms* (Grand Rapids: Baker, 1969), 169.

3. Ibid.

4. Herbert Butterfield, *Christianity and History* (New York: Charles Scribner's Sons, 1950).

5. C. H. Spurgeon, *The Treasury of David,* vol. 1a, *Psalms 1–26* (Grand Rapids: Zondervan, 1968), 244.

6. Leupold, *Exposition of the Psalms,* 174.

7. Gaebelein, *The Book of Psalms,* 87.

Psalm 19: The Big Book and the Little Book: Part 1

1. C. S. Lewis, *Reflections on the Psalms* (New York: Harcourt, Brace & World, 1958), 63.

2. Alexander Maclaren, *The Psalms,* vol. 1, *Psalms 1–38* (New York: A. C. Armstrong and Son, 1893), 188.

3. Robert Jastrow, *God and the Astronomers* (New York: Norton, 1978), 116. The statements of Eddington, Nernst, Morrison, and Einstein are on pages 112, 113, and 128.

4. The second half of this couplet literally says, "their voice is not heard," which has produced a difference among commentators as to how the verse as a whole should be taken. The New International Version inserts the word *where* at the beginning, thereby making the verse mean that the witness of the heavens is heard everywhere (so also Luther, Calvin, Leupold). Purists retain the strict meaning: "They have no speech, there are no words; / no sound is heard from them" (NIV note, Perowne, Craigie). But if they do this, they have to add or imply the word *yet,* linking the first half of the verse with the second: "*Yet* their voice goes out into all the earth, their words to the ends of the world." In the first case there are two parallel couplets, lines A and B being parallel and lines C and D being parallel. In the second case there is a contrasting parallel between the first two lines, on the one hand, and the second two lines, on the other. In either version the meaning is the same: the witness of the heavens is pervasive.

5. John Stott, *Favorite Psalms, Selected and Expounded* (Chicago: Moody, 1988), 21.

6. P. C. Craigie, *Psalms 1–50,* vol. 19 of the *Word Biblical Commentary* (Waco: Word, 1983), 181.

7. H. A. Ironside, *Studies on Book One of the Psalms* (Neptune, N.J.: Loizeaux, 1952), 112.

8. C. H. Spurgeon, *The Treasury of David,* vol. 1a, *Psalms 1–26* (Grand Rapids: Zondervan, 1968), 269.

9. Lewis, *Reflections on the Psalms,* 80.

10. Ibid.

Psalm 19: The Big Book and the Little Book: Part 2

1. H. C. Leupold, *Exposition of the Psalms* (Grand Rapids: Baker, 1969), 181.

2. Derek Kidner, *Psalms 1–72: An Introduction and Commentary on Books I and II of the Psalms* (London: InterVarsity, 1973), 99.

3. C. H. Spurgeon, *The Treasury of David,* vol. 1a, *Psalms 1–26* (Grand Rapids: Zondervan, 1968), 273.

4. P. C. Craigie, *Psalms 1–50,* vol. 19 of the *Word Biblical Commentary* (Waco: Word, 1983), 182.

5. Quoted by H. A. Ironside, *Studies on Book One of the Psalms* (Neptune, N.J.: Loizeaux, 1952), 123.

Psalm 20: God Save the King

1. The commentators vary in the extent to which they see liturgical words or a liturgical structure in the psalm, as well as in the individuals to whom they assign the various parts. Much of this is sheer conjecture. But even Leupold, who generally resists this kind of speculation, admits that in this case at least "the psalm bears a half-liturgical stamp" (H. C. Leupold, *Exposition of the Psalms* [Grand Rapids: Baker, 1969], 185).

2. J. J. Stewart Perowne, *Commentary on the Psalms,* 2 vols. in 1 (Grand Rapids: Kregel, 1989), 1:229. Original edition 1878–1879.

3. From the *Winthrop Papers,* published by the Massachusetts Historical Society, vol. 1, 196, 201. Quoted by Peter Marshall and David Manuel, *The Light and the Glory* (Old Tappan, N.J.: Revell, 1977), 149.

4. William J. Johnstone, *George Washington, the Christian* (Nashville: Abingdon, 1919), 23–28. Quoted by Marshall and Manuel, *The Light and the Glory,* 285.

5. Charles E. Kistler, *This Nation under God* (Boston: Gorham Press, 1924), 71. Quoted by Marshall and Manuel, T*he Light and the Glory,* 309.

6. Norman Cousins, *In God We Trust* (New York: Harper and Brothers, 1958), 42. Quoted by Marshall and Manuel, *The Light and the Glory,* 342–43.

7. See Derek Kidner, *Psalms 1–72: An Introduction and Commentary on Books I and II of the Psalms* (London: InterVarsity, 1973), 101.

8. See P. C. Craigie, *Psalms 1–50,* vol. 19 of the *Word Biblical Commentary* (Waco: Word, 1983), 185. Others allow for either possibility, for example, J. J. Stewart Perowne, *Commentary on the Psalms,* 2 vols. in 1 (Grand Rapids: Kregel, 1989), 1:229. Original edition 1878–1879.

9. The difference between the way Jewish armies fought in David's time and before (on foot) and the way they fought from the time of King Solomon's rule and afterward (with chariot and cavalry units) argues for an early date and thus also a Davidic authorship for the psalm.

10. The generally neglected story of the role of the church in the changes that have come to Eastern Europe is told in part in the January 22, 1990, issue of *National Review,* "How the East Was Won: Reports on the Rebirth of Christianity under Communism," 22–28.

11. *Voice of Truth,* Romanian Missionary Society, January–February 1990, 2.

Psalm 21: A Day of National Thanksgiving

1. Rudyard Kipling, "Recessional" in *The Literature of England,* George K. Anderson and William E. Buckler, ed. (Glenview, Ill.: Scott, Foresman, 1953, 1967), 1134.

2. Derek Kidner, *Psalms 1–72: An Introduction and Commentary on Books I and II of the Psalms* (London: InterVarsity , 1973), 103.

3. P. C. Craigie, *Psalms 1–50,* vol. 19 of the *Word Biblical Commentary* (Waco: Word, 1983), 189.

4. Ibid.

5. Cf. J. J. Stewart Perowne, *Commentary on the Psalms,* 2 vols. in 1 (Grand Rapids: Kregel, 1989), 1:232. Original edition 1878–1879. Also Arno C. Gaebelein, *The Book of Psalms: A Devotional and Prophetic Commentary* (Neptune, N.J.: Loizeaux, 1965), 97.

6. Craigie, *Psalms 1–50,* 192.

7. Alexander Maclaren, *The Psalms,* vol. 1, *Psalms 1–38* (New York: A. C. Armstrong and Son, 1893), 205.

8. In the Hebrew text the tenses in Psalm 20:6–8 are perfects, though they are rightly translated by present-tense English verbs since they refer to a victory which, though certain, had not
yet finally occurred (The LORD *is saving* his anointed). The tenses of the Hebrew verbs in
Psalm 21:8–12 are imperfects, which could also be rendered by present tense English verbs but
in the context seem to require explicitly future translations.

Psalm 22: The Psalm of the Cross: Part 1

1. Derek Kidner, *Psalms 1–72: An Introduction and Commentary on Books I and II of the Psalms*
(London.: InterVarsity , 1973), 105.
2. *The New Scofield Reference Bible* (New York: Oxford University Press, 1967), note to Ps. 22:7.
3. Kidner, *Psalms 1–72,* 107.
4. The technical possibilities are discussed by most of the commentators, but the most thor-
ough is probably J. J. Stewart Perowne, *Commentary on the Psalms,* 2 vols. in 1 (Grand Rapids:
Kregel, 1989), 1:246–48. Original edition 1878–1879. However, Kidner (*Psalms 1–72,* 107–8) and P.
C. Craigie (*Psalms 1–50,* vol. 19 of the *Word Biblical Commentary* [Waco: Word, 1983], 196) also have
helpful discussions, the latter with many references to additional scholarly material on the subject.

Psalm 22: The Psalm of the Cross: Part 2

1. J. J. Stewart Perowne, *Commentary on the Psalms,* 2 vols. in 1 (Grand Rapids: Kregel, 1989),
1: 245. Original edition 1878–1879.
2. For some reason the New International Version does not reflect this abrupt declaration
though it is clear in the Hebrew text, where the verb (translated "save" by the NIV) is placed
last. See the previous chapter for a more extensive discussion.
3. John Murray, *Redemption, Accomplished and Applied* (Grand Rapids: Eerdmans, 1970), 51.
4. Arthur W. Pink, *The Seven Sayings of the Savior on the Cross* (Grand Rapids: Baker, 1976),
119–20. The discussion of the full sufficiency of Christ's atonement is borrowed in part from
James Montgomery Boice, *The Gospel of John: An Expositional Commentary,* vol. 5, *John 18:1–21:25*
(Grand Rapids: Zondervan, 1979), 240–42.

Psalm 23: The Shepherd's Psalm

1. C. H. Spurgeon, *The Treasury of David,* vol. 1a, *Psalms 1–26* (Grand Rapids: Zondervan,
1968), 353.
2. J. J. Stewart Perowne, *Commentary on the Psalms,* 2 vols. in 1 (Grand Rapids: Kregel, 1989),
1:248. Original edition 1878–1879.
3. Alexander Maclaren, *The Psalms,* vol. 1, *Psalms 1–38* (New York: A. C. Armstrong and
Son, 1893), 226.
4. Phillip Keller, *A Shepherd Looks at Psalm 23* (Grand Rapids: Zondervan, 1970), 35.
5. Derek Kidner, *Psalms 1–72: An Introduction and Commentary on Books I and II of the Psalms*
(London: InterVarsity, 1973), 110.
6. Keller, *A Shepherd Looks at Psalm 23,* 61.
7. See John R. W. Stott, *Favorite Psalms, Selected and Expounded* (Chicago: Moody, 1988), 32.

Psalm 24: Letting the King Come In

1. Psalm 24 was used on the first day of the week; Psalm 48 on the second day; Psalm 82 on
the third day; Psalm 94 on the fourth day; Psalm 81 on the fifth day; Psalm 93 on the sixth day;
and Psalm 92 on the seventh, the Jewish sabbath.
2. David Dickson, *A Commentary on the Psalms,* 2 vols. in 1 (Edinburgh and Carlisle, Pa.:
Banner of Truth Trust, 1985), 126. Original edition 1653–1655.

3. C. H. Spurgeon, *The Treasury of David,* vol. 1a, *Psalms 1–26* (Grand Rapids: Zondervan, 1968), 377.

4. Ibid.

5. See Franz Delitzsch, *Biblical Commentary on the Psalms,* vol. 1, trans. Francis Bolton (Grand Rapids: Eerdmans, n.d.), 332–33. Original edition 1867. Also Arno C. Gaebelein, *The Book of Psalms: A Devotional and Prophetic Commentary* (Neptune, N.J.: Loizeaux, 1965), 117–18.

6. Spurgeon, *The Treasury of David,* 1a: 378.

Psalm 25: A Bible Acrostic

1. G. Campbell Morgan, *Notes on the Psalms* (Westwood, N.J.: Revell, 1947), 51.

2. Arno C. Gaebelein, *The Book of Psalms: A Devotional and Prophetic Commentary* (Neptune, N.J.: Loizeaux, 1965), 121.

3. This may not be the whole story, however. Although the first word of verse 2 begins with *aleph* rather than *beth,* the word involved means "my God" and may actually belong at the end of verse 1, which would then read: "To you, O LORD, I lift up my soul, O my God." If that is a proper handling of the text, then the pattern holds at verse 2, since the second word of the text as it stands does begin with *beth.* As far as two other variations are concerned—the omission of a verse beginning with *waw* and the final appended verse beginning with *pe*—the same pattern is found in Psalm 34, the next of the acrostic poems, which suggests that the pattern is not an error but rather is deliberate. In the case of *waw* the two psalms may reflect an early form of the Hebrew alphabet, which could have left out that character.

4. P. C. Craigie, *Psalms 1–50,* vol. 19 of the *Word Biblical Commentary* (Waco: Word, 1983), 222.

5. H. A. Ironside, *Studies on Book One of the Psalms* (Neptune, N.J.: Loizeaux, 1952), 157–58.

Psalm 26: Standing on Level Ground

1. Derek Kidner, for example. "In Psalm 26 the worshipper, as he approaches, is searched by God's demand for sincerity (cf. Pss. 15 and 24) and, in the last verse, rejoices to have found access. In Psalm 27 he sees this house as sanctuary from his enemies, and as the place of vision, face to face with God. In Psalm 28 he brings forward his petition, spreading his hands as a suppliant towards the holy of holies, and receives his answer" (*Psalms 1–72: An Introduction and Commentary on Books I and II of the Psalter* [London: InterVarsity, 1973], 117).

2. H. A. Ironside, *Studies on Book One of the Psalms* (Neptune, N.J.: Loizeaux, 1952), 153.

3. C. S. Lewis, *Reflections on the Psalms* (New York: Harcourt, Brace & World, 1958), 71.

4. P. C. Craigie, *Psalms 1–50,* vol. 19 of the *Word Biblical Commentary* (Waco: Word, 1983), 224, 227–28.

5. C. H. Spurgeon, "The Saint's Horror at the Sinner's Hell" in *The Metropolitan Tabernacle Pulpit,* vol. 9 (Pasadena, Tex.: Pilgrim Publications, 1969), 454–55.

Psalm 27: My Light and My Salvation

1. For further discussion see P. C. Craigie, *Psalms 1–50,* vol. 19 of the *Word Biblical Commentary* (Waco: Word, 1983), 230–31, and H. C. Leupold, *Exposition of the Psalms* (Grand Rapids: Baker, 1969), 234–35.

2. Craigie, *Psalms 1–50,* 231.

3. John R. W. Stott, *Favorite Psalms, Selected and Expounded* (Chicago: Moody, 1988), 36.

4. Alexander Maclaren, for example. "This aspiration of the psalmist . . . depends not on where we are, but on what we think and feel; for every place is God's house" (*The Psalms,* vol. 1, *Psalms 1–38* [New York: A. C. Armstrong and Son, 1893], 141).

5. C. S. Lewis, *Reflections on the Psalms* (New York: Harcourt, Brace & World, 1958), 50–51.

6. C. H. Spurgeon, *The Treasury of David*, vol. 1b, *Psalms 27–57* (Grand Rapids: Zondervan, 1968), 10.

7. The verse creates a problem for the interpreter, because it seems to say that David's father and mother had forsaken him when, in fact, they had never forsaken him, as far as we know. Some have suggested that the words should be referred to the time David took his parents to the Moabites for safekeeping, during the years he was pursued by King Saul (1 Sam. 22:3–4). But in that instance it was David who left his parents, not they who left him. Other writers have suggested that by the time of the writing of this psalm David's parents had died and that this is what is referred to. On the whole it is probably best to regard the verse as a hypothetical statement, which is what the New International Version tries to do by words meaning, "If my father and mother should forsake me. . . ."

8. Spurgeon, *The Treasury of David*, 1b:4.

Psalm 28: Hope in God Alone

1. C. H. Spurgeon, *The Treasury of David*, vol. 1b, *Psalms 27–57* (Grand Rapids: Zondervan, 1968), 21.

2. Alexander Maclaren, *The Psalms*, vol. 1, *Psalms 1–38* (New York: A. C. Armstrong and Son, 1893), 271–72.

Psalm 29: The Lord, the Lord Almighty

1. The closest psalm parallels are Psalms 8 and 19, but even they have some additional elements. The best parallels are the Song of Moses (Exod. 15) and the Song of Deborah (Judg. 5), but they are not as concentrated in their praise as Psalm 29.

2. H. A. Ironside, *Studies on Book One of the Psalms* (Neptune, N.J.: Loizeaux, 1952), 171.

3. C. H. Spurgeon, *The Treasury of David*, vol. 1b, *Psalms 27–57* (Grand Rapids: Zondervan, 1968), 29.

4. The phrase which the New International Version translates "O mighty ones" is an unusual one, occurring in the psalms only here and in Psalm 89:6. The Hebrew phrase *(beni 'elim)* literally means "sons of gods." On the surface this might suggest an inferior rank of gods, that is, "sons of the gods." But this idea is so out of place in Hebrew theology that it needs to be abandoned. Actually the phrase is similar to the more common words *beni 'elohim* ("sons of God"), which refer to angels (cf. Job 1:6; 2:1; 38:7), and this is the meaning it seems to have in Psalm 89:6. The strange double plural may be only an unusual plural form, or it may be a way of heightening the term to mean many, many angels. The latter explanation seems to fit well here.

5. The actual temple did not exist in David's lifetime, of course. It is possible that David wrote "tabernacle" or some equivalent and that this was changed to "temple" by a later editor for worship purposes.

6. Spurgeon, *The Treasury of David*, 1b: 31–32.

7. Franz Delitzsch, *Biblical Commentary on the Psalms*, vol. 1, trans. Francis Bolton (Grand Rapids: Eerdmans, n.d.), 373.

Psalm 30: A Litany of Uplifting Contrasts

1. The chief possibilities are: the temple, which is how the Revised Standard Version translated the word (the chief difficulty being that the first temple had not yet been constructed), and David's own house, that is, his palace. This is the first time since Psalm 18 that a title has linked a psalm to a specific historical event or function.

2. P. C. Craigie, *Psalms 1–50*, vol. 19 of the *Word Biblical Commentary* (Waco: Word, 1983), 253.

3. H. C. Leupold believes this incident actually lies behind Psalm 30 and was the occasion for it. According to his view, "the house" of the psalm's title would be the future house of God, the temple soon to be built by Solomon. The psalm would have been used for the first "dedication" of the site when the land was purchased. He lists a number of significant parallels between the two passages, concluding, "The psalm fits this historical situation as a glove fits the hand" (*Exposition of the Psalms* [Grand Rapids: Baker, 1969], 251–52).

4. H. A. Ironside, *Studies on Book One of the Psalms* (Neptune, N.J.: Loizeaux, 1952), 175.

5. See note 3.

Psalm 31: Rock of Refuge

1. C. H. Spurgeon, *The Treasury of David*, vol. 1b, *Psalms 27–57* (Grand Rapids: Zondervan, 1968), 58.

2. J. J. Stewart Perowne, *Commentary on the Psalms,* 2 vols. in 1 (Grand Rapids: Kregel, 1989), 1:284–85. Original edition 1878–1879.

3. Alexander Maclaren, *Expositions of Holy Scripture*, vol. 3, *The Psalms, Isaiah 1–48* (Grand Rapids: Eerdmans, 1959), 184–85.

4. If the background for this psalm is the time of David's flight from Saul described in 1 Samuel 23, as some think, then the besieged city was Keilah, from which God delivered David by an oracle.

5. H. C. Leupold, *Exposition of the Psalms* (Grand Rapids: Baker, 1969), 263.

Psalm 32: A Great Man's Great Testimony

1. The significance of the term is uncertain, but this seems to be its meaning, particularly in the Book of Daniel (cf. 11:33; 12:3, 10).

2. Psalms 32, 42, 45, 52, 53, 54, 55, 74, 78, 88, 89, 142.

3. H. C. Leupold, *Exposition of the Psalms* (Grand Rapids: Baker, 1969), 269.

4. Alexander Maclaren, *Expositions of Holy Scripture*, vol. 3, part 1, *Psalms 1–49* (Grand Rapids: Eerdmans, 1959), 197. Maclaren has a full discussion of these terms on 196–201.

5. John Bunyan, *The Pilgrim's Progress* (New York: Dutton, 1954), 39. Original edition 1678.

6. J. J. Stewart Perowne, *Commentary on the Psalms,* 2 vols. in 1 (Grand Rapids: Kregel, 1989), 1:292. Original edition 1878–1879.

Psalm 33: A Praise Psalm for Everyone

1. P. C. Craigie, *Psalms 1–50,* vol. 19 of the *Word Biblical Commentary* (Waco: Word, 1983), 272.

2. Alexander Maclaren, *The Psalms*, vol. 1, *Psalms 1–38* (New York: A. C. Armstrong and Son, 1893), 312–13.

3. H. C. Leupold, *Exposition of the Psalms* (Grand Rapids: Baker, 1969), 295.

4. Craigie, *Psalms 1–50*, 272.

5. Maclaren, *Psalms 1–38*, 1:314.

6. C. H. Spurgeon, *The Treasury of David*, vol. 1b, *Psalms 27–57* (Grand Rapids: Zondervan, 1968), 120.

7. Maclaren, *Psalms 1–38*, 1:319.

Psalm 34: A Poor Man's Rich Legacy

1. Psalms 3, 7, 18, 30, 34, 51, 52, 54, 56, 57, 59, 60, 63, 142.

2. Some scholars find difficulty in the use of the word *Abimelech* in the title of Psalm 34, since the king of Gath is called Achish in 1 Samuel. They imagine an editor's blunder in confusing this man with the king mentioned in Genesis 20, 21, and 26, though it is hard to imag-

ine any writer or scribe so foolish as to make such an obvious error. Actually, there is an easy explanation for the change of name. As P. C. Craigie says, "It is more plausible to assume that 'Abimelech' (literally, 'my father is king') was an official title for Philistine kings, just as *Pharaoh* was an official title for Egyptian kings. The word 'Abimelech' in the psalm title, in other words, presumably refers to the Achish of 1 Samuel 21:10" (*Psalms 1–50,* vol. 19 of the *Word Biblical Commentary* [Waco: Word, 1983], 278). Support for this reasonable assumption is found in the fact that the time span between Genesis 20 and Genesis 26 probably indicates that two different individuals are involved in these accounts, though given the same name, and that the name is therefore more accurately a title.

3. The others are Psalms 9 and 10 (which together make up a single acrostic psalm) and Psalms 25, 37, 111, 112, 119, and 145. The most elaborate, as well as the best known, is Psalm 119.

4. C. H. Spurgeon, *The Treasury of David,* vol. 1b, *Psalms 27–57* (Grand Rapids: Zondervan, 1968), 122.

5. Derek Kidner, *Psalms 1–72: An Introduction and Commentary on Books I and II of the Psalms* (London: InterVarsity, 1973), 140–41.

6. Craigie, *Psalms 1–50,* 282.

Psalm 35: No One Like You!

1. See J. J. Stewart Perowne, *Commentary on the Psalms,* 2 vols. in 1 (Grand Rapids: Kregel, 1989), 1:305. Original edition 1878–1879.

2. So Perowne, Leupold, Maclaren, Gaebelein, Spurgeon, Craigie, Kidner, and some others. It is surprising that the New International Version does not follow this pattern. It would have been better, in my judgment, if the fourth stanza in the NIV had been broken at verse 18, the first half being attached to stanza three and the second half to stanza five. The stanzas would then comprise verses 1–3, 4–10, 11–18, 19–25, and 26–28.

Psalm 36: An Oracle

1. J. J. Stewart Perowne says, "Transgression is personified, and is represented as uttering its counsels to the wicked man, and finding the same ready obedience in his heart as the voice of God himself in that of the good man" (*Commentary on the Psalms* [Grand Rapids: Kregel, 1989], 1:310). Arno C. Gaebelein says, "The wicked carries in his bosom an oracle" (*The Book of Psalms: A Devotional and Prophetic Commentary* [Neptune, N.J.: Loizeaux, 1965], 161). But in order to get these meanings, "my heart" has to be changed to "his heart," that is, the heart of the wicked, which is not what the text says. John Jamieson asks, "How could the 'transgression of the wicked' speak within the heart of him who in the inscription of the psalm declares himself to be the servant of Jehovah?" (cited by C. H. Spurgeon, *The Treasury of David,* vol. 1b, *Psalms 27–57* [Grand Rapids: Zondervan, 1968], 161).

2. H. C. Leupold wisely takes this view, saying, "The psalmist means that deep down in his heart insight was granted to him about what really is wrong with the wicked" (*Exposition of the Psalms* [Grand Rapids: Baker, 1969], 294).

3. Gaebelein, *The Book of Psalms,* 161.

4. Condensed from one of Jonathan Edwards's sermons by Spurgeon, *Psalms 27–57,* 1b:162–63.

5. Perowne, *Commentary on the Psalms,* 1:310.

6. Alexander Maclaren, *Expositions of Holy Scripture,* vol. 3, *The Psalms, Isaiah 1–48* (Grand Rapids: Eerdmans, 1959), 229–30.

7. Spurgeon, *Psalms 27–57,* 1b:159.

8. Ibid. 1b:166.

9. David is probably also thinking of a river (or rivers) in the Garden of Eden, when he writes of "your river of delights." But this is a multifaceted image in Scripture, and other pas-

sages may be in view (cf. Pss. 46:4; 65:9; Ezek. 47:1–12; John 4:13–14; and Rev. 21:6; 22:1–2, 17).

10. Perowne, *Commentary on the Psalms,* 1:312.

Psalm 37: Not to Worry: Part 1

1. See Derek Kidner, *Psalms 1–72: An Introduction and Commentary on Books I and II of the Psalms* (London: InterVarsity, 1973), 148.

2. Verse 1 is found again at Proverbs 24:19, apart from one synonym.

3. H. C. Leupold, *Exposition of the Psalms* (Grand Rapids: Baker, 1969), 303.

4. Blaise Pascal, *The Mind on Fire: An Anthology of the Writings of Blaise Pascal,* ed. James M. Houston (Portland, Oreg.: Multnomah, 1989), 96.

5. P. C. Craigie, *Psalms 1–50,* vol. 19 of the *Word Biblical Commentary* (Waco: Word, 1983), 297.

6. This is the theme of Herbert Butterfield's classic study, *Christianity and History* (New York: Charles Scribner's Sons, 1950), written shortly after the Second World War. See especially the chapter "Judgment in History."

7. Craigie, *Psalms 1–50,* 299–300.

Psalm 37: Not to Worry: Part 2

1. H. C. Leupold, *Exposition of the Psalms* (Grand Rapids: Baker, 1969), 303.

2. P. C. Craigie, *Psalms 1–50,* vol. 19 of the *Word Biblical Commentary* (Waco: Word, 1983), 298.

3. H. A. Ironside, *Studies on Book One of the Psalms* (Neptune, N.J.: Loizeaux, 1952), 220.

4. C. H. Spurgeon, *The Treasury of David,* vol. 1b, *Psalms 27–57* (Grand Rapids: Zondervan, 1968), 176.

5. Ibid. 1b:177.

6. Alexander Maclaren, *The Psalms,* vol. 1, *Psalms 1–38* (New York: A. C. Armstrong and Son, 1893), 371–72.

Psalm 38: A Sick Man's Cry for Help

1. P. C. Craigie, *Psalms 1–50,* vol. 19 of the *Word Biblical Commentary* (Waco: Word, 1983), 302.

2. C. H. Spurgeon, *The Treasury of David,* vol. 1b, *Psalms 27–57* (Grand Rapids: Zondervan, 1968), 198.

3. Derek Kidner, *Psalms 1–72: An Introduction and Commentary on Books I and II of the Psalms* (London: InterVarsity, 1973), 155.

Psalm 39: Creature of a Day

1. Arno C. Gaebelein, *The Book of Psalms: A Devotional and Prophetic Commentary* (Neptune, N.J.: Loizeaux, 1965), 175.

2. See Derek Kidner, *Psalms 1–72: An Introduction and Commentary on Books I and II of the Psalms* (London: InterVarsity, 1973), 157.

3. See also 1 Chronicles 9:15–16; 2 Chronicles 29:13–14; and Nehemiah 11:17.

4. J. J. Stewart Perowne, *Commentary on the Psalms,* 2 vols. in 1 (Grand Rapids: Kregel, 1989), 1:328. Original edition 1878–1879.

5. Alexander Maclaren, *Expositions of Holy Scripture,* vol. 3, *The Psalms, Isaiah 1–48,* (Grand Rapids: Eerdmans, 1959), 264–79.

6. See also 1 Chronicles 29:15; Job 19:15; Psalm 69:8.

7. Maclaren, *Expositions of Holy Scripture,* 3:277.

Psalm 40: Up from the Pit

1. In Hebrews 10:5–10.

2. For a fuller discussion of this point see P. C. Craigie, *Psalms 1–50*, vol. 19 of the *Word Biblical Commentary* (Waco: Word, 1983), 313–14; H. C. Leupold, *Exposition of the Psalms* (Grand Rapids: Baker, 1969), 321–22; and J. J. Stewart Perowne, *Commentary on the Psalms*, 2 vols. in 1 (Grand Rapids: Kregel, 1989), 1:332.

3. The Septuagint text has "a body you prepared for me" for the words "my ears you have pierced," which explains the different rendering in Hebrews 10:5 (see NIV footnote). The author of Hebrews used the Septuagint, because that was the text most familiar to his readers.

4. Derek Kidner, *Psalms 1–72: An Introduction and Commentary on Books I and II of the Psalms* (London: Inter-Varsity, 1973), 159.

Psalm 41: A Weak Man's Strong Tribute

1. H. C. Leupold, *Exposition of the Psalms* (Grand Rapids: Baker, 1969), 330–31.

2. J. J. Stewart Perowne, *Commentary on the Psalms*, 2 vols. in 1 (Grand Rapids: Kregel, 1989), 1:343. Original edition 1878–1879. By a similar line of reasoning, Spurgeon wrote, "The strained application of every sentence of this psalm to Christ is not to our liking" (C. H. Spurgeon, *The Treasury of David*, vol. 1b, *Psalms 27–57* [Grand Rapids: Zondervan, 1968], 259).

3. Leupold, *Exposition of the Psalms*, 334.

Subject Index

Scripture Index